ABOUT
THREE BRICKS SHY
. . . AND THE LOAD
FILLED UP

ABOUT THREE BRICKS SHY

...AND THE LOAD FILLED UP

THE STORY OF THE GREATEST FOOTBALL TEAM EVER

ROY BLOUNT Jr.

UNIVERSITY OF PITTSBURGH PRESS

Published in 2004 by the University of Pittsburgh Press, Pittsburgh, Pa. 15260

About Three Bricks Shy of a Load was originally published in hardcover in 1974 by
Little, Brown and Company and in paperback in 1980 by Ballantine Books.
Portions were first published in *Sports Illustrated*.

ISBN 0-8229-5834-1

Manufactured in the United States of America

Printed on acid-free paper

10 9 8 7 6 5 4 3 2

■   ■   ■

TO ANDRE LAGUERRE, WHO CONCEIVED THIS PROJECT,

ART ROONEY, WHO CONCEIVED THE STEELERS,

AND MR. AND MRS. R. A. BLOUNT

WHO CONCEIVED

     THE AUTHOR

MAY ALL OF THEM PARDON SOME OF THE LANGUAGE

CONTENTS

■ ■ ■

INTRODUCTION

$\mathbf{F}$ranco Harris, who hated getting hit, told me something once, about running with the ball, that I didn't get down in my notes. It was something to this effect: as much as he wanted to comprehend the whole problem of a long run, to anticipate the whole open-field maze and to improvise a continuous mind-body flow of cuts and angles that could only end in the end zone. . . .

Essentially what he said was, you can see too many possible tacklers. Not so much because you're anxious, hearing footsteps in that sense, as because you're trying for too ingenious a solution—wanting to fake out more tacklers than necessary. Coach Chuck Noll's catchphrase, "paralysis of analysis," cuts to the quick of the matter—too quickly for my satisfaction, but then I'm wary of coaching (and I didn't give Noll enough credit in this book). As I get older I register more tacklers, and feel tired. But I wrote this book when I was young, for a writer, and my mind was bursting with Steelers.

In the seventies giants walked the earth, and they didn't waddle, either. Guards didn't weigh three to four hundred pounds. When Moon Mullins was pulling out ahead of Franco on a sweep, he weighed about the same, 230 or so, as Franco. He was a positive addition to the run's complexity. A 400-pound blocker can't pull. Mean Joe Greene, with his insistent sense of fitness (he picked the ball up from the line of scrimmage once and flung it into the stands), would have harpooned and rendered a 400-pound blocker before the fat stopped jiggling.

Not only are today's linemen too big, they aren't funny enough. I see Warren Sapp of Tampa Bay holding forth in interviews, and to me he's a cover act, trying to do Dwight White without the sparkle.

So I sound like an old fart. So sue me. When I was a thirty-something fart, the Steelers were in their golden age, winning four Super Bowls in six years, and I was hanging with them. Actually "loafing with" was the Pittsburgh term, then. I don't know whether it still is or not.

I do know that since this book was published in 1989—as an expanded, updated version of my 1974 book about the '73 Steelers—history has proceeded.

Twelve of the people involved in the great Steeler teams of the seventies are now officially immortalized: Art Rooney, Joe Greene, Jack Ham, Mel Blount, Terry Bradshaw, Franco Harris, Jack Lambert, Chuck Noll, Mike Webster, Dan Rooney, Lynn Swann and John Stallworth are in the National Football League's Hall of Fame. And there's no reason in the world that L. C. "Lover Cool" Greenwood isn't among them, and how about Dwight White? Donny Shell? Andy Russell? How about me?

Okay, I didn't play. But I did do a lot of heavy-duty listening, and I did write the original core of this book in three months, on a manual typewriter, sleeping from nine to five and writing all night, busting a gut to see the whole field presented by the material, and feeling the book constantly getting away from me, because the stuff I had to work with was so good. When I hit a wall, I would remember what Ray Mansfield and Bruce Van Dyke told me you had to do when you were hurt: play through it. (A perhaps less salutary corollary to that was, when you feel like you're getting drunk, drink through it.) "Iron men and wooden ships!" Mansfield used to exclaim, by way of evoking old-school values. I wish I were back there wrestling with that raw material instead of sitting here adding another layer of varnish. (In the second chapter, by the way, there's a typo where Mansfield says to Van Dyke, "I drove it." That's supposed to be "I'd've done it.")

Since my day the Steelers have been to the Super Bowl once. And—get this— they *lost* it. In the seventies, the Steelers had the biggest payroll in the NFL, but their highest paid player was Terry Bradshaw, who never got more than $400,000. Lambert got $200,000. The offensive linemen made considerably less than $100,000. Even adjusted for inflation, those figures are maybe a third of what players that good today can get, because they can become free agents represented by hotshot agents who negotiate multimillion-dollar contracts. In 1998 Ed Bouchette of the *Pittsburgh Post-Gazette* asked a leading player agent to estimate how much the old Steelers would be worth on the '98 market. To sign just twenty-two starters from the seventies, the agent figured, would cost $91.8 million. In '98 each NFL team had a salary cap, for all fifty-three players on the roster plus injured ones, of $51.5 million.

Bouchette quoted Jim Boston, who was the Steelers' chief negotiator in the seventies, as saying the dynasty Steelers could never have been kept together in the nineties: "They would have gotten a cup of coffee as they passed through." Market freedom has prevented the Steelers from holding on to Rod Woodson, Levon Kirkland and other horses who might have started a new dynasty.

Any such dynasty, however, would get its butt kicked by the dynasty of my day. Only now can we realize how irreproducible this book is. You had to have great characters who were athletes rather than mounds of flesh and were funny without being derivative, and you also had to have the right—which is to say, exploitative—economic conditions. Toward the end of this book's chronicle of the '73 season, you may notice, there is a reference to L. C. Greenwood's having signed with the rival World Football League. As it happened, that league folded before his Steeler contract ran out. Otherwise L. C. would have been somewhere else, making money commensurate with his uniqueness. Can you imagine the dynasty without L. C.? Wearing that gold chain with the bangle formed by the letters TFTEISYF, which, he explained when I asked, stood for "The first time ever I saw your face"? Right there in that corner of the locker room, L. C. of Mississippi next to Craig Hanneman of Oregon, numbers 68 and 67, respectively, you had the cast for a great buddy movie. And panning around to the right, we see, for instance, number 63, Ernie Holmes. Where else would I have gotten to know a man who shaved his head in the shape of an arrow?

So it was a rare moment in history that I had the great fortune to be a tangential part of. Heady times—see particularly the chapter herein regarding Super Bowl '75. Even some of the players have said they didn't realize how good it was until it was over.

Art Rooney, the Chief, died in 1988 after a long, full life. But another of the Steeler immortals, Iron Mike Webster, died in 2002 at the age of fifty. He'd been hit in the head too many times, suffered too many concussions, resulting in brain damage. In his last years he was sometimes homeless, sleeping in his car or in bus stations. When old teammates greeted him at get-togethers he snarled, or wouldn't acknowledge them. Joe Willie Gilliam, such a great passer, died the same year, four days shy of his fiftieth birthday. In the latter part of this book, as of 1989, I reported that he had broken his drug habit. He broke it several more times after that.

A number of years ago Sam Davis was found mysteriously battered. He's in an assisted care facility. Steve Furness died of a heart attack at forty-nine. And the last time I saw Ray Mansfield, the Old Ranger, who was my age and my best friend on the team, he was lying in his coffin—smiling, to be sure, and holding a big cigar. That was 1996. I wrote a little memorial piece about him for *Sports Illustrated*, under whose auspices I took on the Steelers in the first place. Here's a modified version:

Nobody ever hung in there any stronger than the Ranger, who still holds the Steeler record for consecutive games played. Even in the insurance business, Mansfield remained a warrior. When a man reneged on an agreement to buy a big policy from him, he went back to the man's office six times and finally kicked a hole in his desk. Then he couldn't get his foot out. Not long before his death he ran into the formerly ferocious Dick Butkus, got right up into the old Bear's face and said, "Dick, I owned you," and Butkus didn't argue.

Mansfield also set the unofficial Steeler record for hours enjoyed. Until he was sure there was no more conviviality to squeeze out of it, the Ranger would never call it a night. He had stories to tell that stretched from Bakersfield, California, where his family was living in a tent in an itinerant labor camp when he was born, all across the country. And he appeared prominently in other people's stories. The night before his funeral, Andy Russell told one:

"One night in training camp, Ray told me, 'It's embarrassing. You've been my friend all these years, and you've never once sneaked out after curfew. Tonight's the night.'

"I said, 'Aw, Ray, I can't be doing that, we've got to play Baltimore tomorrow.'

"The next thing I know, Ray, Jack Lambert and I are stealing through the darkness. Ray is dodging from tree to tree—here's big wide Ray, tiptoeing from one skinny little tree to another ...

"So we get to this bar, and I can't just keep on drinking, I'll get sick, so I'm sitting there with coffee and Jack is dancing on the bar with his shirt off and Ray is arm-wrestling with the bartender ...

"So I'm the designated driver, and Ray and Jack are in the back seat hitting each other on the arm or something, and here comes a big white horse toward us right down the middle of the road. I swerve to miss it, and Ray and Jack are outraged. 'You're supposed to be the sober one!'

"There was a big white horse! I tell them, and they're even more outraged. 'We don't see any white horse. And we're the ones drinking!'

"Then the next day, Baltimore was on our one yard line, about to beat us—it was just an exhibition game—and Lambert came over to me and said, 'Andy I think I see the white horse.'"

The Ranger's father died laughing, as I thought Ray might one night in my apartment in Pittsburgh in 1973. Pete Gent, the ex-Cowboy turned novelist, was in town, publicizing *Dallas North Forty*. After he and Andy and Ray did an interview together, they came to my place to do something that people who are now old farts would sometimes do back then: smoke a joint. Mansfield loved authors and books, and he was having a fine time discussing differences between art and life with Gent and Russell and me, even though he was in serious pain. A couple of days before, he had cut-blocked Jon Matusvak, bringing that enormous Raider down onto his, Ray's, neck all but completely separating a cervical connection. Suddenly one of Gent's off-in-the-ozone reflections—something about getting from point A to point B by way of point D—hit the Ranger's funnybone so hard that his top rib separated from his spine completely. He rolled on the couch, alternately laughing and crying. That injury plagued him until he died. Once he told me, "It hurts so bad sometimes that I think about killing myself," but he always spoke of that evening fondly.

Even more than merriment, he enjoyed the Grand Canyon, which looked like a cathedral to him, he said, and where he backpacked many times. The last time was with his son Jimmy, then twenty-four, and a friend of Jimmy's. The Ranger loved camping out. Eulogizing him, Russell told the story about Butkus and the one about kicking the desk, and also about the time he and Ray spent the night outdoors on the ground, and Andy was freezing, "and Ray, who was never cold, said, 'Andy, you can cuddle.' That was one warm body."

His blood pressure was way too high. No medication could correct it. He was still up around his playing weight of 250 or so, and he still indulged enthusiastically in big cigars, beer, salt on his food and physical exertion. He had business worries. His older brother and sister had both died of congestive heart failure. He had told Jimmy, "I'm going to die in this Canyon." Along toward evening on their second day of hiking, he told the young men to go on ahead and set up camp, his ankle was bothering him, he'd be along. But he didn't show up. They couldn't look for him in the dark.

Next morning they found him sitting with his back against a big rock, a water bottle in one hand and a disposable camera in the other. He hadn't taken a farewell snapshot, the foil wrapper was still on. But his expression was serene, and the breathtaking vista he faced must have been even more so at sunset.

I gather from *Steelers Forever*, by Jim O'Brien, that most of the old Steelers are alive and thriving: Bradshaw and Swann on TV, Russell and Mike Wagner and "Mad Dog" White and Terry Hanratty in the money business, L. C. a CEO, Rocky Bleier in demand as a motivational speaker, Mel Blount running two youth homes, J. T. Thomas and Larry Brown owning and operating thirteen of whatever is the plural of Applebee's, and so on. Most of them limp.

Occasionally I talk to Russell, who has written two books about the old Steeler days himself. At the suggestion of my son Kirven, who has loved the Steelers steadfastly since he met them at age five, I sometimes go on Yahoo.com to catch the inimitable Myron Cope broadcasting the last few minutes of current Steelers games. I still remember phone numbers by Steelers' jerseys: 201 223-2733, say, is Bleier, Bradshaw, Wagner, Edwards, Fuqua. I wear one of Mel Blount's old jerseys on special occasions.

And I'm still trying to tell myself, when I see the white horse, "Play through it."

INTRODUCTION
TO THE 1989 EDITION

$\mathbf{I}$n 1973 I had the great fortune (except that this was back before sports books started making people rich) to spend a season amidst the Pittsburgh Steelers. And I wrote a book. And *then* they became the greatest football team of all time. (That is what *Sports Illustrated*'s pro football maven, Paul Zimmerman, recently called the '74 and '75 Steelers, and since that is what he said, I agree with him.)

Even though the Steelers waited until after my residency to win four Super Bowls in six years, I did not hold this against them. I kept coming back. The first part of this volume—the original *About Three Bricks Shy of a Load*—is about the Steelers when they didn't quite have their act together, which I have been gracious enough not to take as a reflection on me. The second part—*And the Load Filled Up*—consists of stories and columns I wrote about them in their full fruition.

Four of the Steelers in this book—Joe Greene, Jack Ham, Terry Bradshaw and Mel Blount—have already been enshrined in the Pro Football Hall of Fame, and others are likely to join them. None of the Steelers in this book are still playing. When Dwight White, in retirement, was asked what was wrong with the uninspired 1986 Steelers, his judgment was succinct: "They don't have any gizzards. We had gizzards, man." But that's not all the Steelers had. They had a certain lift to them.

In 1989, when Pete Rozelle announced his retirement as commissioner of the National Football League, he said the brightest moment of his nearly thirty years in that office was when he presented the Steelers' first Super Bowl trophy to Art Rooney, the team's founder.

When Art Rooney died in 1988, I was in the south of France eating *mousse de chocolat amer avec les tuiles morbreés* and beholding naked Frenchwomen for the *National Geographic*. If somebody had said, "Would you rather go to the south of France and do all that or to Pittsburgh and pay tribute to Art Rooney?," I would have been there in Pittsburgh. But since I was already in the south of France I sat in a café in St. Tropez reading about the Chief's death in the *Inter-*

national Herald Tribune. I thought about mortality, immortality, and a time when the Chief was distinctively down-to-earth in an elevator.

The Chief and I were riding in this elevator in a motel in Oakland, I think it was, back around 1974. A man got on, identified himself as an assistant trainer with some California junior college team, and started telling us about the Steelers' chances the next day. He filled us in on who was going to be able to play and what the coaches had in mind, and he added a few words about the team's tradition. He spoke as a nonpartisan expert. A representative of the smart money. He held forth. The Chief put in a friendly word.

The expert looked at the Chief as an informed person might be expected to look at a harmless-looking, nondescriptly turned out old gent with a rumpled face who had presumed to put in a word. "Whadda we know, though, huh?" the expert said indulgently, and then he winked in my direction.

The next floor was the Chief's. The expert saw him off with a condescending smile, but then something seemed to strike him, and he said to me, "That old guy... *connected* with the Steelers?"

"Created he them," I said, or words to that effect. The expert gave me a funny look as I got off at my floor, but what I remember is the expression on the Chief's face when he saw that the expert did not know who he was.

The Chief's eyes lit up. After all, whadda we know indeed? The Chief's lips puckered loosely with delight. I'm told he had the same expression one afternoon a couple of years later as he picked himself up on the sidelines, in Three Rivers Stadium, after a Steeler running back ran full tilt right over him, during practice, when he was seventy-eight. It buoyed the Chief, to be patronized by an assistant junior-college trainer or flattened by a young employee. Unlike too many leaders, he liked good solid irony. His amusement had both gizzard and float, and his team lived up to it.

· O N E ·

ABOUT THREE
BRICKS SHY

■ ■ ■

□ **1** □

ABOUT THE TITLE

I got all my stuff together one time, and then I couldn't lift it.

—ROGER MILLER

Pro football players are adults who fly through the air in plastic hats and smash each other for a living. I now know a bunch of them, and I think they are good folks. They are made up, loosely speaking, of rickety knees, indoctrination, upward mobility, pain tolerance, public fantasies, meanness, high spirits, brightly colored uniforms, fear, techniques, love of games, Nutrament (a diet supplement used, sometimes with steroid drugs, for "bulking up"), corporate kinesthesia, God-given quickness, and heart. Sober, one of them told me, "What it boils down to is, sacrifice your body with a picture in your mind." Drinking, one of them told me, "When I'm on the football field I'm a knight in shining armor. When I'm selling insurance I'm just an asshole." Stoned, one of them told me, "You can be hit so hard it *burns.*" High on the game he had just played, one of them told me, "There was no other world outside it. There was nothing."

But there was a rich penumbra. I recall the afternoon of November 11, 1973. The Pittsburgh Steelers were beating the Oakland Raiders, 17–9, in a tempestuous game, in Oakland, on national TV. It was drizzling rain, great hunks of ill-rooted sod were flying through the air, sea gulls were frenetic overhead, Oakland fans were roaring and pulsing ambiguously . . . it was like standing in the eye of a tumbler washing machine, only noise and throat-figures all around instead of soapsuds and clothes. Steelers were running off the field with snot on their moustaches and glee and strain and grass blades in their eyes, and Craig Hanneman, a reserve defensive end from Oregon with whom I had often chewed snuff, turned to me on the mushy sidelines and cried:

"You picked the right team! Oh, a great bunch of guys! And a bunch of crazy fuckers! I'm crazy too! We're all about three bricks shy of a load!" Hanneman's last sentence—as an expression of wild approval, which I shared, tinged with then-unintended undertones of fallibility, which I tried to register as the year went on—summed up my six months with the Pittsburgh National Football League team better than anything else.

I spent the 1973 NFL campaign, from the first day of training camp in July

3

through the draft in January, loafing with (to use the old Pittsburgh term for hanging around with) a rich mixture of Steeler or Steeler-related persons: players, coaches, scouts, fans, wives, girl friends, relatives, media people, front office people, hangers-on and prospects. I fooled around the periphery of practice, habituated the dressing room, experienced games from the bench, and followed people home. I helped Mean Joe Greene, the tackle, buy his wife a birthday card; lost 11–10 in electronic Ping-Pong to Franco Harris, the running back; heard Terry Bradshaw, the quarterback, sing his own songs and speak of welding; considered stereo buys with Frenchy Fuqua, the running back; chatted up nurses with Moon Mullins, the tackle-guard; played the horses with Art Rooney, the patriarch; and listened to Center Ray Mansfield's little girl play "Faith of Our Fathers" on the clarinet. I talked labor–management with vice-president Dan Rooney (management) and player rep Andy Russell (labor, but he sells tax shelters). I threw my arm out returning Kicker Roy Gerela's field goals to him in the cold; elicited catcalls from Palm Springs residents by dropping (in street shoes) eight end zone passes from Quarterback Terry Hanratty; and sprained my ankle and had it taped up with a vengeance by trainer Ralph Berlin. I reminisced fleetingly about candy bars with head coach Chuck Noll, met a man who steals phonograph records for a living (can't give his name), saw tackle Jon Kolb's goat, and was helped up off the floor by Bill Nunn, the scout, at 3 o'clock in the morning in a black after-hours club in Jackson, Mississippi. I gained some thirteen pounds of Steeler-related beer and perhaps an ounce or two (from pushing on the leg-weight machine while talking to people with knee injuries) of Steeler-related sinew. I shared linebacker Jack Ham's shampoo, interviewed at her insistence Mrs. Bruce (guard) Van Dyke's obstetrician, and heard the word "collision" used as a transitive verb. I hardly ever did anything *I* wanted to do.

By just sort of drifting around, and not having any readily discernible immediate objective, I became more intimate than a press person, more detached than a football person, and possessed of a certain amount of gossip from all angles. As the bricks in the load shifted, I acquired interstitial inklings of how players, coaches, scouts, fans, press and front office people fit together and how they viewed each other. (Generally, as necessary evils.)

On the one hand the Steelers in '73 didn't make the Super Bowl, or even, as they had the year before, win a playoff game by a miracle; on the other hand none of them was caught up by tragedy—though two of the coaches were fired, two of the marriages broke up, and Mansfield, the veteran center known as the Old Ranger, did once offer, if it would help my narrative, to die of a pinched nerve. The Steelers won ten of their fourteen regular-season games and made the playoffs, but they were proved not to be as inevitable as they and their supporters thought they were. The previous year was the year the franchise lost its maiden, winning its first title, but '73 was a year that innocence was lost. I never had a headier year in my life, though, than I did checking out the various feels and levels of the Pittsburgh load of bricks.

I doubt that Chuck Noll—a constrainedly low-keyed man and reputed gourmet cook who speaks in terms of programming, preparation, adulthood and "good experiences"—would like to think of his team as being three bricks shy of a load, which is comparable to playing with less than a full deck. But what deck that is worth anything can ever be said to be full, and what is so boring as a complete, neatly squared away load of bricks? "We don't have the peaks and valleys," said a member of the NFL champion Miami Dolphins; neither do expressways through Kansas. The great thing in sports and nature is the way bricks slip and reassemble in unexpected combinations. That, for all the coaches' planning, is how the Steelers won games and lost them. The Steelers and the people around them were a great miscellany of minds, bodies, backgrounds and visions of reality, held firmly but hazardously together by the goal of winning all the marbles. In '73 they won only a good share of them— like most enterprises they fell short at the end, and heads rolled and players felt bleak and the fans in Pittsburgh very nearly started saying "The Same Old Steelers" again. But the Steelers' mix was more than their aim.

I want to thank the Rooneys, Noll, engagingly upfront publicists Ed Kiely and Joe Gordon, and everybody else in the Steeler organization for the access and help—not to mention the almost unlimited Vitamin-E-and-wheat-germ pills and cigars—they afforded me, and Andre Laguerre, Roy Terrell, Ray Cave, Gil Rogin, and Tex Maule of *Sports Illustrated* for their guidance and sponsorship; and the men in Black and Gold—Hanneman, just for instance, for the title and the snuff.

□ 2 □

A LITTLE BACKGROUND

Après moi, le déluge, i.e., first things first.
    —FATHER ORFE IN *CARDS*
    OF IDENTITY, BY NIGEL
    DENNIS

One day late in December 1972, Andre Laguerre, then managing editor of *Sports Illustrated,* summoned me, one of the staff writers, and said he wanted somebody to live with a pro football team for a season and write a book about it.

Well. I was thirty-one years old and just divorced, so I was at suitably loose ends, but otherwise I wasn't sure about the idea. I came into sportswriting unexpectedly from a newspaper job in which I made fun of, and occasionally deigned to talk to, politicians. I was the natural man, the politicians were the connivers. I was primary, they were secondary. In sportswriting I found it to be the other way around: the athletes were instinctive artists, just trying to stay inspired and exercise their craft, and I was in the position of trying to get them to conceptualize, to say something that they tended to feel would somehow get them into social, financial or ontological trouble. I will never entirely get over the sensation of realizing that my boyhood idol Willie Mays disliked me on sight. The fact that every other writer I know who ever tried to talk to Mays came away with the same impression does not really help. "Willie," I said to him at one point, "do you realize that the last eight innings you've led off, you've gotten on base seven times?"

"Man," he said, "I don't keep up with that shit."

All I want to happen to me in heaven is for Willie Mays to come up to me and say, by no means humbly, but appreciatively, "Do you realize that in the last eight descriptive sentences you've written you've used only one adjective?"

"Man," I will say (*nicely,* but firmly), "I don't keep up with that shit."

I prefer doing outré sports stories—coon hunting, synchronized swimming, an eighty-two-year-old lifeguard. I like to hang around with people I feel I am in the same boat with, which is to say that we are all confused but have visionary flashes occasionally and like to argue and tell stories. Then I like to go back to my office and render these people as semisympathetic characters, which entails a certain amount of betrayal I–Thou-wise, but after all, if you

6

hang around with an eighty-two-year-old lifeguard you put up with certain things, and the same goes for hanging around with a writer. Everybody, as subject or object, is a semisympathetic character at best.

But whoever did this book was going to have to spend a lot of time in a big-time dressing room. Big-time dressing rooms had always made me nervous. For one thing I could never spend longer than a few minutes in one without being galled by not having my own stool and uniform and helmet, or glove, and some of those cleated shoes that click on hard floors like the bears' claws on the cement in the zoo. Faulkner said a novelist is a failed short-story writer who is a failed poet. I am a failed linebacker, or defensive end. I have gotten over those ambitions, at least vocationally, altogether (now I want to be a man who operates a steam shovel), but still my reaction around football practice is like that of my four-year-old boy Kirven. When I took Kirven to watch the Steelers practice he enjoyed it until he realized nobody in uniform was going to chase him. Then he wanted to go home. So he missed meeting Johnny Unitas, which was probably just as well considering the moods he and Unitas were in. (While the two moods were not identical, they were perhaps comparable, as we shall see.)

Another thing is that I had never liked being around a lot of people each of whom could so easily beat me half to death that there wouldn't be any point to it. It's not that I actively fear or feel antagonism toward football players. Many people do, I think, including football fans. And so might I, if I had gone to a college where jocks were more freely indulged than they were at Vanderbilt in the early sixties, where several Commodores were my friends—which may bear a relation to how seldom the Commodores won. Some drunk Georgia Bulldogs once threatened to kill my sister Susan and peed on her date's foot at a house party, and when she complained to Coach Vince Dooley he said the boys were under a great deal of pressure.

I never saw any Steelers bully any civilians, and in fact I saw some of them contain themselves when people were being pointedly obnoxious. "Lemme at them," I remember crying one night. "I'll pee on the bastards' *feet.*"

"No," I was told. "It would reflect adversely on the organization."

I just made that up. But whenever I heard of Steelers being involved in barroom brawls I did wish, irrationally, that I had been there and had pitched in by doing what I once did as a fraternity pledge raiding the Sigma Chi house in college: leapt from the top of some stairs onto a crowd that was dragging a fellow pledge up the stairs toward the shower and knocked a good dozen people all the way down the whole long flight, in a thrashing heap. And ran.

But it wouldn't have been that way for me in a pro football brawl. I would have been hit spang in the middle of the face so hard that not only were my glasses broken and I had to be led back to the car but I also lost forever my sense of taste. That's what happened to a man I know who was fool enough to get in a fistfight because it seemed like the thing to do at the time. And the boys would have told me, "Well, you certainly took all the fun out of that

7

donnybrook." (Or whatever the appropriate term would be. In Pittsburgh they call a brawl a "hey-rube.")

I had always felt uncomfortable in a big-time dressing room because everybody who belonged in it had laid his body on the line. I imagine that if you hang around a showgirls' dressing room for very long without making an advance you feel like a eunuch. Hanging around a sports dressing room without ever having knocked anyone in it down, or tried to take his job, or helped him knock someone else down, tended to make me feel wispy.

Not that I am, by any means, of a mind with the civilians who come up to Van Dyke in Pittsburgh bars and try to get him to go one-on-one with them—the civilian rushing some imaginary quarterback, Van Dyke blocking—in the parking lot. "I know you'll beat me," such a man once said, "but I just want to see."

"This one guy was so nice about it," Bruce said. "I almost did it, he wanted me to so bad."

"I drove it," Ray Mansfield said. "And I'd've killed him."

"Well, but you can't . . ." said Van Dyke.

"I think I'll start carrying a couple of helmets in my car. And when some guy comes up with something like that, I'll do it."

"Well, but . . ." said Van Dyke.

"And I'll kill him," Mansfield said.

I don't have any desire to test myself against the best hitters, or to make a living hitting, any more than I want to make a living punching cows. I just want to *act* like a cowboy, and sing cowboy songs. (Interestingly enough, there are no pro football player songs, in the sense that there are cowboy songs. I thought about trying to write one during the season, but the closest thing I could produce was the title to an Ode to a Stewardess: "My Seat Back, Tray-Table and You Know What/Are in a Full Upright Position Over You.")

But there is a shared sense of hardiness around a sports dressing room which a reporter pointedly does not share. Often have I watched a fellow reporter prying away (most often deferentially) at a sports figure in his cubicle after a game—trying to get him to say something catchy and courageous about the trials and tribulations of being the only Jewish defensive end on a team run by Arabs, say—and felt that I shared with everyone in the dressing room this unvoiced assumption: Well, old B. B. (short for Booger Bear, the sports figure's cognomen, richly earned in hand to hand combat with people justly named Hercules Koskov, W. W. "Bad" Tydings, C. M. "Crazy Mother" McFarlane and Boulder Feoli) could just stand up suddenly and with the updraft of his chest knock old Herb (the reporter) over into that pile of peeled-off bandages over there, if he wanted to.

Not that the likelihood of B. B.'s physically squelching Herb was high. (Though such a thing has certainly happened—I remember a New York baseball writer saying how much he liked Ralph Houk of the Yankees even though Houk had once picked him up by the shirt, in answer to a question, and held him against the wall of his office.) But the very fact that B. B. was refraining from the use of his physical presence against Herb—when that physical presence was the primary reason both of them were there—diminished Herb's stature. Conceivably, though by no means necessarily, Herb could have squelched B. B. intellectually, but there would never seem to be any point to that in a dressing room. For one thing, if Herb tried it, then B. B. probably *would* put him over into the pile of bandages, with some justice.

Andy Russell, the Steelers' all-pro linebacker, may read the above and shake his head, and even without the condoning chortle with which he greeted my assertion that a fluttery forward pass is like a flaccid penis ("And you're going to *write* things like that, aren't you?" he said, with bemused delight). Russell's hero is James Ling the businessman (or was, until Ling spoiled his record by going ill-advised into the steel business in Pittsburgh). Russell goes about linebacking the way Kissinger goes about negotiating (except that Noll doesn't give him as free a hand as Nixon gives Kissinger). But I would like to point out what Russell's friend Mansfield said about Russell and Joe Greene: "When they're in there on defense it's like knowing your big brother is there, and if anybody tries to push you around he'll beat them up." Football takes us back to certain fundamental concerns. And I felt a resistance to the idea of hanging around, in their element, with 47 people who, if all 48 of us were on a desert island with 47 coconuts (see Noll's remark, in a later chapter, "the strong will arise . . ."), I would naturally be on welfare, at best.

Of course, as in the children's hand game, paper covers rock. What remained for the aforementioned Herb, after B. B. had either squelched him or declined to respond meaningfully at all, was to go to his typewriter and deal high-handedly in prose with B. B's output or attitudes. And B. B. may well have deserved it. But that prose, sportswriting being what it mostly is, would probably not be so sound or compelling, in any primal sense, as the way B. B. moved on the field of play, or even as the way B. B. sat on his stool with sweat running down his neck and gauze unraveling down his legs. Among themselves, of course, Herb and his colleagues would have their own bonds and hardihood, highlighted by talk in some ways more rounded and venturesome than the players'. But the stories told would be *about* players, mostly. Check out the sportswriter characters in pro football novels. "Chumps" would be a player's word for them. "Somebody you slap in the face and he don't do anything. That's the definition of a chump," Dwight White told me. And Joe Greene once referred to $50 as "chump change." A player makes more money than a scribe, and yet has stayed truer to his fiercest childhood dreams; he pushes the equivalent of a dozen people down the equivalent of a flight of stairs on a normal working day. He lives firsthand, and doesn't like to admit, by and large, that he is in the same boat with a man who asks questions and describes.

9

"He looks like a fag," one Steeler said to me about a member of the local media who was as straight as Vince Lombardi. "What does he know about football?"

What I should have said to that was, "You look at least as much like a gorilla as he does like a fag. What do you know about journalism?" But I was too deep into the scene by then—in a sense, I knew what he meant—and anyway that's not what a reporter says to a sports figure. What he does is take a mental note. It's not a very dignified role. But then again neither, if you think about it, is flying through the air in a plastic hat.

It was true that I had in a sense appeared in the bestselling pro football novel of all time (I guess), Dan Jenkins's *Semi-Tough*. But that was no real recommendation of me as the man for this job, since the character Elroy Blunt, a country singer, did not resemble me: I am not a *professional* country singer, I can't afford to give parties where beautiful, young, scarcely clad women try to get people to go upstairs and urinate on them in the tub, and I can't imitate a cricket (after the book came out I wore all the hair off the insides of my calves trying to learn). All I had done to merit such a place in literature was sing in Jenkins's company my song, "I'm Just a Bug on the Windshield of Life," whose actual lyrics are as follows:

> He drove up in his big new car
> And gave a little toot on his horn,
> And drove off with the prettiest girl
> That ever was born.
> He's in the driver's seat now,
> Beside him sits my wife,
> And I'm just a bug on
> The windshield of life.
>
> Now they're driving down the road
> And never think a thing of me.
> Two in the front seat's company,
> You know what they say about three.
> Now my wife looks over at him,
> Her words cut like a knife:
> "Old Arnie's just a bug on
> The windshield of life."
>
> The Lord above looked down on me
> And said, "I tell you boy,
> Where you are is just misery,
> There is no earthly joy.
> You and him and your wife are all
> In a world of sin and strife.
> On down the road I'll cleanse you from
> The windshield of life."

I figured football players would have little sympathy for that kind of senti-ment—that they were always in the front seat (I was wrong).

I have never claimed to be a fanatically interested or technically advanced student of pro football. Since I am an American it can stir my blood, of course, but here I was being told that somebody was needed to spend most of a year dwelling upon a pro football team, in a capacity somewhere between that of a tick and that of a consultant. I said, well, I would. And after some weeks of discussion, my preference for Pittsburgh was indulged.

□ 3 □

WHY PITTSBURGH

"Have you heard of these people before, Georgiana?" "Certainly not, Serena. Nobody has heard of any one in Pittsburgh."

> —TWO BOSTON LADIES IN
> 1874, QUOTED IN
> *VALLEY OF DECISION,* A
> PITTSBURGH NOVEL BY
> MARCIA DAVENPORT

Losing has nothing to do with geography.
> —CHUCK NOLL

A good many of my colleagues could not understand why I chose Pittsburgh of all the places in the NFL. Members of the *Sports Illustrated* staff are always tearing off to exotic places. I remember photographer Jerry Cooke pulling up in front of me in a taxi outside the Time and Life Building one evening. He noticed I was standing there with a suitcase.

"Where are you going?" he asked.

"Pittsburgh," I said.

There was a pause.

"Where are *you* going?" I said.

"China," he said, and then he rode away.

Well, I had never covered the Steelers but I had done several stories about the Pittsburgh Pirates. I once asked Pirate catcher Manny Sanguillen about his hitting. "My weakness is I swing at the first pitch too much," he said. "I know this."

"Well, why don't you stop?" I asked him.

"Because it makes me feel good!" he cried, beaming.

I once got on a plane behind Pirate pitcher Steve Blass, who for fun had tied his tie so that it was only about four inches long.

"Hello," the stewardess said.

"Hello," said Blass. "I'm the one in the short tie."

Dock Ellis, another Pirate pitcher, was once called upon suddenly to pinch-run. He ran out of the dugout wearing a Steeler warmup jacket. An umpire told him he couldn't run the bases dressed like that. So Ellis took off the warmup jacket and had nothing on underneath. I once asked Ellis about the Cadillac El Classico he had driven to spring training. It was white with red-leather outside trim and a grille that looked like the Parthenon in chrome. "It ain't nothin'," he told me, "but a DC-8."

I once sat with Pirate slugger Willie Stargell in a dugout in Bradenton, Florida, on a hot, sluggish day. Stargell commented on how little electricity, everything considered, was in the air.

"A great day to be in the outfield," I said.

"Yeah," said Stargell. "To just stay out in the outfield all day. And every ball that comes out there, paint it a different color."

I figured any town with a baseball team that sportive ought to have a football team worth loafing with. I knew the expression "loafing with" already because I had been to Pittsburgh on various assignments and had met some of its people, including a man who sat down next to me in an ice cream parlor and said, "You're looking at me—you may never see me no mo'. I may die before I get out of here, we don't know. That's one thing we don't ever know. Gimme a butter pecan, lady.

"I prophesy," he added. "I don't use no cards. That's gifted. That's from the Lord. I *broadcast* tonight at 7:30."

I knew Pittsburgh, by reputation, as a town full of locally famous eccentrics, past and present—such as the late Baldwin McMoney, the late Yutzy Pascarelli and his assistant One-Way, the extant Maniac McDonough and the man, whatever his name may be, who walks the downtown streets wearing two huge sandwich-board signs and carrying a third sign on a stick. In June 1973 (they change), the three signs were hand-lettered as follows, in part:

"President Nixon Vice President Agnew and Congress has the Power and Authority to Redress My Grievance Against All the Federal Courts of America But Purposely Failed to Redress My Grievance to Help U.S. Steel and the Steelworkers Who Has Tortured Me for Over 8 Years and They Will Abuse Me Until the People of America Bless Me With Their Help to Get My Grievance Against the Federal Government Properly Redressed. Please Show the World You Can Do It. . . ." The sign man is usually struggling with the wind and often seems about to be carried away by it, especially as he goes around corners. But if you evince a glimmer of interest in his message, while walking or driving past (not many people do) he will turn gradually so as to remain readable to you for as long as possible.

People—including a good many in Pittsburgh—tend to look upon Pittsburgh as a Loser town. Perhaps it is the "Pitts" in the name, suggesting depression. Perhaps it is the immigrant millworker image of the population. Perhaps it is the fact that Pittsburgh has never been westerly enough to imply frontiersmen, easterly enough to imply sophisticates, or middle enough to imply stolid prosperity. Perhaps it is the fact that the Steelers went forty years without a championship of any kind. Perhaps it is the soot.

13

"That's all people otta ton think of the Burgh as," a local bartender told me: "Soot." (Burghers sometimes refer to their town as "the Burgh." For the "ow" sound in words they say something which I have tried to render here with a short *o,* as in "donton longe," but which is more precisely, to take the case of "town," a blend of "tehn," "tahn" and "tan." It falls somewhere in between the Boston version of the short *a* and the East Tennessee version of the long *i.* The Pittsburgh accent is unique.)

And to be sure, the city's air before 1946 was so bad from the smoke of steel mills that the streetlights often had to be lit at noon. "Here was a scene so dreadfully hideous, so intolerably bleak and forlorn," wrote H. L. Mencken, "that it reduced the whole aspiration of men to a macabre and depressing joke."

James Parton, writing in 1868, called Pittsburgh "Hell with the lid taken off," a phrase which Lincoln Steffens used as the title of his exposé of the shame of the town. Anthony Trollope, after stopping in Pittsburgh in 1862, called it "the blackest place . . . I ever saw." At his hotel, "on coming out of a tub of water my foot took an impress from the carpet exactly as it would have done had I trod barefooted on a path laid with soot. I thought that I was turning Negro upwards."

But there are ways of putting a better face on the soot. (Not, to be sure, that I want to imply that there need be anything abhorrent about turning Negro upwards. Many a white defensive back would love, would give his eyeteeth, to have black feet.) "There was an eternal mist, an everlasting fog in the air," writes Stefan Lorant in *Pittsburgh,* the richly celebrative photo-and-text book he published in 1964.

> The silhouettes of the buildings and those of the boats were soft, at times hardly visible, more felt than seen. The figures of humans as they walked through the streets seemed unreal, like in fairyland. The world was quiet, one could hardly hear the steps of the men who emerged from the fog, coming from nowhere and disappearing into nowhere. The city had about it a dreamlike quality—a phantastic and romantic paradise for photographers and painters. It is strange that no more works of art were done during Pittsburgh's smoky decades.

I gather that the Burgher in the street took the air's condition in his stride, and even developed a certain proprietary feeling toward it. For one thing, the open-hearth (pronounced "open-herth") furnaces gave the mills a bright side, too. "Nobody ever said anything about the soot and smoke," Steeler owner Art Rooney told me once. "This used to be some town, Roy. When those mills lit up the rivers. I remember coming in on the train with [Chicago Bear owner George] Halas from Chicago to New York, we came by Pittsburgh at night and those mills lit up the rivers all the way along."

"Little pieces of soot if you had oily skin used to sit on your nose," added

Rooney's friend and driver Richie Easton, nostalgically, almost as though he were recalling a small pet that perched on his shoulder.

Nobody else in the country but Pittsburghers could boast that they had to live in such interesting air. I know I would rather live in a town that had been described as Hell with the lid off than, say, Cleveland.

But even in a town where politics have traditionally taken their own sweet time, and their own sweet advantage of the populace, there comes a point when twelve hours of evening followed by twelve more of night is too bad for business. After World War II there began what was called the Renaissance, whose first big step was requiring the mills to filter out most of the visible pollution.

Pittsburgh air is still bad, but the Renaissance has lifted the soot and brightened up the downtown to the point that what may be the nation's most compactly dramatic city vista is disclosed. Suddenly, as you drive through the Fort Pitt Tunnel from the airport, you come upon a beautiful blend of hills, rivers, bridges, boats, old and new buildings, surviving smoke columns, and lights. You can see it best from Mount Washington, across the Monongahela River from downtown. They call downtown Pittsburgh the Golden Triangle; it comes to a vigorously focal point, called The Point, where the Monongahela and the Allegheny conflow to form the Ohio. Across the Allegheny from the Triangle is Three Rivers Stadium, the handsome modern bowl where the Pirates and the Steelers play. The birthplace of George S. Kaufman, Gertrude Stein and Bill Cullen was never merely a spot of smuts, and now it is not that at all. (The furnaces up the rivers from town are not as vivid anymore either, and some are inactive, but they can still be seen to glow. Molten! That is what something inside a productive pro football player must be.) I liked the view from Mount Washington best when the buildings appeared to be held lightly by a vaguely visible atmosphere, held tenuously like a tipped-in basketball just hanging in the net or breasts suspended braless in a softly clinging sweater: the skyline rendered more palpable by seeming just-contained in the air's gauzy embrace.

Speaking of bad air, the Los Angeles Rams were considered for the subject of this book. But the last time I spent any time with a group of people in Los Angeles they seemed to be divided between people who said they were going to stop doing dope because they had started seeing faces in their food, and people who said they were going to start doing more dope because seeing faces in their food was not enough. I am not avid to condemn, and have been known myself to border on such behavior, but it was not the atmosphere I wanted to work in. I like to be surrounded by a certain *kind* of decadence—a digestion, rather, of something hard. Pittsburgh, like its leading beer, has the name Iron City. It has a literary magazine called *Ferrous Oxide.* It is the place, after all, where *The Night of the Living Dead* was filmed and where Strom Thurmond, at a school board meeting, was pelted with marshmallows. But things don't happen too readily in Pittsburgh. As the feller says on "Hee-Haw," "The news

15

is the same tonight, it just happened to different people." Pittsburgh is a town with roots. In Pittsburgh I encountered four or five different single or divorced women in their middle or late twenties who still lived with their parents. One of them had lived her whole life in the same house. Walter Iooss, who made the photographs for this book and who joined me off and on during the season in loafing with the Steelers, once told me he needs to keep his "New York edge"—the quickness you need in New York to preserve yourself and to keep up with what is going on—in order to take good action pictures. I know what he means, but I also need to keep my Georgia drag: the sense of ballast you need in Georgia, where I grew up, to appreciate the powers and even the uses of inertia. There is plenty of drag in Pittsburgh.

And yet—or, accordingly—Pittsburgh is the source of many of the nation's great fortunes. The history of the Burgh is studded with inventors and entrepreneurs. Andrew Carnegie started out there as a bobbin boy. George Westinghouse proved the practicality of Alternating Current there, and later a Westinghouse engineer there set up KDKA, the first commercial radio station in America. After making aluminum in Oberlin, Ohio, Charles Martin Hall came to Pittsburgh for financing and the result was Alcoa. The money came from Pittsburgh's Mellons, whose interests still control or dominate not only Alcoa but God knows what. H. J. Heinz started pioneering in packaged foods in Pittsburgh. There are more corporation headquarters in Pittsburgh than anywhere in the country except New York.

I don't know where all those corporate-executive types loaf, though, if they are transfers from out of town. Everybody I met in Pittsburgh was from Pittsburgh, or some small town outside it. Pittsburgh often calls itself "a big small town." It has an Old World sort of integrity. There are streetcars, cobbled streets and innumerable publike bars, not to mention the national headquarters of the Croation Fraternal Union of America, the Ancient Order of Hibernians, Italian Sons and Daughters of America, Polish Falcons of America, the Serbian National Federation, the National Slovak Society of the United States of America and the Ukrainian National Aid Association of America.

"You know what I mean?n" is an expression I never heard anywhere else but in Pittsburgh. That is as closely as I can render the inflection: "You know what I mean?n." The drift of it is, "You know what I mean, don't you? I would think so." It is expressed by a rising and then suddenly a falling inflection on the last word, "mean?n." It reflects, I think, a sure but not complacent sense of shared assumption.

There is a dug-in, inveterate quality to life in Pittsburgh. By that I don't mean a peaceful quality. Pittsburgh has always been one of the drinkingest towns in the nation. "A shot-and-a-beer town," its inhabitants often call it. You don't have to drink too many shots and beers (I did a couple of nights, though, in a spirit of research) in a Pittsburgh bar before you begin to feel the frustrations perking all around you.

16

The frustrations, however, are not fly-by-night ones. Pittsburgh is a town of classic grievances, and also of characters in the old sense, of raffishness. You see freakishness around the country, but you don't see that much raffishness anymore.

Pittsburgh was a big town for fighting, too. Art Rooney, the Steelers' owner, and his brothers Dan (now a priest, who is said to have spent some time protecting Chinese nuns from Communist troops with his fists) and Vincent (who fought professionally under the name Duke York) were all prizefighters of note half a century ago, but it was in the streets that the Rooneys really shone. North Siders used to meet groups from the other side of the Allegheny and fight in the middle of the bridge, throwing each other off into the water. There was a man named McCreary, the Rooneys' old friend Dago Sam told me, "a big dig-ditcher, who would stand out in front of the Rooney saloon and say 'Who wants a bit of a scrap and a roll mit' me?' " Once a visiting carnival boxer was getting the best of the Rooneys' friend Squawker Mullen and Dan reached into the ring and belted the carnie and his friends hollered "Hey Rube!" and in the ensuing melee the tent collapsed and the disturbance raged on lumpily within the great folds of canvas.

Pittsburgh today is not much of a mugging town, as major league cities go. (On a local radio talk show, however, I heard a lady call in to say that she'd had three elderly friends mugged and she wondered why the Pittsburgh police couldn't dress up as decoys to catch muggers. "Maybe they can't find a Pittsburgh cop who's willing to wear a dress," said the host. "Well, how about a pants suit?" asked the caller.) But it is a good town for walking past a bar and having somebody sitting outside it offer to whip your ass for you. When Pittsburgh had a pro basketball team, the ABA Pipers, it was noted primarily for its drinking, its losses and its brawls. Piper Coach Mike Binstein once went into the stands to fight a heckler while his team sat on the bench laughing and rooting loudly for the heckler.

I never heard the word "Jagov" so often in my life as I heard it in Pittsburgh. There was an iron imperative not to be accounted a Jagov. The word is "jack-off," but in Pittsburgh it sounded like a Russian name. It means a person who doesn't take care of business, who makes a lot of noise and motions but doesn't connect. "Schizophrenic" is not too much further down the road. "Are you just jagging me off, or do you mean that?" a reasonably nice young woman in Pittsburgh (young women in Pittsburgh tend to be nicer, in the sense of demivirginality, than young women in many major league cities) might say, without any apparent awareness of the root sense of the term. "Brian's mother is a Jagov," I heard one high-school-age girl say to another in a Pittsburgh grocery store. If a lady wouldn't talk to him in a bar a Pittsburgher might well walk off grumbling, with a hint of desperation, "I'm a Jagov, right?" Pittsburgh tended to be thought of even by many of its citizens, with a certain strange pride, as a loser's town.

I had learned some of these things about Pittsburgh while in town researching a story about the Rooneys—Art and his sons, Dan, Art Jr., Tim, Pat and John, who own not only the Steelers, but now, since the sons have expanded the empire, several racing operations around the country as well. Art Sr. founded the team in 1933, buying an NFL franchise for $2,500 as soon as the Pennsylvania blue laws were repealed, and for decades he ran it the way you might run a good, rowdy, but respectable saloon, such as his father used to run on a spot just across from where the Three Rivers Stadium parking lot is now. Rooney is an offhandedly self-made man who once played football against Jim Thorpe, led the Middle Atlantic baseball league in batting and boxed professionally, and kept the Steelers going through lean years by winning money on the horses.

He likes to loaf with groundskeepers more than millionaires, though he has befriended some of the latter too, and he attends wakes and finds people jobs in something like the manner of Frank Skeffington in *The Last Hurrah*—although Rooney ran for only one office in his life, registrar of wills, and blew that race when he said in a campaign speech that he had no idea what the duties of the office were. He lives serenely on the unfashionable North Side, in a neighborhood where Lillian Russell and Harry K. Thaw used to live but which later turned into a neighborhood of, in the words of Rooney's late friend Owney MacManus, "mostly hillbillies and sword-swallowers," and is now, except for his household, a black ghetto. His big house is the same one he moved up the hill to, from the sub-lace-curtain neighborhood just below, in 1928 when he was married. "I only lived in one other house in my life," he says, "and that was just out the door and across the street from this one." He commutes by foot to his office in the stadium.

Rooney is the only NFL owner who has lived his whole life within easy walking distance of where his team plays its home games, and who once nearly drowned on the stadium's site. In those days Exposition Park stood there, and whenever the waters rose—which could happen, he says, "if you spit in the Allegheny"—it was flooded. Rooney, his brother Dan and Squawker Mullen were navigating left field in a canoe when Squawker stood up, capsizing the boat, and Art, being dressed in boots and an overcoat, had to swim hard for his life. Just as he was going under he grabbed the bleachers.

The Steelers', then, is a franchise with roots. Rooney could have lined his pockets by moving to Atlanta, Boston, Baltimore, New Orleans or Houston, but he always said, "I'm a Pittsburgh guy."

The Steelers also had a loose, open family administration in the persons of the Rooneys: Art Sr., a presence still richly felt; his eldest son Dan, who had become the team's chief front-office executive; and the second son Art Jr., called Artie, who supervised the scouting operation. There were other Rooneys around the Steelers too: Art Sr.'s nephew, Vincent's son Tim, who scouted and helped make trades; Art Sr.'s elder brother Dan, the priest and ex-boxer and ex-brawler; and their younger brother Jim, the former college punter and Pittsburgh politician.

It was Jim who had told me about the figurehead legislator elected out of the North Side by the Republican Coyne machine: Asked by a jocular member of the press for his position on the Monroe Doctrine, this legislator said, "If the boys are for it, I'm for it." Then he showed up at the train station with a ticket to Washington. "What are you going to Washington for?" he was asked.

"I was just elected to the Congress," he said.

"No, no," he was told. "You were elected to the state legislature. You're supposed to go to Harrisburg."

The Rooneys struck me the way Pittsburgh did: down to earth, stoutly localized and full of lore.

Another good thing about the Pittsburgh situation was what one heard of and from the fans. The Steeler fans were widely acknowledged as peerlessly vocal (their recorded clamor was used by NFL Films as the audio portion not only of the Steelers' '72 highlights but also of several other teams'), and as a model of pungent heterogeneity. The Poles of Dobre Shunka, followers of linebacker Jack Ham, whooped in harmony with the Ukrainians of Gerela's Gorillas, who backed place-kicker Roy Gerela under the leadership of an infectious enthusiast named Bob Bubonic, The Gorilla. Whatever the weather, Bubonic wore a full gorilla suit. He would pound his great gorilla chest and bellow, and a man sitting near him would pull up his shirt and pound his considerable Ukrainian belly and shout. Then there was Franco's Italian Army, which boosted half-black, half-Italian sensational rookie running back Franco Harris. The Army actually brought together Italian fans (including Frank Sinatra, who kissed Harris in a special ceremony in Palm Springs) and black fans in the same loosely woven effort.

As for the Steelers themselves, I had never been around them, but I knew that they, too, provided a study in *e pluribus unum*. The quarterbacks were a white small-college Southerner (Terry Bradshaw), an Irish Note Dame All-American (Terry Hanratty), and a black predominantly black-college Southerner (Joe Gilliam). The head coach was regarded as more of a technician than a character, but also as a commendably nontotalitarian overseer and an opinionated student of everything from history to viruses. There was a running back named Frenchy Fuqua, who dressed in such things as capes and a Three Musketeers hat, and there was a tackle named Mean Joe Greene, who brutalized quarterbacks but received reporters.

We were still deliberating which team to pick, however, when the Steelers won their first championship ever—that of the American Conference's Central Division—and took on the Oakland Raiders in the first round of the playoffs.

With just over a minute to play, the Steelers were leading the Raiders 6–0, when Oakland quarterback Ken Stabler, on a broken play, ran 30 yards for a touchdown. Suddenly the Raiders, bested all day, led 7–6.

But the Steelers were not dead. They took the kickoff and with 22 seconds to go had advanced to their 40. It was fourth down. Bradshaw went back for

19

one last pass and confronted a bad situation. A surge of Oakland rushers was about to break over his head and his primary receiver was covered. But he slipped away from the people banging and clawing at him and threw to Fuqua. Fuqua and Oakland defender Jack Tatum, famous for nearly breaking folks' backs with his tackles, went up together, and the ball hit them, bounced off, and disappeared, as surely as Dave Garroway, from the TV screen.

Ah, well. The Steelers had a tradition of being done in by fate. Three times in previous years they had lost the NFL's old Eastern Division title on one quirky play: a bad snap by a rookie center; a line-drive field goal attempt by one Joe Glamp—there's a name—that hit the crossbar and bounced back; and a receiver who caught a pass, tucked it in, romped downfield all alone with it, and somehow or other allowed it to pass from his hands in midstride. This, '72, had seemed at last to be the Steelers' year, but maybe some franchises are born to lose. Art Rooney had already conceded and was on his way by elevator to the dressing room, to console the team.

However, in the split-second it might have taken for these reflections to pass through my mind, had I not been occupied in kicking a hassock (like a great many other neutral observers around the country, I had already become an emotional Steeler fan), Pittsburgh's fortunes were reversed.

The ball reappeared on the screen, borne by Harris, who had caught it, off-camera, at his shoetops on the rebound. A plane would crash on him as he ran. The head of The Gorilla's costume would by some freakish mischance fly off and land on Harris's head, backwards, obscuring his vision so that he ran out of bounds. Something would happen to frustrate the Steelers again.

But it didn't. Harris turned the corner, so thrustfully you could *feel* it, around a couple of pursuers and held his course just perilously within the sideline—showing what I would call "marginal feet," though scouts use the term in a different sense—against the pressures of centrifugal force and hard-angling Raiders, for 42 yards and the touchdown that won the game.

That was what came to be called The Miraculous Reception. Pandemonium! What a great thing football is, that allows us at rare moments to be pandemonious. I happened to be watching the game with four uncomprehending children, each of whom, with the possible exception of the eleven-year-old, I threw up into the air. Gerela's Gorillas and Dobre Shunka and Franco's Italian Army and Maniac McDonough and everybody went crazy.

The next week the Steelers outplayed but lost to the Miami Dolphins on another quirky play, a fake punt by Larry Seiple. The Dolphins went on to win the Super Bowl; but I had my team. We wrote a letter to the Rooneys, they said I could loaf with their organization the following season, and that June I visited Pittsburgh while the rookies were in Three Rivers Stadium for a week of pre-training camp workouts.

But before we get into that I had better lay down one more chapter of groundwork. The only way in which this book is going to be like a Russian novel* is that it will entail a plethora of names. The best way, I think, to keep track of all these names is to provide an expanded roster right up front. Thereafter I am just going to call a player by his name and if you forget who he is you can turn back to this roster. If you want to get on with the story of the Steelers' doomed Super Bowl quest (as well you might, I should think, by this time), skip this chapter and refer back to it at leisure. While laying out this roster, we can also consider the whole question of Names.

*Aside from the Jagov concept and the fact that one of the Steelers, rookie Glen Scolnik, said his family name was originally Raskolnikov. "That's something to be proud of," I said. "Well, I don't know," Scolnik said. "A guy that killed an old lady with an ax . . ."

□ 4 □

NAMES

Miss Paradise surveyed it all with the equable look that marks lunatics and the newly-risen: the world (her look said) is furnished with many sightly shapes; it is not for me to try and name them.

—NIGEL DENNIS, *CARDS OF IDENTITY*

Judging from the roster, none of the Steelers had what you could call a really great name. No such name, that is, as Fair Hooker of Cleveland or Jubilee Dunbar of the 49ers or Coy Bacon (Coy Bacon! How about Arch Spareribs!) of San Diego, or Tyrone Daisy and Drane Scrivener, rookies in camp with the Cowboys, or Dallas veteran Jethro Pugh, who named his daughter Jethrolyn Jo; or Ivan Cahoon of Gonzaga, who played tackle for the Packers from 1926 to 1929; or Wesley Leaper, who played end for the Packers in 1921 and 1923; or Veryl Switzer, a back for the Packers in 1954–55; or Cephus Weatherspoon of the Saints; or Billy Mantooth of West Virginia, who went to camp with the Eagles; or, of course, the Redskins' Herb Mul-key ("He had that done, that hyphen," a scout told me, "to give him individuality"); or Haven Moses of Denver; of course Miami's Jim Kiick and Larry Csonka: with whose surnames you could, fittingly, give someone a concussion by calling him up on the phone and abruptly pronouncing them into his ear. There being hardly any Latin influence in pro football, there was no Steeler name on the order of Marcelino Lopez, the Baltimore Oriole pitcher whose name has always seemed as pretty to me as Cielito Lindo. If not prettier.

The lack of a really grabby name among the Steelers was a shame, especially inasmuch as the team had had some fine ones in the past: Bob Balog, Byron Beams, Maurice "Mule" Bray, Rocco Canale, Shipley Farroh, Urban Henry, Max Kielbasa, Booth Lusteg, Gonzales Morales (*hardly* any Latin influence), Mel O'Delli, Myron Pottios, Dick Riffle, Loran Ribble, Marty Rosepink, Walter Szot, Lou Tsoutsouvas, Lowe Wren and Joe Zombek.

And Chuck Cherundolo, the greatest Steeler center of all time. I don't know any more about Cherundolo than that he is called the Steelers' greatest center, but I would rather hear his name over and over than birdsong. Cherundolo. Elements of *andale* and bungalow, churl and undulate, chirrup and trundle.

22

One of the great charms in sports is the high incidence of magical names. The Vanderbilt basketball team when I was a student at the university had a 6–9, bone-thin, deft, eagle-nosed center and forward named Snake Grace. He was the second-best-named person I have met personally. (First was a WAC lieutenant colonel named Ariel Stout. I have never met the public relations director of the *New York Quarterly*, who, if the masthead is to be believed, is named Zenith Gross.)

But I'm not sure that I realized what a great name Snake's was while we were in school together. He was in my fraternity and out of Hopkinsville, Kentucky, and whenever you saw him coming up you would automatically say "Snake!" and everybody around would feel good. He was a funny-looking but together-looking person. You could see how readily he must have come by his nickname and at the same time how ill it suited him: snakes are low-down and Snake was 6-9; snakes are sneaky and Snake was not only as long but as upright as the day is.

In other words my sense of how good a name Snake had was different from the fan's or the sportswriter's sense. It was only when I went with the Steelers' Tim Rooney on a scouting trip to watch the Vanderbilt-Tennessee game, and got to reminiscing about Vanderbilt names, that the combination Snake Grace seemed as great, in a purely literary and theological sense, as it would have seemed arising from a strange team's roster. One of the periodic delights of scribes is to scan the agate-type draft lists or training camp rosters in various sports and pick out the great new names. When one first became aware that Penn State had a defensive lineman named Steve Smear, that the Boston Red Sox had a pitching prospect named Richard Pole from Trout Creek, Michigan (did he have a friend named Line? Was he tall enough to be called Bean?), that the Cardinals used to have a pitcher named Bob Duliba whose nickname was "Ach"—those are moments of pure verbal appreciation that have nothing to do with the people involved. One loves to invent nicknames for sports figures based on nothing but their names: Curt "Watsa" Matter of the University of Washington, former pro receiver Jimmy "Either" Orr and baseball's Don "Bird Thou Never" Wert. Imagine the verse that could have been written about Snake Grace by someone who didn't know him from Adam:

Oh Snake (he glides and wiggles) Grace!
We know he'll ne'er stink out the place!

("Stink out the place," or ". . . the joint," or ". . . the house," is a player's common expression for doing badly, as in "My hands stunk out the joint tonight.")

One of my greatest regrets during training camp was that Loren Toews's last name turned out not to rhyme with Loew's. Even if he couldn't kick, he would have made a great counterpart to pitcher Rollie Fingers of the Oakland A's. But Toews rhymed with Raves. Had someone formed a fan club called Toews's

Broews, that would have been some consolation. But what the sportswriter's soul cried out for was the chance to dub the young prospect, however obviously, Twinkle. That is what sportswriting is for, and such a chance may come along once in a scribe's lifetime.

However, that would have been silly anyway, I realized after being around the Steelers personally. If L. C. Greenwood had thought of it, it might not have been silly, come to think of it—but anyway the only nickname I heard applied to Toews during the year was "Flake." I heard trainer Ralph Berlin call him that once, after Toews showed up on the team plane wearing only (from the waist up) a T-shirt. "Way to dress up, Loren," teammates told him. (The word "flake" as a sports term for eccentrics derives from the remark by Wally Moon—there's a name—of the baseball Cardinals, to the effect that things seemed to "flake off" the mind of his roommate, Jackie Brandt, and disappear.)

Toews seems likely to be a Steeler for a long time. He was distant, never said much, and had gone to Berkeley, but he hit very hard, and one could detect a still-amorphous favorable feeling growing up toward him among the players. He had not opened up enough, however, or done anything engagingly strange enough to warrant a nickname. What people on a team call each other has to do with the kind of feeling people had toward Snake, knowing him. As the year went on, I realized that there were some great names on the Steelers at that.

OFFENSIVE LINE (BEGIN WITH THE MOST OBSCURE BIG NAMES)

Ray Mansfield, starting center, 6–3, 260, white, born in 1941 in Bakersfield, California, University of Washington, eleventh year in pros. Mansfield and Jim Clack felt deprived of recognition potential by having to share the first-string center's job (Mansfield in the first and third quarters, Clack in the second and fourth). I suggested that Mansfield was a bad name for recognition anyway, compared to such more widely known centers' names as Forrest Blue, Mick Tinglehoff and Jim Otto. I suggested that he and Clack turn themselves, for publicity purposes, into one center named Manclack. "Mansfield is a pretty good name," he said a little severely. But his best name was "The Old Ranger." Or "The Ranger," or "Ranger." Several players were watching "Death Valley Days" on television a couple of years back. That program's narrator, the Old Ranger, came on the screen and spoke for a while through his moustache. A teammate turned from the screen to Mansfield and said, "The Old Ranger."

A beefy burr-headed person throughout his youth, Mansfield had by this time become a veteran and had grown hair and a bushy moustache; and he told a lot of stories. And his life had provided a lot of story material. By the end of 1973, through grit and frontier resourcefulness (once, in 1971, he inserted himself into a game for one play, a kickoff, to keep his streak going), he had sustained a team-record consecutive-games-appeared-in string of 154. And for his bulk and years, he ranged. In films, when a Steeler play seemed to have just about ground to a halt, the Old Ranger would come flying into the frame, the towel in his belt flapping like a tail, to knock some unsuspecting defender down flat. "He's just like a little kid," a Steeler scout observed once, watching Mansfield do this on film. It gave Mansfield, himself, a great deal of pleasure to reflect on this aspect of his game. People would look over at Mansfield sitting on his stool in the dressing room, boyish, seasoned, blockish and sprightly, and say, "The Oooold Ranger." And people, including Mansfield most of all, would smile with satisfaction.

Jim Clack, starting center, 6–3, 250, white, born in 1947 in Rocky Mount, North Carolina, Wake Forest, third year. Clack's nickname was one of the few that had no real connection to the bearer's personality. It was, however, inevitable. It was "Clickety." Why no group of fans ever had enough sense to start a fan club called Clack's Claque, I don't know. If I were *inventing* the Steelers I would give them a wide receiver named, say, Ezell Split, with the nickname "Lickety."

Bruce Van Dyke, all-pro guard, 6–1, 255, white, born in 1941 in Lancaster, California, University of Missouri, eighth year. Sometimes "Dyker," but most notably "Moose," or "Moosie." Fan club, Bruce's Mooses. Part of the humor involved here, one might infer, is that "Bruce" is an interior decorator's name and therefore should neither apply to Van Dyke nor rhyme with Moose. Bruise Van Dyke would have seemed more simply appropriate. Then too, Van Dyke did not look like a moose exactly. He had a huge moose jaw and was no doubt strong as a moose, but he was built, on an NFL scale, more like a fireplug. A moose compressed into a fireplug was about right; a man who was unloaded upon by Van Dyke, one may speculate, felt like a dog who approached a fireplug which suddenly unfolded into a moose. Then again, Van Dyke did have a certain creditable Bruciness; "super gentle" was the word a lady in the party used to describe him after an evening with the Van Dykes. Hence, perhaps, the diminutive: Moosie.

Sam Davis, starting guard, 6–1, 255, black, born in 1944 in Ocilla, Georgia, Allen College, seventh year. On an NFL information form a few years back Sam wrote, under *Nickname,* "Rock." *Who gave?* "High school coach." *What prompted?* "Because of my solid hitting power." But on the Steelers he was called "Tight," or "Tight Man," "because," as one teammate put it, "he keeps us tight." That would be tight in the sense of together—Davis was the Steelers' offensive captain, and he had a dedicated, disciplined, responsible air. He also exuded the tightness of a drum. On that same publicity form he said his *greatest experience in football* was as follows: "During my sophomore year I executed ten successful tackles in the backfield unassisted." But he was too short to be a defensive lineman in the pros; and offensive linemen don't get nicknames like "Mean Joe," "Mad Dog," or even "Hollywood Bags" (see later). Tight Man suits an offensive lineman. "Being on offense you can't be vicious, violent, destructive," he explained once ruefully. "Pass-protectionwise you want to stay away from violence. You can't ever get mad. Man hits you on the side of the head, you just laugh, stay there in front of him, let him hit the other side of your head. Then, on a running play, you can explode on him." "Explode" was, of course, the standard term for what a lineman is supposed to do—"explode off the ball"—but Sam used it more often in discussing his craft than anybody else I talked to. Sam had a nice laugh but with pain behind it.

Jon Kolb, starting tackle, 6–2, 262, white, born in 1947 in Ponca City, Oklahoma, Oklahoma State, fifth year. "Kolb" was in itself a good slablike name that fit Kolb—the strongest man on the team and one of the strongest weight-lifters in the league, with a top benchpress of 550 pounds—as well as any nickname could have. I did hear Kolb called "Jon Paul" once, and for some reason that seemed appropriate, perhaps for its overtones of Oom Paul. He was sitting next to Gilliam in the bus going to the hotel in Houston before the first Oiler game. Gilliam was wearing high-heeled shoes, a felt cap, low pants and an open-front shirt. Kolb, who lived in the country, was wearing cowboy boots and nonfancy pants and shirt. (Sometimes Kolb came to practice in Levi's and a Levi jacket with a turkey-hunting license pinned on the back.) Gilliam and his roommate Ernie Holmes were exchanging threats to pass the time. Gilliam said he had a gun in his bag, so Holmes had better look out when they got up to the room. Besides, he said, "ain't nobody going to threaten me. 'Cause Jon Paul ain't going to let 'em. Are you, Jon Paul?" Up until that point I hadn't realized that Kolb was droll. Kolb's straight-faced response to Gilliam was to unbutton his own shirt and pull his T-shirt up and his pants down far enough that his navel showed, like Gilliam's.

Glen Ray Hines, starting tackle, 6–5, 265, white, born in 1943 in El Dorado, Arkansas, University of Arkansas, eighth year. Hines, an accomplished pass blocker acquired early in the year from Oakland, was probably the slowest man on the team. Once L. C. Greenwood, a big one for giving people nicknames, looked over at Hines in the dressing room and said, "Super Speed!" Hines smiled. "Got to look quick to see me," he said, and he moved steadily on.

Gerry Mullins, reserve or starting tackle, guard, and on occasion tight end, 6–3, 244, white, born 1949 in Fullerton, California, University of Southern Cal, third year. "Moon." Moon was called "Moon" because of the comic-strip character, but the name fit him more intimately than Clickety fit Clack. Moon had a big, full face trimmed with bushy muttonchop whiskers and frequently

26

expanded by a large semi-evil smile; he was also called "Mooner," "Moon-chops" or "Chops." Angie, the girl friend who visited him from California, called him "Chops." One of the best athletes on the team, Moon hadn't settled into a starting job and was nagged by Noll, but anybody who is called "Chops" by as wonderful-looking a girl as Angie, in the tone Angie tended to use, doesn't really have much more to achieve in life. He and Sam Davis also called each other "Hero," for vague reasons. "Why do you call him Hero?" I asked each in turn. " 'Cause he's my Heee-ro!" they each replied.

Gordy Gravelle, reserve tackle, 6–5, 250, white, born in 1949 in Oakland, California, Brigham Young, second year. Gravelle was always in on badinage between Mullins, Clark, Van Dyke, Mansfield and others, but the only nick-name I heard applied to him was "Squint." He squinted without his glasses. His father was well-off, the owner of a big trucking company, and he perhaps accordingly did not seem particularly driven, or explosive. He regretted having gone to Brigham Young (where he was an All-American), though.

I told Gravelle's engaging wife Molly a sort of shaggy-dog story whose punch line was "Pardon me Roy, is that the cat that chewed your new shoes?"—a story which Van Dyke, Mansfield, Hanratty and Russell often requested that I retell—and discovered that she didn't get it because she was too young to have heard of "The Chattanooga Choo-Choo." I wonder whether the next generation will even know what a choo-choo is. If they don't they may not appreciate the famous name story about the TV interviewer who, looking forward to a nice lively chat, asked Choo Choo Coleman of the New York Mets on the air, "How did you get your name, Choo Choo?" and heard him answer simply, "I don't know."

Mel Holmes, reserve guard, 6–3, 251, black, born in 1950 in Miami, North Carolina A & T, third year. Once known as "Leo, because during a sandlot game when young I was so mean, they called me the lion," Mel had not emerged as a mean pro. But on the team bus he said, "I had to nearly kill a man one time to convince him I wasn't Ernie Holmes."

RECEIVERS

Ron Shanklin, all-pro wide receiver, 6–1, 190, black, born in 1948 in Hubbard, Texas, North Texas State, fourth year. His most widely used nickname was "Shank," but his black teammates also called him "Booker," or "P. B. Booker," a name which mystified me until, and to some extent after, I asked him and L. C. and Dwight about it on the team plane. "I guess it's because I keep getting up," Shanklin explained. Seeing that I still hadn't mastered the concept, he said to L. C., "Run it down for him, Bags."

"P. B. Booker: Pretty Bad Booker," said L. C. Seeing that I had still not entirely caught on, Dwight took over.

"Keep on Bookin'," he said. "Like keep on truckin'."

White Steelers tended not to have any idea what the bases of black Steelers' nicknames were.

Frank Lewis, starting far and wide receiver, 6–1, 196, black, born in 1947 in New Orleans, Grambling, third year. No known nickname. He may have been too fast to pin one on.

Barry Pearson, starting (when Shanklin or Lewis was hurt) or reserve wide receiver, 5–11, 185, white, born in 1950 in Genesco, Illinois, Northwestern, second year. During one poker game, at least, he and Dennis Meyer were both called "Leprechaun." Presumably because they were small, by the standards of their profession, and white, which is to say more or less Irish. There was, to be sure, something gnarled and mystical about the way Pearson kept catching passes despite a notable lack of size or speed.

John McMakin, starting tight end, 6–3, 232, white, born in 1950 in Spartanburg, South Carolina, Clemson, second year. Blond, gangly, low-talking, boyish-looking. L. C. got a good deal of pleasure out of calling him "Junior." One of the things McMakin and I had in common was that we both got a good deal of pleasure out of whatever L. C. said.

Glenn Scolnik, reserve wide receiver, 6–3, 190, white, born in 1951 in East Chicago, Indiana, Indiana University, first year. Called "Tomato" because of his vegetarianism. Once he told Dennis Meyer he wouldn't eat meat because it would weaken him. "How weak would you be *then*, Tomato?" crowed Meyer.

Chuck Dicus, reserve wide receiver, 6–0, 183, white, born in 1948 in Odessa, Texas, University of Arkansas, third year. After Bradshaw began thinking of himself as Hose Manning, the quarterback in *Semi-Tough*, he began calling his steady companion Dicus "Shake," after Shake Tiller, the receiver in that novel. But I never heard anybody else call Dicus that.

Dave Williams, reserve wide receiver, 6–2, 207, white, born in 1945 in Cedar Rapids, Iowa, University of Washington, seventh year. Like Dicus, acquired from San Diego during the year, too recently to have a teamwide nickname.

Dave Davis, reserve wide receiver, 6–0, 175, black, born in 1948 in Alcoa, Tennessee, Tennessee State, third year. Newly acquired and quiet, no nickname. But his acquisition gave the Steelers clear claim to the league lead in

28

Davises, with four. On the sidelines during the first Oakland game, with Clarence Davis playing for the Raiders, Mansfield and I speculated that all the many black Davises in the NFL might be traced back to the same slaveowner. Jefferson, maybe. Or Al. This was insensitive of us, but that's the way you get when you think of people in terms of roster names. When the Steelers drafted still another Davis, Charles of TCU, there was some speculation that Noll might want everybody on his team to have the same name so that they would be interchangeable.

Larry Brown, reserve tight end, 6–4, 229, black, born in 1949 in Jacksonville, Florida, University of Kansas, third year. The only talk of any length I had with Brown was about what a great all-star football team could be put together of people named Brown. Paul, Jim, both Bobs, Bill, Tim, Larry, Aaron, Booker, John, Johnny Mack, Willie, Ed, Pete, Rosey, Barry, Charlie, Fred, Roger and Ray would be very strong. Especially if they played the Steelers in Cleveland. Larry's wife was named Vanessa.

SPECIALISTS

Roy Gerela, kicker, 5–10, 185, white, born in 1948 in Sarrail, Alberta, Canada, New Mexico, fifth year. Called "Good Foot," "Big Foot," for obvious reasons (though oddly enough he had the smallest feet on the team), and "Easy Money" because kickers are considered to work less hard than, say, interior linemen or steel puddlers. Besides being one of the NFL's best kickers Gerela was felicitously named for the formation of a fan club. If you want your boy to grow up to be a pro football star, feed him well, keep him poor, and name him Mosby or Hooper or Ben-Gurion, so that his Raiders or Troopers or Centurions can flock to him.

Bobby Walden, punter, 6–0, 190, white, born in 1938 in Boston, Georgia, University of Georgia, tenth year. Two data that jump out of the Steelers' press book are that Walden lives in Climax, Georgia, and that his wife is named Scarlett. Scarlett Walden, then, and what would Thoreau have said about that?
None of which is to be interpreted as a reflection on Walden, because he told me he would bury me on his farm if I wrote anything about him that was bad. Tom Keating called Walden "Sterling" because he once heard Mrs. Walden call him that. "Because he has a sterling personality," she explained. "He never uses it." Walden was the oldest and most resolutely crackerish Steeler. He was the only Steeler to ignore the last players' strike (he claimed he hadn't heard about it), and in the '73 training camp the rookies presented him an award as the crabbiest veteran. Toward the end of the year, however, Walden was occasionally addressed as "Geek." For some time he had himself been calling

anyone with long hair "Geek," and yet his own hair had gradually filled out pretty considerably. He had even taken to using a hair dryer. He was not at all defensive about using a hair dryer. (Most often he was called, with I think "affection" would not be too strong a word, "Bo.")

RUNNING BACKS

Franco Harris, starter, 6–2, 230, black-Italian, born in 1950 in Fort Dix, New Jersey, Penn State, second year. Franco was sometimes addressed in fan letters as Frank O'Harris, Frank O. Harris and even Frank Oharis, which I guess would be Greek, but he didn't have a nickname; and didn't need one. Anyone whose name ends in *o* and has any flair at all has a great advantage in becoming a household word, viz.:

Brando, Garbo, Monroe, Valentino, Groucho, Harpo, Chico, Zeppo, Gummo, Geronimo, Satchmo, Bronko, the Bambino, B. O. (Plenty), Pogo, Cisco, Pancho, Pinocchio, Gambino, Gallo, Sambo, Coco, Bobo (Newsom, Olson, Rockefeller), Bevo, Bardot, Joltin' Joe Di Maggio, Jersey Joe, G. I. Joe, Shoeless (Say It Ain't So) Joe, Roberto, Trevino, Rizzo, Toto, Dino, Basilio, Charley O., Johnny O., Big O, Jackie O., Mighty Mo, *(Story of)* O, Little Mo, Columbo, Sacco, Romeo, Yevtushenko, Marco Polo, Frodo, Hero, Zero, Nero, Miro, Spiro (nolo), Rothko, Tito, Pluto, Thoreau, Poe, Ralph Waldo, Perry Como, Rollo, Arlo, Marlo, Marlowe, Nemo (Little or Captain), Godot, Bo, Jumbo, Dumbo, Ringo, Ingo, Bozo, Rebozo, Dynamic Duo, Kingston Trio, Yoko Ono, Harriet Beecher Stowe, Hondo, Apollo, Desalvo, Jojo (the dog face boy), Sluggo, Mineo, Ezio, Mario Savio, Sonny and Cher Bono, Mr. Moto, Bilbo, Bilko, Garo, Nogood Boyo, Boudreau, Harthorne Wingo, Captain Video, Fats Domino, Wells Fargo, Jell-O, Gonzo, Colonel Stingo, Oh (the last name of the Babe Ruth of Japan), Ho, Mao, and Quasimodo.

Franco was the most commercial property on the Steelers, even while having an off-year. He was also perhaps the most private Steeler.

John Fuqua, starter or reserve, 5–11, 205, black, born in 1946 in Detroit, Morgan State, fifth year. "Frenchy." Also "The Frenchman" or "The Count," because he claimed to be a French count who, while vacationing on the Riviera, was turned black by fallout from a nuclear test. If this story may be credited, the Steelers had two star running backs that were black and European. And if Franco is not exactly Italian for Frenchy, it is close. "When I was at Morgan," Frenchy said, "they just called me 'Fuqua.' I think it was Rowser who named me—Rowser and Myron Cope to some extent. Rowser and I were in high school together and he couldn't say 'Fuqua.' I took French and I used to say 'commontalley voo' in the halls and he would call me 'Frenchy Fuckwa.' I used to get on his case when he called me 'Fuckwa.' "

* * *

Preston Pearson, starter or reserve, 6–1, 205, black, born in 1945 in Free-port, Illinois, University of Illinois, seventh year. Called "Press." A slithery runner who sometimes broke away impressively, he pressed harder in the public press for recognition of his abilities than he sometimes did under pres-sure for tough yardage. If the above seems a stupidly self-conscious stretch of punning around, it is because I liked Preston, as did his teammates, and I feel awkward about pointing out what seemed the weakness of his position. By the end of the season I had to keep reminding myself (by such means as trying to catch passes) that I was ultimately a member of the press. I was infected by the players' I think honorable (as well as self-protective) disinclination to criticize other players publicly. I have to resist the inclination to be oblique in discussing the players I got to know personally, even though that is the journalistic equivalent of "dancing"—which is what Preston was accused of doing, and what he and others accused Franco of doing, as a runner. And what Preston, by God, did not do when it came to speaking his mind.

Rocky Bleier, reserve, 5–11, 210, white, born in 1946 in Appleton, Wiscon-sin, Notre Dame, fifth year. I don't even know what Rocky's given name was. It's not listed in the press book; he was nicknamed "Rock" in the cradle. "He was a very robust baby," his father told me. "Somebody looked at him in the baby bed and said, 'He looks like a rock in there,' so I started telling people, 'Come in and have a look at the Rock.'" Hence the fan club, Rocky's Flying Squirrels, and the banner in Three Rivers Stadium that read "Bleier. We Love You. Like a Rock." Something about Bleier—earnest hard-working midwest-ern Catholic Notre Dame Vietnam veteran—made one assume that at bottom he was a clean-cut bedrock type. What I mean is, one of the Steelers' publicity people said he was "Middle America at its best," and he was manifestly straight, solid and fresh-faced, especially in his 1972 picture, in which he appeared clean-shaven, short-haired and choir-boyish. But in 1973 he had grown a moustache and longish thinning hair, and in the dressing room he had a way of rolling his eyes like a midwestern mad scientist, so that he presented himself as an engagingly askew-looking, not to say rocky-looking, rock: huge-chested, gleam-eyed and proclaiming to those about him, "Don't knock the Rock!" Not that anybody ever did knock him, except to his face—for instance, making fun of his war wounds.

Steve Davis, 6–1, 218, black, born in 1949 in Lexington, Virginia, Delaware State, second year. Another quiet Davis, Steve was, however, an extremely hard runner and the Steeler about whom one most often heard informed sources saying, "He's going to be *some*thin'." Somethin' Davis is a good name for a fullback, especially since a consistently physical runner was one of the somethings missing from the Steelers in '73.

31

QUARTERBACKS

Terry Bradshaw, starter, 6–3, 218, white, born in 1948 in Shreveport, Louisiana, Louisiana Tech, fourth year. None of the names Bradshaw was called by teammates were particularly distinctive: T.B., Terry B.B., Brad. "The Blond Bomber" sounded like a press creation on the order of "the Nollmen" and "Rooney U."—two collective terms for the Steelers favored by the *PostGazette* and hated by the players. "How would you like to be called 'the Nollmen,' in your work?" one Steeler asked me. I don't suppose Bradshaw, who was interested in branching out into entertainment circles, minded having a name like "The Blond Bomber"—which was given to him by a college teammate he didn't like—though he would have preferred an offensive system which allowed him to throw bombs; but there was a certain lack of immediacy about such an appellation. I can't think of any other player in the NFL with such a Golden Age of Sport cognomen. Bradshaw was also called "The Louisiana Rifleman," too, briefly, because of his arm and his considerable physical resemblance to Chuck Connors, who played the Rifleman on television. But players today tend to be called more familiar names by fans and press than in the days of the Galloping Ghost and the Georgia Peach. Incidentally, the best-sounding "The" name I ever heard was twenties goalie George Vezina's: "The Chicoutimi Cucumber."

Terry Hanratty, reserve, or starter when Bradshaw was hurt, 6–1, 210, white, born in 1948 in Butler, Pennsylvania, Notre Dame, fifth year. Hanratty was a man to whom familiar nicknames stuck: "Rat," for his name and appearance, and "Hook," for his nose. Sometimes "Rat" was lengthened to "Ratso Rizzo," which was interesting since if you had to pick two Steelers for the Dustin Hoffman and Jon Voight roles in *Midnight Cowboy* they would be Hanratty and Bradshaw, respectively. After the Cincinnati game, in which Bradshaw was hurt and Hanratty took over and rallied the offense, Ernie Holmes used the phrase "Han the Man," but that—thanks no doubt to Hanratty's own injuries—never caught on. Which was a shame because it evoked Stan the Man Musial, and Hanratty's mother, the parent who had by far the greater influence on him, was a Cardinal fan who named her son after outfielder Terry Moore. It was also a shame because in '73, at least on offense, no Steeler ever became the Man.

Joe Gilliam, reserve, or starter when Bradshaw and Hanratty were hurt, 6–2, 187, black, born in 1950 in Charleston, West Virginia, Tennessee State, second year. In college Gilliam was "Jefferson Street Joe," because Jefferson was the main street in black Nashville and the man whom Gilliam "idolized to the max," as he said, was Broadway Joe Namath. During the first part of the '73 season, when he was on the taxi squad, Gilliam said he wasn't Jefferson

Street Joe anymore, "just Joe," and trainer Ralph Berlin called him "Ragoo," because "he's on the rag all the time." But Gilliam was too mercurial to be just Joe. Teammates called him Joe Gillie; and when, after he came in to save the Redskin game, somebody called him "Joe Willie number two," invoking Joe Willie Namath, Gilliam said, "No. It's Joe Willie *Gillie*. The *original*."

DEFENSIVE LINE

Joe Greene, all-pro tackle, 6–4, 275, black, born in 1946 in Temple, Texas, North Texas State, fifth year. As everybody knows: "Mean Joe." Or, to his friends, just "Mean." Greene could have been named Freddie Perkins, or Cynthia something, and still have been a palpably great defensive lineman, but there is no doubt that the name furthered his national recognition. He got it not for meanness, the story goes, but because his college team was known as the Mean Green. In fact, the story often goes on, "Joe Greene is not mean at all." I always felt that those who pronounced this opinion most energetically were subtly boosting their own substantiality, like acquaintances who say of Henry Kissinger, "He's just good plain folks." I mean Greene was a pleasant, well-spoken person; but it was hard to look at him without also thinking, "Now he's . . . *bad*." Asked if being named Mean bothered him, he said, "As far as football goes—it doesn't hurt me as much as it does in my personal life. I like to think of myself as a nice person. I am a nice person. As far as being mean, I think I'm capable of being mean. Very capable."

Once I was watching Greene when he pulled off his huge cowboy hat, gunbelt and guns, threw them down on the field, said "Joe, this is child's play!" to Steeler publicist Joe Gordon, and clumped off to the dressing room in his practice uniform. Someone had been trying to pose him with the rest of the front four as "Greene's Gang," in exaggerated Western garb, and he had decided it was silly. "Bad enough the way people look at pro football players already," he muttered.

"What is there about pro football players that people don't realize?" I asked him.

He looked at me darkly. (It is hard for me to keep touches of what may be respectful racism from creeping into my reactions to defensive tackles: he looked at me darkly.) "Human," he said. Human Joe Greene.

Ernie Holmes, starting or reserve tackle, 6–3, 260, black, born in 1948 in Jamestown, Texas, Texas Southern, second year. Holmes was first called "Fats" by his grandfather: "I was a very large baby." He was also a very large adult, and although he was built much too well to be considered fat by civilian standards, he had a great tendency to put weight on, even though he said he only ate "two major meals a week." But when he took a whole package of wienies out of his refrigerator and ate them cold, he did not consider that a major meal. He had a wide face and an almost wider smile and a big gold tooth, he often danced (like Gilliam, White and Blount) while dressing after practice, and "Fats" fit him. But if you wanted to sum up the way he played ball, rain or shine, practice or game, you couldn't do better than to say his given name: Earnest Lee. (In camp it was said that his new nickname would be "Quick Draw," because in the off-season he had shot a policeman in a helicopter, but that name didn't stick. Once when a helicopter flew over the practice field Tom Keating said, "Don't get anxious, Fats.")

Dwight White, all-pro end, 6–4, 255, black, born in 1949 in Hampton, Virginia, East Texas State, third year. "Mad Dog." "Hey, it was one of those foolish things, man. I transferred from Lincoln High School in Dallas, where we had Duane Thomas and Abner Haynes and Sticks Anderson, to Madison. We were playing Lincoln then in the city championships and Sticks was their quarterback, and they were beating us, and on the last play of the game they were just running the clock out. I was just . . . man, they beating us! Sticks just lay on the ground with the ball. I ran up and boom, hit him on the back. He looked up and said, 'Hey, man, that was cold-blooded.' But I didn't want them to win! After that they called me Mad Dog.

"I came here I thought I'd lost that Mad Dog shit. Everybody: 'Dog! What's happening, Dog?' That has some kinda slanderous implications, you know. It could be taken all different ways. Everybody started calling me that. That's my name, now."

But Dwight White was a catchy name in itself: Fight, fight, Dwight White. His fan club was Dwight's Whites. "I don't know who they are," he said, but then he did an imitation of a white fan looking down on him and saying, "He's a *big* un, inny?" Another name I heard directed toward Dwight by people around the club was "Dee-wight." Like "dee-light."

I might say that White sometimes called me "The Hemingway of Western P-A."

L. C. Greenwood, all-pro end, 6–6, 245, black, born in 1946 in Canton, Mississippi, Arkansas A. M. & N., fifth year. One of the first things I asked L. C. was what his initials stood for. "Lover Cool," he asserted, but then he went on to say that they didn't stand for anything, L. C. was his name, but that people in his fraternity in college had kept after him about it so that he had told them it stood for Leonard Carl, but they wouldn't believe that so he changed it to Leonard Charles, so if I ever heard anybody address him as Leonard Charles, that would be why. "I think he's hiding his real name," said Fuqua. "As a matter of fact, I betcha it's something funny. It's probably Lenore or something like that. Almost a girl's name or something . . ."

But then I saw a form L. C. had filled out which called for his full name, and I learned something that very few people know: L. C.'s middle name. His full name, I found out, was L. C. Henderson Greenwood.

His full nickname was "Hollywood Bags." He had a T-shirt that said "Hollywood Bags" on it. The Hollywood part was given him by former Steeler Chuck Beatty, in recognition of his oft-repeated desire to go to Hollywood and act. (By '73 he was more inclined toward TV broadcasting.) The Bags part was more obscure. It derived from his other nickname, which was "Baggit," or "Bag It." "You know, like . . . bag it." In other words, I guess, "give up on it," but L. C. didn't give up on anything in '73. I would say he had the best year on the team.

Tom Keating, starting or reserve tackle, 6–2, 247, white, born in 1941 in Chicago, University of Michigan, ninth year. Keating's acquisition from Oakland complicated the problem of a name for the Front Four, along the lines of the Rams' Fearsome Foursome.

The Front Four was the rock on which the Steelers were built, on the playing field at least, and a suitably ominous or at least celebrative name seemed called for. The *Pittsburgh Courier,* the town's leading black paper, called Greene, White, Greenwood, and Holmes the "Baaaaad Black Front," "The Soul Patrol" was suggested, and "AfFront" occurred to me. But Keating eventually played as much as the naggingly injured Holmes, and except for a bush of hair and a moustache that covered a good part of his face Keating was basically white. Besides, the Baaaaad Black Front always sounded to me like a weather condition. Other proposed names for the front four were the Steel Curtain, the Anvil Chorus and—because first Greenwood and then Greene, White and Holmes took to gilding their game shoes—the Gold Rush. This last was perhaps the best, but then they gradually—as some of the starch went out of the team—stopped wearing the gold shoes. I kept this question in mind all season long, it being scribes' responsibility to verbalize mythic forces, but the best names I could come up with were Fore Front, the Popular Front, the PreFrontal Front and the Sore Fore Four. Consultation of *Bartlett's Familiar Quotations* yielded, from *Hamlet,* the Front of Jove Himself ("See, what a grace was seated on this brow;/Hyperion's curls; the front of Jove himself;/An eye like Mars, to threaten and command. . . ."). I toyed with the idea of Baptismal Front, on the grounds that the Four had made a Christian, as the saying goes, out of many a quarterback and blocker. Or, The Nameless Dread.

But just before the San Francisco game I had the privilege of sitting around swapping fart stories with Greene, White, Greenwood, and Holmes. I forget how the subject came up, but I spoke of Le Petomane, I remember, and they of T. J. Lambert's farts in *Semi-Tough* and of friends who lit them. "There's nothing that relieves you," Holmes said in summation, with a big smile and great feeling, "like a good belch or a good faht." There is nothing like farting to drive people apart, but there is nothing like *talking* about farting to bring them together. The way the Front Four played ball had nothing to do with farting. As a matter of fact Greene said he put underarm spray and a little

cologne on before a game. "That's how you blow by guys. They go 'Sniff
. . . sniff . . . what's that?' And you blow by 'em." If any element of the Steelers
was flatulent, it was the offense. So you wouldn't want to call the Front Four
the Poot Troops.

Craig Hanneman, reserve end, 6–3½, 245, white, born in 1949 in Salem,
Oregon, grew up in Turner, Oregon, Oregon State, second year. Hanneman,
as a solid values conservative out of the Oregon woods (he discussed abstract
issues that he cared about, notably environmental matters, as cogently as
anyone on the team), came like Walden to be called "Geek" occasionally after
he let his hair get shaggy, but his primary nickname was "Copenhagen," or
"Cope." At the age of twelve, haying around Turner, he had taken up chewing
Copenhagen snuff because you couldn't smoke around hay. "It got to be a
habit when I was fourteen. I chew two cans a day when I'm nervous. That's
when I'm at the attic stage." (As I recall, he said "attic," not "addict"—he
said he was always at the addict stage—and he explained that he meant the
stage when he should be locked in an attic.) "A can and a quarter when I'm
not. I'll chew a can before game time. I roll out of bed at 7:30, put a pinch
in, soon as breakfast is over put another pinch in, go to the stadium, put in
a pinch, spit it out soon as I take my morning shit and puke. At halftime I'll
put a pinch in. After the game I'll put another pinch in and I'll chew it till
I go to sleep at night."

After the Cowboys' Walt Garrison appeared in a TV commercial for Skoal
snuff (which is mentholated Copenhagen, and smells about as dubious as
anything in my experience), I told Hanneman he ought to offer his promotional
services to Copenhagen. He said he'd thought about it but had concluded that
his name wasn't big enough: "The first thing they'd say, 'Who the fuck is Craig
Hanneman?' And they'd be right."

"Cope" was an interesting name for Hanneman ("Cope! Cope!" the cry went
up when he belted people in the Oklahoma drill in camp) because he was
redolent of a desire to prove to doubting coaches that he could cope with a
regular job. A vaunted brawler and hatchetman, he was also an earnest friend
whose feelings were easily touched. He didn't complain about football's physical toll, but he did say it hurt him for coaches to address him by his last name.

Steve Furness, reserve tackle-end, 6–4, 255, white, born in 1950 in Providence, Rhode Island, University of Rhode Island, second year. The only
name-talk I had with Furness was when I asked him whether he was related
to Betty. He said no. He dipped snuff too, but had not made a name for himself
that way. If he ever becomes big in Pittsburgh he is a natural to be called
"Blast."

LINEBACKERS

Andy Russell, all-pro outside, 6–2, 225, white, born in 1941 in Detroit, University of Missouri, ninth year. The quintessential thinking player, a prominent businessman off the field, team player rep and defensive captain, Russell was convivial.and warmly respected, and he was like Fran Tarkenton in being an unsettlingly imaginative player though an unabashedly white suburbanite person. But how many tax-shelter salesmen do you know with really pungent nicknames? "A.R." was sometimes heard, but the closest thing to a pet name for him was "Captain." "Old Captain," said Moon Mullins to him one afternoon in the Jamestown Inn after a trying practice, "this beer is going to taste better than any beer has ever tasted."

Henry Davis, starting middle, 6–3, 235, black, born in 1942 in Slaughter, Louisiana, Grambling, sixth year. The nature of the Steeler defense required this Davis to apply and absorb a punishingly heavy amount of direct hole-clogging contact—he wasn't free to float and pop the way famous middle linebackers have been—and strength and "physicalness" were his strongest points. But the other black Steelers' name for him was not, say, "Hard Henry," but "Scatter." Henry was flashily dressed, keyed up, staccato-talking, and—what's the best way to put it?—alive in several different directions at once.

Jack Ham, all-pro outside, 6–1, 225, white, born in 1948 in Johnstown, Pennsylvania, Penn State, third year. Ham's fan club was Dobre Shunka, which is Polish for Great Ham—or, actually, I was told, for "Good Ham," there being no word in Polish for "great." Every year this club presents him with a big ham. His name on the team was "Hammer." Quickness and reaction—he was one of the best athletes, and best players, on the team, and receiver coach Lionel Taylor would have liked to have him as a tight end—were Ham's game, but he also hammered. Not a sledgehammer, a ball peen (used especially for riveting). His little-known middle name, for what it is worth, was Raphael. "Ham" suggests a kind of blatancy, which Ham didn't have. I remember once when someone asked Gravelle what he'd done the night before and Gravelle said, well, he'd gotten together with his wife's family and they'd looked at slides, and Ham glanced up from his gin hand and said, "Why didn't you *call* us?" One night at a party a man who had been drinking took Ham's wonderful-looking girl friend Joanne Fell aside and offered to help Jack market his All-American-boy image. He took me for $18 once, throwing a Frisbee into a laundry hamper.

George Webster, reserve outside, 6–4, 220, black, born in 1945 in Anderson, South Carolina, Michigan State, seventh year. I don't think Webster had a nickname, but he didn't need one. I don't think he needed anything. By the time he was twenty-five he had already been named an *all-time* all-pro in the American Football League. He had made good money, signing with Houston of the AFL during the talent wars between the then-separate leagues, and his appearance—tall, big-shouldered, long-legged, lissomely stooped, Fu Man-chued, bright white-toothed, relaxedly distant-looking—was so impressive that people sometimes mistook him in hotel lobbies, with a hat on, for Isaac Hayes, whom he actually looked considerably better than. He wasn't the player he had been at his peak with the Oilers, before knee injuries left him less aggressive, but he filled in capably—sometimes impressively—for Russell or Ham. He had a big home in Houston and "I got some diversified stocks, got some Woolworth's and all that shit into it, and I don't even check it," he said contentedly once. After alluding to a certain occasion in a ski lodge, he added, "If I die tomorrah . . . I had some *good* times out of life."

Loren Toews, reserve outside, 6–3, 212, white, born in 1951 in Dinuba, California, University of California (Berkeley), first year. "Loren" is almost "Loner." Rookies seldom entered very freely into team fun, except during the chug-a-lugging festivities in camp. Mansfield said you were slow to get friendly with teammates for the same reason you were with fellow combat soldiers—they were too likely to drop out of your life. For a while Toews roomed with Glen "Knotty Pine" Edwards, but Toews never said anything in the room, Pine said, so Pine asked for a new roommate. When Toews heard of it he went to Pine and asked, "What's wrong with me?"
"*Naw,* it ain't like *that,* man," Pine told him.

Ed Bradley, reserve middle or outside, 6–2, 239, white, born in 1950 in Bridgeport, Connecticut, Wake Forest, second year. Big-chested, strong, Bradley hung around with Furness a lot, and used snuff too. His father, also Ed, played two years with the Bears, and gave him in his cradle a ball with Johnny Lujack's, Bulldog Turner's, Ed Sprinkle's and other Bears' autographs on it. Bradley was marked by those names for life.

DEFENSIVE BACKS

Mel Blount, starting corner, 6–3, 205, black, born in 1948 in Vidalia, Georgia, Southern University, fourth year. One of the reasons I picked the Steelers for this book was that they had a player with my name. "Just think," Blount said at one point, "your great-grandfather probably owned my great-grandfather and here you are writing a book about me." I thought that was an interesting possibility, and suggested that we both change our names to Akbar-Muhammad. Later I asked my father if in fact my great-grandfather might have owned

Mel's. "No," said my father, "because your great-grandfather didn't own anything. He was poor as owl dung."

Mel's nickname was "Supe." Many of the white Steelers thought it was "Soup." But Blount said it was short for "Super." Pete Carry of *Sports Illustrated* tells me that most National Basketball Association teams have a black player called "Supe," short for "Superstar," because he signed for a lot of money and never played much. Blount, an eminently gifted athlete, was, however, in his second season as a full-time regular, and he was always talking about making more money somewhere. When Gilliam told him he wouldn't have any hair by the time he was thirty, he said, "I don't *want* hair when I'm thirty. I want *money.*" One night I was out with the Gilliams, the Blounts, and some other people when Leslie, Blount's wife, asked him why they called him "Supe."

"We got one child and another one on the way," he said. "I thought you of all people would know." He and I called each other "Blount." He wanted me to write his biography, to be called *A Man Called Supe.*

John Rowser, starting corner, 6–1, 190, black, born in 1944 in Gallion, Alabama, but grew up in Detroit, University of Michigan, seventh year. Dirty John, or DJ. Ralph "Sticks" Anderson put the rationale for this as well as anyone: "Because he beats on people so bad. Against Miami last year he beat Howard Twilley *up,* the whole game." A crafty gamesman, who admitted to giving receivers fists and elbows as they tried to run their routes, Rowser was too abrasive a talker for defensive coordinator Bud Carson and Noll, and also for a few of the white players. Though he was relatively small and unswift, Rowser's tackles on receivers were often dramatic in effect, and raised the emotional tone of a game. He complained a lot about how much tackling of big running backs and playing off of guards the Steelers' defensive system required of him. In this connection he and Henry Davis might be called the niggers of the system. The coaches said that Rowser didn't have the range to play any other role. They also thought Rowser was subversive, and although coaches are nearly as quick to spot subversion as southern sheriffs are, "Rowser" did seem in one sense or another as good a name for Rowser as Dirty John was. The Steelers could have used more rousing.

Glen Edwards, starting weak safety, 6–0, 185, black, born in 1947 in St. Petersburg, Florida, Florida A & M, third year. While Sticks Anderson was with the team Edwards was sometimes called "Stones"—he being slightly shorter and almost as thin as Anderson, whom he competed for a starting job with and hung with. Noll is said to have gotten these nicknames backwards once. But Edwards's main nickname was "Pine," or "Knotty," or, in full, "Knotty Pine."

"I got that name my freshman year in college," Pine explained. "I was going to practice one day and I thought I was going to be late, so I jumped out of bed, didn't comb my hair, you know, and had lint all over my head, so when I got to practice a guy pointed to my head. And said, 'Pine. Knotty Pine.' "

"What does lint have to do with pine?" I asked.

"Heh," Pine said. "I don't know."

But that was dumb of me. It wasn't the lint, so much as the scraggly look of Pine's uncombed hair—and of Pine generally, even when he was wearing a magenta hat and a shirt of many vivid flowers. I don't mean "scraggly" in a pejorative sense. Pine didn't look messy, but he did look knotty. His Afro, parted on the side, stuck up in one small and one large clump, and his chin and cheekbones looked like burls, and he hit people like a pine-limb knout. He was also, for all his bumpy corporeality, the Steelers' most evanescent punt-returner. On one return against the Jets he ran into a tackler's arms, spun around 360 degrees in them, and came back out to take off again. Against Houston he went for an 86-yard touchdown although, as Noll put it, "there wasn't a block thrown. He saw a clog, ran away from the clog, came back, and ran away from the whole team. Nobody touched him." Pine himself put his technique, fittingly enough, in terms of grain: "People have a way of floating toward the way the return is going. I have a tendency to look at the man on the end, and if he knifes in I'll turn back and go against the grain." I wouldn't be surprised if the tackler in whose arms Pine spun around came away scratched up, as from sliding down a pine tree.

Mike Wagner, all-pro strong safety, 6–1½, 210, white, born in 1949 in Waukegan, Illinois, Western Illinois, third year. Wagner was named Hitter of the Year after '73 by some ethnic organization in Pittsburgh—and those organizations do not name people such things lightly—but his only nickname was "Wags." He was fast and tough (and waggish) but not innately nifty. He attracted little notice in high school, and he played for a college which had never before had a player drafted by the pros. He was drafted eleventh, which is pretty low down, and yet he was a starter in his first pro year, and in '73 made a big splash. A man with a good solid name and a good solid working background, he proved that application and intelligence can make up for a lack of Great Quick, which some scouts will tell you is the name of the game.

James Thomas, reserve corner and safety, 6–2, 196, black, born in 1951 in Macon, Georgia, Florida State, first year. Never called James, but J. T. "I had a habit," he said, "of writing my initials on everything—including myself. On my arms, desk and other places with an ink pen while in elementary school." He also said, "All through my life, I've figured I can do anything anyone else can. I probably can't, but you won't tell me I can't. I have a basic philosophy in life—I can. I can do anything with the help of God. That's me." After failing to beat anybody out for a starting job—though he played well as a fifth defensive back in special situations—he said he was somewhat disappointed in pro football, "but I'm not going to tell you in what ways."

John Dockery, reserve corner, 6–0, 185, white, born in 1944 in Brooklyn, Harvard, sixth year. Called "Dock." Among his former teammates, the Jets, he was known as "Schnauzer," for his moustached looks. Dockery's, on West Thirty-first Street in Manhattan, was his father's bar—a good Irish place where, in the words of Steeler public relations director Ed Kiely (whom L. C., incidentally, called "Easy Ed"), "They put the bottle up on the bar until you're finished with it. Some people brought in a pizza while I was there and were bringing pieces over to the people at the bar, and Mr. Dockery said, 'What're you trying to do, make a Guinea joint out of this place?'" Having survived in the pros as long as he had at his size and with a Harvard preparation, Dockery would have deserved the nickname "Hickory."

Dennis Meyer, reserve safety, 5–11, 186, white, born in 1950 in Jefferson City, Missouri, Arkansas State, first year (on the taxi squad in '72). Wiry and mildly countrified, Meyer was called "Kamikaze," for being so headlong while tackling or receiving the short punt, which most people would not want to receive at all. He was one of those people who, in scouting terms, "hurls himself with total disregard of his body." Or, it goes without saying, other people's bodies. Off the field, though, he was as unfanatical-seeming a person as you would ever want to meet. It was impossible to have a total disregard of his wife, who looked like Sally Struthers.

Ralph Anderson, traded safety, 6–1, 180, black, born in 1949 in Dallas, West Texas State, third year. Traded to New England during the exhibition season. "Seems like everywhere I go I get a nickname," he said. "In high school they called me 'Suitcase.' "
    "Why?"
    "Well, I had rather large feet. And I was the quarterback. And the coach just called me 'Suitcase.' In college they called me 'Skinner.' Then I got here, and I came into the huddle one day, and somebody looked down at my legs, you know, and said, 'Look like you got some getaway sticks there.' And after that they dropped the 'Getaway.' Everywhere I've been I've had a different name. And if I go someplace else, I guess I'll get another one." The next day he was traded.
    He did have amazingly thin calves. Once in practice Ernie Holmes, in an expansive mood, yelled "Sticks is . . . *Sticks!* Hey Sticks: they pinned you, man. That nickname they gave you." Then he thought a moment and looked even more pleased, and cried, "Should've called you 'Twigs'!"

COACHES

Chuck Noll, head coach, born in 1932 in Cleveland, University of Dayton, seven years as pro player, fourteenth year as pro coach. As an assistant coach he had been called "Knowledge," "Knute Knowledge" and "The Pope," because he knew everything and was infallible. The Steelers addressed him as "Chuck." In the third person they sometimes called him "Chuck" but more often "Noll" or, sometimes, "Chas."

Bud Carson, defensive coordinator, born in 1931 in Freeport, Pennsylvania, University of North Carolina, second year as pro coach, didn't play in pros.

Bob Fry, offensive line, born in 1930 in Cincinnati, University of Kentucky, ten years as offensive tackle with Rams and Cowboys, seventh year as pro coach.

Dick Hoak, offensive backfield, born in 1939 in Jeannette, Pennsylvania, Penn State, ten years as Steeler running back, second year as pro coach.

Babe Parilli, quarterbacks, born in 1930 in Rochester, Pennsylvania, University of Kentucky, sixteen years as pro quarterback with Green Bay, Cleveland, Oakland, Boston, Ottawa and New York Jets, third year as pro coach.

George Perles, defensive line, born in 1934 in Detroit, Michigan State, never played pro ball, second year as pro coach.

Bob Widenhofer, linebackers, born in 1943 in Butler, Pennsylvania, never played pro ball, first year as pro coach.

Lionel Taylor, receivers, born in 1936 in Kansas City, New Mexico Highlands College, ten years as receiver with Bears, Broncos, Oilers, fourth year as pro coach.

Paul Uram, flexibility, Butler, Pennsylvania, Slippery Rock College, never played pro ball, part-time coach.

Lou Riecke, strength, New Orleans, never played college or pro ball, part-time coach.

People called Hoak "Hoakie" and Parilli "Vito" and Widenhofer always "Woody," and Uram and Riecke "Stretch" and "Lift" respectively. I spent some agreeable time with the coaches, but they were the element of the team

42

I felt least at ease with. "I don't like coaches," I went so far as to tell photographer Iooss in training camp.

"And they sense it," he suggested. "Like dogs." Actually it was more a matter of our not trusting each other. Assistant coaches worry about saying anything that will get them in trouble with the head man, even more than players do. And once or twice I felt that a coach was trying to find out from me which players talked to me the most, and therefore which players ought to get in trouble.

A number of the people around the Steelers had nicknames of interest. Trainer Ralph Berlin was known as "the Plumber," in reference to his medical delicacy, and as "Plum"—short for Plumber but also descriptive of his shape—and also, by L.C. at least, as "Witch."

Traveling secretary Jim Boston was "Buff," or "the Buffalo"—it appeared that he weighed as much as a buffalo, and even in some hard-to-describe way that he moved like one.

Flamboyant groundskeeper Steve Denardo was "Dirt," for his medium and his appearance.

Art Rooney, Sr., was called "Boss" or "the Prez" or "the Chief," and he disclosed that as a rowdy street youth on the Irish North Side he had been called "Phoo," because "I never did curse, but I said "Phoo!" sometimes."

Driving back from training camp to Pittsburgh one evening I stopped at the Irwin exit turnpike toll station and found myself handing a dollar bill to a great-looking young woman named, according to her nametag, either Jeannette or Paulette (I can never remember which) Lips. I have always been interested in tollbooth people: their aspirations, their impressions of the people they meet, what it is like touching slightly the fingertips of thousands of people daily. I have also always been interested in lips. "You have a great name," I said to Ms. Lips as she made change.

"Thank you," she said.

I made so bold as to add, in a polite way, "and you're great-looking, too."

She smiled and then, what with the pressure of cars behind me, I drove off. What am I doing?! I thought. I got back on the turnpike, doubled back around, and came by her booth again. She had been replaced by a man named, I believe, Billiard. The toll-takers' shift had changed. All through camp I kept pulling up to that toll station and asking, "Ah . . . where is Paulette Lips?" No one knew. "Ah . . . where is *Jeannette* Lips?" No one knew her either. I told a number of players about this woman. In reply I heard of a girl called "the Squat" because of the position in which she liked to made love. That was not the level of romantic nomenclature I was off into.

"Do you like this girl just because of her name?" one player asked me, insinuating that that was the kind of thing you might expect from a scribe. The bartender at the 19th Hole, the after-practice bar, said he would track her down through friends in the Highway Patrol, but he never did. His name was Rabbits.

43

□ 5 □

FIRST DIP INTO
THE SCENE

Remember: Wherever you go . . . there you are.
—PITTSBURGH BOND
TRADER AND WAITRESS
JAIN QUERY

I made a preliminary visit to Pittsburgh in the middle of June, to get an apartment high atop Mount Washington, in a building whose top-floor restaurant, Christopher's, afforded the city's best view of the Golden Triangle, and to check out the rookies' orientation week.

In the past the Steelers had worked with their rookies in training camp for a week before the veterans arrived, but this year they weren't thinking much in terms of new blood. They were just bringing the new crop in to appraise them briefly in the flesh, to check their times in the 40-yard dash, and to give them some exercise programs to work on before camp.

In 1969 Chuck Noll took over a team that included a good many bad athletes. Bad athletes, the ones who manage to play anyway by hook or crook, appeal to me, but not to Noll. Only six—Bleier, Davis, Mansfield, Russell, Van Dyke and Walden—of the players Noll had inherited were still on the team in 1973. Only the last four of these were twenty-eight or older. Inspired drafting and trades during Noll's first three years—as the team won 12 games and lost 30, and consequently drafted high—brought together a young team with great potential, which became a Cinderella winner in '72. In '73 it had to be brought to maturity, as they say. The Revolution had come; now the new order had to be sustained. Some of the young veterans had been brought along carefully, worked gradually into Noll's emerging system. Now the bad athletes were gone. If a rookie made it this year he was going to have to be lucky, extremely good, or very forceful.

The veteran quarterbacks were in town with the rookies—quarterbacks always work longer hours. I introduced myself to blond, clean-shaven Bradshaw, who looked like Galahad; to hook-nosed, black-moustached Hanratty,

44

who looked more like Iago than Galahad; and to gaunt, goateed, moustached Gilliam, who looked a little like Ho Chi Minh.

The workouts were already underway. I walked out onto the Tartan Turf, a ruglike surface I had trod before, back in the summer of 1970 when it was new and swarms of moths were trying to eat it. It was odd to see players chasing and hitting each other inside a bowl of 50,350 empty seats. When the stands are full and people are yelling and the band is playing and the players are in game uniforms, the green area at the bottom of the bowl seems profound, resonant, deep-set. An empty stadium seems *less* cavernous than a full one. It is hard to pick up any great sense of exertion or urgency from players during practice, with nothing looking down on them but a big orange Gulf sign.

The coaches were putting some forty draftees and free agents through paces and the scouts were standing on the sidelines looking on. The coaches, who would have to make something out of any rookies who were kept, were shaking their heads over them. "I like the coaches," said Artie Rooney, "but coaches are know-it-alls." The scouts, who had studied the rookies for a couple of years before rating them as good material, were boosting them.

"They're intelligent," said Artie Rooney. He is the biggest of the Rooneys, around six feet tall, heavy-set, a former lineman at St. Vincent's College. At thirty-seven, he was also loose around the middle. He has more of his father's rumpled, fleshy-featured looks than any of the other Rooneys. He seemed apprehensive about the rookie crop.

"And they went through agility drills," he said. "We haven't got any spastics." He had been about to chew some tobacco but saw his father nearby. Until recently the Chief, who didn't mind chewing a bit himself, had been unaware that Artie indulged.

"One of the coaches blew the whistle on me," Artie said. "My father was looking for some chewing tobacco and the coach said, 'Artie's got some.' My father told me, 'Jeez, it's a dirty habit, you don't want to do that.' He's also always saying to me, 'You're a fatso.' "

The Chief was standing not far away, seventy-two years old and serene, chewing a cigar. He is almost always working on both ends of a big dollar cigar, burning the one end and masticating the other. From time to time he will bite a piece off, spit it out, hold what is left out in front of him, study it a while and give it a flick before replacing it, firmly, at an angle, so that it blots out his whole mouth when seen from the front.

The Chief looks like a cross between Charles Coburn and Jiggs. He is chunky, big in the middle, not tall. He has shaggy eyebrows and thick white hair, combed back. Since he was not wearing one of his out-of-whack soft felt hats, the hair was stirring a bit in the breeze. He is a man who, once he has become acquainted with you, looks almost comically glad to see you again. For that matter, I have seen him look at a brand-new acquaintance, of no particular prominence, with the expression of a little boy who has just been handed a puppy. The Chief is hard on his sons but I never heard him say one critical

45

word about anybody else. Noll and Dan Rooney—especially Noll—run the Steelers, but the Chief is perhaps the most fondly regarded figure in all of pro football. The people in Pittsburgh who denounce him do so because he got rich, coming up from nothing, without ever giving the city a winner. Asked once how he felt about having the image of a good loser, the Chief bristled. "I *hate* losing!" he snapped. "I *hate* it. I *always* wanted to win." But he probably ran the Steelers too permissively to win. It was in those enterprises where he was least soft-hearted—such as in raising his five sons, who now control the Steelers, Yonkers Raceway in New York, two other horse-racing operations and one dog track—that he has had the most concrete results. Some of the things he permitted to go on before the Noll Revolution were more engaging, though, than victory. When he gets to reminiscing it seems that the things he *enjoyed* the most, at least in retrospect, were the things that went wrong. Comic spirits appreciate incorrigibility. "In 1941 I went up to our summer camp in Hershey," the Chief has said, "and the team had new uniforms on. They looked terrible and when a sportswriter asked me what I thought I told him so. I said, 'The only thing different is the uniform. It's the same old Steelers.' The papers have never let me forget that."

But nobody who has ever seen the Chief start laughing near-helplessly can forget that either. Later in the year scout Tim Rooney told me a story:

"We were riding down to the family farm in Maryland. The other Timmy and I were just kids. We were sitting in the back seat with Dago Sam between us. Sam was a Greek god in his younger days. He was a real dude. And he had on a camel's hair coat.

"We stopped at the side of the road for some buttermilk. Our clan has always had a real craving for buttermilk. We bought a crock of it and Timmy and I were passing it back and forth over Sam. Suddenly Tim spilled it; buttermilk went all over Sam. He stood up in the back seat and started waving his arms and yelling. Whoever was driving the car started weaving in the road. Every time he would weave, more buttermilk would go on Sam and his camel's hair coat. And he would yell louder.

"I was just a kid. I was scared. My uncle turned around and began actually to cry. He was crying, he started laughing so hard. The driver stopped the car, and my uncle opened the door and fell out of it. Like he'd been shot. I looked down and my uncle was on his hands and knees on the side of the road, laughing."

That is my kind of executive. If the Chief had been President and someone had come to him with the story that G. Gordon Liddy and E. Howard Hunt and some Cubans had kept replacing the tape over the door lock of the Democratic headquarters when the night watchman took it off and had accordingly gotten arrested, maybe he would have fallen out of his chair laughing, told the whole story to an appreciative nation, and there wouldn't have been the same kind of crisis.

I went up to the Chief there on the field and he took out his cigar and smiled his rumpled purse-lipped smile. He nodded in the rookies' direction and said, "They're all athletes. In the old days there would be some guys who were obviously out of shape. But these guys are all athletes. That helps."

But I was looking for someone unusual, like the former Steeler whose eyesight was so poor that he once raced downfield and fell on an official's flag, thinking it was a fumble, in a night game years back when a white ball was in use. A promising offbeat rookie was Glenn Scolnik, the sixth draft choice, a tall, slim wide receiver. "Scolnik's a vegetarian," said Artie unhappily. "He ran a 4.9 40, became a vegetarian and ran a 4.55 40. And he credits it all with being a vegetarian. The question is can he be strong enough not eating meat. But of course he brings up the elephant and the horse."

Scolnik dropped a pass. Artie looked over toward him the way someone might look at a kid brother whom he was permitting to go around the neighborhood in a dress. "I just hope he doesn't flake completely out on us."

Scolnik went out for another pass and the number two draft choice, defensive back Ken Phares of Mississippi State, covered him. The two of them tangled in the air and when Phares came down he landed awkwardly—ruining, as it turned out, his knee. No one could foresee it at the time, but Phares had probably ended his football career. Back in the dressing room Ralph Berlin examined him and said he'd have to go to the hospital. "X-ray or orthogram?" asked Phares, stoically. Like most players, he'd had knees mangled before. Eventually he had two operations on this one and developed rheumatoid arthritis. Fortunately he was an agricultural economics major with good grades; but an arthritic knee takes some of the pleasure out of gentleman farming. Later, in camp, Phares was hobbling around after his first operation. "It's hard," he said, "keeping your attitude up. It helps, being a Christian. Knowing that things will work out for the best, whether it's the way you want them to or not."

Now a wiry, hard-looking, bobbing young man wearing wide red suspenders on his pants and a red bandana do-rag on his head appeared. He was Rooster Fleming. A few years before, right out of a local high school, he had tried out with the Steelers as a running back but had been beaten out by Cannonball Butler, among other people. Now he was a star in Canadian football.

And he had a bar in the Hazelwood section of town, a section which was turning black. "They call it Plywood now," he said, "because so many places are boarded up. And in those alleys there's some *mother*-fucking going on. You got to take a stick."

Rooster had been in to a Liquor Control Board hearing that morning about his bar: "Inspector there said he'd come in and observed but he was a liar. Said he got there at twenty till twelve and a fight started. At fifteen till twelve a fight started. At ten till twelve, a fight started. At midnight a fight started. At five after twelve a fight started. And then he left.

"I said he was lying because I didn't see him and I was there. And if there'd been that many fights in a place with ten people in it he'd have been right in the middle. They would've had his wallet, his watch and his shirt. Because guys come up to me in there and say, 'We never saw him before, is it all right to roll him?' And I say," Rooster said with an air of responsibility, " 'Naw. We don't do that in here.' "

"You still enterin', Rooster?" asked the traveling secretary, Buff Boston.

"Yeah. Got to. People know me. See me in my suspenders and they got to take a shot at me. Hold *on* to that egg, guv'nor," Rooster said in the direction of a rookie receiver. " 'Cause you can't score without that *apple.*"

Buff asked him about another Hazelwood bar, did he ever go in there. "Naw. That's a black place now. Right next door and it's a black place. I don't know how you feel about it; I'm not prejudiced, but we don't let 'em in the place. There's a big difference between a black man and one of those big jungle *boogers.*" He did an impression of an extremely loose-hipped individual bopping into a place and pulling a knife. "They try coming in we charge 'em $4 cover and $2 a drink. You don't want one of 'em dancin' with your wife. I don't know how you feel about it, but I'm prejudiced. Up in Canada—why you think they go up there so much? They go out with good-*lookin'* white girls. Tell 'em they're Indians.

"There, that'sa way to catch. Get rid of every one of 'em but him and him and him.

"I'da made it with the Steelers, but they called me off the Cannonball. I'da beat him but they called me off." Rooster bobbed away to talk to somebody else, carrying a paper bag in which he said he had some "herbs and wine."

One reason the rookies weren't catching too many was that Bradshaw was throwing laser beams. "Jeez, he's such a specimen," someone said. The question was, would he develop into more of a scientist. He had been accused, in fact, of being dumb when it came to selecting plays and reading defenses.

"He's got to learn it by rote," a member of the Steeler front office said. "Just like I learned to be a Catholic. 'Why does God love me?' You go over it forty million times, and maybe you don't know all the depths of it, but you know it." After that, when Bradshaw went back to pass, I imagined him thinking, "Why does God love me?" "With your arm, why wouldn't He?" seemed the appropriate answer.

A more comforting subject was The Miraculous Reception. "That catch wasn't good scouting," said Artie. "It wasn't good coaching, it wasn't good playing. It was seventy-two years of good Christian life on the part of my father."

Later that day the Chief was sitting in one of the baseball dugouts talking with Ernie Holmes when I came up. Ernie was thanking the Chief for his help in connection with "the incident"—the one which had culminated in Fats's almost shooting down a helicopter.

Holmes had had a good year at defensive tackle after failing to make the team in his first try in '71. He took home maybe $22,000, counting his playoff share, but he bought a Cadillac and a big wardrobe and had an apartment in town and a house back in Texas. "He asked me if he could talk to me about some personal problems," says Artie, "but I didn't know, I thought he might be one of these guys who just want to borrow some money and stick you . . . I told the team lawyer. He said he didn't want to get involved either."

Then, in the off-season, Fats's marriage broke up. He gave his last $1,000 to a man who said he'd double it for him but who lost it all. In March he called Dan Rooney and said he needed some money. Dan told him to come to Pittsburgh and talk it over. Fats heard about the money Steelers were making playing basketball and thought that might be the answer.

But he needed more release than basketball. On the way to Pittsburgh he jockeyed with trucks, trying to get into town before the Steeler offices closed for the day. But he didn't make it in time. He drove through town and headed back out, on the Fort Pitt Bridge. An accident had backed traffic up. He pulled over and approached a state trooper who was busy trying to untangle things.

"What are you going to do about those guys?" Holmes asked the cop.

The cop wanted to know what he was talking about. Holmes said truck drivers had tried to run him off the road. The cop recognized him as a Steeler and figured he was under the weather. In fact he was under the influence of nothing but a nervous breakdown. The cop put him off. Holmes went back to his car and sat there for a while. Then he pulled back into the traffic, and headed out of town.

He had grown up shooting on an East Texas farm, and he had a rifle and a pistol with him in the car. Somewhere in Ohio he started firing at passing trucks through his window with the pistol. He was a good enough marksman to hit what he wanted to. "I didn't want to hurt anybody," he said later. "I could have but I didn't."

Word had gotten out that a man was shooting at trucks. Two men spotted Holmes and gave chase. He sped away and careened off onto a small side road to give them the slip. He was going so fast he ran off the shoulder and his axle broke, the wheel fell off, and he ground to a stop in a ditch.

So he got out of the car with his rifle, and ran into the woods nearby, wearing a tank-top shirt and some sandals. He ran out of the sandals. He hid in the woods. By now there was a large-scale police search on. An Ohio state police helicopter hovered over the woods and Holmes shot at it, hitting a patrolman in the ankle. Because of the shot the police found him, and he surrendered peacefully. "We could have killed him a dozen times," one of the police said.

This time the Steelers helped him out. Noll and Dan Rooney went to the jail where he was being held and the Chief visited him nearly every day in the Western Pennsylvania Psychiatric Hospital, where he stayed for almost two months. He pleaded guilty on three counts of intent to kill and was placed on five years probation.

"I didn't want to turn to the team," he said later, "because I wasn't sure they wanted to help. But now I'm really grateful. Especially to Mr. Rooney. It's like, if it was possible to add an additional person to your family, I'd like to add him to mine."

Holmes didn't want to talk in front of me, there in the dugout. "Oh, don't worry about Roy," the Chief said. "He's going to be just like one of our coaches." But Fats still looked wary. He can smile big and he can also narrow his eyes and withdraw. Then Rooster came up and the Chief introduced him to Holmes. "I play up in Canada," Rooster said.

"What do you . . . ?" said Fats, and he made a stick-wielding gesture.

"Football," Rooster said.

Holmes leapt up and grabbed him, and swung him halfway around. "I had you playing hockey!" he exclaimed. Immediate bond: the brotherhood of people who make a living trying to crunch each other. I want to infiltrate that, I thought. Without getting crunched.

Other people seemed wary, too. That's another bad thing about being a reporter walking into a dressing room: you feel like a cop walking into a bar where there's a crap game in the back. But then I ran into Noll and felt like a suspect.

It was in the hall that I ran into Noll. I had just been talking with Ed Kiely, the public relations director, and Uncle Jim Rooney. Kiely had said of someone local, "He goes off on toots."

"Heh," said Uncle Jim. "Won't hurt 'im. Heh. I never saw anything wrong with it, in all my travels. What bothers me is all these reformers around. I saw Scanlon today. He had another birthday and he's seventy-nine again. I said, 'Patsy, you better come up a little.' He's been seventy-nine for five straight years. Somebody asked him one time, 'Patsy, don't you have trouble with your liver?' He said, 'I don't have any liver.' A wonderful fella, lifts the whole room."

Then Noll came down the hall, with a bunch of assistants behind him, and I met him for the first time. He didn't seem to know anything about my project. Theoretically, I should have tried to sound the head coach out, see what kind of rapport we were going to have, before I picked a team. But that would have been like sounding out her father before you take a girl out. Noll was too young to be Ernie Holmes's or Jim Rooney's father, of course. He looked strong, sharp and preoccupied. He had blond-brown, close-cropped hair and blue eyes whose focus seemed set on something half in his mind, half straight ahead of him. He looked about the right size and brisk enough, but a bit too chunky, to be an outside linebacker. His walk had about it a hint of the gathering, heavy-shouldered, jut-headed gait of a pulling guard. He moved like a man squarely intent on advancing some line of scrimmage which, along with a running clock, he kept rigorous track of in his head.

A German. Being around the day's previous people and then bumping into Noll was like poking around in a woods full of interesting new trees, bushes, creatures, shadows and noises, and then bumping into one of those modern aluminum light poles you see along an Interstate. Noll had every right to be a pole; it was *interesting* to encounter a pole in the middle of the woods. But it was unsettling. It was like, in a dream, being under rumpled, tangled covers with fourteen variegated members of the opposite sex and suddenly finding their pastor, or their supervisor, or something, in there among them.

> *"What are you doing in my seraglio?"*
> *The Sultan asked. I answered, vaguely, "Oh . . ."*

I knew I wasn't going to be like one of the coaches.

Then again, I didn't aspire to be. That night I rode the incline down Mount Washington. The incline is a track straight down the cliff over which a sort of Toonerville Trolley tramcar moves with a slight moan, by cable. It is the sort of conveyance Pittsburgh would have. Then I walked across the Fort Pitt Bridge, the one Ernie Holmes had crossed.

I looked around at the Steel City; or the Iron City; or the City of Bridges; or the Big Small Town; or the Pothole Capital of the World; or the Friendly City; or the Burgh. I could see the Fort Duquesne Bridge, which linked the Point and Three Rivers Stadium. For years that bridge stood incomplete, 120 feet short of the North Side, and was called the Bridge to Nowhere. Two different people moved the barricade aside, during this period, and drove across to see if they could jump the gap. One car went 90 of the 120 feet before hitting the water.

□ **6** □

TRAINING CAMP

*It is my mission here this morning to introduce you to a
wide variety of physical scourges, torments, and piteous
blood-sweats.*
—POOKA MCPHELLIMEY IN
AT SWIM TWO-BIRDS, BY
FLANN O'BRIEN

I don't know why people quit. Maybe it's in their genes.
—CHUCK NOLL

Training camp was from July 16 to August 24 at a small Catholic seminary, St. Vincent's College, thirty or forty miles east of Pittsburgh near Latrobe. It was in Latrobe that the first game between teams made up entirely of paid players ($10 each) was played in 1895. The country is pretty, green, rolling. Within a couple of miles from St. Vincent's you can buy red, lush, tangy "Vine-Riped Tomatoes" from a roadside stand, or "Refrigerated Eggs" from a man named Clair L. Frye's egg-vending machine on the side of the highway in front of his farm. Nearby towns include Grapeville, Marguerite and Pleasant Unity. That last town, it appeared as camp opened, might have been named after the Steelers.

"For a baker, it's that big pie, or that big batch of donuts. For us it's that Super Bowl," said Ron Shanklin. "We got a glimpse of it last year. Now we want to go back and see—was that what I thought I saw?"

Big-time athletes, of course, always say that their primary and ultimate goal is for their team to win whatever is the highest championship available. (Once at a party later in the year I heard one prominent young Steeler say to another, "If we win, we win. If we lose, we lose." But he may have been out of his head.) For a team-sport figure to come right out and say that his goal was becoming Most Valuable Player, or making enough money to buy another Continental, or attracting enough speaking engagements to get out of the house five nights a week, or putting off having to go back to South Carolina for another year, would be like a Chinese journalist saying he was out to make a name for himself.

Which is not to accuse the Steelers of hypocrisy for talking in terms of team.

52

It's hard to play well on a bad team. "It's like soup," said L. C. Greenwood of teamwork. "A whole lot of good vegetables. Reaching a level of adhesiveness. Feeling each other out." When good players get to know each other, he said, each of them, ideally, is freed to do what he does best, knowing what the others will be doing best around him. The Super Bowl is a great focusing factor, of which there are not many currently operative in American life.

Later in the year Pete Gent, former Dallas Cowboy, was in Pittsburgh promoting his football novel, *North Dallas Forty,* which the ads said "hits with the force of a blind-side paralyzing bone-crushing tackle," and whose near-paranoid severities the Steelers considered far more realistic than the pathos of *Brian's Song.* In the course of a long evening's discussion Gent said, "I always wanted to win the Super Bowl.

"So I could take it . . . and hold it . . . and look at it . . . and see what lies beyond it.

"I think it may be the Sun."

The Steelers in training camp weren't looking that far ahead. Suddenly in '72 they had gone from mediocrity to meteoricity, and they figured they might just as well get themselves set and shoot off in the same direction this year. They were united on that, and also in praising the whole Steeler setup to outside reporters, which is to say, at that point, Skip Myslenski of the *Philadelphia Inquirer* and me.

"Chuck was a smart enough coach to know how he needed maturity to win," said Bradshaw. "He told us, 'We're going to be the best. The best. The best!' You could see the writing on the wall for the guys who didn't think that way. They're gone. He doesn't want sour apples, as he says, to mess up the whole barrel.

"And he's so gol-dang smart he'll make a believer out of you. He teaches and teaches and teaches so much, when you go to bed you go, 'Uh-oh, I don't want to go to sleep, I want to get better.' I tell you, I don't want to play for anyone else. As a coach, I love Chuck Noll."

"No one in this organization doesn't believe we're a better football team than Miami," said Joe Greene. "I'm not blowing smoke. Everybody on this team is convinced we'll win the Super Bowl./It's not a lax attitude, but it'll just be a methodical march making our way there.

"You know, at the beginning of last season, it stopped being fun. I was really, seriously considering quitting. Maybe I was in the process of maturing. But I just went flat. Then we played a game with Dallas. We lost, but for the first time I could remember we didn't give a game away. That made it all enjoyable again. Chuck made a speech after that game, saying this team could win, all we had to do was want it."

Andy Russell had been with the Steelers through seven bad years before '72. "I was never cynical when Noll came in, because he low-keyed it. He said it would take time. You never lost respect for the guy—because he thought with his brain, not with his heart. He's never irrational, he's never petty, he doesn't

53

talk from a gut emotion. You feel what he's saying is so logical he *should* be saying it.

"We never really doubted him. If we played an awful game, a real debacle, we'd be sitting at a meeting wondering what he'd tell us, how in the world he could get us in a positive frame of mind. But he did it. He wouldn't come in and start screaming about you bastards this and that. What he'd say, it would be the right thing, ten times out of ten.

"You may lose so many big games through so many years, you start to doubt your own abilities. You even start to doubt the fates. Say you have a good first half. A losing team won't start thinking of how it will win, but how will we screw up this time.

"So before the San Diego game, I thought, Christ, here we are. We've had a great season and now we can screw it up, then that stigma of the losing Steelers will still be there. That's what my heart told me. My brain said, Hell, we should win this game because we're the better football team. But for the old-timers, Ray Mansfield and me—we had this haunting feeling.

"Then when we won, that sense of delirium . . . There's a picture of Ray and myself on the plane. We were like two feet over the seats, just floating."

"I came here from the Eagles in 1964," Mansfield said. "I found the ugliest uniforms I ever saw. The idea was to emulate the Golden Triangle."

There was an apex-down triangle on the front and another on the back of the jersey. This was before Dan Rooney took over direction of the club. Dan recalled that he was in Dallas one day before a game and a radio interviewer asked him, seriously, if the uniforms were especially for Halloween, which happened to be the next day. "They thought we were Batmen," Rooney said. "So it was a question of telling everyone what the jerseys meant, the triangles. Then it was a question of getting rid of them."

In those days the Steelers practiced at South Park, whose main function was to house a Labor Day–weekend county fair. They dressed in the basement of a dilapidated building. It had six showers, four of which worked. The toilets didn't have seats; you had to sit on the porcelain.

In the old days, under Buddy Parker, said Mansfield, they used to do their running in camp through the woods. The veterans would sit down as soon as they got out of sight, then cut across and meet the younger players just before they all emerged from the woods. Parker would have practice in the morning, then let the players take off for lunch before afternoon movies. During lunch they would get drunk. One afternoon the offensive coach sent a player to the defensive room to get some film. When he switched on the light, everyone on the defense, including the coaches, was asleep. The film had run through the projector and was going thwap . . . thwap . . . thwap.

"When I'm speaking to groups," Mansfield said, "I tell them the equipment manager came in one day and said, 'I got good news and bad news. First, the good news: Everybody gets a change of T-shirts today.' Everybody cheered.

'Now, the bad news: Mansfield, you change with Van Dyke. Russell, you change with . . .'

"There used to be a saying," Mansfield said, "if you can't make it somewhere else you can make it in Pittsburgh. It was the last-stop town. When Noll came in and talked about winning, it sounded like a broken record. I'd heard it so many times before. But in that first year, when we went 1 and 13, I couldn't believe his patience. He noticed the minutest detail.

"The lowest point was the game against the Bears in 1969. They beat us 38–7. It was the most I've ever been humiliated in a game. We were looking for volunteers from the stands. Kolb was playing center and Dick Butkus was backing up ten yards, running full speed, and hitting him just as he snapped the ball."

"I used to be 6–3," said Kolb. "I've been 6–2 since that game."

"One time Kolb just fell to the ground and Butkus tripped over him. Butkus got up in a rage and chased Kolb off the field, yelling 'I'll kill you, you son of a bitch, I'll kill you.'

"Then in 1970 we went into the new stadium, and that beautiful dressing room. That place wasn't in any way connected with the past. And Noll knew what was doing and could see what would happen. He kept his cool. He was like George Washington must've been at Valley Forge.

"Then we won in San Diego. Clark was playing guard, filling in for Moon— Moon was sort of crazy, he'd been being hit in the head for the last three weeks. I went up to Clack before the last play and said, 'Kid, you want to go down in Steeler history?' So we're in the famous picture, carrying Noll off. We carried him halfway across the field before anybody came up around us. Noll was embarrassed by it anyway. 'You guys are going to hurt yourselves,' he said. Jim had one leg, I had the other. Jim went left, I went right. Rocky was in back holding him on."

Noll, for his part, said, "In 1969 we decided we had to do certain things technically to win, and we decided to do them then, even though we knew some of the personnel couldn't do it. In other words, instead of adapting the system to the players, we just installed our system. Then we set out to fill our team through the draft."

Wasn't he worried during that terrible year? "I guess it's a philosophy. I don't concern myself with eventualities. I just competed the best way I knew, and let the chips fall. I did it the only way I knew how. There's nothing else.

"When I was playing with the Browns," Noll went on, "we made fun of Pittsburgh. Sometimes different Steelers wore different-colored helmets. But when I talked to Dan, interviewing for the job, I was convinced they were committed to changing.

"When we went out into the new stadium for the first time, the players couldn't contain themselves. They were looking around, smiling. We went out for the pregame warm-up and they were so excited I had to cut it short, to take them in and settle them down, or we'd have shot our wad right there."

After San Diego, did Noll celebrate? "No, not really. One thing I learned very early, you never have it made. You never relax, never rejoice very long. One thing I realized early in my football career, you play a game, it's a very emotional thing, you get all up for it, you work like hell, you get keyed up. Then when it's over, you take a shower and go out and sit down on the bus, and it's like someone stuck a pin in you. For me. For me, the doing is the pleasure, not the rejoicing therein. Once you get the goal, it's over."

But Noll had to admit, "It's a great feeling, to turn history around."

"He's very young-player-oriented," said Artie Rooney of Noll. "He was patient with them. He kept their spirits up, kept the enthusiasm of the kids." He also, Artie pointed out, abolished the rule requiring players to wear blazers and slacks for traveling. "Now we have the reputation of being one of the wildest dressed teams in the league."

"Judging a football player," said Noll, "doesn't have anything to do with the accidents of appearance." (Frenchy's cape and Three Musketeers hat were "accidents of appearance"?)

"Noll seldom gets emotional, maybe only when it's really going bad," Terry Hanratty said. "I remember after Stabler scored the touchdown against us in the playoff game. Seventy-three seconds to go and we were behind. You could look at Noll's face and see he thought we'd still win. He called those last pass patterns very calmly. He knew something would break. It was weird."

Hanratty, Tom Keating and John Dockery discussed the new-style Steelers as a top-notch firm. Keating had just come in on the trade with Oakland (because Noll, though he wouldn't admit it to a member of the press, was worried about a recurrence of Ernie Holmes's breakdown).

"I turned in my airplane ticket for reimbursement," Keating said. "In Oakland that would've taken three weeks and I'd've had to keep reminding them. Here, I got an envelope the next day with the money in cash, plus an extra $5 for cab fare. I've never been on a team with so many happy people."

"Now Pittsburgh is being used as an example of how to build an organization," Hanratty said. "Because of the way we're treated. We're all persons, not just a bunch of numbers. When I negotiated my first contract, my agent wanted to put incentive clauses in it. Dan said no, we don't want to put that kind of pressure on Terry. And he just gave me the money."

"You know," said Dockery, "an athlete can have a very fragile ego. It has to be reestablished, by performances and by appreciation for them. And by what you're surrounded with."

Well. All that sounded good—too thoroughly good to be the last word, as we shall see. I was poking tentatively around trying to get a less victory-oriented fix on the training camp scene.

The Steelers had St. Vincent's pretty much to themselves. There were nuns around, serving in the dining hall, but not many students. For some reason there was often a cluster of nuns under the film tower, from which

Mac McCartney was filming every practice. The Steelers had bought a film-developing truck so they could see rushes of the day's practice that evening, and Mac was always rushing up to Noll with film hot out of the truck. Mac was sometimes called, because of the way his hair stuck out from his head, Dr. Einstein. His predecessor had been Les Banos, still the Pirates' photographer. During World War II Banos had been a Hungarian secret agent, and Adolf Eichmann's chauffeur. Banos was disgruntled with the Steelers, but I was more interested in the espionage. I asked him, when I met him later in the year, whether the Nazis ever came close to finding him out.

"Well, I was hung," he said. He was branded a spy and strung up in a barracks, he said, but a compassionate German soldier cut him down. He escaped and hid flat on his back in a sewer for three weeks. When the building the sewer was under was bombed, it settled and cut his breathing space down to a few inches. He said it wasn't just Eichmann he drove around, it was Hitler too.

"What was Hitler like?" I asked him.

He was temperamental and had to have his way, Banos said. "He was like some of these football coaches."

There were also a few traces around St. Vincent's of the students: the graffiti on study tables and in the men's room outside the snack bar. "WHO STRANGE PEOPLES YOUR DREAMS?" for instance.

The Steelers worked out on two full-length fields side by side; a scruffy field where the linemen hit each other and where everyone lay down and did flexibility exercises, and a lush one especially sodded by the Steelers that they used for scrimmages and passing drills and that no one else was supposed to use at all, even after camp was over. These fields were in a broad open area bordered on three sides by hills and on the other by a line of weeping willows. Up one hill was a softball diamond, and beyond that was the square new brick dormitory where everyone staying in camp slept. Behind the dorm was a cemetery full of crosses where a Steeler had once enabled a girl to have what she asserted to be the first orgasm of her life. "But I don't know what all those things she had before were, then. It was right in there among the stones. But not the monks'. Over there among the civilians. I thought those guys would appreciate it," he said.

There were also big oak trees around, and cornfields, and if you stood up by the softball field you could watch practice against a background something like that of the Mona Lisa: interlocking hills, winding roads, a McDonald's golden arch, light planes landing on a small airfield, mountains in the misty distance. For the first time, after the big winning year in 1972, there were sizable crowds watching, standing in roped-off areas to one side and on one end of the sodded field.

Generally the schedule of training camp was this: Monday through Friday, optional breakfast at 7 A.M. Most players opted out. Around 8:30 they began to get their ankles taped and by 9:30 they were suited up for a 9:30 meeting.

At 10 a 90-minute practice session began. Mandatory lunch was at noon. After lunch players napped, read, played cards in their rooms. At 3 there was another meeting, followed by a practice session that lasted until around 5:30. Mandatory dinner began at 6, and you had to be there—key point—by 6:30. At 7:30 there was another team meeting, and until 9 or so the team broke down into segments with the various assistant coaches to watch films of their performances during the day and be critiqued. Lights out was at 11. On Saturdays there was one practice or a scrimmage, and then everybody was free until Sunday night. After the first few weeks the number of daily practices was reduced to one.

Stated flatly that way, the camp regimen sounds oppressive, like army camp. It was oppressive. Imagine being, say, thirty years old and fairly famous and making, say, $30,000 a year and having to be in with the lights out every night at 11 o'clock. "Say you're lonesome and want to call your wife," one Steeler said. "You can't even go out into the hall and use the phone after 11." Lionel Taylor would come down the hall telling everybody it was 11 and Craig Hanneman would say, "Lionel, have you got a dime?"

"Lights out, now, you guys."

"Lionel, have you got a dime?"

"Come on, it's 11."

" 'Cause if you have got a dime, use it to make a phone call to somebody who gives a shit."

But the rule held up—there wasn't a lot of sneaking out after curfew, and there was often pell-mell rushing to get in before it. I remember somebody telling a story about playing ball in Canada with the fabled Cookie Gilchrist.

"Everybody'd be coming in, going into the head before turning in, and there would be Cookie, in there tying his tie. Everybody coming in, and Cookie be just puttin' on his *suit.*"

I had imagined being introduced at a team meeting, so that it would be established right away who I was, and then I could just blend in and absorb what was going on. Dan Rooney said it was up to Noll.

I went to Noll. Nobody from the outside got into his team meetings, he said. One of the important things about a football team was that it was them against everybody else in the world, he said. He always announced and explained things affecting the team—trades, fines—to his players first and to his players only, so that they would hear things from him and not through rumors or the press.

Well, I said, I wanted an inside look at how his system worked.

He didn't want to give me one, he said. It might help other teams if they found out how his system worked.

"But they won't find anything out until the book comes out, next year."

"It might help them next year," he said. If they didn't find out until ten years from now, it might help them then, he said. "It might hurt the football team. And if it hurts the football team . . ." He shrugged. That was an absolute value.

Of course players on other teams told Steelers after the year was over that the Steelers' offense was so predictable that they could anticipate it easily, but that may have been Bradshaw's fault. And Manny Fernandez told Clack after the Miami game that the Dolphins knew all the Steelers' line signals because they were the same as the Dolphins'. Tackle Bob Heinz was relaying them to the Dolphins on each play. (Fernandez said, however, that he didn't rely on that intelligence because the Steelers were too likely to take advantage of it with a fake audible.) Anyway, Noll believed that the media, in general, went around exposing too many inner workings.

Later in the year a Rooney in-law told me he had always listened to Myron Cope on the radio and TV to learn what was what with the Steelers—"until one day I heard him and Noll talking in the Steelers' offices. From then on Myron Cope as an oracle to me was dead."

I'm glad this in-law never heard Noll and me talking. I could seldom think of anything to say that would *advance* a discussion with Noll. He tended to make the kind of flat statements that invited a challenge, but he didn't seem to enjoy a challenge and didn't respond to one. The difference between Cope and me as Steeler interviewers is the difference between a bulldog and a hound who hangs around the front yard picking up scraps, snuffling under the stoop, and angling to be taken out into the woods to trail scents of semimutual interest. But no matter how he was approached, Noll didn't seem to feel that other people's notions were interesting unless they could be framed throughly and cogently in the terms of his own system. He wasn't going to get down and tangle with Cope, nor was he going to take me into any woods or leave me any scraps, if he could help it. I could have been William Blake with a creative research grant from Pete Rozelle, and Noll wouldn't have been tempted to yield an inch to interact with my vision.

Why that realization irritated me, I don't know. For my purposes I liked the idea of a head coach who kept to himself. But Noll was Power, which only a Jagov reporter could ignore. "The Virgin and the Dynamo," I thought. To Henry Adams in 1900 the Virgin symbolized the force which had inspired cathedrals and the Dynamo the force which drove the future. On the Steelers the Chief was the Virgin and the Pope, Noll, was the Dynamo. "All the steam in the world could not, like the Virgin, build Chartres [or the Immaculate Reception]," Adams noted, but he was also fascinated by what the Dynamo's steam could miraculously produce.

I said to Noll, "Well," because in my discussions with him my voice tended to trail off. But I was thinking, Okay. Like Johnny Unitas I will take what you give me. If you won't talk to me I'll write about your face. If you won't look at me I'll write about the back of your head.

I had hoped that Noll's reputed intellectual drift would be the chink through which I could get inside an NFL coach's head. But Noll was tough. He was almost always polite—though once later in the year he stood in the Steelers' kitchen as Cope and I talked to each other and to him for five minutes and he never said a word—and even cordial, but if anybody strange peopled his dreams, or even his defensive backfield, he wasn't going to let on about it. Later on during camp he said, "Well, they've taken my hero off television."

He was referring to John Ehrlichman in the Watergate hearings. "I never saw anybody with more balls than that guy," Noll said.

"Haldeman's coming on," someone pointed out.

"Yeah," said Noll, "but he's not in a class with the guy with the eyebrows."

Maybe that was something of a Who-Strange-Peoples revelation at that. We went on to argue a bit about politics after Noll mentioned Ehrlichman, but we didn't have enough patience with each other's positions for the discussion to be fruitful. The Watergaters' strongest justifying argument, Noll said, was that "the other side"—peace demonstrators and the like—"went so far the other way. When that starts happening," he said, "the strong will arise. They talk about rules of the game, but . . ."

I tried to talk about the Bill of Rights.

"I just hope Ellsworth gets a thousand years," said Bud Carson, meaning Ellsberg.

You could chat with Noll in camp, but he wasn't in the business of giving things away. He would sit with the press at lunch and answer questions as he ate fruit.

"What's caused Gilliam to lose weight?"

Noll pulled a peach off its pit. "His metabolism."

"Maybe you ought to get a metabolism coach."

Smile.

"What's the big thing you're working to improve?"

"The passing attack. Better pass protection from the line, better pass routes from the receivers, and then the quarterback's contribution."

"You think Bradshaw is on the verge of a dramatic improvement?"

"Yes."

"Why?"

"His development. We've evolved past the burdensome stuff, of being a good quarterback. That's automatic now. He's at the stage of getting down the fine points now."

What about Miami quarterback Bob Griese's allegation, that Bradshaw didn't study enough before games?

Not true, said Noll.

"If your wife looked like Bradshaw's, would you take films home?" asked Phil Music of the *Press.* The reporters at the table laughed. Noll didn't. Went on eating fruit. Was this too serious to joke about? Did he make it a policy never to acknowledge jocular references to his players' home life? Or maybe his wife *did* look like Bradshaw's. And Noll certainly took films home.

These interviews aside, Noll's training camp was far more accessible to the press than most coaches'. Washington's George Allen wouldn't let reporters visit the players' dorms or even sit down during practice. He considered it unseemly for observers to be resting while Redskins whanged together. Like the regular members of the Steeler press corps, I had a room in the players' dorm.

My first night there I went down the hall to Hanneman's and Kolb's room. Hanneman was a pretty formidable person, I had been advised. He had once punched out a Steeler fan who was making too much noise in the hall outside his hotel room the night before a road game. He did not seem overjoyed that I was going to be around all year. He urged me, however, to stick a pinch of snuff under my lower lip.

I had never done this before, but I had experience with chewing tobacco. "A friend of mine named Dan Mayfield," I said, "knew a man who would keep a chaw in each cheek, and when he drove his pickup into the parking lot of the place where he ate lunch, he would pull out his two chaws and clomp them onto the dashboard. They would stick there until he came back." I had always thought of this as a pretty funky story. I mentioned Red Man as a good chew.

"That Red Man," said Hanneman. "That's just like candy. Baseball players chew that. Baseball is a titty-pulling sport."

"Well," I said. I took a dip of Copenhagen. After a not entirely casual moment Hanneman handed me his paper cup to spit into. I spit all over the front of my shirt.

"It don't spit like tobacco," I said.

"That's all right," said Hanneman, "you're just a rookie at it." Most people's reaction to Hanneman's offer of some Copenhagen was that it smelled like cowshit. I hung in with mine, and there was never a hitch in our relationship after that.

Did he chew during games, I asked him.

"I stopped doing that my junior year in college. I got hit and threw up my dinner from that day and my breakfast and my dinner from the day before. It was dripping all off my face mask and onto people's feet. Then I got the dry heaves."

Bad?

"Well, I was leaving the ground."

We ruminated for a while. Holding snuff next to your gums is something like mainlining nicotine, or smoking the strong end of a camel (not a Camel). It was the first time I had ever gotten a rush off a cud.

"I have been known to recycle it," Hanneman said. "Run out, and have to go back and scrape it up off the bottom of the can I was spitting in. I got a little growth on the inside of my lip, the dentist told me. But the Lord giveth and the Lord taketh away. And if that ain't true you can kiss my ass."

Bobby Walden happened by and said to Hanneman, "Hey, Geek," in reference to his shaggy hair.

"That's right," Hanneman said, tongue in cheek, "got my hair long and now I'm on drugs. Got my head together." He clenched his fist like a mock black athlete.

61

"Naw, I admit it," Hanneman said of his hair, "and I'm ashamed. But these other guys got their hair halfway to their ass and they've had it *cut.*"

Somehow or another the question of marijuana came up. "It's up to every man," said Walden. "But if I ever see anybody giving it to my son, I'm going to kill him."

The conversation swung back around to chewing. Walden said he had given his boy Bobby, seven, some tobacco to chew.

"There," said Kolb, "you talk about giving . . ."

"I was going to break him of it," Walden said. "It was Sunday. I drove all the way into the store for it. I was going to break him. Gave it to him and he was still chewing and spitting it thirty-five minutes later."

"You were chewing something out there in practice today," Hanneman said.

"That was a peach seed," said Walden.

Somebody said something about a spitting, belching and cussing contest. "I could win that," said Hanneman, and then he emitted a single belch that rumbled low and built steadily for a good fifteen seconds. "No kidding. I think I could belch with Fats."

"He'll do that," said Kolb, who was into his second year of rooming with Hanneman. "It gets to where you have to hold onto the ground."

At other points and other moments along the dormitory hall there were John Rowser playing chess or lying in bed reading *The Science of the Mind*: "It's about metaphysics. It has to do with positive thinking. It teaches you that there are certain laws in the universe that are available to you. It shows you how to use them, how to apply yourself."

And Frenchy Fuqua, lying on his back in his room with his red-white-and-blue eyeshade on and his cigarette holder in and his earphones on, listening on his quadraphonic system to Dr. John singing "I Been Hoodooed" or Millie Jackson singing "My Man, a Sweet Man," or War or Tower of Power or Al Green or The Five Blind Boys of Alabama, a gospel group, singing "Too Sweet to Be Saved." Sometimes he had the earphones off and there was a white ballboy lying on each side of him listening too. "Did you see Dr. John on the Midnight Special?" Frenchy asked. "See him come out in that thing on his head with all the feathers? Had that beak on it?" He had more than one fancy marble chess set in his room. "I am the chess champion of Pittsburgh," he said. "Andy Russell, he's supposed to be the smart person on this team, he's afraid to play me. Ron Bell, the rookie, he's supposed to be an intellectual, I dusted him six times in a row. I don't even let him in here anymore. The only difference between me and Bobby Fischer is color."

Another time, in Bradshaw's and Hanratty's room, "Untamed World," an animal documentary, was playing on the portable television. Hannenman was semidozing on one of the beds. The show included an ape smoking a cigarette, a chimp teasing a hornbill, and an aardvark palling around with a pangolin.

"I tell you I got a pet alligator back home?" said Bradshaw. "Six foot long."

"What's his name?" I asked.

"Call him Hanneman," said Bradshaw.

"Shit," said Hanneman.

"Got him in a pond. He migrated in from Clear Lake."

"How fast're those things on the ground?" asked Hanneman.

"Pretty fast."

"Really? I mean compared to a human."

"Nawwww."

"No, I mean *compared* to a human."

"They're pretty fast. He's quick."

Gilliam came in and he and Bradshaw messed around with each other for a while. Then Gilliam rose to leave, went over to Bradshaw, and said close into his ear. "Okay, Cajun Sugar."

"Okay, Sweet Nigger," said Bradshaw.

I still felt alien and tolerated, but I appreciated being free to loaf in the dorm. And Noll never tried to stop me, all year, from getting into anything involving the players except the meetings, whose few dramatic moments the players would eventually fill me in on. (One player offered to wear a tiny concealed tape recorder into a halftime meeting toward the end of the season, but this notion, though offered in a spirit of fun and information, struck me as too Nixonian to use on an organization which had been mostly open with me, and which by all accounts had dull meetings.)

In *Rolling Stone,* right after the '73 season, Dr. Hunter S. Thompson wrote of his difficulties with the Oakland Raiders. Thompson had resolved to follow the Raiders for the last half of the regular season to "try to document the alleged—or at least Nixonian—similarities between football and politics." (Someone told Thompson that there were only two teams in the whole League flaky enough for him to identify with in any kind of personal or human way: One was Pittsburgh and the other was Oakland.) The Raider organization received him at first but then decided to bar him. The stated grounds were that he was identified with drugs, but the actual grounds were doubtless more general: that he was liable to stir things up along some kind of non-victory-producing lines. Thompson writes that Tom Keating advised his former team-mates not to talk to the author of *Fear and Loathing in Las Vegas.* Toward the end of the season Keating and I spent some time in the Steeler weight room fondly recalling passages from that very book.

"Throw the fucking radio in the bathtub with me!" Keating cried rapturously in the weight room, quoting the voltage-seeking Dr. Gonzo's appeal to Thompson. Anybody who has played pro football can appreciate, I suppose, an openness to be jolted at an insane level of force. But there are strict channels for such things in the NFL. A football team is not an open society. It is a society at war. And whereas, on most of the scenes *Rolling Stone* covers, the writer's instincts may well be to loose all the demons and let oppressors and anal compulsives worry about the consequences, in pro football the consequences are likely to discommode not management but the visceral, flavorful types—the players. The clubs control the players' schedules, pay, job assignments, and even medical care (consider the paranoia-inducing possibilities of that last factor). Labor-organizer Keating had had trouble enough with Raider management to know the risks of stirring things up uncontrollably. I was careful all year not to appear to be interfering with the Steelers' advance toward the Super Bowl. Noll's stance impressed the necessity of this upon me.

"If it hurts the football team . . ."

In his researches into the Dynamo, said Henry Adams of himself in the third person, he "mixed himself up in the tangle of ideas until he achieved a sort of Paradise of ignorance vastly consoling to his fatigued senses. He wrapped himself in vibrations and rays which were new . . . while he lost his arithmetic in trying to figure out the equation between the discoveries and the economics of force. The economics, like the discoveries, were absolute, supernatural, occult; incapable of expression in horse-power."

"Green. 41. 41. Hut'n-hut'n-hut'n!"

"MF." *"Eunh."* "Ff-ff-ff *hunh*-ahh."

"C'mon Steve—blow!"

"Pass!"

"Ball Ball Ball."

"Yeah, KNOCK 'IS ASS OFF. Everybody knock their ass off—now!"

Those were the sounds of the Steelers running plays and hitting each other in training camp, as heard from the sidelines.

There is less hitting in pro football practice than in the colleges, where quarterbacks and ball carriers are more often "live," which is to say tackleable. But there was incessant contact in Steeler practices all the same. Everyone was live during the Saturday scrimmages and the lineman hit during "thud," or "team" scrimmages, in which everyone acted out their assignments at a three-quarter-speed pace that was hard to keep down to three-quarters. Then there was the drill called the Nutcracker by coaches who like to use meaty language and by Noll the Oklahoman. Two six-foot dummies were laid down and an offensive lineman stood in the three-foot gap between them. A defensive lineman or linebacker stood nose-to-nose with this blocker, behind whom stood a running back. The offensive lineman would fire out and try to block the defender out of the way long enough for the runner to make yardage through the space between the dummies. The defender would try to fling or batter the blocker aside in time to hit the runner, or just try to shove the blocker and runner straight back together. Two sides wanting the same piece of real estate: the heart of football and of war.

There were various solutions to this problem, on both sides. A wily blocker like Van Dyke or Mansfield might fling his body across the rusher's legs suddenly to trip him up—or he could fake forward, step back, allow the rusher to lunge forward off-balance like a man through a suddenly opened door, and then fall on top of him. A rusher could just keep banging inexorably straight ahead—"Hoyt Wilhelm used to throw all knuckleballs!" George Perles would cry—or he could sidestep, grab the blocker with his hands, and club him with his sledgehammer forearm.

Essentially, though, it was a simple matter of leverage. Stay low enough to hit the other man at his fulcrum and bend him back, but not so low that he could fold over and push you down. Especially you had to keep *driving,* administering force upward and forward from your purchase on that real estate.

"Stay square! Don't you take the side. Make him take the side," Fry would shout.

"Right through his face, L. C.!" Perles would cry.

"Keep that face up, right through him."

"That's what we want, stuff him right in the hole!"

"You didn't work your feet at all, just lunged."

"A tired football player can't go."

"You left your feet. You got to work those feet."

"Be strong now. Quicker quicker quicker."

"Come off the ball, Roger. You got to come off the ball. Good sustain, but let's see a little better blow."

"He's getting underneath you, Fats, you got to get under him!"

"Stay square! Stay square, Larry, huh?"

"E-*oonmph.*"

"*Yunh. Yunh,* nng*Omph.*"

It is strange and a little unnerving to hear this sort of thing for most of a morning or afternoon while watching people spit and lunge and blow their noses in their hands and heave against each other over and over again, doing the fundamental things repeatedly, not for the immediate purpose of advancing or stopping a drive, but for the sake of the fundamental things. It was something like watching a pornographic movie. ("Unbelievably real!" said a sign outside a porn theater in Pittsburgh.)

But there was a redeeming purpose. "You put a football team together from the bottom up," said Noll, "and you start over every year. You build a football team by building up the individuals in it. You build their habits. Program them with habits, techniques. So when the time comes to do it in a game, they react automatically."

The Steelers' offensive line, for example, had to learn blocking assignments for each of the team's 170-odd plays against the five or six different fronts—4-3, 4-4, Over, Under, Stack Over, and five-man rush—that defenses would use against them. The defensive backfield had to learn how to operate in a Cover One (man-to-man), Cover Two and Cover Three (different combinations of man-to-man and zone), and Cover Four Red or Blue (pure zones). The receivers had to learn how to run a Smash, a Fly, an I-Cut, or an O-Cut pattern in spite of being jammed—that is, in spite of having the bump-and-run administered to them, which is to say in spite of being beaten on with elbows, fists or shoulders while trying to go a certain distance downfield and cut at a certain angle. (In '74 the bump-and-run was made illegal.)

All of these assignments had to be learned, for starters, by studying the Xs and Os in the playbook and on the coaches' blackboards. (Actually the Steelers didn't use Xs, but other letters, to designate defenders. Defensive ends and tackles were indicated by Es and Ts, the middle linebacker by an M, for Mike, the outside linebackers by Ps, for Pluggers (linebackers plug holes), the corner-backs by Cs and the safeties by Ss. Offensive players were Os, except for the center, who was an O with an X inside. ("I thought of myself as a square for years," said Mansfield, "because that was the way centers were drawn. Now I have to think of myself as an O with an X in the middle.")

Offensive play systems in the pros are not as easy to learn as they might be, because their codes are not entirely consistent. For instance a G appended to the number of a play may mean that the "on" or strongside guard is to pull, and an O that the "off" or weakside guard is to pull, but a GO doesn't necessarily mean that both guards are to pull. The Steelers' P36 didn't mean fullback (the 3 back) plunge up the middle, or 6 hole, but a *fake* P36. The 36 sucker meant a fake 36 which turned out actually to be a 33, or fullback through the 3 hole, between the right guard and the right tackle. In some coaches' systems, the odd-numbered holes are to the right side and the even-numbered ones to the left; in other coaches', vice versa. In some cases play-designating terms varied between the defense and the offense even within the Steelers. I once heard Jack Ham and Terry Hanratty trying to explain to each other the meaning of a Ram—a type of defensive stunt—and their mutual confusion was almost as great as mine.

The hard part, however, was not learning the plays in the abstract but executing them bodily. First of all, you had to be in shape. Noll's approach to conditioning was that of a modern, rational, unhellish coach who uses the most scientific, rather than the most testing, methods available.

For that matter, practice in the pros generally—both before and during the season—is less of an ordeal than it is in college. "I couldn't make it through a college practice today," said Hanratty. There is less waste motion in pro ball. The players presumably know their own bodies well enough to get them in shape, with proper guidance and hard looks from coaches, in a businesslike manner.

When Bill Austin became Steeler head coach in 1966 he instituted grass drills, which entail a lot of frenzied flopping up and down and landing on your belly and rolling over and jumping up again. The starting center got up off the ground in the midst of grass drills and walked out of football forever.

Noll, said Andy Russell, "wants everybody to be in perfect condition, but he emphasizes we shouldn't push ourselves so far that we do more damage than good. The old idea of 'get out there and run yourself into the ground' is out."

"Running for conditioning: Why?" said the Steeler playbook.

The body has two systems of converting glucose into usable fuel for the muscle (1) Aerobic System (oxygen system) (2) Anaerobic System (lactic acid system). Explosive activities depend on the anaerobic system but sustained activities depend upon the oxygen system. The oxygen system supplies energy for submaximum efforts and also converts lactic acid into fuel for use by muscles. Lactic acid is an irritant and must be quickly removed from the muscle area and this depends upon the body's ability to supply oxygen.

Noll's device for building the oxygen system was "the 350s." These consisted of five 350-yard laps. At the end of each lap, each runner rested briefly and applied his finger to the pulse in his neck while a coach counted out ten seconds. If his pulse was 30 beats for ten seconds, he was running the right speed and getting the most from the drill without hurting himself. A faster pulse meant that his pace was too fast, a slower one meant it was too slow. The idea was to increase your speed in the 350 gradually while keeping your pulse the same. (Later in the year I ran a mile in Three Rivers at a fairly brisk pace for a scribe and then took my pulse while Hanratty counted to ten. When it came out 29 I concluded that I was in better shape than I could push myself to reflect in my speed of running, so I quit running for the season.)

Explosive strength, drive, and thrust the Steelers built up by lifting weights, under the direction of strength coach and former Olympic lifter Riecke, part of whose credo was, "Everyone can develop tremendous strength. In contact you need a driving movement." "Hit 'em in the numbers and climb 'em—hit 'em a rising blow. Receivers and defensive backs want to be able to jump high." These powers were developed by squatting, pulling, and pressing in Riecke's weight-lifting machine, a frame fitted with bars and counterweights which could be set to pose the resistance of varying weights.

The chipper, white-haired Riecke looked about half the size of the defensive linemen, but he said, "I could probably squat with more than anybody on the team. Possibly with the exception of Kolb."

Riecke did not acknowledge the concept "musclebound." "There is no way to get strong without lifting weights," he said. Push-ups, he said, were just a less economical way of lifting weights. "The players that are the strongest pound for pound and for the training they've had are the defensive ends and running backs. And they're the best athletes." Granted, heavyweight lifters were fat: "The body has to work to carry all that fat around. Fat men are strong. You check a fat man out some time. But there are two kinds of weight—the weight you carry around and the weight that carries you around. That's extra horsepower. And you can *feel* it. Do those squats and walk down the street and you can *feel* that power. I was a skinny little kid. When I got stronger I got more confident, I could do things in gymnastics I couldn't do before. There's no way to be strong and not *know* you're *strong*.

"But what is natural strength? Nobody knows. Nobody ever uses all of their muscle fibers. Take the case of a hundred-pound woman with her child caught under a car. She lifts that car. It's concentration on the moment. The only thing she has in mind—it was a complete focusing of attention. She may have broken her back doing it. You can break your arm by your muscle's contraction. But mentally you can't. Your mind restrains you.

"I tell you what: that word motivation. I think that word motivation can make you do just about anything in the world."

All the Steelers lifted weights during camp, then; but not all of them did before or afterwards, when they didn't have to. Joe Greene, for instance, had little patience with lifting. Later in the year, when Greene appeared to be less dominant than he had been in the past, one Steeler suggested that the game's foremost active tackle had reached the point in life where he was going to have to lift regularly to keep up his natural strength. But Sam Davis said in camp, "My honest opinion about strength—I'm beginning to believe it's a mental thing. Joe, he may not can lift two hundred pounds [he could of course lift much more than that, but he wasn't among the team's mightiest weight men], but on the pass rush he can lift two guys. I've seen him hit guys with one hand, rushing in, and knock them flat on their behind. If that ain't strength I don't know what is."

Besides thrust and wind, the Steelers needed flexibility. This was in the hands of Paul Uram, a high school coach and the author of a book of exercise entitled, fetchingly, *Refining Human Movement.*

One of the things Uram emphasized was, when you are doing a stretching exercise you should hold it at the point of greater stretch for a while. Bending over to touch your toes and making several short up-and-down dips while bent over, as athletes are often coached to do, was actually bad for the muscles and tendons involved, Uram held. He also advocated cracking your knuckles and stretching your fingers and toes frequently. His exercises included one where you balanced on your coccyx with both legs straight up in the air and your forehead clamped to your knees. When Kolb did this he looked like a huge drumstick, or a ham. Then there was the "Extreme Quad Stretch," where you knelt and then, while your knees and lower legs continued to kneel, you put your hands over your head and laid everything from the back of your thigh up to the backs of your hands flat on the ground.

It amazed me that all of the Steelers could come close to doing these exercises, and some of them could actually do them the way they looked in the drawings in Uram's book, which I would have thought could be simulated only by the use of deftly placed screens and two different bodies for each position. I could see doing some of those exercises with my own upper body and someone else's lower, or vice versa, but kneeling and lying supine at the same time, or kissing my *own* knees without bending them, was beyond me. The more I worked at the exercises, even over a period of a few minutes, the closer I could come, it was true, to doubling up in several directions. But how anyone as blockish as Mansfield could sit with his legs stretched out in a rigid V and then bend straight over and touch his forehead to the ground, which he could do, I don't know. It was like folding a full sandbag over double. Uram was leading all the Steelers through these contortions one afternoon in camp when one of them cried, "You'd be great in bed, Coach."

Unfortunately the stretching exercises did not keep the Steelers' muscle pulls down during the season, as they were supposed to do. One of the stretches, however, was of great importance. It cured the sore arm Hanratty had had since high school and made him a better passer.

As advanced as all these modes of conditioning seemed to be, they nonetheless produced distress in most of the Steelers. After practice the players would come dragging up the steep hill, pictures of fatigue, thinking of Juice. The Juice was a pale Kool Aid-like liquid available in coolers in the dressing room.

"Juice!" cried Dockery, walking bent over from the waist. "I'm driven to it. *Drawn* to it."

"Take two salt pills and jog it out," said Ralph Berlin to rookie Lee Nystrom, who had been beaten on by Joe Greene. If there was one thing that irritated Greene, it was playing across from someone who didn't know what he was doing, and Nystrom—though approved of as "fluid" by the scouts—had played at tiny Macalester College in Minnesota and therefore had a lot to learn about technique.

"I've run myself to death already," Nystrom sighed.

Franco Harris came trudging up the hill looking like a Rouault engraving. Franco usually looked nobly stricken anyway, even while being kissed by Sinatra, but the postpractice tiredness made him look tragic. There were fans who pointed and laughed at the sweat-and-dirt-streaked players as they toiled up the hill. No one seemed at least consciously envious of the dignity hard labor had conferred upon them.

"Isn't being so tired a kind of distinction? Isn't it even almost a kind of high?" I asked Mansfield at the 19th Hole after practice.

"Maybe," he said grudgingly. "I sure do hate it, though."

The 19th Hole was where I concluded that relaxing with the Steelers wasn't going to be a problem, although driving home afterwards might be. Ed Kiely had suggested that the Hole would be a good place to get familiar with a number of the players, and he introduced me to Van Dyke, who was glad to take me along. So was Mansfield. Offensive linemen don't get much publicity.

The 19th Hole was a bar down below a nearby motel. Its virtue was that it was the closest bar to St. Vincent's. Over the stairs leading down to it was painted "The Steelers Will!" and inside it were Steelers' pictures and a Bruce's Mooses banner. There was also, over the bar, a picture of a boxer named Slugger Klingensmith. By the jukebox hung photographs explained by a framed newspaper clipping:

ONE-ARMED GOLFER MAKES "WILLIAM TELL" SHOT

> While reclining Lee Bollinger, Grapeville, holds a tee between his teeth, one-armed Al Monzo, professional golfer of East McKeesport, sends the ball to parts unknown, his assistant none-the-worse for his experience. . . .
> As a youngster Monzo fell down and broke his arm while caddying and an operation followed. . . . He doesn't have a right hand since his arm was amputated at the shoulder. "I don't need two hands to correctly teach fundamentals," he says. . . . But it took a lot of courage for a 16-year-old youngster to laugh off the loss of an arm and bring into force enough determination to follow thrugho [sic] with a boyhood plan.

There was usually less than an hour between the time the Steelers finished practice and the last moment they could be in line for dinner. Van Dyke and Mansfield would shower, dress from the waist down, and emerge from the dressing room—as teammates cried, "Way to be quick, Moose!" "Good time, Ranger!"—running and pulling on their shirts. Then they would jump into Van Dyke's car and button their shirts as they rode, moaning, past the cornfields and half a mile up the highway to the Hole. Then, as five to twenty-five other Steeler regulars arrived not long behind them, they would fall to drinking as many beers, poured into pilsener glasses filled with ice, as they could before around 6:25 or 6:27, which left them five or three minutes to reach Placid Hall to be served by the nuns.

Mansfield said that he thought he averaged twelve to fifteen beers a day during training camp. "You get so dehydrated out there," he explained. "I'll tell you how dehydrated you get: You know when you drink beer you piss? In camp you never piss. You drink all this beer and at night you'll piss once. And it's completely yellow."

The problem of a reporter in that situation is that reporters don't go into it that dehydrated. My bladder held up, but eight quick beers on a hot evening before dinner sometimes went to my head. And sat there, like eight bricks. Noll looked up once as I straggled in to dinner with a bunch of 19 Holers and asked, "What did you find out at the Bucket of Blood?"

"Everything," I told him. "But I forgot it all."

I did remember, however, the conversation which followed my attempt there to draw out a tableful of guzzling Steelers on the question of tiredness.

Van Dyke conceded that there might be something dignifying about being so tired. "But you feel so bad. You see spots. You're *dry*. Your legs are rubbery. You lose ten pounds of water in a day. Five quarts."

They discussed the possibilities of conniving with opposing defensive linemen to go mutually easy—to form a "union." Joe Greene, one of them said, "used to be a good union, but he's not anymore."

"Keating is. Keating says, 'Okay, on this play defense are the good guys. Defense wins! Now it's your turn.' "

"Ernie Holmes is always going all out. So you back up and hit him a couple of cheap shots. It doesn't faze him."

"Fats don't know whether it's day or night out there."

"My feet were like 120 degrees out there," said Gordy Gravelle.

"On the coast," said Mansfield, "you never have hard ground."

"*What?*" cried Gravelle.

"Well, I've played up and down the coast . . ."

"You have *adobe* out there," Gravelle said.

Mullins: "Oregon must've been worse than hard ground. Mud up your ass."

Mansfield: "Yeah, in the old days. You'd look over the field and couldn't see the other team. All you could see was heads."

Van Dyke: "In Atlanta they took mowed grass and sprinkled it over the hard dirt field and then sprayed it with green."

Mansfield: "In Yankee Stadium there were horse turds."

Someone sat down with an armload of beers.

"The other day my wife was working in the yard," said Mansfield, "and it was really hot and afterwards she had a beer and said, 'Now I know how good beer tastes to you after practice.' 'No you don't!' I said to her. 'You'll *never* know.'

"It used to be," Van Dyke went on, "that drinking was the big thing on this team. We had this guy Bill Saul who would bet he could beat a rookie chug-a-lugging no hands. He had this big mouth and he'd fit it around the glass and turn his head up and just inhale it. He'd drink ten beers in thirty minutes."

No one seemed to prefer the old days, though. "Noll does things to psych us up that I'd do if I were coaching," Van Dyke said. But he was hard-pressed to cite a specific example. "Today," Van Dyke exclaimed one afternoon, "Noll said, 'All right, we've got to bear down. You know what today is. It's eleven days until our first exhibition game.'

"Eleven days till our first exhibition game! Damn! We went out there and *hit* it.

"Then . . . 'Eleven days till our first exhibition game!' What the hell does that mean?" Van Dyke said. He shook his head. "I don't know how he does it."

In the Hole the Steelers impressed me as a good, loose, homogeneous group. You would see most of them in there—blacks, whites, stars and reserves, mixing relaxedly. The black-white socializing had come only in the last few years, Van Dyke said.

"Thousands of young men all over America are feeling the way we do now," said Mansfield wearily in the car, as we rushed back to dinner, drinking the beers that had been unfinished at 6:28.

"Couldn't be more than two thousand," said Van Dyke.

"That's not *one* thousand is it? That's thousands."

"Two thousand."

"You can say thousands."

"No."

"How about all the college and high school kids?"

"They start in August."

"*Well?*"

"It isn't August yet."

Mansfield looked out the window. He was wedged into the front seat. He took a long rattly swallow of beer and little chunks of ice. Each of his limbs was the size of a grade school child and as discontent as a large, beached, not-quite-dead fish. "It seems like it," he said.

It seemed late to Noll, too. After the first few days he answered a press question at lunch, "How is camp going?" by answering, "So well I don't want to talk about it." But he was leaning hard on the players.

In his first years Noll had been firm, authoritative and easy-going. But the closer the team came to Super Bowl caliber, the players agreed, the harder he pushed, the more he "wound it tight." He exploded during practice sometimes now—"Why the fuck can't you *learn?*"—and rode players who made mental mistakes or who didn't seem to him to be going all out, who therefore "didn't give him a picture."

One of the mental habits several players said was important was "having a picture in your mind" of what you are supposed to do: visualizing yourself breaking through each blocker likely to present himself and then driving your shoulder into the quarterback, for instance. A coach's picture is more complex, and it must be frustrating when the lines of your system—whose kinks you are trying to work out and whose validity you are trying to establish—are obscured by aberrant Os and Es and Ts. It often seemed to me, in talking to coaches, that they would be a lot happier with the game if it didn't have to be played with players. How anybody can aspire to fit Mad Dogs, Frenchys, Moons and Dirty Johns into a finely tuned machine, I don't know, but the most successful coaches do it, and Noll's image of himself and his team depended on it. (You know who was from Pittsburgh? Edward Hicks, the primitive painter of, among other things, *The Peaceable Kingdom*, in which lions, a bear, a wolf, a jaguar, a bull, a cow and human children are shown lying down or standing around with a lamb and a goat. The landscapes in the backgrounds of Hicks's paintings are Pittsburgh, without the industry.)

Another expression commonly used regarding practice, besides "giving him a picture," was "getting everybody on the right page." The image was of a classroom following Noll through his design, inscribed in a text, line by line.

As a matter of fact the Steelers' practice picture was never thoroughly reliable. The quarterbacks, not being "live," would take longer to pass than they would be able to under a game-conditions rush, so the secondary would have to play differently from the way they would in a game. (When Babe Parilli—his desire to be a player again shining all over him—stood in at quarterback, however, he gave the defense a good picture, delivering the ball with dispatch and even rolling out zestfully when the rush came too close.) The defense also took advantage of the difference between practice and the real thing. Russell would gamble and blitz more in practice, because if he made a mistake the consequences weren't crucial—"They don't run the plays all the way out anyway," he pointed out. Rowser would guess what the pass was going to be on the basis of his knowledge of the Steeler offense. Instead of playing it safe and giving a rookie receiver a chance to beat him man to man, he would "read" the play, which was relatively easy against his own offense, and jostle the rookie out of his pattern or position himself right where he knew the pass was to be thrown.

"I'm readin' the shit out of these rookies," he would cry, grinning hugely.

"Yeah," some veteran receiver would grumble. "You better watch out."

"Rowser ought to just call out the numbers," Tim Rooney said on the sidelines. "Like telling jokes in prison: Just call a '301' and everybody laughs because they've got the jokes all numbered."

Such exploitation was inevitable, however, because all the individuals— notably the quarterbacks and Rowser—were fighting to win or keep a starting job. When it came to beating other people Noll was no idealist himself, and he didn't want to discourage his people from using every advantage that came to hand.

With the veterans cheating on them and the coaches pressing them to fit a collective pattern, however, the rookies were in a bind.

"People say, 'How the hell is this or that guy going to make your team?' " Noll said. "I don't know how the hell they'll make the team. That's their problem." After practice he would call the whole team together on the field and say, "All we can do out here is to provide a learning situation. What you get out of it is up to you."

Noll admitted, "Once you're functioning effectively, it's hard to keep patience with people who come in and screw things up. We bring in people we feel can come quickly. I'm doing things the only way I know how. There's no other way."

It was hard for the rookies to find any way. But one reliable principle was to hit when in doubt.

Lou Angelo and Ken Jackson, two free agent defensive back candidates, were talking on the sidelines. "I don't know whether to hit them or not to hit them," said Angelo of the receivers who were catching passes against him.

"Shit," said Jackson. "Hit 'em till they tell you not to hit 'em. We're trying to make the team too."

The year before, as a rookie, John McMakin had been having trouble holding onto passes, and veteran cornerback Chuck Beatty was banging away on him the way veteran cornerbacks will bang away on rookie receivers, especially ones of a different race. But once when Beatty hit McMakin, McMakin hit him back, and caught the ball. Beatty responded by jumping on McMa-

73

kin's back, and McMakin grabbed him, slid him around to his front, and hit him seven or eight times on the head. His helmet notwithstanding, Beatty had to go lie down in the camp station wagon. McMakin started catching the ball consistently and Beatty was traded.

Glenn Scolnik, the vegetarian, 42 pounds lighter than McMakin, received the same kind of treatment. Knotty Pine Edwards hit him twice in one day. "I kept going, foggy as hell," Scolnik said, "but the second one got me. I started blowing plays . . ."

He was the one who had to take a rest. There was some confusion about the nature of the blows—Scolnik described them both as elbows to the face, but he was foggy. Dick Haley, formerly a Steeler defensive back, watched one of the blows close-up. He said Scolnik had been looking back at the passer and just as he relaxed and turned to look upfield Pine drove the top of his helmet into Scolnik's face. It is hard to imagine a ruder awakening than running along and turning your face into what must have looked, for a flash, like a yellow-striped bowling ball coming straight into your mouth. "I did that to a friend of mine in a game once," mused Haley with a grim face, "and it put him out of football. He looked up at me and said, 'Dick . . . Why'd you do that?' "

At any rate Scolnik had been out of the play, so the blows were cheap shots, and they gave him a concussion and a broken tooth. "I shoulda turned around and hit him right back," Scolnik said. "That was my impulse. But I don't know how Coach feels about fighting. They kicked guys out of practice for fighting in college. In the second week I ran out and hit Rowser with my fist. That's what I do now—deliver a blow. So they don't play tight on me. It's just part of football. Trying to jam a guy. But that cheap shot stuff . . .

"They haven't been hitting Marvin Foster [a rookie wide receiver who was black]. Maybe the brothers are sticking together."

But "Kamikaze" Meyer, white, had been roughing Scolnik up too. And if there was racism in the jamming, it didn't carry over, at least so pronouncedly, into off-the-field activity. "I know Pine," Scolnik said. "I played cards with him the other night. It's nothing personal."

Scolnik was a thoughtful, Consciousness III sort of person who liked the outdoors and animals: "If you're going to be a pro football player you have to live where the most people are, because that's where they build stadiums. But in the off-season I'm going to live in a tent in a state park."

He had trouble getting the kind of food he wanted in camp. "They said they'd cook anything I want, but I'm not going to ask those nuns to spend four hours cooking wild rice. They have yogurt here, but it's custard-style, not the kind I like. I go to the China Inn and have egg foo young and rice."

The meat in camp revolted him. "Overcooked carcass," he called it. "I'm not ever going to eat meat again. Meat bogs the peristalsis in your system and leaves you feeling irregular. And I don't want anything to be killed for me to eat. In a way it's like setting up a contract for a hit. I'm not a health food nut. Broccoli cooked right with a Velveeta cheese sauce is just like ecstasy to me.

I used to feel bad when I smoked cigarettes—I mean because people didn't expect it from a vegetarian. But I said fuck, I got the right. In college I trashed up my whole body. A lot of things, you know, that go with long hair, being a sophomore. But cigarettes make me relax. And they don't affect me out there playing."

Scolnik got as much wire service publicity during camp, because of his vegetarianism, as anybody on the team. And I liked his looks while he was loosening up on the sidelines during exhibition games—jogging bing bing bing with his knees high while holding his torso bent in a sneaky-loose sort of crouch like the coyote's in the Roadrunner cartoons, and shaking his fingers as though he'd just hit all ten of them with a hammer. A vegetarian amongst behemoths (but weren't mastodons vegetarians?) was good copy.

However, although Scolnik hung on with the Steelers all year, he never loomed large. "I like to catch the football," he said during camp, "but I don't like to block." Neither did any other receiver, but the others didn't *admit* it. Mike Shannon, the smallish (232-pound) rookie defensive tackle who was Scolnik's roommate, quit the team after sustaining a pinched shoulder nerve, a sprained ankle, "an unreal assortment of bruises" as one veteran put it, and a noticeable slot in the bridge of his broken nose.

"Shannon tries to run through people," said Scolnik. "I try to avoid them." But when someone is trying to push you out of your pass pattern, you have to run through him. The new rule in '74, banning the bump-and-run, may be a boon to vegetarians.

Since I was usually in the 19th Hole until late, I didn't see much of the traditional rookies-standing-up-on-the-dining-hall-table-and-singing action. The Steeler veterans didn't take much interest in such hazing anyway. I did, however, catch Scolnik's Lollipop Kids song. It was from *The Wizard of Oz.* Scolnik put his thumbs in his armpits and sang in a loud tough-guy voice out of the side of his mouth, "We represent the Lollipop Kids, the Lollipop Kids, and in the name of the Lollipop Kids, we welcome you to Munchkin Land." The only reaction this number elicited from the dining regulars were some blinks. "In college," Scolnik said, "everybody was always yelling for it."

The other two standout rookie dining hall performances were Bracey Bonham's and Ron Bell's. Bonham was a 6–1, 253-pound, ebullient guard out of North Carolina Central. He sang soul numbers from the table so well that veterans actually applauded. "The first day I got here, I went up against Joe Greene," he said. "I was thinking, 'I wonder what will I do.' If you see 'em on TV, you say 'There goes Bruce Van Dyke! There goes Joe Greene!' They're a terror on the TV. But when you get to know 'em . . . At first it's, you know, Joe Greene going to beat me up. But then you realize, he just playing the game and so are you. In pro football it's the same old *unh,* and crunch, and whatever. Football's gonna be football."

But Bracey kept making mistakes, which interfered with Noll's picture. "He got the worst case of offsides," said Dwight White, "I ever seen."

Bell's case was more complicated. The scouting reports on him said things like "Good physical qualities but sure is dog at times. Tough kid, good strength, well built, wouldn't want him with any of our teams." "Fine physical skills but doesn't use them." "Ran the fastest 4.7 I have seen."

When asked what that last assessment meant, Bell had a good answer. "It means I ran a 4.6." He had looked so good in some game films—he gained 239 yards and scored 44 points in one performance for Illinois State—that the Steeler scouts had decided in his favor, in spite of the bad word on his attitude. Franco Harris, after all, had had attitude problems at Penn State. But the way Bell performed in camp left the scouts shaking their heads. He jogged like Gale Sayers on his way back to the huddle, but when he carried the ball he coasted, and dropped as though poleaxed on slight contact. "He had to have had his eyes shut that time," Haley marveled once. The veterans thought he was arrogant, if not crazy, and were shoving the blocking dummy into him. Joe Greene really belted him once, the way you might kick a dog that was acting unnatural. When Bell was told to get up on the table and sing his alma mater, he got up and recited it, softly, to general disapproval.

Bell lay back on his bed in the room he shared with Bonham and stroked his lips meditatively. His features were fine, his body heavy but compact, clean-lined. If I had to pick a sports figure he resembled facially it would be Muhammad Ali, in a solemn mood. The lights were dim and the radio was playing the theme from *Shaft* at low volume.

"People who don't know me well," he said, "might say I was out of touch with reality. I don't talk to many people. But reality is part of my thinking. I have never idealized football. I never idealized players—such as Gale Sayers. I studied them. I try to see the reality of football. I have studied psychology. It has helped my perception. I think I'm *more* mature than most people.

"You know, to be frank," he said, laying his finger alongside his nose, "I've been trying to quit football for four years. But I haven't been able to. Football life to me is six months of hell and six months of pleasure. To people who enjoy playing football, I can see how it is all pleasure. Football itself as a game, I don't enjoy. Sometimes I think, 'What are grown men doing out here, playing a game?' I see it as the best opportunity that came along.

"I'm creative. I'm studying the flute. I see football as an art expression, and I see myself as a long run artist. When I make a run I'm painting a picture. My objective is to run the length of the field for a touchdown, completely untouched. I want to be original."

"What's original about your running style?"

"Rhythm. Ability to make my body a pawn and my mind the overseer."

"Have you learned anything from watching Franco?"

"About life?"

"Well, okay."

"Yes."

"What?"

"To be frank, again . . . This is deep. This conversation is getting deeper than I . . . No, I'd rather not say."

"Do you enjoy contact?" I asked him. Rookies were supposed to say they had a craving for contact.

"No," said Bell, "Can't stand it." I must have looked startled, because he added, "I will *tolerate* it."

Bonham came into the room and sat down on the other bed. "I *love* to hit," he had told me. He looked at Bell as if trying to make him out. "I'm going to dinner, Bro," he said. The scouting reports on Bonham had said, "Works hard in practice—not a loafer. Very coachable—good second effort."

"It's never entered my mind that I won't make the team," Bell said. "I have not known much failure in my life." He had had trouble getting underway in life, he said vaguely, but football had come along as a way to get somewhere. At one point he said, "Existentially speaking . . . do you follow me?" The next day I said hello to him on the field and he said, "Generally speaking, have you made any interesting observations today?"

"Bell says he is an artist in the long run," I said to Haley. "He says his ambition is to run the length of the field without being touched."

"In the Oklahoma drill," said Haley, "he kept running into the back of his blocker."

"This is the big intelligent draft," said Artie grimly. "These guys got alternatives. When it gets tough—not just getting your head beat on, but that element of doubt, about whether there's room for you on the team—they've got alternatives. That guy Klippert's a civil engineer from Stanford. Honor student. He may not stay out here and be used as a tackling dummy. He can go out and build a bridge somewhere."

I asked Noll about the problem of intelligence, or reflection, among rookies. It was a question of special interest to me because I have always felt that one reason I was such an inconsequential athlete myself was that I had too much inner life. Noll said intelligence helped a player to "assimilate quickly," but "if you have to rely on thinking, you're in trouble. You have to react." A phrase he had used before was "paralysis of analysis."

"Then, too," I said, "maybe some kids with degrees in engineering or something figure they could be making it in the world somewhere without getting hit in the head."

"If you are doing it right," said Noll, "you don't get hit in the head. You hit the other guy."

I never met anybody else in the Steeler organization who believed that it was even theoretically possible to play pro football, no matter how aggressively, without getting hit in the head a good deal. But Noll's was a mind that looked straight downfield. "Hit that ye be not hit" is a maxim to which you do indeed need to bind yourself with bands of steel if you are going to move steadily downfield.

Another rookie running back who underachieved was Leo Allen, picked up by the Steelers for a look after being cut by Oakland. "I took him aside," said Bill Nunn, whose job besides scouting was to run the camp administratively, "and I said, 'Do you know what the word "lethargic" means?'

"He said no. I said, 'Well, you better realize that word is stuck on you and you got to get it off.' But it don't look like he is."

"Maybe he isn't able to," said Artie. "Maybe he's lethargic."

J. T. Thomas, who after signing his contract some months before had said, "Now that all the rush is over maybe I can find time to get down to Orlando and visit Disney World," was looking good, and so was the reticent Toews, whom Artie Rooney went so far as to call "the best player in camp." Noll said long-shot Lee Nystrom was giving him a good picture, and Scolnik got a break when veteran receiver Al Young's heat prostration was diagnosed as the product of a rare, incurable ailment which would most likely keep him out of football for good. But nobody else seemed to have much of a shot.

A number of rookies were still around, however, for the rookie show and chug-a-lug festival about halfway through camp. Jack Hart, the field manager, tried to chase me from the rookie show. I was perhaps linked in Hart's mind at that point with the women's movement, but even if I hadn't been he would have tried to chase me. Hart is a wizened, burr-headed, leather-skinned native of the North Side who has been with the Steelers in various capacities since 1946, except while he was being a Korean War hero. He grew up on the North Side. Until he approached puberty he was retained by one of the famous madams to sweep up in front of her sporting house. He started on with the Steelers as a ball-boy.

As field manager, Hart was in charge of the playing fields at St. Vincent's and at Three Rivers. He also helped Tony Parisi with equipment, and he was in charge of balls—in the sense of pigskins, and also in the sense of having them. Anybody who seemed to Hart unauthorized, he kept away from the Steelers. During a previous camp he had chased Arnold Palmer, who is Latrobe's most famous son, and Palmer's sister off the practice field. When Artie Rooney tried to bring a friend's kids into the dressing room after a game in '72, in violation of a new rule Artie was unaware of, Hart barred the way. Then, when Artie persisted, Hart slugged him. Artie then shoved Hart into a dirty-clothes hamper, but Hart had had the satisfaction of punching the owner's son in pursuance of his duties, and the Steelers was not an organization that would fire an old hand for that.

"The first time I saw Hart, when we were kids, he was beating up his brother in a garbage bin," said Artie. "Garbage was flying up in the air . . ." When Hart hit Artie he cut his hand on Artie's tooth and the cut got infected. "He wore a bandage on the field for five games," Artie said. "Every time somebody saw it, I was embarrassed. People were calling me Rattlesnake."

A few days into camp I was standing on the field with a local TV announcer of the sporting news, Lee Arthur, watching practice. Women were barred from the practice field and Lee Arthur was an obvious woman, with auburn hair, who had appeared in a Broadway musical. She had press credentials. It was a historic moment in Pittsburgh sports. She said she liked the "concentrated sexual energy" in football. "If I could ever get a man to look at me the way they do at a player after a great touchdown run . . ." Several men in the vicinity were trying. But Hart came up and said she would have to leave.

Hart has a consistent gleam in his eye which sometimes is jocosity and sometimes is zeal. We thought he was joking. He came back after a while and said, "I'm telling you, don't give me any trouble, you got to get off. *No women on the field.*" Just because she was on television didn't keep her from being a woman, Hart said. He said he would get a cop.

I forget all the backs and forths of the incident, but at one point Artie Rooney said, "I'm the last person to talk to," and at another point publicity director Joe Gordon came down on the field and told Lee it was all right for her to stay, and someone said Hart was a Jagov, and then Hart came up again and Lee, assuming she was set, tried to smooth things over with Hart by putting her hand on his arm, and he drew away, snapped "Watch it!" (though he was said to be a ladies' man), and still insisted she had to go, and Van Dyke yelled "Way to be a meanie, Jack!" and Lee went away and came back in short shorts! and said she didn't see why her shorts would affect the issue, she didn't have very good legs, and everybody said yes she did, yes she did, and at some point she told Hart *his* legs (which were very spare, brown and knotty) were better than hers, and he didn't take to that notion at all, and Dan Rooney came up to Lee and said, "We're delighted to have you," and I thought, Well, he doesn't laugh as well as his father but he has a good smile, and Hart was seen lying rigid in his bunk. At one point Lee tried to discuss the liberation of women with Hart. She asked him when blacks had first gotten into pro football significantly and he said, "Marion Motley, 1946," and she said now women were breaking down barriers, and if Hart saw any connection he didn't let on. "For the first time," she told me, "I feel like a Negro."

Hart had also chased Iooss (who grew up as the only Flemish kid in his high school in New Jersey) a couple of times when he felt Iooss was getting too close to the action with his camera, and I heard that Hart had once, pursuant to some new policy, locked and refused to open the dressing room door in camp when Joe Greene wanted to get into it. So Greene picked up an iron bar and knocked the door down. Which is another way of feeling like a Negro.

"No newspaper guys!" Hart cried when I tried to attend the rookie show. I appealed to Noll and he let me stay.

Tom Keating, the movie authority, told me later in the year that he thought the rookie show was the best one he had ever seen. Marvin Foster, a 175-pound wide receiver free agent from the University of Kansas, had such stage presence as the show's emcee that I wished he weren't too skinny to make the team. (When Gene Austin was head coach he kept a rookie around for a long time just because he was so good in the rookie show, but Noll was not likely to do that.) Bracey Bonham did a good job of hobbling the way Ralph Berlin did on his ruined knees. There was a skit in which Bonham/Berlin left a gravely injured Phares lying prostrate to go see about a hangnail on someone playing Andy Russell. There was a re-creation of the famous incident when the police came for Frenchy, a few years back, to haul him in for nonpayment of alimony. ("I woke up one morning," Frenchy told me at the 19th Hole, "and I was hung over, nineteen and married.") The rookie playing Preston Pearson, Frenchy's roommate at the time, ushered the officers in saying, "No, *I'm* not John Fuqua—but *he* is." Russell was awarded the annual Jacques Cousteau award—a pair of goggles—as the veteran who spent the most time in the tank, which is to say in the whirlpool nursing injuries. The whole offensive line was presented the Bleeding Pussy award: a Kotex for each man. "I've stopped going to the rookie show," Artie Rooney told me later. "I went in there with some people who had been following the team and there was a skit that suggested they were homosexuals."

The show was followed by an hour or so of ritual beer-drinking. I believe I have this right:

"Here is Cardinal Puff for the first time tonight." Tap right forefinger on table once. Tap left forefinger on table once. Take one gulp of beer. Bounce in your seat once.

"Here is Cardinal Puff for the second time tonight." Tap right forefinger on table twice . . .

And so on, up through Cardinal Puff for the fourth or fifth time tonight. But I think I've left out a few touches. Anyway, if you make a mistake you have to swallow your whole beer and start over. One year a rookie who had never drunk before wound up drinking so many beers so fast that he had to be thrown in the shower, and in the process he bit down on a coach's finger so hard the coach barely got it out of the rookie's mouth whole.

There weren't any coaches around for this occasion, just the players and Berlin and Parisi and Hart, who glared at me. It took many of the rookies a long time to finish Cardinal Puff. Whenever one got close Van Dyke would start crying, "Oh, he's got it now! Let's just give it to him. Oh, he can't miss," and he would miss. I will never forget the look on the face of Roger Bernhardt of Kansas, a guard, the third draft choice. Bernhardt's lack of zest in the trenches had been a great disappointment to the coaches and scouts. The scouts called him a "computer player," that is, one whose specifications—6–4, 244, 4.9 in the 40—were excellent but whose intangibles were lacking. They implied that Noll was a man who would fall for a computer player. "Nobody would have drafted him if they'd *seen* him," Noll said accusingly to the scouts, who pointed out that *Noll* had seen him, in the Senior Bowl. What someone should have noticed was the expression on his face; but then it may have been different in college. Bernhardt had thinning hair and a dour look, and every time I saw him in camp he looked like he had grave misgivings about whatever he was doing. He reminded me of myself in graduate school, when I realized that everybody else took footnotes and the poet Wither seriously. Or at any rate they discussed the poet Wither knowingly. I remember this conversation in graduate school:

"He's im*por*tant. He leads you into *Davenant*."

"Oh, he doesn't count. Nobody reads Waller, he's like Wither. Wither and Waller. Waller and Wither."

I remember also going to a class of Robert Lowell's, which was conducted by I. A. Richards because Lowell had had a breakdown. I saw Richards nearly swoon, literally, from the emotion he derived from reading Shelley. I remember thinking, I *like* literature and all, but . . .

I figured Bernhardt was feeling similarly about football. He looked like a normal person who'd been invested with an ideal offensive lineman's body and had always sort of liked to play the game, but now was being looked at scornfully *because he couldn't work up an appetite for colliding in all sorts of complicated ways with Fats Holmes and Joe Greene.*

Never had Bernhardt looked so dead certain that he was in the wrong place, however, as he did during the Cardinal Puff. I mean a person likes to relax and have a few beers with friends, but . . . I don't know that I've ever seen anybody having as bad a time at a party as Bernhardt was. He kept making mistakes, and looking sick, and trying to chug-a-lug just part of his beer, and a veteran would say seriously, "Come on, Roger, we won't cheat you, don't you cheat us," and he would groan and start trying to be Cardinal Puff again.

After all the rookies had made it through Cardinal Puff there were chug-a-lug relay races between rookies of the offense and those of the defense. Then there were eliminations to determine the best individual rookie chug-a-luggers—Bonham, a nondrinking preacher's son, and Shannon, the battered social education major who had won Oregon State's Attitude Award the previous year. These two were pitted against the best two veterans—Fats Holmes and Mansfield. Mansfield had been the champion for years, but in 1971 Fats arrived on the scene and took over the crown. He could chug-a-lug in one second flat. "He just puts that big mouth around the glass," Mansfield said.

When the foam cleared this night Holmes was still the nonpareil. Everyone said there was less vomiting this year than usual. In '72, Bradshaw sat across from Gilliam, egging him on, until suddenly Gilliam threw up in Bradshaw's face. Bradshaw, who hadn't even been drinking, was so taken aback that he threw up on Gilliam.

Nothing that dramatic happened this year, but there was puke all over the floor even so. "Sick, sick, sick," said Van Dyke. Scolnik, who had Puffed and chug-a-lugged adequately (as had Bell), shouted, "It is a tradition, unquote, to throw beer on Ralph Berlin," so the rookies who were able all ran over and threw beer on Ralph Berlin. Off in the corner Virgil Robinson, a quiet, handsome running back from Gretna, Louisiana, who'd been cut loose by the Packers and was soon to be waived by the Steelers too, sat with his back to the revelry, softly playing the piano.

81

"You never had an experience like this before, have you?" Sam Davis asked me. "After this, there's no more rookies. Everybody's everybody." For the first time during camp veterans brought rookies with them to nearby places like Bobby Dale's, where you could drink beer, play electronic Ping-Pong (Andy Russell was the team champion), eat pizza, and, if you were unattached, dance with school-teachers and secretaries from surrounding communities to the music of bands like The Deuces Wild.

The next morning people had some trouble applying themselves to the business of running 350s and imprinting each other's numbers on each other's chests (that's what you were supposed to do, hit people in the numbers that hard), but they did it.

Bodies thrashing around now not as guzzlers, whooping and lurching, but as pistons in an engine, straining for the right compression, which required seizing split-second, foot-long opportunities for vantage.

"What are you fooling around for?" George Perles would be yelling at a rookie who wasn't holding his own in the hitting. "What are you going to get out of this? They're all trying to impede you. You're going too slow."

"Be soft with your feet," Lionel Taylor would be yelling to receivers going through a sideline drill—he would throw them the ball just inside the line and they would have to catch it and put both their feet down before going out of bounds. "Run through the ball," he would say to receivers when they slowed down to concentrate on catching. He would run over toward them as they went up for a catch and then cry, "You're thinking about me! Old man like me!"

"Stay off your heels, stay off your heels, stay off your heels," Fry would cry. Or, "All you want to do is bump him and wall off the inside."

"Tits! Tits!" players would yell appreciatively in the direction of Ron Curl, the amiable guard from Michigan State who was going to fail in his second attempt to make the Steelers. Tits was his nickname because of upper-body bulk.

"Way to run, Lydell!" cried Mike Wagner to Franco Harris. Lydell Mitchell was the back in whose shadow Harris had played at Penn State.

"This woman was six foot nine and weighed three hundred pounds!" said a Pittsburgh newsman, describing an incident he had seen in town. "She whipped two bus drivers and four policemen. Said to the driver, 'Come out here!' Thought she was a big bluff. Knocked him flat with her open hand."

Kolb and Hanneman, each with a leg in a cast from a camp injury, watched the hitting for a while and then went hobbling off, stiff-legged like Frankenstein monsters, in white shorts and T-shirts. They stopped for a moment to get down and square off, to illustrate mutually some point in their conversation, and then they went on across the empty field.

"Let's get it on, let's jiggle!" Greene cried as the defensive linemen ran from one field to the other. He was dragging behind himself though. He was good enough to lag.

The kickers, Gerela and Walden, stayed to themselves, doing flexibilities and a little kicking. Walden said you could kick too much and wear yourself out. Some of his punts would pull, draw, and switch from side to side. Others would seem to hesitate in flight and then take off, climb higher. These latter were the ones that turned over, he said. "It adds ten or fifteen yards when it turns over." The point of the ball that led on the way up was supposed to trail on the way down. Like a two-headed salmon that leaps, is bent back, but swings its trailing head around to shoot forward farther. Or like an acrobat swinging, legs trailing, forward on a trapeze, then, as he is about to peak, kipping forward with his legs to make a midair thrust. A punt that sawed back and forth, like a struggling kite, was a punt that came down the same way it went up. That turning over and taking off was like what the best runners did—after they got through the line they "reaccelerated" or "generated," igniting a second stage. The roots of the word "punt" are obscure—it may just be onomatopoeic—but they may be the same as those of the words "pontoon" and "Sputnik." The livelihood of the Waldens of Climax had been depending for years on whether the ball crested right, turned over, sixty or seventy times a regular season. A beautiful punt is a beautiful thing to watch. But it's bad to catch, Pine Edwards pointed out. The ones that settle down flatly instead of turning over and nosing down like an artillery shell are easier to handle, just as a man who presents his ventral surface instead of his nose is easier to block, tackle, or run over. It is by remembering first principles such as these, not by thinking existentially, that you keep your bearings in football.

"Look him straight in the eyeballs!" cried Perles. "That's right, L. C."

"Bracey keeps on doing like that," someone said, "somebody is going to go pft and tschooo. Grab him, hit him upside the head, knock it down his throat."

"Look at his belly button," cried Fry. "You didn't move with him. You saw him but you didn't move with him. Stay in front of him, stay in front of him. Work. Look at him. Look at him. Be strong. Be strong."

"Way to ball-react!" exclaimed Lionel.

"Ball-react?" I asked Dick Haley.

"React to the ball," said Haley. "Lionel's got some new terms for us this year. He says 'em backwards."

"That's right, Gail," cried Perles to rookie Gail Clark, "that's the way they'll kick the shit out of you. And we're going to do it right back to them."

Oh, there were diversionary matters to consider on the sidelines of camp. For instance I told Artie that Wojciechowicz S. "Bow-Wow" Wojtkiewicz, a West Coast football figure, had been sending me pictures of naked women with lurid captions ever since I mentioned him in my story on the Rooneys. "He sends me holy pictures," Artie said.

But the business at hand boiled down to the offense—hard-pressed progressiveness—against the defense—high-powered destructiveness, entropy and chaos. The difference between Fry of the offensive line and Perles of the defensive was instructive: Fry steady, low-key; Perles emotional, ebullient.

Even their young sons scuffling on the sidelines: Perles's, red-faced, bumping against the older Fry boy, forcing him off of a dummy they both wanted to sit on. Fry's son giving ground eventually because Perles's was acting childish and there was nothing to be gained from fighting a smaller kid over a seat on a tackling dummy when there was another one right next to it.

Pro football first became glorious through long scoring passes: bombs. But defenses around the league were now stifling the big pass attack. Noll said this was primarily because of the advanced evolution of the pass rush. A new improved breed of defensive linemen, weighing 260 pounds and faster than linebackers, were "putting their ears back and rushing the passer," said Noll. "He doesn't have five seconds to think anymore." The Steeler linebackers were taught to break in the direction a quarterback first cocked his arm to throw in, because the front four wouldn't give him a chance to cock it more than once. The rush of Greene, White, Greenwood and Holmes in '72 had forced opposing quarterbacks to hurry passes so that they were easier to intercept. The Steelers had the wild, head-knocking rush up front and the quick, highly organized linebackers and secondary to back them up.

But so did a number of other teams they would be playing. The whole question seemed to be whether the Steelers could put together a sustained offensive attack. Noll's byword was poise and control. But the team's greatest strength was the way his system deployed the Mad Dog defensive forces at its command. Could the creative, the offensive side of the system generate and sustain a flow? The games would tell.

Camp—the most grueling time of the pro football players' year, the time when they are most thoroughly enclosed like monstrous boys to be integrated bloodily into the system which should carry them, with constant attention, through the season—was ending. St. Vincent's students were showing up in greater numbers on campus, at least one of them—perhaps the author of "WHO STRANGE PEOPLES YOUR DREAMS?"—wearing a T-shirt that said "Property of City Jail, San Juan, Puerto Rico." Tony Parisi would soon direct the packing of the team's equipment into three twenty-two-foot trucks.

In the evening after dinner, Stenger, Gravelle and Clack sat in the grass talking about how bad camp made them feel. "I feel like I'm thirty-four," said Gravelle, who was twenty-five.

"I don't see how Moosie and the Ranger do it at their age."

"I guess they make a joke out of everything."

"It's all in your mind."

"That's right."

□ 7 □

MOOSIE AND THE OLD RANGER

This football business is like a day off compared to what I did on the farm as a youngster. You don't get patted on the back or written up in the press for picking cotton.
—LEE ROY JORDAN,
DALLAS COWBOYS

The road to easy street goes through the sewer.
—FAVORITE EXPRESSION
OF OAKLAND HEAD
COACH JOHN MADDEN

Mansfield and Van Dyke were indeed humorous company, but they didn't see football as any kind of joke. "Well, Bruce and I laughed our ass off about this," Ray said, when I asked them for a funny game story. "We were playing the Baltimore Colts. We were backed up to the 1-foot line, it's cold, we were losing bad, we wanted to get the game over. They're booing us, throwing snowballs at us, at home. Guys were ducking snowballs in the huddle. Well, in those days we had girls called the Steelerettes doing dances and shit behind the end zone. Larry Gagner looked over there at them and said, seriously, 'Come on, you guys! At least the girls are still with us.'

"The girls are still with us! Great! But even that wasn't a laughing matter at the time. Only later. At the time it was a chuckling matter."

"You're not in a humorous mood," said Bruce, "on the field."

"When I was born," Mansfield said, "my family was picking prunes and living in a tent outside Bakersfield. About the time I was born my father was bit by a rattlesnake on the wrist and my oldest sister died of pneumonia. There were nine kids in all. We moved up to Washington, my father drove a truck for the Walla Walla Canning Company. My brother went out to Arizona and said there was great work out there, so we all went there and my father got a job as a carpenter. He'd never been a carpenter in his life. After a while he

85

went into the concrete business for himself. He went back to Missouri for a while and while he was gone his partner bought himself a new car and bankrupted the concrete company, so we had to sneak out of Chandler, Arizona, in the middle of the night.

"We went up to Kennewick, Washington, and my father hired the family out as asparagus cutters. I was in the third grade at the time. Four of us cut ten acres of asparagus every morning before school. My Dad went back into the construction business—the hardest fucking thing in the world, concrete. That's slave business.

"My father was 6–4, 235, the meanest guy who ever came out of Arkansas, Mo. A long-legged guitar player. He tells about the time some guy name of Henry hit him over the head with a beer bottle. My dad drew back, his brother put brass knuckles in his hand, and he hit Henry in the eye and just opened it all up. But I always saw him as a gentle man. My brother was going to run away from home. My dad caught him in about three steps.

"We lived in an old run-down motel: Campbell's Cabins in Kennewick. This punch-drunk boxer who lived there got me out, put gloves on me. He was a grown man, I was in the third grade, he was beating the hell out of me. My eyes were closed, my nose was bleeding. My dad went out there, grabbed that man and beat the shit out of him. I thought it was fun, he was teaching me how to box.

"There's been a Mansfield on the Kennewick team since 1949. My cousin's playing there now. My younger brother—the Pirates were looking at him to play baseball. But he came up to make a tackle, he was a defensive back, and got his leg caught, tore up his knee, and it atrophied. He's still crippled a little bit. We used to play against a high school across the border that had a family, the Pentagos. There was always a Pentago and he was always great. I can imagine what they say about the Mansfields now. 'How you related to Ray?'

"I'd be finishing concrete, pouring basement walls, and then I'd go play Little League baseball. The other kids came in from farting around all day. A guy named Rich Alpac was writing a doctoral thesis in psychology about Andy Russell and me. We talked about what makes a successful athlete. I said you've got to be hard-nosed, stick to it, outfight, outscratch the other guy. Andy thought it was more analytic, you had to outthink the other guy. My background was a scratching, fighting background. Andy's dad was an executive for Monsanto, my dad was a guy who scratched it out of the ground. I probably outsmart guys as much as anything now. But I still like to get tough with them.

"Football's like my father's work, because it's hard, grinding work. And because it grinds you down. It makes for a short life. At least a very uncomfortable life later. You get arthritic conditions. I have prostate trouble, from standing, I guess. Right where the quarterback slaps his hand. My neck always hurts from being broken in college. They thought it was sprained so I played with it. It hurts all the time now.

"My first game in high school, I thought I was God's gift to football. I thought I was going to beat the shit out of everybody. I went up against this big kid who was a senior. He ate my cookies.

"I couldn't understand it. It turned out, this guy I played against in my first game was Bob Lilly. But ever since then, I've been afraid that everybody was going to beat me. I was an All-American at Washington, but I still felt that way. About the time you should be relaxed and enjoying yourself, you're worried, afraid of failure. You know, I think people like that do better."

Van Dyke was born in a small town in California too, but he grew up on a farm in Missouri. "My family was poor, and I worked my ass off as a kid. The first thing I told myself, I'd never live on a farm when I grew up because I hated it so much. I said I'd never do physical labor.

"Football is hard labor, especially in training camp. But you don't look at it as such. You're only doing it for six months, and it's kinda worthwhile. Not the same as digging ditches. People are looking at you. Being entertained.

"I went to a small high school, but my senior year my coach said I'd have a shot at a scholarship, and I got one to Missouri. I played defensive tackle there mostly. I always had this ego thing—there was no question after my senior year I'd play pro. Even though the coach, Dan Devine, said pro football was a rat race, I'd be better off not going out for it. I thought I was a lot better than the scouts must've rated me. I thought I'd be drafted high and be great. The paper in Columbia, Missouri, quoted a scout, saying I would be a number one choice. I had the biggest head in Missouri: they know how good I am.

"The day the draft began I waited up until three in the morning and nobody called me. I went all through the second day. Not believing it. Then finally the next day Kansas City in the AFL called me, said 'Hey, Bruce, we're thinking about drafting you, in the tenth round. Will you sign?' 'Hell, yeah.' But they didn't draft me until the fifteenth. Philadelphia in the other league drafted me in the twelfth, and I never heard anything from anybody. This was the '66 season, when guys were going for big money. A good kid got $200,000, maybe he never played a down of pro football. And here I am a Jagov. I hear nothing from nobody for two weeks. Then Philadelphia called, said they were thinking about a $1,000 bonus. I said I wasn't going to play for that, I'd get a job somewhere else. Every time they called they raised it $5,000. Finally they got up to a $20,000 bonus, a $12,000 salary, if I'd guarantee I'd sign after the Sugar Bowl. They kept pressuring me. So, $20,000, I'll take that. I gave the guy my word.

"Kansas City never called me. But I got a note from them saying they hoped they'd be seeing me in red and white. That was their colors. So . . . After the Sugar Bowl, there's the Philadelphia guy. But I hadn't had a chance to talk to Kansas City. I said, 'Well, I'm a little bit dizzy and nervous from the game . . .'

"The Philadelphia guy had the contract and a pen in his hand. Right there

87

in front of everybody in the dressing room, he starts ranting and yelling: 'God damn—I had to leave my wife and come down here. You think I wanted to come to this damn game? Sign the goddam thing!'

"So I'm sitting there, feeling like the biggest ass in the world, and I took the pen and signed. I never heard from Kansas City.

"I believe in the mental aspect of the game. I'm from the old school. You can do what you want to do. That's probably wrong. I'm not extremely fast or extremely strong. But then that could be bullshit too—because I am, you know, pretty fucking big."

Van Dyke laughed, "Heh, heh," down in his prominent jaw. Of all the Steelers he may have been the most thoroughly reflective, as in the paragraph above: plus, but minus, but minus times minus equals plus—with an undertone of minus, with a tone under that of plus. Van Dyke admired James Whitehead's novel *Joiner,* whose hero is a gargantuan but endlessly analyzing and synthesizing pro football player who kills a man with his bare hands. Van Dyke thought the killing part was overdrawn.

But he was a devastating if not a lethal hitter. About half of the pictures of Franco Harris picking up yardage show him following Van Dyke, pulling. And you didn't see Franco's hand on Van Dyke's behind pushing, either, the way you see running backs doing to guards who are less brisk. Van Dyke looked about the same size with or without his shoulder pads; he was short, 6–1, for a guard, and his breadth made him look even shorter. In the '74 Pro Bowl he looked like a bowling ball amidst all the other star linemen. He had the Pittsburgh franchise's most prominent trapezius muscles—the ones that extend from the base of the skull to the shoulders and enable the shoulders to *lift.* Against Cincinnati at Pittsburgh in '72 Van Dyke so dominated the Bengal's great tackle Mike Reid and whoever else got in front of him that he was named the league's Offensive Player of the Week, an almost unheard-of distinction for an interior lineman. On one play he pulled, blocked a linebacker, went sprawling, scrambled on all fours along the turf, and threw another block on a defensive back, springing Harris for 21 of the 101 yards he gained that day.

In '73, though, he was feeling his twenty-nine years—and the fruits of years of rollicking off the field, some observers suggested. "I used to stay hard just walking around," he said. "Now I have to lift weights whenever I feel like I'm getting slack. In order to hit hard—just sell out—and make the guy's back snap, you've got to plant your foot in just the right place. A couple of inches make the difference. I've always had that knack. Some guys have to learn it. But this year, I haven't been hitting as hard. The films don't show it, but I can feel it." He had missed the last regular game of the '72 season with a pulled calf muscle and he was gimpy again in training camp. A lump appeared in his leg and there was talk of phlebitis.

The day that possibility arose Van Dyke broke his team-leading string (several years) of consecutive post-practice appearances at the 19th Hole.

(Mansfield had missed once a couple of years before when the centers had to stay late and snap to the kickers.) He stood in Bobby Dale's that night and said, "The thing that gets me—this is my eighth year, and you figure an offensive lineman should have four more. And now that we're beginning to win . . . If I had to quit now, I don't know whether I could watch a game. If we'd win the Super Bowl, and I had that, then I could come back and sit in the stands. But to just go to nothing . . . Football players have to eat so much shit. Practice, and coaches yelling at you. To just go to nothing, to become just one of the guys you hang around with . . ."

Fortunately it turned out not to be phlebitis. Van Dyke remained a player, a star, a team leader, a rollicker, a familiar face in a local TV beer commercial. He and Mansfield roomed together, ran together, and played side by side. Mansfield often helped him block the best opposing tackles—one of the ways Reid was handled in the '72 game that won Van Dyke the award was for Mansfield to hit him behind the legs and Van Dyke to fold him over. Reid has knee problems. "You got to make him aware of his knees," Mansfield said.

I talked to Moose and the Old Ranger for two or three hours one afternoon, trying to get an idea of what it was like in what are known as the trenches.

One of the things defensive linemen hate is to be "cut"—hit low, around the knees, and cut down. "I don't let nobody get my knees," Fats Holmes had said. "Come in and cut me, I say, 'Pleeze don't do that again.' Come in again, cut me, I got on him and hold him down, grab his old balls and twist 'em and say, 'Don't you do that again.' "

"Yeah, well," Van Dyke said, "they're embarrassed by being cut. It's sort of humiliating. But Joe Greene will chase an offensive lineman around kicking him. I wouldn't let Joe intimidate me like that. I cut Curly Culp once, he jumped up and got his cleats in my back, and made sure he stepped on my hand. But usually they don't do anything."

"What did you do when Curly Culp did that?"

"I hurt."

"Ray and I have different philosophies. He provokes guys, makes them mad. I try to stay friends with 'em, because if you don't they're going to hurt you more. They've got those great big forearms and they can beat the shit out of your neck. Once Walter Johnson beat me on a pass and Ray came across the middle from three or four yards away and stuck his helmet in Walter's ribs. Then Ray said, 'Way to hit, Bruce.'

"Well, there was Walter Johnson with veins just sticking out of his neck and forearms, and on the next play he just beat the shit out of me. It's a difference in philosophy. A sleeping giant like . . . We better keep personalities out of this. Don't want to make 'em mad. A sleeping giant, you don't fuck with him."

"Alex Karras," said Ray, "would have a personal vendetta against you. He'd come after you to the point sometimes he forgot about doing his job. Course he never could see. He saw objects, but that's about all.

"In the days of the 4–3 defense the center was the intimidator."

"Ray could sit back there all day and take those cheap shots."

"That's why you could be a 225-pound center. Now, with these uneven fronts, you've got those 280-pounders right over your head most of the time. But still . . . Karras—I used to like to get him mad. Some guys I like to mouth off to. Say 'Old Cunt. You must be having your period.' The defensive guys have to do a job. If the ball carrier's there they've got to get him, not you. But we can seek them out.

"I'll tell you a case when somebody got me, though," Mansfield said. "When we opened against the Bears in '67, our receiver caught a pass and I went flying downfield and blindsided Butkus. He was screaming the whole game, and I was cutting his ass down the whole time. Then there was a fumble. I fell on it. Butkus landed on me and his forearm caught me across the back of the neck. I got up. I couldn't tell which end of the field was mine. I said, 'Dick, I didn't even feel it.' They penalized him 15 yards. Course it didn't help my neck any. I would go after a guy like Joe Greene. I wouldn't let him intimidate me. I'd go after him till they threw me out of the game. I'd blindside him, whatever it took. When I meet my match and more than my match, I've always had the dogged attitude, I don't care how overmatched I am, I'm going to make it as hard as I can on that guy."

"I've been intimidated," said Bruce. "Before they changed the rule on clubbing. Now the defensive guy's supposed to be able to hit you with his arm only once, on his first step. It used to be—Walter Johnson would slap me in the head like a sledgehammer. Left, right, I was dizzy on my feet, I'd start to worry."

"I've been humiliated," Mansfield said. "By Bob Lilly, when Dallas beat us 56–14. But I've never been intimidated."

"I remember sometimes Walt didn't even rush the passer," said Van Dyke. "Just come across the line and wham, wham. Nothing I could do but put my hands up. He found it pretty easy to beat me after that. In the last exhibition game . . . no names . . . a guy complained, said I hit him a cheap shot. I said 'You motherfucker, you're not that good, that I have to cheap-shot you. You better watch your ass, cocksucker.'

"Then he said, 'Oh . . . Well . . . I didn't mean . . .' "

"It doesn't really get so intense, as far as the animalism of the attack," Mansfield said. "You can't just be an animal on the offensive line. You've got to be calculating and cunning."

Bruce: "You're graded on consistency. You've got to approach it as a business."

Ray: "You're playing a psychological game with these guys."

Bruce: "In your mind, you're trying to make yourself perform. To think the right things at the right time. I go over the play as I go to the line. First I look at what defense they're going to be in. Then I think of the count the snap's going to be on. If it's a trap play I think of my route real quick, or if it's a pass I think to myself, I'll have to set up real quick. Then I listen for an audible.

Then if there's no audible at the snap I uncoil and do it.

"Everything's in my mind. All the plays and my assignments. All I do is flash back in my memory and make sure. If I don't sometimes I'll mess up. If I don't think 'I've got to set,' I'll mess up on the pass-block. It's easy to get complacent about your assignments. You're wired for it all but you've got to remind yourself every time."

Ray: "I think harder on the number the snap's going to be on. My primary responsibility is to get the ball up on time. I keep saying '2,2,2' or '4,4,4' to myself going up to the line. Once in a while I've forgotten it. Once in a while the quarterback forgets it. Thank God most quarterbacks anticipate a little bit by pushing their hands up. So I've got to think about the snap. Then the play and my blocking assignment. I see myself using the type of block I'm going to use."

Bruce: "The snap. It's like a sprinter getting off. Everybody has to get off at the same moment. Exact. Everybody anticipates just a little bit, everybody together."

Ray: "It's a relative thing. It amazes me, really. When is the exact time everybody gets off? It's not on the number, really. Say the snap is on 2. 'Hut 1, Hut 2 . . .' "

Bruce: "Usually it's just before the second 'hut.' "

Ray: "Yeah. I guess so. 'Hut 1, Hut . . .' "

"Then, too," Ray said, "sometimes the center has to make an adjustment. The guy who was supposed to be over me may be over Bruce. After the audible, then the center may make a blocking call. Sometimes a tackle or tight end will repeat it, so the whole line hears it. It's hard to hear down there. Guys will be saying, 'What? What?' I may call 'Stack' or 'Solid' or 'Gap.' Change the blocking assignments. A 'Gap' call can mean so many different things, according to what the play is. We have a gap call just about every play. We used to just have two calls: even and odd.

"Then the defense is trying to react. They can tell when the quarterback's calling an audible, by his voice. And they can see guys in the line picking their heads up."

Bruce: "You know we used to have a play on defense called the Fake Fake-the-Blitz Blitz. We would fake a fake blitz, and then blitz."

"Did it work?" I asked.

"I don't know," Ray said. "That's why we didn't win then maybe."

"What do you see and hear down there?" I asked.

"You're not aware of noises," Ray said.

"Everything flashes by," said Bruce.

"I always see eyes," said Ray. "I'm looking at eyes down there, not so much at faces. I'm looking to see where they're looking."

Bruce: "It's funny when your eyes do meet. You think, 'Wow, this is some kind of freak, looking right at me.' You feel guilty. You think you're going to do something wrong."

91

Ray: "I eye-fake. If I'm going to block a guy straight ahead I'll look down the line."

Bruce: "Lot of times if I'm going to the right I'll look to the left first. Then to the right. You've always got to look in the direction you're going to go."

Ray: "You know, I don't even know what guys on other teams look like."

Bruce: "Yeah. I remember seeing what somebody looked like recently, after a game. I was shocked. I never thought he looked like that. Guys look different in helmets."

Ray: "Hanratty looks like Yosemite Sam in his. Big nose sticking out of his helmet with a big moustache under it."

Bruce: "If you're on the field with the other team afterwards you may shake their hands. But not some games when you lose. Some games, there's no way I'm going to talk to any of 'em. No damn way. But last year after the Oakland game, after the Miraculous Reception, I felt compassion for those guys. They were down on the field with their hands down, their heads down, like they were praying to the East. I knew how I'd felt a few seconds before. I walked up to Art Thom. I thought he was Tony Kline. I said, 'Good game, Tony.'

" 'How soon we forget,' he said."

"How do you feel when a teammate makes a big mistake, that costs you a game?"

"It's like when your little kid hurts you accidentally," said Ray. "Like when Jimmy kicked me in the ribs two days after they were broken. You want to hit him, but your reason takes over."

"You know it could've just as easily been you," said Bruce.

Toward opponents their feelings were more complicated.

Bruce: "We were telling Bill Bergey, for Cincinnati, that we were going to get him for giving Hanratty a cheap shot. He was saying, 'Bruce, watch the film, it wasn't a cheap shot. You'll be wrong, you'll see. Bruce, that's publicity, you don't believe that, do you? They're trying to get me!'

"I said, 'You're a good football player, why do you do that stuff? You just piss people off.' He said, 'Well, I don't mean it. Bruce, you're always giving me the hard-ass.'

"You get to know guys. It makes it tough for me to play guys two games. Only way to play a good game is intensity—you've got to get mad. I'm not vindictive, I don't carry a grudge. But you've got to want to hurt people.

"But maybe you like the guy. He talks on the field to you. And I really want to hurt him because we're losing the game. How can I have these feelings? But they're temporary feelings."

Ray: "The impulse is to hurt a guy while you're out there. Then if you do hurt a guy you feel like a horse's ass."

Bruce: "I remember Lou Cordeleone said, 'Bruce, why'd you have to do that?' "

Ray: "Et tu, Bruce."

Bruce: "It was in LSU stadium. We were running a sweep the other way.

I've got to take two steps and jump toward Cordeleone's legs. His knee is sticking out . . . 'Bruce, you hurt me bad,' he said. He never played again after that. I knew the guy. I'd been to his bar.

"Reid'll talk to you. Instead of jumping around me on a pass he'll try to run over me. Then he'll say, 'God damn Bruce, it's like trying to climb out of a fifty-foot deep well.'

"Bergey's a clothesline guy. Like Mel Blount. He does little goofy shit. A guy recovers a fumble and Bergey'll push him, for no reason. 'Oh, knock it off,' you say."

Ray: "I admire a guy who never gives a cheap shot. Bob Lilly. I always watched and admired him. He'd taken all kinds of cheap shots and never retaliated. We were playing Dallas last year. I came over and caught him with my helmet right under his chin. He pulled back and gave me a punch in the head.

" 'Bob,' I said. 'I never thought you'd do something like that.' I think it embarrassed him that he did. But he was frustrated. He had a bad ankle, a bad instep. For thirteen years guys had just been double-teaming his ass. Same thing Joe Greene has to put up with. I'd like to see what Joe could do if he went one-on-one with a guy.

"You know," Ray mused, "when some guy gets blindsided, they run the films of it back and forth, back and forth. I got blindsided against New York last year—I just saw people's faces and lights flipping over and over. But it's sort of . . . *firing*. It *fires* you when you see a hit like that. That's what football's all about. See some poor defenseless guy get blindsided, and you just feel the emotion run through the crowd.

"When the guy getting hit is your quarterback, it's a cheap shot. But a cheap shot is a relative thing. I'm a cheap shotter in a way. Those guys are going to be diving on the pile when I get there. Sometimes I have to jump over the pile to get to a guy—stick him and knock him over."

Bruce: "When we're losing, I like to see a guy really crumple some people."

Ray: "I stepped on a guy in high school once. I didn't like it then, and I'll never do it again. I remember my cleats crunching into his back."

Bruce: "Wally Hilgenburg, the Vikings, is a cheap shot."

Ray: "Yeah. He'll go out of his way to hurt somebody. He stepped on Moon's back. He went out of his way to step on Moon's back.

"But you know, everybody always laughs, watching the films, when you get hurt. Even when I saw my ribs getting broken, in the films, I laughed."

Bruce: "I remember once I was going full speed and hit the defensive end. He hit me in the head. I go down on my knees. I just go down on my knees and fall over. It's really funny in the films. Even when the quarterback gets hurt, it's funny."

Ray: "It's sort of like a nervous laugh."

Bruce: "We all know we could get it any time. If you laugh at it, it keeps it on a lighter plane. And it makes it . . . tougher."

Ray: "You don't want sympathy. You don't want guys saying 'Aw, Ray, you got hurt man.' I'd rather they laughed.

"I remember when Bradshaw jammed his finger against Houston last year. It wasn't funny at the time, looked like we'd lost our quarterback. He came off the field, on national television, acting like he'd really been killed. It was funny in the films because he was acting too dramatic for it to be the injury it was. I remember Gary Bleeker, our quarterback in college. He gets up off the ground, starts spinning around, falls down. He jammed his thumb. We all thought some sniper had got him from the lower deck.

"At [the University of] Washington they never helped you off the field. I saw guys making it off with broken legs. The only guy who I saw just laying in the mud, staying there, was a guy who'd split his spleen. It was in practice. I'd just seen a movie of Wild Bill Elliott dying in the mud. Bleeding from the mouth. I said, 'This guy's shot!' He damn near died. But they wouldn't help him off. They just moved practice further down the field. The school nearly got sued on that. I wish they had.

"They used to tell us wild-ass stories. We'd imagine the superguy, playing with his neck broken, coming off under his own power after the game with the bone sticking out. Guys laugh at stories like that today. We thought it was great. Today they say the guy musta been nuts. 'Hey man, funky dude.' Look at you like you're a weirdo if you do things like that. A guy like that is a short-haired guy, too far to the right. 'You've only got one body,' they say today."

Bruce: "We were brainwashed, maybe: it should feel good to get pain. Like my little kid—he sees blood on his finger and likes it. Feels tough."

Ray: "Yeah. I don't think it's good, even now, to be sissy. But it's not good to be stupid either. I've got hemorrhoids. The urologist said it was from stress."

Bruce: "Younger guys ask you, how can you put up with the pain? As you get older, bumps and bruises bother you more. The artificial turf, age, playing against bigger guys."

Ray: "Pro football is a different animal from college. In college it was animalistic. The only thing in the world that mattered was the fucking win."

Bruce: "Well, that's the same in the pros."

Ray: "Yeah, that's not different. But it's . . . There was a purity between the players and the fans in college. I rarely remember a Husky being booed. The fans were part of you. Here you're a fucking pro. You're not part of them. Still you're somebody to be admired, though."

Bruce: "Yeah, I think football's a good and just and nice and reasonable thing to do."

Ray: "And booing. When the Pirates are fucking up I'm sort of booing down inside. I knew some of them, guys like Giusti and Blass. But it's not Giusti and Blass, the guys you know, when they're playing. It's the Pirates.

"It used to piss me off that people didn't recognize me. Now I hate to be recognized. The other day a little skinny guy came up to me and wanted me to feel his shoulder separation."

The conversation swung back around to hitting. "The only reason we like to hit people," said Bruce, "is because we've been conditioned to. We know we're going to be commended."

Ray: "The things I do I don't try to put 'em in any perspective. Whether it's right or good . . . I don't want to figure it out. I don't want to know myself. I like myself the way I am."

Bruce: "But that's rationalization."

Ray: "No, it's not."

Bruce: "I try to figure . . ."

Ray: "I got thinking after reading Gent's book and talking to Gent. I don't want to put it on a plane where I have to justify it."

Bruce: "But you have to justify it, when the coach is screaming at you, and . . ."

Ray: "But then I justify it because I was brought up under the old system. That's what coaches have to do. I really do enjoy hitting. More for approval than for anything else."

Bruce: "Yeah, that's what I said."

Ray: "But not from the coach. From teammates more than anything else."

Bruce: "And from the guy you're hitting."

Ray: "Right. You want respect from the guy you're hitting. And if you're really good, attention is going to come. When Tinglehoff got all-pro center all the time—he's getting respect from guys he's hitting. I'm not."

Bruce: "Well, but the way people vote for all-pro. Guys get reputations off the field. Like Ben Davidson in Oakland."

Ray: "Yeah. Ben is the most publicized third-team tackle ever. He played behind me in the Rose Bowl. I remember when Tim Rossovich went to the Pro Bowl as a defensive end. Hear how tough this guy is. Huh.

"But you always question yourself. No matter how good you are, you wonder, is this real? Always worrying. I'd like to have one summer of happiness. There was a movie called that.

"Maybe we're a dying breed. Maybe football will become flag football."

Bruce: "I remember you and I used to be the only ones who liked training camp."

□ **8** □

CONTACT

Fear not to touch the best.

—SIR WALTER RALEIGH

The reflections of Moosie and Old Ranger have led us directly into an essential subject, of which eye contact is only an interesting sidelight. At the heart of every sport except pure races is some form of hitting, of solid connection—the merging for a fruity instant of good wood and fat pitch, a firm forehand's flowing thunk, the shwunk of a round leather ball through stretchy cords. ("Shooting and hitting is a sensation unlike any other."—Bill Bradley.) "Only connect . . ." "Right on the button." Two hard things meeting in a moment of give.

Football, especially. "That battle of the hitting" is what Chuck Noll kept saying must be won. We have seen that purposeful contact in football is not a matter of thrashing out, but one of transmitting power, as in electrical contact, from the earth through the muscles and frame to a spot of sufficient but not superior resistance on the body of the opponent. A taste for contact is the common touch which all pro football players—quarterbacks and wide receivers alone excepted—must have. And quarterbacks and wide receivers must be able to take contact literally in their stride.

To some extent the taste for contact is universal, I should think. I am close to whatever is the opposite of blood-lusty, but on sandlots I always enjoyed the sensation of banging into my peers. A clean blow with your shoulder into the right-sized person's trunk makes your back feel good, like stretching in the morning or sex. It discharges the dead air between your shoulder blades. "Unload" and "sell out" are players' terms for what you do when you put all of yourself into another body. When a batter hits a baseball on the nose he says, "I got it all." But the hitting I observed on the sidelines during Steeler games went beyond, or fell short of, that kind of gratification. Sometimes it sounded like bags of cement being dropped from the top of the cab of a truck. From the back of a truck sounds regrettable enough—WUMP with an undertone of dusty rupture—but it's the kind of thing that will happen from day to day. The percussion of a bag dropped from the cab's top sounds uncalled for, perversely bad. "Oh, come on, you guys, that's not necessary," I felt like saying sometimes on the sidelines, as if the game were a scuffle turned ugly. The contact

96

was not all shoulder-in-the-gut. It was, for example, a linebacker's upper body flung sideways in front of a runner's surging knees and concrete thighs while the bulk of the linebacker's and the runner's bodies in such a situation give off a sound like that of a racehorse running through a picket fence. Then there is the contact of separated shoulders against broken ribs and damaged knees. Hitting people with parts of yourself that are hurting and threatening to tear apart must be worse than belting out a song with strep throat. How people can have any kind of taste for contact along those lines I don't know.

"You hit him where he's soft," said Noll. "In the numbers. Come in low and strike a rising blow. Then he can't hit you hard. It's an aggressive act, it's a good experience. If you do it right, you feel good. If you do it wrong, he feels good. It's a better experience for him. The person who has the good experience, he'll want to do it again." Like a good many of Noll's positions, this had a Platonic undeniability, but it failed to account for a great deal that went on. I saw a lot of collisions that must have been poor experiences, at best, for all parties. "People who say football is dehumanizing," said Noll, "I'm sure have had a bad experience. If you lose—if you're not up to the challenge—it's going to be a sour thing for you. There are some people who are not going to be up to the challenge. But that doesn't mean the challenge is wrong."

Bo Schembechler, the head coach at the University of Michigan, once spoke of contact to me in what seemed a suitably resonant way. In a way, that is, which left room for a certain presumption of dreadfulness: "I'm not saying it's natural. A guy throwing his body around and hurting people, that's an unnatural thing. It has to be instilled at around the junior high school level." But Noll steered away from pain and kept coming back to technique:

"Some coaches have an obsession with toughness. Someone told them their team had to be tough so they're gonna teach toughness. I was on the road one time, watching schools practice, and at one place I saw offensive linemen working on roll-out pass protection. The quarterback was rolling to his right and the tackle on the left set up almost like he would on a dropback pass—so the defensive lineman on that side took the inside and broke through and chased the quarterback down. And the coach, from the other side of the field, ran up screaming at the top of his lungs at this kid, 'You're not tough! You're not tough! You're not tough!' Well, toughness had nothing to do with it. He broke down because his technique was wrong. When you come screaming up to a kid who's shaky, trying to learn the game, and you tell him he's not tough ... One of the things I think you have to do in coaching is not screw up people you're working with."

"Do you think that with the right talent and technique, any kid can be tough?"

"My personal experience is that it wasn't just natural to go out there and run into people, so you had to learn how to do it and not come out the worst of it."

"What was your experience in learning how to hit? Starting out as a kid."

"Well, it goes back into high school, and you started out with the blocking sled. Most kids, when they hit it, they kind of turn sideways and lean against it. Learning how to hit it with a pop and with each shoulder was an accomplishment. You learn how to hit it with your right shoulder first, and you can't hit it worth a damn with your left, so you work like crazy with your left shoulder until it became better than your right shoulder, you know. Of course the first time you break the spring on the sled is a big thing. It's like aggressiveness, it's something that has to be learned on the field."

"Is there a problem at all in teaching people to be aggressive and then worrying about how they apply it off the field?"

"I don't see where that has anything to do with it. Aggression on the football field, in a game—it doesn't cause him to go out and murder people. There are people who are aggressive . . . talkers, for instance. But it doesn't carry over into other areas. The most aggressive football players you run into are those feisty little kids—the only way they've made anything in life is by being aggressive, and it carries over into football. But learning it in football—it doesn't carry over the other direction."

"Radical critics of football talk about it fostering aggression. Whereas defenders might say that it enables fans to work off aggressions. Do you think about that at all?"

"Well, the only thing I've learned is that most people who are against something—they're knocking the game for a reason. Usually, it's not a good reason. So I've never really put much stock in what people like that have to say. They're trying to upgrade their departments by tearing down football. They don't understand what football is. Football is the greatest learning experience that I've ever had. You can peck away at anything—but the fact is that it's there."

I am conservative enough to agree with Noll that being there is a big point in football's, and accordingly in contact's, favor. But there is a lot more to be said on the subject. The Steeler playbook's prescriptions on hitting were not so antiseptic.

"Don't be a 'nice guy' and just tackle the receiver, make him remember you and never want to catch another ball in your area again," reads one playbook passage. The middle linebacker was adjured to punish a receiver who tried to cut through his territory on a pass route: "Mike, if ends try to cross you, pop them good with a shoulder-forearm shiver. Never let ends cross on you."

When an opposing man had bad knees, the Steelers focused on them. And Noll, when an opposing player had put a Steeler out of the game, was known to say on the sidelines, "*Get* that sonofabitch."

"Hurt the other guy," said Van Dyke, "and he'll bend a little bit. That's how you win football games. You hurt the other person. Bend him backward, get him a little gun-shy. When the guy's right in front of me all I can do is finesse him, drive him back. But on these traps, when I can get two or three steps and he's not expecting me, I can hurt him physically."

"I guess you have to be some kind of neurotic to play this game," said Hanneman. "When I was away from it for a year I never went through such hell. But anybody who says he enjoys hitting heads in practice day after day is a liar. You do get pleasure from a good hit. But it's bred into you by coaches. And then it's true that there aren't many clean shots in life."

Rocky Bleier said he'd had a better camp than usual in '73 because he'd decided to commit his body recklessly all the time in practice, the way he did in games. "When you're doing it in a game, it's sort of a romanticist concept— you're a knight in shining armor. You go balls-out. You get hit, all right, it's in a noble cause. But in practice it's an unnatural thing. You *know* the guys. It's not *nice.* And somebody steps on your foot and you jam your finger and it's all . . . aggravating. But you have to do it. You have to show that you don't care about your body. The game does superhuman things to people."

"Killing people is unnatural too, isn't it?" I asked Bleier. He was the only NFL player to see active duty in Vietnam. His was a story which a major production company had expressed interest in making a movie of. He'd been captain at Notre Dame, but when he made the Steelers in '68 everyone figured it was because he was a well-spoken, immediately likable Catholic kid whom the Chief was therefore partial to. When he got drafted (due, it was said, to bad blood between him and a member of his local draft board) it looked like the end of his career. As an infantry PFC on patrol near Chu Lai, he was caught in a Viet Cong ambush and shot through the left thigh. While he crawled toward the rest of his platoon a grenade went off in his path; he rolled away, and shrapnel pierced his right leg and foot. He dragged himself 150 yards through the underbrush to what was left of his platoon and was pinned down with them for seven hours. After three leg operations he returned to the Steelers in 1970 and kept making the team, year after year. By '73 he was actually faster than he'd been in college, from working with weights and running to strengthen his wounded leg.

"No," he said about combat contact. "It's different. You're fighting for self-survival, and that's one of your first instincts. In football you're thinking about making the team and producing. In combat, you're just thinking about getting through it and getting back home. And if you get wounded, they're going to pull you out of there. So you drink, smoke, and do what you're told."

In other words combat was psychologically easier than football. Incidentally I asked Bleier what his thoughts were while lying near Chu Lai, bleeding. "Well, the only things to do over there are read books and think about R and R, which I never got to take," he said. "So I had just been reading this war story, about a guy who gets hit and prays that if he gets out of it alive, he'll become a priest. And he does.

99

"So the first thing I thought was, I'm not going to be a prick about this. I mean when you confess, you're really just saying I *hope* I won't do this again, but you know that if the occasion arises, nature is going to take its course. So I prayed and said I'm not going to promise to be a priest. I'm just going to say that I'll put my life in Your hands, to do whatever You want with it. Now I realized even at the time that that was a pretty chickenshit move. I mean I could do anything and say, well, that must be what God wants me to do."

Keating grew up going to Catholic schools where they used a driver with the head off or a paddle with holes in it on you. And gym class was sixty minutes of calisthenics. "It was no fun at all. It was awful." Playing pro ball, he said, was also a grind: "You get one guy beating on your head, or another guy." He shrugged. "I can't tell the difference. One day you've got it, and another day you don't."

But there were bright spots: "The other night I hit a guard right in the stomach, where it was soft." Keating said. "He went 'Phuhh.' I doubled him right over me, his feet were off the ground, he was out of it. But you don't go to injure a guy. If you did, Namath would be out of football. If a guy's got bad knees you'll block at them, to get his hands down to protect himself, get him thinking about them. You'll do that. But not just to hurt a guy."

Of course, Keating acknowledged, there was such a thing as smashing a quarterback good, and even late. "When I was with him at Oakland Ben Davidson hit a quarterback once—I was in there ahead of him and I had already come to a stop, the ball was thrown, and Ben ran past me and smeared the guy. What I love is to come in and reach out with an arm when the quarterback doesn't see you, he's not expecting it, and just catch him as you come in and take him down. I got Namath once that way—caught him right up in here [Keating indicated an area around the collarbone] and he went phuuuuh. That's fun, sure. I shouldn't say that, I guess, but you work so hard the whole game to get there . . ."

Keating said he by and large didn't take special measures to intimidate men who were blocking him. "I did against Oakland though, Gene Upshaw and I exchanged blows." A man with the Steelers who watched that game's films closely said he noticed Keating, in fact, toward the end of the game when he began to wear down, sticking his fingers in the eyes of people in his way. "It's hard to play against good friends," said Keating. "It was no problem with Upshaw, because with him I knew it'd be hello before the first play and that'd be it. But if I were ever a defensive back playing against Freddie Biletnikoff, it'd be hard."

"I never thought it was a rough game until after I broke my rib this year," Mansfield said, and indeed the Steelers tended by and large to take contact for granted, or at least not to speak of it too lustfully.

"I never think about it," Ham said of contact. "We do it so much, I don't know . . . Andy and I are similar linebackers: We're not real strong physical linebackers, we use finesse, technique. I get as much out of faking the offensive tackle as I do out of really sticking somebody. I'm more concerned with making tackles and not making mistakes than I am with decking somebody."

"I think of myself as a finesse-type player," said George Webster. "I like to hit people. But I'm not peculiar about it. I don't like it more than . . . oh . . . kissing a nude lady."

Once on the sidelines I stood with Dockery as an awful-looking tangle of limbs came cracking and sprawling toward us like three sheep and a buffalo caught in a net. "It's funny," Dockery said. "When you're standing here it really looks rough. You say to yourself, 'How do I do stuff like that?' But when you're out there playing, you don't think of it. You're caught up in it, just gliding. You're reacting to your keys—you can't think about fear. Can't have second thoughts. If you do, that's when you get trampled. And some days, you know, I really look forward to contact—a simple collision. Untarnished. In a world that's getting softer every day. It's certainly unnatural for a cornerback to take on those guards. But you get conditioned.

"But coaches will tell you—if you get a chance to break a leg, do it. I don't like to hear that kind of thing. I was George Sauer's roommate with the Jets, and he quit football because of things like that. I think it's possible to win and emphasize some of the other things you get out of football." (I might report that I spent an enjoyable evening with Dockery and Sauer in San Francisco, and Sauer said he had made up the following story: A man had murdered a woman and was dismembering her and throwing the pieces out the window when he heard the police arriving. But even though it meant capture he went on with the task of cutting off her remaining leg. "The maim is never over," he explained, "until the last gam is out.")

Sam Davis put the pleasures of hitting in clear-cut, goal-oriented terms: "I get a pleasure out of putting a man on his back. Because you know, then, there's no way in the world he's going to make the tackle. You can tell when you hit a guy whether you really hit him. If you stand him up—you can feel that sensation. On the other hand, you can feel that sensation of, gee whiz, I can't go nowhere on this particular block. If they ever get a little spark, they're going to be hard to beat. So you want to take that spark, and break their morale."

Gerela had played defensive back in college and he made several solid tackles on kickoffs during the season. He was no Garo Yepremian. But he saw football contact with a certain detachment: "It's brutal. In soccer, you might get a bump here and there, that'll throw you a little off-balance. You might get a little bang on your shin with a boot. But you're not talking about bumps when you're talking about football, you're talking about *hits*. Collisions. You're talking about a 250-pound guy hitting a 190-pound guy—that's what you call a *hit*. Especially when you weight 189."

Certainly there is more to being a hitter in pro football than just knowing how to do it. "I'm sick," said Dwight White expansively, as we shall hear later in more detail. It helps to grow up in a tough neighborhood or in the country: "I was always aggressive—by growing up on the farm," said Mel Blount. "My brother used to put me on bulls. I used to do a lot of rugged things, like breaking horses. I applied a lot of that to football."

Will Walls, the legendary scout, tended to see good hitting as an aspect of certain people's nature. If he ever once saw a prospect shrink from an impact, he wrote that prospect off. "Once a flincher, always a flincher," he said.

"You know when they say about a player, 'He hangs around bars all the time and gets in a lot of fights,' " Walls told me. "Well, he likes contact."

The Steelers had their share of bar fighters. When Hanneman mentioned having participated in a state arm-wrestling tournament I told him I had heard that Van Dyke was the team arm-wrestling champion. Hanneman said well, he'd like to challenge him, but "I was in a fight out on the coast last season and I threw a big roundhouse right and something popped in my forearm." Hanneman and a friend once in their youth were trying to get together some money so they could go into a loggers' tavern. They were standing outside. They saw somebody back a car into a pickup truck, and although it wasn't their pickup they said, "Well, just give us $50 and we'll forget about it." One thing led to another and before the evening was over they had whipped nine men and three women. "Jess took six men and I took three men and three women," Hanneman said. "The whole place was torn up. There were people stretched out on tables. I had a knife sticking out of my arm."

"You try to get as much of your momentum into the other guy as you can," Wagner said. "To protect yourself. When you go"—and here he flinched, wincing inward with his shoulder—"that's when you get hurt. But what I hate to see is a fullback coming through untouched. He weighs 235 pounds and he's got an 8-yard start and he can go two ways, and you just say to yourself, 'I hope I get a piece of him. And I hope I don't get hurt.' "

The players with the shortest career expectancy are the ones who make the most effort to avoid contact—shifty running backs. Those who last the longest in the game—aside from quarterbacks, who are either ruined early or last for years and years, like men in combat—are the offensive linemen, who are supposed to welcome punishment, or value it more highly than daylight between themselves and their opponents. But then, offensive linemen are bred for size and solidity, and the collisions they are involved in are not usually ones in which several long strides' worth of momentum have been generated. Getting as much of your own momentum into the meeting, though—that seems a valuable principle, one that might be applied to daily life.

But off the field most of the Steelers seemed to want just to have fun and go with the flow, to operate less in terms of give and take than the civilians around them did. That was probably because off the field the flow tends to come to pro football players, when they are recognized, without their having to make much of an effort. The magnetism of their station in life is momentum enough (which makes things hard when their careers are over).

I was at a party with a Steeler who was wearing a Steeler T-shirt. There were a number of girls from an eye-ear-nose-and-throat hospital there, and I had some pretty interesting and germane things to tell them, I thought. I said that according to Van Dyke, the first place a person loses weight is under the eyelids. I said I had played softball against the actor who plays the doctor in *Deep Throat*. And I told the story Roy McHugh of the *Press* had told me about Pie Traynor, the all-time-great Pirate third baseman. It seems that Traynor was asked on the radio about spitballs, and he said that in the old days he'd had to face a pitcher named Wheezer Dell, "and Wheezer had what we call no nose at all. He'd hold the ball up in front of his face and wheeze on it, and . . ." I was trying to think of a good ear story when I noticed that the Steeler was getting more attention by just saying "Oh, wow."

A couple of the girls surrounding him were kidding him about going to a party in a Steeler T-shirt. "How do you know whether people like you for yourself, or because you're a football player?"

"I don't give a shit," he said. "I'll probably never see anybody here again except him and him," he explained, pointing to me and another companion. That struck me as a perfectly realistic response in context, but that kind of reality probably makes it hard to keep as firm a sense of yourself in contact off the field as in contact on it.

And after a while the aggressive sense of yourself on the field may wear thin. No matter how technically well you hit another man, you get hurt, too, doing it.

"I've always loved to hit," said Kamikaze Meyer. "I don't know if that means something's wrong with me, but it never bothered me. It just feels good to knock hell out of a guy. Only sometimes it hurts you more than him—you'll be getting up saying. 'Boy, I knocked the hell out of that guy.' But you'll be getting up thinking. Oh, my God."

Sacrificing your body serves the team and in some ways, for a while, it serves your body, more than flinching does. But in the long run it wears most bodies down. Both Frenchy and Rowser got injured in '73 while driving all of their momentum into another, larger man. Rowser was a gritty and deft hitter, but toward the end of the year the coaches' feeling was that he had been doing it too long, for someone as small as he was. The coachly phrase applied to Rowser was this: "He may be hit out."

A hit-out case. A man who's sold out all he has to sell on the field. Whether such cases are an indictment of football's challenge or not depends on how valuably recreational you think pro football is, if you're an observer, or where it can get you, if you're a player. Rowser didn't think he was hit out, though he said he was playing with a slightly dislocated shoulder toward the end of the year—"I got one cannon here that won't go off. I can point it, but it won't go off." He was going to go on knocking people flying for as long as he could with the Denver Broncos, to whom the Steelers traded him, and in the off-season he was involved in a black-owned business in Detroit, Young Men on the Move, which made small plastic items like desk calendars.

At any rate, as Noll said about the challenge, and as Scolnik might have said about the top of Pine's helmet when he turned his face into it, there is no denying that contact is there.

□ 9 □

THE EXHIBITION SEASON

You see the pigskin
Way up high.
You feel the clench
In your thigh.
You fight to win,
You fight to lose,
You do it any
Way you choose.
Beware the big guys,
All tall and full.
Smash the small guys
To a pulp.
—"FOOTBALL," BY STUART
DUFF, AGE ELEVEN

The afternoon of the first exhibition
game, against Baltimore in Three Rivers, I ran into the Chief and his son Tim
in the lobby of the Pittsburgh Hilton as they were meeting Cardinal Cooke.
You were likely to meet anybody, from Horse Czarnecki, the groundkeeper
at Pitt, to Jack Warner of Warner Brothers, with Art Rooney. He had earlier
introduced me to two noted old-time Pittsburgh fighters: Billy Conn, who told
about a time when he was visiting a rich woman in Florida, and she complained that the coons were stealing and eating from her fruit trees, and he said,
"Yeah, them Coons'll steal and eat anything"; and Charley Affif, with regard
to whom the Chief said fondly, "This here's Kid Zivic," Affif having fought
under that name once. I wish I could report that the Chief said, "This here's
Cardinal Cooke," or even that he introduced him under a name he once fought
under, but toward the cardinal the Chief was more nearly formal. He genu-
flected. Tim didn't.

"Do you go to the Jets and Giants games?" I asked the cardinal.

He said something vague.

105

"He used to a lot more," a younger cleric accompanying him said, "before he became archbishop."

The Steelers ran roughshod over the Colts, 34–7, and two people were shot in the stands.

Bell, the rookie enigma, ran the first kickoff of the season back to the 29, and Joe Greene said something friendly to him on the sidelines. Then Preston Pearson, trying to beat out Frenchy for the second running back job, took Bradshaw's handoff on the first play from scrimmage, stumbled, regained his balance, swept to the left, beat linebacker Ray May to the corner, picked up a block by Frank Lewis and went 69 yards. Bradshaw sneaked over.

The defense came in and stopped the Colts cold—Russell blitzing to hit quarterback Marty Domres as he tried to pass on third down. As the Captain, the Hammer, Mean Joe, Hollywood Bags and company left the field for the first time there was a great standing ovation. DEEEFENSE! Hot dog.

Everything went right. Preston improvised, turning a 5-yard loss into a 39-yard gain. Franco scooted wide so suddenly he went off the instant-replay screen in the press box, like the ball going off the screen in The Immaculate Reception. Pine fumbled a punt, recovered it, and went 30 yards. A Colt fumble went through four or five people before Sticks Anderson fell on it. Bradshaw went back to pass and stood looking for receivers, holding the ball with one hand, while a rusher pulled on the ball and Bradshaw's wrist with both his arms; Bradshaw didn't get the pass off but he held the ball. The Colts had first and goal at the 7 and the Steelers stopped them on the 1. Hanratty, who relieved Bradshaw in the third quarter, pumped twice to fake out defenders and threw to Steve Davis for a picture-pretty touchdown.

It was during the half that Charles Cooper, a former Duquesne basketball All-American, and Mrs. Rose Marie Bell were shot in the leg and the foot, respectively. "Some guy just shot two people," said son Tim in the press box. "The cops are chasing him."

"Where?"

"Outside, I hope. This doesn't happen even in Yonkers."

The police were looking for a man dressed in white and posing as a Liquor Control Board agent, or a man wearing a yellow shirt and khaki pants. The first man turned out to be a Liquor Control Board agent and the second never materialized. The final theory was that the shots were fired from outside the stadium and lofted into the crowd, though a detective said "Nobody's sure. You can't ever second-guess bullets." After the game a couple of the Steelers took the news of the shootings hard. "The only person that hasn't been assassinated yet is a football player," one of them said. "It would be so easy." The next week a spectator was shot mysteriously in Atlanta Stadium and for a while it appeared to be a wave, but there were no more shootings during the year.

"They exploded on us and executed letter-perfect," said Baltimore coach Howard Schnellenberger.

"I'm in heaven," Keating said. "Football's fun again."

John Kolb hurt his knee and said it "feels like a revolving door."

Noll was happy. He even had a good word for the part of the team he had been pushing most impatiently in practice: "The offensive line was something to behold."

Next week the Steelers lost to Minnesota, in Bloomington, and Noll used for the first time a term he came back to all year: "We didn't play with enough intensity." Intensity, he said, was a matter of doing things hard. "We better sustain it. That's the thing that protects you from injury, from everything. You've got to be the aggressor. You've got to be doing the hitting."

"Last year," said Minnesota coach Bud Grant, "it was easy to get a team like Pittsburgh aroused week after week. Because they had that possibility of a first title year constantly going for them. But now they've had a taste of a title, and it might be tough to keep them fired up."

"It is hard," said Noll evenly when advised of Grant's comments, "for a person from the outside to know what's going on on a team."

What clearly let the Steelers down was the offense. All ten Minnesota points were attributable to Bradshaw interceptions. Pittsburgh seemed set for an easy touchdown when Clack recovered a fumble on the Viking 19, but Bradshaw passed badly to the sideline and it was intercepted and run back 93 yards for a touchdown. Another interception set up the Minnesota field goal. Blount stopped the Vikings with an interception but on the next play Bradshaw was intercepted. Wagner intercepted and returned the ball to the Viking 38 but the offense had to settle for a field goal.

Bradshaw seemed confident enough after the game, however. "Tell Francis he has the weakest arm in the league," he said jokingly to a Minnesota newspaperman, and Noll referred to the Vikings' "three-yards-and-a-cloud-of-dust passing game." Francis Tarkenton, in fact, had been administered a rebuke by the home crowd, which cheered lustily when Bob Berry came in to spell him.

The year before was supposed to be the Vikings' year, Tarkenton having arrived from the Giants to give Minnesota the only thing it seemed to lack: a solid quarterback. He had never been on a winner before and this seemed to be his chance to prove that a scrambler could be as productive as he was exciting. Andy Russell was a believer in Tarkenton, as a businessman and field general.

"I had a product I wanted to get him to identify himself with a couple of years back," Russell said. "I was in Dallas and heard he was there too. So I went to his hotel room while he was getting ready to go somewhere, and I went through my presentation. I'd been through it a hundred times. I thought I knew all the answers to all the questions about it. He listened and then he said, 'I tell you what, Andy,' and he pulled his tie into place with a flourish, 'I'd say these things: One . . .'

"And he made eight comments, bing bing bing, and I knew I couldn't answer five of them. Then I remember we played an exhibition game in Montreal with the Giants. We were leading 16–10 with 42 seconds to go, the ball on the Giant 20. Francis came onto the field, looked at our defense, and smiled.

"And he started completing passes, and scrambling for first downs, and running out of bounds, and I thought, This guy is going to get them in. I knew he was. And he got down to our 10 and threw a screen, and if Joe Greene hadn't hit the receiver from behind and made him fumble into the end zone, which wasn't Francis's fault, he would've."

The Vikings had had nagging injuries in '72, however, and opponents stopped trying to pass long against the fabled rush of the Purple People Eaters but ran at them, trapped them, faked them out with play-action passes, and the Vikings finished 7–7. And Tarkenton was no local hero.

But in '73 the Vikings, with Francis being a wizard, were going to go all the way to the Super Bowl. And things very similar to what happened to the Vikings in '72 were going to befall the Steelers.

The Viking game was an interesting one for Van Dyke because Fry and other Steelers had been telling him that Carl Eller, the Vikings' great defensive end, had threatened to kill him. The year before Van Dyke had been called twice for clipping, cutting Eller down from behind just outside the zone where it is legal. That was the only way to catch Eller on sweeps to his side, because he moved sideways so quickly, and that was what Van Dyke was supposed to do, but the Steelers had received an official warning from the league office. And Eller, who had bad knees, was said to be in a murderous mood.

"I've never been in that position before," Van Dyke said after the game. "I was worried about going down and people stepping on my back. But Eller just laid into me a couple of times on extra points." (The Steelers said "laid into" to mean going easy on contact, whereas I grew up understanding it to mean a desperate assault: "He laid into that old boy and like to tore his ear off.")

"Then on one play," Van Dyke said, "I passed up a chance to really hit him hard when it wasn't necessary, and he said, 'Hey, thanks Bruce.' "

What the Steelers did to Eller in this game was for Mullins to stand him straight up and Bleier to shoot in and pop him in the knees. Twice he was flipped over onto his head that way.

Ron Bell's brightest moment with the Steelers came during the Viking game. He leapt over a tackler and ran a kickoff back 45 yards. "I almost had my masterpiece that time," he said after the game.

I asked him if I'd heard him reciting a poem on the dinner table in camp.

"No," he said, "that was my alma mater. But I do write poems. Want to hear one I wrote for a girl recently?

"Buzz Buzz Buzz / Come into my parlor, brother fly . . ." was part of it. "I wrote that after getting beat in Ping-Pong," he said. Ten days later he was cut.

"When I tried to tell him about the technicalities of being placed on waivers," said Bill Nunn, "he said 'I know that.' You know they tried to run him off in college his senior year." In college when a coach decides a player doesn't fit into his plans he tries to get him to quit his scholarship by running him through brutal extra contact drills over and over. "But he wouldn't run off," said Nunn. "Not only that, he gained a thousand yards." Bell was a mystery. The last straw for him with Noll, one of the players said, had to do with the signal word "Peter." When you're back to receive a kick and the ball is bouncing around and you want your teammates not to touch it you yell "Peter!" Which must derive from some forgotten coach's strict upbringing with regard to genitals and means "Hands off." Bell wouldn't yell "Peter." He would only mutter it.

The Steelers were complaining about having to play on the Vikings' grass after Three Rivers's Tartan Turf. "You put your feet down differently," Russell said. "Your cleats grab the grass and pull. On the Tartan you glide." I was glad my work never required me to put my feet down differently from week to week as I ran and huge men threw themselves at my legs.

Franco Harris didn't play in the Minnesota game because, Noll said, a bad thigh incurred in the Baltimore game had bothered him in pregame warm-ups. Nobody thought too much of this at the time.

During the Philadelphia game I sat next to the Chief in the press box. He wasn't much of a talker during games, he watched solemnly. "We don't look like the champs," he said as the Steelers floundered against the Eagles during the first half. But Bradshaw led a 33-yard scoring drive after rookies Thomas and Toews smeared the Eagles' punter, and Hanratty came in during the last quarter and on his second play pumped twice and threw 53 yards to Shanklin for a touchdown. Wagner, Dockery and Edwards intercepted. Star Eagle receiver Harold Carmichael, 6–8, smashed Pine's nose with his elbow and Wagner jumped Carmichael. A huge inflated blue-and-white plastic football player was passed around hand-to-hand overhead through the crowd until a bunch of boys got hold of it and merrily tore it to shreds. The Steelers won, 17–3. After the game in the dressing room Dwight White pointed to a mouth semifilled with jagged teeth and said, "See what they do to me out there. Make me *ugly* and shit."

Noll showed that he could sometimes be candid, if not directly candid, under questioning. "Would you say this defense is easy to throw against?" asked a member of Philadelphia's aggressive press corps.

"I wouldn't say that," said Noll. "I wouldn't say that about anybody. Not even my son."

Noll was pressed further to size up the Eagles, coached by his former Cleveland teammate Mike McCormick. "One thing they may have," he said, "is a defensive line."

* * *

The next exhibition, a 29–24 loss to the Giants in New York, was the one in which Noll really lost his poker face. In the first drive of the game the Steelers looked great, with Preston running for 8 and 10 yards a crack through good holes, Frenchy sweeping for 6, and Bradshaw hitting Shanklin neatly over the middle for 16. But they couldn't push it over, had to settle for a field goal, and thereafter the offense was awful. Bradshaw threw three interceptions in the second quarter. Two were returned for touchdowns and the third set up one of the Giants' five field goals. Before one of the interceptions Bradshaw looked over and saw Noll pointing to the ground. "We had discussed on the sidelines what we were going to do," Bradshaw said later. Noll had said for him to call a run. "But then . . . I saw him pointing to the ground," Bradshaw said. "Did he want me to run or did he want me to pass?" Bradshaw interpreted the point as a sign to pass. Noll descended upon Bradshaw as he came off the field and began to berate him in front of everybody in Yankee Stadium. Bradshaw began to move away to get a drink of water and Noll grabbed him and jerked him back. A man in the press box was watching the scene through binoculars, "Noll's not a swearer," he said. "And he said at least five fucks."

"I lost my poise," admitted Noll after the game.

"That stuff's hard to take," Bradshaw said. "But he's the head man. I guess things have been piling up for him, and then all the interceptions. Especially the third one."

"He hasn't begun to reach his potential," Noll said of Bradshaw.

The offensive line was terrible. Van Dyke was out with a pulled calf muscle. He'd sustained it the previous week and taken his family for a holiday outing before advising the team of the injury. (When Van Dyke was ready to go again in practice he went in with the starting line and Noll snapped, "You're not the first-string guard." Then Noll told Musick of the *Press* that Mullins would be sharing the position with Van Dyke. This in fact didn't happen, and Musick felt Noll had been using him to take a slap at Van Dyke.) The raggedness of the offensive line against New York made Noll give up on rookies Bonham and Klippert. The latter was supposed to get a chance to prove himself in the last series of downs but didn't because the Giants controlled the ball until the end of the game. "People make it in pro football because of circumstances," Mansfield said later. "Everybody does." Klippert had been practicing with a broken toe. "This was a real throwback," Noll said of the team effort. "You'd have to get a psychiatrist," he declared uncharacteristically, "to dredge up the reasons for it."

The Steelers showed a general distaste for the big city. Art Rooney said, "New York, New York, Big Daddy [Lipscomb] used to say. 'So big they had to say it twice.' " But the game depressed them more than the town did. The mood was solemn in the bus to the airport for the flight back to Pittsburgh. "Get the feel of this and multiply it six times, and you'll know how it used to be," Artie said. "Dan's friend Mossy Murphy said after one loss back then that they ought to close all the windows in the bus, fill it full of shit so it smelled bad, and ring a bell every two minutes so nobody could go to sleep. One time we were in the bus coming from a game in New York and the driver had the radio on. A sports show came on and the announcer was going down the Steeler roster, cutting up each guy. They were listening, yelling 'Turn that damn thing off!' "

I talked to Bonham the morning he was cut. "Coach told me, 'Bracey, you put out an outstanding effort. You really stuck with it,' but I was on waivers. I didn't hear much after that. When I first got to camp not knowing the system it was hard. But I don't know. I found myself daydreaming between practices. Picture myself playing. See myself not jumping offsides anymore.

"You know, Joe liked me, and Dwight. Holmes, he say, 'Well, Rook . . .' You know, they liked to call me Rook. Specially L. C. Say, 'Well Rook, you got to hold your head up.' I just enjoyed it. I was going to walk to the Superburger, and Holmes got mad 'cause I didn't ask to use his car.

"Well, see, I started playing football when I was in the fourth grade. You know, I can't see playing this long and then got to stop. If I keep applying my physical self and my mental self . . . I'm gonna keep working out, and I'm gonna give it another try next year.

"My father's a minister. If a person wants something, it's up to him to apply himself to get it. Coming up through college I had a lot of deaths in my family. My father's mother, my mother's brother—that really worked on me mentally. I had three brothers, and this year one of 'em got killed. On my birthday. This worked on me to make me try harder. He was a year older than me. He was smaller than me. He would say, 'This is my little brother,' and people would say 'Huh?' He got off with . . . he was on his own, really. But still he was my brother. I'm the type of person, I don't like to run in a crowd. My brother . . . He got shot, is how he died. Yeah, I guess football is kind of a crowd. Once you get into it, and put all you have into it . . . You just love it.

"My younger brothers look to me. It's pressure. It's more than just going out on the field and letting people see me. It's . . . My brothers say, 'That's my brother!' You know. The youngest one, sometimes he will take some of my trophies, take 'em in his room.

"I just regret I wasn't two inches taller. It really plays a role I guess. But if you got the heart to apply yourself . . ."

I asked him if it would be hard to go back to his younger brothers after being cut. "Naw, it's not going to be hard. First thing they'll ax me is what happened. And I'll start telling 'em about camp, and they'll enjoy it."

During the week after the Giants game the Pittsburgh papers were already running stories about people in the street asking "What's wrong with the Steelers?" By and large the press was defending Bradshaw, but Bill Christine of the *Post Gazette* quoted "a Steeler offensive regular" as saying "Terry Hanratty has twice the grasp of the game that Bradshaw has." In the dressing room after that came out, offensive regulars were going around saying loudly, "Who would say a thing like that?"

111

But the Steelers bounced back against the Packers in Green Bay, coming back in the second half to beat what looked at the time like a strong team, 30–22. Pine ran a punt back 70 yards for a touchdown. Bradshaw threw two passes in a row, the first of which should've been intercepted and run back for a touchdown but was dropped, and the second of which was intercepted, but after that he settled down, completing 9 of 17 for the night. "He was mentally ready," Noll said.

"The Coach—it was beautiful tonight," Bradshaw said. "He let me alone. Let me get it straight. You got to be involved in the game, do what you can do. Get smashed, start hitting a few long ones, maybe make a sprint. That's when I really enjoy it. That New York game, I was ready to hang it up in pregame warm-ups. You get those feelings, people don't realize. Sometimes you do a good radio show, sometimes you don't. Sometimes I play a good game, sometimes I don't."

Harris continued to run sparingly and not well, but Preston had another good game, and with Steve Davis healthy and Rocky Bleier showing early foot the Steelers seemed to have all the running backs they would ever need.

One of the arguments advanced by people who defend the structure of pro football against the theory that players ought to be able to play wherever they want to and can get a job is that nobody who could get a job anywhere else would want to play in Green Bay. Ed Garvey, executive director of the Players' Association, would suggest in response to this argument that maybe Green Bay didn't deserve a franchise, then. It would be hard to imagine Green Bay without the Packers. In an attempt to find a corner of town with no signs about the Packers, no copies of the Packer newspaper and no Packer postcards, I went up a flight of stairs into a suitably musty used-book store and found there, amidst volumes of Schopenhauer, Halliburton, Jerome K. Jerome and Herbert Read, the proprietor eating his lunch off a napkin that said "Go Pack."

Lambeau Field looked somehow like a huge high school stadium—everybody sitting together in serried circular rows of wooden benches. The press box had a glass front so reflective that it was hard to watch the game through it without feeling like shouting at yourself, "Down in front." If you had been wearing by chance a shirt with little football players on it you'd have been hard-pressed to separate them from the ones on the field. In the press box there were firemen in uniform and a Farmer's Market pamphlet distributed by the City Sealer which disclosed that an average twenty-four-year-old northern pike weighs 48.4 pounds, that the Green Bay market's champion hubbard squash of 1972 was grown by Mrs. M. Fischer of Brillion and weighed 51 pounds 12 ounces, that the argument of " 'new left' extremists" that "human rights are more important than property rights" was "phony, for several reasons," and that "what this country needs is dirtier hands and cleaner minds." As "The Star Spangled Banner" was being played before the game by the Crown Point High School Marching Band featuring Cadettes (Captain Cindy Head, Co-Captain Lark Jennings) and a female Color Guard (Drill

Captain Sue Gumm) and a female Rifle Drill Team (Captain Robin Mees)—
"Tonight," said the band's "Media Guide," "the band will present a show consisting of precision drills, routines by pom-pom girls, rifles . . ."—Musick of the *Press* said to me, "We are in the heart of America," and we were glared at for talking. I think it would be a shame if the NFL were ever to stop playing games in Green Bay.

After the Packer game the Steelers were in good humor. Dwight White got on the bus grumbling, however: "Now I got to dry off my cheese. I give the man my cheese I got specially here in Green Bay, and tell him to keep it cold during the game, and what does the fool do? He puts it in a bucket of water. After the game there's my cheese, floating around. It's getting harder and harder to find competent people anywhere."

Ernie Holmes entered the bus, gold tooth flashing. "Hey, Bodacious," somebody said to him. He said, "I ain't bodacious, I'm *tired.*" Holmes saw the cheese, which White was peeling layers of cellophane off of. "Hey, gimme some that cheese, man," yelled Holmes. "Come over to my 'partment, eat all my goose liver, won't gimme any cheese. Eat that cheese with some *crackers.*"

"All of a sudden," said Dwight, "we got a bus full of cheese connoisseurs. Hey, it ain't wet!" and he started eating it.

"Cheese'll constipate you," said Holmes. "I hope you don't shit for a week."

"You just don't worry about it. I can handle it," said White.

"Little peanut butter with this cheese'd be good," said Holmes, having pulled off a hunk.

"Man!" screamed White. *"You don't eat peanut butter with this cheese!* Ya big *dommy!* This cheese is cold-*blooded.*"

"I'm a wine connoisseur," said Holmes. "Little rosé or Chablis, don't like it too heavy."

"Little Lancers," suggested Gilliam. "Little Thunderbird."

"Get your hands off my cheese, man!"

"I need a knife. I know somebody on this bus carrying a knife."

"I haven't got a knife but I got a gun," said J. T. Thomas, sitting behind ex-gunman Holmes.

"Some peanut butter *would* be good with it though," Holmes said.

"I got a headache," said White. "Stuck my head in there on that maximum protection and they tried to pull it off!"

Holmes winced. "Yeah. That time Joe hit me." He and Greene, going after the passer, had run into each other with a sound like that of a side of beef dropping two stories onto a marble floor.

"Everything considered, though," said White in his standard-coach's-voice intonation, "I'd say it was a pretty good effort."

And so was the 19–0 exhibition win over the Atlanta Falcons at Three Rivers, where a banner in the stands read "Atlanta Is No Falcon Good" and McMakin made a leaping one-handed catch of a Bradshaw pass and Frenchy ran for 121 yards and the Falcons were never in the game. Falcon quarterback Dick Shiner, a former Steeler, dropped back to pass and Greene chased him into the end zone and almost back out the other end of it before he frantically threw the ball away. Some of the Steelers and their wives were sitting around after the game when one of the players said that Shiner was an intelligent quarterback. "If he only had Bradshaw's arm," he said.

"Or if Bradshaw only had his head," said one of the wives.

"Um," said the players.

There still were obvious answers, however, to the hypothetical question "Why does God love you?" in Bradshaw's head. Even if there also were answers to "Why doesn't Noll?" At his best in the exhibitions Bradshaw had looked capable of anything. "He's a big stud," said Falcon coach Norm Van Brocklin. "He's matured in the last couple of years. I remember when he couldn't hit his ass with both hands. He's a big stud. If he doesn't know what he's doing, I'd like to get me a half-dozen ballplayers like him who don't."

"What do you have to be to throw a pass?" asked Bradshaw, for his part. "An Albert Einstein?"

What seemed more thought-provoking at the moment, in terms of the Steelers' chances for the year, was the head of Chuck Noll.

□ **10** □

NOLL

A head coach always puzzles everybody.
—BRACEY BONHAM

"**T**here is no way you can have a beer with Noll and relax," more than one Steeler person said. I was finding that true one Saturday night early in the season, having a Heineken's with him in the lounge of the Sheraton Inn south of town, where the Steelers ate hamburgers and slept the night before every home game—"so they won't be bothered by two o'clock feedings," said Noll. A thirtyish diminutive fan whose tie was hanging outside his buttoned sport coat came up, wobbled slightly, beamed, and said, "We love ya, Coach. By God, ya just don't know . . . After last year . . . You prob'ly think I'm just an average jerk, but . . . Mansfield sold me insurance. We love ya, Coach."

Noll smiled opaquely. I may be a Jagov or something in this respect, but it seems to me that smiling is a better contact experience than either end of the essential one of scrimmage. The Chief when laughing appeared to feel like a man seized by friendly hands, thrown onto a blanket, and tossed into the air, and he liked it. Van Dyke would thrust out his chin, go heh-heh-heh deep in his throat, and get a slightly glazed look in his eyes, like a man just roused agreeably from sleep. Mansfield would sink into himself and close his eyes and twitch and jiggle, and wince from the pain of injuries, and twitch and jiggle harder. Once in my apartment he got to laughing so hard that he went ahead and completely snapped the rib he'd cracked in the first Houston game, and had to go home. "That was the worst I ever hurt," he said later, but as he left my apartment, bent over with the pain, he was still chuckling as well as he could. Greene would take on a sort of spoofy evil look, sidelong, and roll his eyes. Dan Rooney would duck his head and look up beaming shyly like a boy who's been found out knowing something precociously wise. Walden would get even more hard-lipped in the front, but his eyes would soften and the very corners of his mouth would twitch up in almost a flutter. McMakin's mouth, which was always close to grinning, would get so big it looked like he was about to swallow his face with pleasure. Greenwood would drop his head as though acknowledging divinely ordained hopelessness, go slack all over, and then look up, his teeth flashing off and on, and say something apposite. Mel

Blount would flash a bright off-center smile, cocked to the right, which implied, Yeah, you found me out, I'm happy, handsome and full of love. Keating, whose forehead looked like it had been pounded down over his eyes like a hat, would come burgeoning out of his brows and moustache with delight as he told the most drastic stories of player abuse. Ham never changed expression much but always seemed to be confronting the ludicrous.

Noll's smile was dimply, powerful and very nearly winning. It brought his cheeks way up against his eyes in a sort of "big lug" look, only more steely-eyed. If I reach way back I can summon the memory of a "hyeh, hyeh" laugh and his head rising vulnerably higher than usual and bobbing back and forth. But I may be imagining that part—imagining what amusement would do to Noll if he let it carry him. Generally Noll's smile, however big it was, lacked something: release. It never suggested "Whoops!" It was Noll's responsibility to keep the whoops element out of life. He had a sharp wit, in fact, but once he said, in response to a reporter's obtuse reaction to a postgame sardonicism, "That's my trouble: I never could tell a joke." Like most everything Noll said, that had an edge to it, and if the reporter had been more attentive he would have felt it. But that remark also had the ring of near-confessional, or concessional, truth. At any rate Noll never looked truly tickled. He did sometimes look pissed to the point of release. I have literally never seen a meaner thin-lipped, hot-eyed, near-to-seething look than Noll could throw at a reporter's effrontery or a player's lapse.

Anyway he smiled opaquely at this unsteady fan's affection, in the lounge of the Sheraton Inn. I think I could have sold this fan insurance at that point of the evening, but there was real feeling in his words. Noll had turned Steeler football, and therefore Steeler fans' conceptions of themselves, around.

His predecessors had been more vivid and less productive. In the late thirties Johnny Blood, poet, orator and vagabond halfback, came in from Green Bay, where he had added to his legend by jumping from one sixth-story hotel window ledge to another six feet away in a driving rainstorm to enter Coach Curly Lambeau's room when summoned. Blood said of himself, "I'm a schizophrenic personality. I was born under the sign of Sagittarius, which is half stud and half philosopher." Once while he was player-coach at Pittsburgh he went to Green Bay to visit friends, and took in the Packer game. "I thought your team was playing today," somebody said to him.

"No," he said. Just then the first-quarter score of the Pittsburgh-Philadelphia game was posted on the scoreboard. "You couldn't rely on John a whole lot," says the Chief fondly.

In the franchise's fourteenth year, by which time it had had two winning seasons, the Chief brought in Jock Sutherland, the great college coach, and it looked like a new era might be dawning. Sutherland established the hard-nosed, beat-'em-up-so-they-can't-play-next-week Steeler tradition. Most years that tradition helped whatever team their opponent was playing the following week more than it did the Steelers, but Sutherland was a man of disciplined

116

vision. His single-wing, power-sweep, good-blocking system may have had a formative influence on Vince Lombardi, who played against it often and became the most influential strategist in pro history by fitting the same sort of attack into the T formation later. Under Sutherland the Steelers went from 2–8 to 5–5–1 in '46 (the year the all-time best Steeler, sixty-minute halfback and kicker Bill Dudley, became the only Steeler ever to be named the league's MVP) and then 8–4 in their first playoff game. Then one evening at dinner Sutherland suddenly jabbed his fork into his seat and shoved the meat over into the lap of a young lady at the table. A doctor advised him to wear a big-rimmed hat against the sun. He died of a brain tumor.

The Steelers didn't convert to the T until 1952, by which time the single wing was embarrassingly quaint in the pros. With Joe Bach as head coach and Jimmy Finks at quarterback, the T produced a lot more offense but fewer wins than losses. Bach, who had been one of the Seven Mules—the linemen who blocked for the Four Horsemen at Notre Dame—was once taken into the men's room and knocked down by the Chief, according to a family legend which the Chief pooh-poohs, during an argument over the color of the team's uniforms.

Then Walt Kiesling came back for his third shot at running the Steelers. He was an inflexible man who dismissed rookie Johnny Unitas as dumb and insisted that exciting halfback Lynn Chandois was lackadaisical. When Chandois ran back three kickoffs for touchdowns in one game Kiesling said to the Chief, "Can you imagine that lucky bum?"

Next came Buddy Parker, who had been highly successful at Detroit before quitting suddenly in the middle of a banquet. Parker said the Steelers had "a loser's complex" and got rid of most of them. He acquired his friend Bobby Layne from the Lions as quarterback and had four winning seasons in eight years at Pittsburgh. But Parker had a tendency to drink and brood and deal personnel the night after a loss. One Sunday night while he was still at Detroit he had sent a telegram to the league office saying he wanted to waive his entire team. Once at Pittsburgh, Parker waived Dick Hayes, a linebacker, and another Steeler to the Bears, and two Bears were waived to the Steelers, with the agreement that after the Steelers and the Bears played in Houston they would all be waived back. But Hayes made a tackle that saved the game for the Bears. Afterwards, the Bears' and the Steelers' planes were parked back to back in the Houston airport. Hayes came on board the Steeler plane. "What are you doing here?" demanded Parker, irate. "They said I was a Steeler," said Hayes. "No you're not!" said Parker. Hayes went back to the Bear's plane. "Coach Parker said I was a Bear," he said. "No you're not," they said, "get back on that other plane." So he went back and friends hid him in the restroom so Parker wouldn't see him until the plane got off the ground. Then there was the time Parker, after a few drinks, had the trainer tape up his fists like a boxer and went around announcing that he was going to hit Big Daddy Lipscomb when he came in after curfew. Fortunately, the trainer had taped Parker's wrists so tight that his circulation was cut off and he collapsed before Big Daddy got in.

"Parker had complete authority," says Dan Rooney. "When he came here I was twenty-four years old, and I had to get into the business end of it. For which I'm thankful. I would get things ready for the draft and sign players. Buddy wasn't interested. In time, whenever there was a call from the league they called me." When Dan was thirty-one he made the move by which he began to assert himself as, in effect, the team's general manager. "I didn't like the format of the way trades were being made. They were all made spontaneously, without any thought. So my father told Parker, 'All right, when you're going to make a trade, I'd like you to talk to Dan.'" Parker had just made the famous "Dial for Nothing" trade, in which the Steelers gave up star receiver Buddy Dial for the right to negotiate with college star Scott Appleton, who signed with the rival AFL and never amounted to anything as a pro anyway. Then one night after the Steelers had been run off the field Parker told Dan he wanted to trade top linemen Ben McGhee and Chuck Hinton for quarterback King Hill, who never did much in the pros. "I told him no. Nobody had ever said no to him. He said, 'Then I quit.' I said, 'Fine, you quit.'"

The next man who was going to make something out of the Steelers was Bill Austin, who had been an assistant under Lombardi at Green Bay. "Let's try something new this time," Dan said to his father. "Let's hire somebody we don't know." So for the first time the Steelers went outside the Chief's circle of cronies—undoubtedly the richest, but not the most managerially gifted, such circle in football—to hire a no-nonsense disciplinarian. Austin turned out to be as stern as Lombardi but not as good, which must have been a bleak combination. His first year the Steelers were 5–8–1 and during the next two years they got worse.

Enter Noll. "We offered the job to Joe Paterno at Penn State," says Dan, "and we had very big discussions with Nick Skorich [now head coach at Cleveland], who was a worthy candidate. Maybe what he said was the reason he wasn't offered the job. I liked Noll's forthright answers. He said he was not going to come in and do any miracles. A lot of candidates said they were, said they were going to come in and turn this team around in a year." So Noll was offered his first head-coaching job and he took it, after demanding that his assistant coaches be fully involved in the draft. This did not sit well with Artie Rooney, who was building up the Steelers' scouting department and wanted to affirm its influence over the draft, but Noll won the concession. In the first draft Noll was involved in, the Steelers pulled a coup. They took Joe Greene, now their mainstay, in the first round instead of Hanratty, the Irish Catholic native of Butler, who'd been the local favorite as first-round choice and whose suspect knee the Steelers had examined. Cagey old George Halas of the Bears called halfway through the first round to discuss the possibility of a trade involving the Bears' choice, which would have given the Steelers a chance to get Hanratty too in the first round. Halas might have been feeling the Steelers out to see what they thought about Hanratty's knee, with an eye toward taking Hanratty for the Bears (who could certainly have used him the last few years). Dan and Noll refused to evince any interest in the idea, at any rate, and on the second round Hanratty was still available and they got him. That maneuver, in that it worked so well, was not a typical Steeler episode. Over the next four years there was a new sense of progress, of command over the Steeler destiny. Their record got better each year and in '72 they hit it big.

The Rooneys still give their head coach full authority over the matters of what players are obtained and kept and how they are used on the field—as do most NFL organizations, Washington, Dallas, and Miami, for example (but not Oakland and Houston). "I never use the term general manager," says Dan, whose title, like Artie's, is vice-president. "I don't think football is a general manager business, the way baseball is, where a general manager connotes someone who's going to act on trades and get involved with trades and oversee the business too. What I try to do is operate, direct—assist might be a better term—everything that's going on. Noll doesn't even know what anybody is paid, and I don't even talk about strategy. I might ask him how come this guy isn't playing and expect an answer from him, but I never say you got to play this guy. Someone has to be responsible for everything that happens here—if Noll makes a bad deal it's my bad deal as much as his. And this year, Tim originated a lot of the ideas for trades." But in practice Noll has the last word. "If there ever comes a time I don't want him to make a trade," Dan says, "I'll say wait a minute, and I'll supply input. But he puts in more input." And Noll's input, into anything, is not capricious.

Noll grew up poor on Montgomery Avenue in Cleveland, "almost in Hough," and football has enabled him, as it has most of his players, to generate and sustain momentum onward and upward.

"I've been interested in the way you respond to the press," I said to him one evening when I was still trying to draw him out of the solid four-point stance he presents to the world. "You keep refusing to speculate, and when you're asked to compare the present to the past you say, 'One thing I don't have is a sense of history. I can't remember yesterday or last year.' Do you have a rule about the kinds of things you shouldn't talk about?"

"Well, I don't want to reinforce a negative thing. There was a negative situation . . ."

"Here in the past?"

"And part of it was history and—it was something we had to overcome and my dwelling on it was just going to keep it alive. That's one of the reasons for that, and speculation can get you no place but trouble."

"Has it gotten you in trouble in the past?"

"I just don't like to speculate, as an individual, as a person. I like to make decisions based on real facts, and if you haven't got enough facts to make a decision, you obviously can't make it."

(Later I asked him what kind of reading he preferred and he said, "Not fiction." I think Noll would have agreed with B. F. Skinner when he said, "I myself would choose to live in a world in which no one could understand what the devil was eating Dostoevsky.")

"So you just wait?"

"There are times when you have to make what they call a 'guesstimate.' But I don't like to do that—just by nature. I would rather go to work to get the facts."

"Do you get any of that from the way you were brought up? Is that a German trait or anything?"

"I don't know, I really don't."

"Was your father that way?"

"No. You know, you always like to think that you are the way you are because of yourself, but you're not. You're a product of everyone you bump into. I was taught very early that you try to not just grab facts, that you try to understand the theory or substance for something, and if you do that, then you can apply it. I don't know who taught me that, all I know is it stuck with me and I'm sure someone exposed me to it. Background, religion had a lot to do with it."

"Are German Catholics different from Irish Catholics? I mean, do you have any sense of being in a tradition . . ."

"No, but I grew up in a neighborhood—a poor neighborhood, that's probably the best way to describe it—and the one thing I got from, let's say, the religious background is hope. You know, it was drilled into me very young, that if I wanted to accomplish anything, it was up to me. There was hope, there was always . . . that."

"Did you grow up in a tough neighborhood, I mean did you fight in the streets?"

"I would say that, yes. It could be classified as tough. I wasn't the fighter, though, I was the watcher."

And a learner of techniques whereby to have good experiences hitting blocking sleds and people. At Benedictine High School Noll played guard and middle guard on a team that won the school's first city football championship. At the University of Dayton he was an offensive tackle, a linebacker, a defensive halfback and co-captain. Since he was small—6-1, 215—and had played for a minor football college, he was only a twenty-first draft choice, but his quickness, both afoot and in mastering his assignments, caught Paul Brown's notice right away and he became a regular at guard and then at linebacker with the Browns for seven years. He was still playing well when he quit at twenty-seven to coach the defensive for Sid Gillman's then Los Angeles Chargers for six years and then the defensive backfield for Don Shula at Baltimore for three. In sixteen years of professional playing and assistant coaching, under three of the most notable modern coaches, Noll had a part in eleven divisional and five NFL or AFL championships.

John Sandusky, offensive line coach of the Eagles, played with Noll in Cleveland and coached with him in Baltimore. "As a player he beat people with quickness, by being in the right place," says Sandusky. "He would study opponents on film, and he had good speed. He wasn't a head-hunter type, he was just a smart football player. At Baltimore, he and Shula got into some heated arguments about a defensive back using certain techniques, which way to play your help. Chuck never backed down from an argument. Some guys used to kid him in a way that in my opinion was a slur. He'd always venture an answer on things, so they called him 'Knowledge Noll.' "

I never heard any *heroic* stories about Noll the player. Once at a banquet honoring Noll, Chuck Bednarik—the great old Eagle, "Concrete Charley," of whom it was said, "if you hadn't played both ways in the pros, like he had, he didn't feel obliged to talk to you," which meant he didn't feel obliged to talk to many people alive—got up and told a a story. During a game, he said, Noll suffered some affront and told Bednarik, "I'm going to get you." The game went by and Noll didn't get him. Next game, it was the same thing. After that game, finally, Noll came walking toward Bednarik with his helmet in his hand and Bednarik decked him. That was the story. You might bear that in mind if you're thinking of having Bednarik speak at your testimonial dinner.

Leo Murphy, long-time trainer of the Browns, remembers Noll as "a first-class gentleman. I never remember hearing him swear." During his first year a reporter asked him (this was in 1953) about his "interest in girls."

"First I've got to make good," Noll said. "Then maybe I can get serious about girls." (Noll now has a wife named Marianne, whom I never met, though I met most of the other coaches' wives, but who is said to be a strong-willed woman, who keeps a sharp eye on the media for unfavorable reference to Noll. Their teenage son Chris, a Steeler ballboy who gave up high school football for soccer, is said to be a nice kid, but I never heard him say a word. They go on vacations together, skin-diving, visiting places of historical interest.)

Mike McCormack, the Eagles' head coach, also played with Noll. "Charley, more than anything else, fit right into Paul Brown's methods of doing everything by the numbers," McCormack says. "He was so well schooled in techniques. He was a very intense player. Very competitive—he was smaller and felt he had to be. We were single our first two years and he was a lot of fun. We played golf and bowled."

I can just see the movie ads for *The Chuck Noll Story* now: "He came out of Cleveland, well schooled in techniques!"

But Noll was not perfectly cool. "I think Noll never loses his poise," said the Chief. "I thought he was a good coach his first year, when he lost thirteen. He never lost his poise. Not only that, he never lost his team. However he does it I don't know. I've seen coaches that were tough guys, worked them real hard. And they won, or they lost, doing it. I've seen easier coaches. And they won or they lost. Keep the team, keep their confidence in you, keep them together." That was the kind of thing the players were all saying when I first talked to them.

Noll had admittedly lost his poise berating Bradshaw in New York, however. And it was not the first time, several players told me after I got to know them. In another game Noll had grabbed at Bradshaw, trying to pull him back so he could yell at him while Bradshaw was trying to go onto the field, and Bradshaw had pulled away, cursing back under his breath, and gone on. Against Oakland in the Miraculous game Noll had indeed been almost eerily collected, but against Miami the next week he had been rattled on the sidelines. "Sometimes," one player said, "he babbles." Against the Cardinals in '72 he had run out toward the offensive line yelling, "You guys aren't blocking worth a fuck!" when, according to the offensive line, Bradshaw had been throwing the ball away. Charley Sumner, the linebacker coach whom Noll had fired after '72, was said to have once snapped, "God dammit, it's third down," when Noll was trying to send the punting team in. "Noll is so cool in strategy," said one Steeler, "but he loses it on the sidelines. He prepares us well. But the best generals aren't always the best leaders."

"We have to get fired up early in the week," said Noll, speaking of coaches. "Breaking down films, getting prepared to teach them what to do against the opponent. It tapers off at the end. I'm not going into combat. The players are. By the time of the game, the hay is in the barn. There's very little adjustment after the game starts." He also took the position, which struck me as curious, that players ought to ignore his yelling at them during a game. "If they're more concerned about me chewing their ass out than doing their job, they won't do it. They've got to screen out everything but the job. It's like self-hypnosis. People who achieve, concentrate. Get themselves locked in."

Maybe Noll stayed locked in so tightly that he lost his bearings sometimes. "He's very intelligent and a tremendous person," says a former Cleveland teammate of Noll's. "But at times he does things that belie his intelligence. Like in one game, we had called a stunt, 'Li and Rip,' which meant I was supposed to go left and Noll was supposed to go right. Before the snap, Noll is screaming 'Liz! Liz! Liz!' Then we both ended up going to the left and bumping into each other. I got on him about it and you know what he said? That the other team was being tipped to what we were doing so he wanted to throw them off by yelling 'Liz.' Can you imagine that?"

Certainly Noll locked other people out. Even the Chief, who prided himself on being able to chew the fat with anybody, got nowhere chatting with Noll. No one in the Steeler organization spoke of him in terms of companionship. "If I died and needed somebody to raise my kids," said one man, "Noll would be the guy I'd choose. But if I was going to a football game, I wouldn't want to go with Noll." And I never heard Noll speak of anyone else with personal warmth. Someone described him doing a biting imitation of Paul Brown, "his little hands and high voice. Noll seemed to get more pleasure out of it than he should have." But then Brown is no Santa Claus either.

Jack Ham said, "There are a lot of similarities between this team and the one I played on at Penn State. All of us together, there, disliked Paterno. It made us closer together. He was very cold to his players, very impersonal. Though he made sure of us getting through school. And Paterno's like Noll in the sense he's very very disciplined. They're both fantastic defensive coaches, very conscious of the big play, and very conscious of special teams and doing little things correctly."

That emphasis on the little things could be abrasive. When Dave Williams came to the Steelers from San Diego he said his former team was a "zoo" and "all the animals are angry. Sometimes after a film session I came home with an empty feeling in my stomach. I'd feel like somebody had called me a dirty name." The Steelers weren't a zoo in that sense, but a number of them showed deep resentment at the way Noll chewed them out. Noll's direct supervision of the punting, kick-off and kick-receiving teams was often cited as an example of his diligence, but members of the special teams, after Noll had heatedly dissected their performances on film, often came home with feelings that were empty or worse.

Some of the Steelers, including regulars, felt that Noll did not merely think of them as faceless elements to be programmed, but actively disliked them, individually. Talking to players I put together this surprising list of Steelers Noll seemed to pick on most: Hanratty, Russell, Mansfield, Van Dyke, Fuqua, Hanneman, Mullins. Since the majority of these were among the team's least touchy, most easy-going and self-motivated people, I suggested to one of them that when Noll was frustrated over the team's imperfections he vented his spleen on the players who could take it best. But this notion did not make the spleen-object in question feel any better.

After every game Noll made it a point to come around and say a few words to each player before the press was allowed to enter the dressing room, but he wouldn't say more than a couple of words—"Are you hurt?" usually—to anybody but a few players: for instance Greene, Sam Davis and Ernie Holmes, in front of whose cubicles he would linger. Greene was a big chunk of the franchise, and tended to apply himself according to the dictates of his own state of mind, and was indulged—appropriately, I would say—more than anybody else on the team. Fats and Sam were brooders who needed bucking up. "He'll try to talk to L. C. after a game," one player said, "but L. C. won't talk to him."

It was Greene who spoke of Noll most sympathetically. "He really cares about his players," said Greene. "He has a hard time to keep from showing favoritism. Sometimes he wants to come up and say, 'Mel, that was a hell of a game!' But he's not that kind of person. He wants to keep everything on an even keel. He gets a lot of pressure on him. The first couple of years he had a staff, but he did most of the coaching himself."

There was general agreement around the club that Noll dominated his assistants. At the end of the season he fired Fry and Parilli, leaving him with none of the staff he had begun with five years before. It was announced that Fry and Parilli had resigned, but Noll had called Fry up on New Year's Day and told him he didn't teach fundamentals well enough and that was that. I heard about Parilli's resignation before Parilli did. People who had been in on quarterback meetings said that Parilli was cogent before Noll entered the room, but he wilted under Noll's cold stare and Noll's impatience with imperfectly substantiated arguments. Fry may have put Noll off by being too loose with his charges, and, one scout suggested, by being too friendly with the scouts. Fry got a job with the Jets right away, and Parilli became head coach of the World Football League's New York Stars. He tried to take first Hanratty, then Bradshaw, away from the Steelers, but they stuck with the more established firm.

The Steelers prided themselves on being a nonracist organization and this pride was, at least relatively speaking, justifiable. Noll, especially, was pointed to as unprejudiced. "I'm convinced Noll is color-blind," said black scout Bill Nunn quite voluntarily, and it seemed to be true and accepted by the black players that while Noll didn't have any tolerance for uppityness from *anybody,* he didn't discriminate against blacks in general and did relate to them at least as well as to whites. In fact three or four white Steelers claimed he was prejudiced in favor of blacks—that he would chew a white player for something that he wouldn't chew a black player for. "I'm not aware of his color," he once said of Gilliam. "At least I don't think I am." That is the one single time I ever heard of Noll's qualifying an assertion with a touch of uncertainty. That seemed healthy.

Of one of Noll's colorful predecessors Artie Rooney said, "He didn't hate blacks exactly, but he didn't like them much either." Another Steeler head coach slept occasionally with a white woman who also kept company with some of the black players (a practice utterly alien to Noll). The players put the woman up to asking this head coach at a confidential moment whether he liked blacks. "I try to," he told her, "but I just can't." She could, and she reported back to the players, who had the coach's number after that.

Buddy Parker kept around a black mascot named Boots Lewis. The story was that Parker had been losing in a card game in college when he called Boots, a custodian, over and rubbed his head for luck. And won. So when he was coaching at Detroit and had a big game in Los Angeles he sent back to Texas for Boots—"Find him," he said urgently—and Boots was found, Parker rubbed his head, and the Lions won. So Boots accompanied Parker to Pittsburgh, where his job was to fetch the kicking tee from the field and to have his head rubbed before games.

Noll had less soul than many of his predecessors, a man in the Steeler front office conceded, but he also was hip to the necessity of not offending blacks. "With the race thing, he's the modern coach. He's what you need today."

Noll once walked up to Dwight White in the dressing room when Dwight was doing the loose booty, or some other massively undulant step, to the strains of "Bad Bold Beautiful Girl" by The Persuaders, or something on that order. Noll started dancing more or less along with him. Dwight yelled in presumable delight and ran off into the bathroom. "You guys think you're the first to do anything," Noll said. "I'm always telling my son, 'Just because I'm forty doesn't mean I never danced or went to a drive-in or got beer at fifteen.'" That incident may not have proved that Noll could be truly loose, but it proved he *knew about* being truly loose.

It was impressive, the things Noll knew about. Football, of course. As the coaches watched the Cleveland–Minnesota game on television, commentator Al Derogatis said a ball carrier was slow hitting a hole. "Expert!" snorted Noll. "He was supposed to be slow. You don't know your ass from first base. They didn't have the 'I' when you were playing." (But most of the players, too, were impatient with TV football authorities. A lot of them derogated Derogatis.)

Once Myron Cope told Noll he'd had a negative reaction to a penicillin shot. "Noll, who is full of inside information on such matters," said Cope, "asked me if I'd had milk before the shot. I said yes, I'd had milk for lunch. 'That's what caused it,' Noll said. 'They treat cows with penicillin.'"

Before one of the road games Iooss, Mike Wagner and I were in the hall of the motel remembering candy bars.

"Remember Zagnut?" I said.

Iooss came up with "Butternut."

"How about Milk Shake?" said Wagner.

"Milk Shake!" we cried.

Noll wanted to know what we were doing. We told him we were remembering candy bars. He nodded. "Powerhouse," he said.

"Very good," we said, but he wasn't finished.

"Mr. Clark Bar took Miss Hershey back behind the Powerhouse," he said as he walked away, "and laid her on the Mounds."

We stood there openmouthed. "And he said, 'Forever Yours,'" I added finally, in a subdued voice.

"And she said, 'Butterfingers,'" said Noll over his shoulder, disappearing down the hall.

"He's so frigging knowledgeable," marveled George Perles. "At the end of the day, when we go out to eat, or drink, or something, he takes a big book on metallurgy or something home and reads it." Maybe it wasn't metallurgy, but it was something like that. "He's so knowledgeable about the things he's really knowledgeable about," said one man who worked with Noll. "But he has such a penchant for being knowledgeable about the things he's *not* knowledgeable about. I don't think he knows how to open up to people. So he tries to open up with his knowledge." Noll was by all accounts an accomplished gourmet cook and mixer of Margueritas. But once in camp he walked into the room of a couple of the players, where Keating, who like Noll considered himself an oenologist, was discussing wines. Noll made a flat statement about wine. "No, that's wrong," said Keating, and began to argue. Noll walked out.

In 1971, a player told me, when the Steelers were on their way somewhere the night of a changeover from daylight saving time, Noll announced that they should all set their clocks up.

"No, no. Back," people cried.

"When you gain an hour," Noll insisted, "you set your clocks up."

"No, back," people said.

"Just make sure you're on time for the pregame meal," he said stiffly.

Noll put people off that way. He was good at marshaling his facts and making declarations, but he wasn't one for taking a matter on from an angle that might not support his momentum. In training camp he and Dan Rooney were agreeing that government was getting into too many things. "Because of these gas and meat controls, there won't be any gas and meat," Noll said. "Because people won't have any reason to sell it. People don't sell things for social reasons."

"Well, but . . ." I said.

"Government's getting too big. It's like a mycelium. It spreads. Watergate's just going to cause more government intervention. Congress should meet four days a year. There's too much legislation. Everything's too big."

"Isn't football getting too big too?" I said. "I mean with big money, corporate structures, television and everything, doesn't it take away from the spirit of the Johnny Blood days?"

But Noll moved on into inveighing against government's intervention into football. "Now the government's going to start telling us the teams can't even control the television announcers!" he cried on another occasion.

I thought maybe we could get something going on *I'm OK—You're OK*. Noll read that book and found its thesis—that everyone was divided into a Child, an Adult and a Parent element, and should engage other people on an Adult–Adult level—persuasive. Noll was high on adulthood generally. When a reporter asked him whether Hanratty hadn't handled being relegated to the second string rather well, Noll snapped, "He's handled it as an adult." I thought the I'm OK—You're OK idea made sense as far as it went, but it seemed to be that football contact boiled down to something like "I'm OK and I'm going to kick shit out of you, because if I don't I won't be OK anymore," or at any rate, "I'm OK, you're in my way."

"In football, on the field," I asked Noll, "isn't there a lot of Child versus Child, or I'm OK, You're Not?"

"Well, I haven't got that much experience with it, to apply it to football," Noll said.

Tom Keating, who was no organization man and who perhaps hit the requisite note of detachment when he said, "I decided very early, I'm not going to let a coach's personality fuck me up," was a great booster of Noll. "It's like working for your family. You do things not because you're afraid of the guys in charge but because you don't want to disappoint the people you work with.

Noll's the one who has control over your life, no doubt about that. But it's all made clear. If Noll says the plane's leaving at six, it's leaving then. He announces fines in meetings. In camp Joe Greene came in late for bed check with a pizza and Noll said the next day, 'Joe, that pizza's going to cost you $50.' And that was that. In Oakland this year, Jeff Queen fell out with [head coach John] Madden in camp, and then when Warren Bankston pulled a hamstring and Madden asked Queen to play tight end, Queen said, 'Listen, Fatso, I know you don't run things around here, but I'm not playing tight end.' Because Al Davis runs things. The next day, Queen was gone. And nobody ever said anything, explained why. Noll would've gotten rid of him, but he would have announced it to the whole team.

"And Noll gets right down on the ground with everybody and does all the exercises, gets as wet and shitty as anybody. He never wears anything heavier than the players when it's cold. It looks like he waits to see what everybody's wearing before he finishes dressing. If you're supposed to be in by eleven, you know he will be. He eats the same food as the players—Madden would put in an appearance at the training table, but then he'd go eat somewhere else."

On the other hand Madden seemed comparatively appealing in another Keating anecdote. "We called Madden 'Pinky' because he turned pink when he got mad. After he got fat we called him 'Bimbo the Elephant.' One time he chewed out Biletnikoff and Freddie turned away and said, 'I'm tired of this shit, Pinky,' and Madden heard it. Everybody was laughing and trying to hide it, and finally Madden laughed. Madden was something. He'd go crazy. A receiver would drop a pass and he'd scream, 'You motherfucker!' and jump up and down, his shirt would come out and his tie would go flying. Then he'd say later, 'I'm sorry, I didn't mean that.' "

I can't imagine Noll laughing if a player called him a derisive name (not that the Steelers had one for him). But then, he had to be the strong man in the operation, whereas not Madden but Davis was the man in Oakland.

Noll drew things on the blackboard, gave carefully prepared, written-out speeches about being "men of substance," and sometimes snarled. It wasn't a formula that inspired affection. But it largely held together. "Everybody resents being told what to do," he said. "You have to show people that it works, that it leads to good experiences. You can have too much jawing. 'Let's have a little false chatter,' some of the players used to say to each other."

Football players expect to be driven. "Guys are used to coaches screaming and hollering," said Joe Greene. "It was different when Chuck came in with his teaching philosophy. He was patient. He wasn't a screamer. He just tried to instill his philosophy into the people he was going to have to use. He was hurt lots of times. He'd sit down there after a game and tears come into his eyes: Was he doing that bad? It would've been easy for him and Dan to panic. They hung in there. And Chuck becomes more forceful every year. Each year there's more pressure. Yes, he can scream occasionally. We all look and listen, too. A lot of times we as humans mistake kindness for weakness."

"I had a coach in college," said the rookie Bracey Bonham, "who would say, excuse the expression, 'Aw Hail.' Coach Stonewall Jackson. Throw down his hat every time something went wrong and say 'Aw Hail.' Everybody on the team started saying it. In college coaches are always staying on you, more than here. In college I would hit the dummy. I figure I hit it 'bout as hard as I can. And Coach would say, 'Aw Hail.' And I find out I can hit it harder. Not that I like to hear a coach yell at me, but deep down inside, you apply yourself harder."

Noll didn't drive his players steadily. His approach was too refined, or impersonal, for that. It may have offended him to have to scream at people. He held his anger back until it was so pinpointed, or jagged, that it came with a flavor of despite, or sometimes of frenzy. His anger would have been more engaging had it been as thoroughly abandoned as Madden's or as ritualistic as Stonewall Jackson's, or if it had been balanced by comparable flashes of softer emotions. I mean he never exploded with *joy*.

Bradshaw confided to someone, some time after the chewing out incident in New York, "Chuck told me he's been working on controlling his Child on the sidelines." And after I started watching games from there Noll refrained from raging. There would still be set looks in Steelers' eyes after practice, though, and someone would explain, "Noll cut him up pretty bad today." An element of mystery, as to how Noll's Parent and Adult and Child stood toward each other and toward his players and his work, remained. As it no doubt does in the cases of most winning, or losing, generals.

Noll's life depended on winning week after week over the systems of men who were approximately as obsessed with winning as he was. The men who brought his system into play, who had more control over its effectiveness than he did, were many of them erratic, wayward, moody, fun-loving spirits. Noll's definition of goodness was to win. As more and more damaging things came out about the Nixon administration Noll did not repeat his admiration for Ehrlichman, or for Agnew, whom he had known in Baltimore and whom he had earlier championed in arguments with Steeler Democrats. "What happened," he said in accounting for the Nixon team's erosion, "was that the losers got elected."

□ 11 □

BEATING THE LIONS, THE BROWNS AND THE OILERS

So use to it, that's why they do it. And you can't beat that with a baseball bat.

—FROM AN INTRODUCTION
OF THE SHIRELLES

The Steelers opened their regular season by beating the Lions 24–10. The defense stopped Detroit on the ground, made Greg Landry pass, and Pine Edwards and Supe Blount each made crucial interceptions—typically the big defensive play was the saver. And this time the offense showed some sustain, as they say. "We don't one-two and then bingo," said Bradshaw. "We boonk, boonk, boonk and then TD." The age of Detroit middle linebacker Mike Lucci was a big help—Lucci was slow, in his last year as a pro, and the Steeler offensive line pushed him around. Frustrated, he kicked Mansfield and drew a personal foul. Words were exchanged and defensive end Larry Hand found an occasion—on an extra-point play, a prime time for personal vengeance—to punch Mansfield in the ribs. "But my buddy Bruce wasn't going to let him get away with that," said Mansfield warmly. "He then hit old Hand."

Bradshaw started slowly in Detroit, throwing an interception on his first pass, to take a great deal of the emotion out of an expectant, surging home crowd, but in the second half he ran for one touchdown and threw for two—McMakin making a great leaping fingertip catch on the first one, and how anybody can apprehend something so much like an artillery shell with literally his fingertips I will never know. "Bradshaw's I.Q. is way up this half," said Roy McHugh of the *Press* in the press box, as the Burghers who had been grumbling about Bradshaw cheered. When Terry B. twisted around and surged through a bunch of tacklers to score from the 2, McHugh said, "I guess he was too dumb to realize they had him stopped." Franco Harris's knee was

129

still bothering him and he didn't play, but Fuqua, a Detroit native who had said, "I'm going to give the Lions the coop de grah. I bet you can't spell that," ran for an even 100 yards and Preston Pearson and Steve Davis ran well too. When asked whether Frenchy hadn't been dangerously provocative toward the Lions, providing them "bulletin board material" by telling the press that they were "venturing into the valley of the coop de grah" during the preceding week, Noll said, "I want our football players to be themselves."

The first Cleveland game, which the Steelers won 33–6, was what Noll later called his team's most nearly perfect of the year. The defense fully merited the crowd's great-bodied cries of "DEE-FENSE." The Browns were forced to try passing and the rush ate them up. Fats Holmes won the game ball by sacking Browns quarterback Mike Phipps three times—once with one hand—and hitting him several other times as he threw. Once he knocked Phipps down, sat on his chest, and tried to talk to him. "I was trying to get him to say something," said Holmes, "but he wouldn't. I don't know whether he was just p.o.'d because I was getting to him too much or what it was." His strategy against offensive linemen, he said, was, "I make them use more energy than you normally want to use, blocking." Russell, Ham and Edwards intercepted.

And the offense was full of itself. Bradshaw underthrew Shanklin, who suddenly stopped and caught a 40-yard pass as the defender on him continued toward the goal. After evading a strong rush Bradshaw threw a desperation pass into and out of a defensive back's hands and into those of Frank Lewis, who held it and scored. Hanratty entered the game in the fourth quarter and went downtown on his first play. "Frank Lewis did his thing down the left sideline," as Harris put it. "The secondary saw someone go by. Hanratty lofted the ball perfectly and Frank had another score." Frenchy bucked and banged and flung himself and Preston glided and wriggled, and both got yardage. The Browns tried some fancy maneuvers that fell flat. A fake field goal, for instance, and a pass to a receiver who wasn't there because he had been held up at the line of scrimmage. "If this be what they mean by imaginative coaching," said the Steelers' mascot, Father John Duggan of Ireland, "Then God deliver me from it."

The year before Greene had gone after the Browns' Bob Demarco, hit him in the jaw, and knocked out several deep-set teeth. There was some question whether Demarco might be vengeful.

"At the beginning of the game," said Russell, "Bob got down in his stance, looked up at Big Joe Greene and said, 'Okay, Joe, let's have a nice clean hard-fought game.' Which shows that Demarco is not only a nice guy but quite intelligent, too."

After the game, in the locker room, Noll was asked what he thought about the gold shoes L. C. had worn in defiance of Pete Rozelle's directive that everybody on a team wear the same uniform, even down to the same color tape, black tape on black shoes, to insure a "standard uniform product." The

Steelers didn't like the idea of being a standard uniform product. Russell recalled that former Steeler tackle Mike Sandusky insisted on wearing his jersey-tail out. When he was nagged to look neater, he just cut the bottom of his jersey off so that it hung down evenly to his waist. "What shoes?" said Noll.

"Gold shoes."

"I don't watch shoes. That's Peter's [Rozelle's] province."

Was that Noll's final word on shoes?

"Well, shoes are part of the uniform. I'd feel bad if he went out there barefoot."

Frenchy dressed for the evening in a long white cape, floor-length.

"Frenchy's dressed like the Pope today," said Father Duggan.

Greene was not impressed with the tone of the game. "Cleveland was easing, easing," he said, "and we got into that same kind of game. You can get in a lull in a football game." He also said, "We still got to play them again."

At Houston the Oilers were fired up and led at the half 7–6. The Oilers' touchdown followed one of Bradshaw's two interceptions. But the defense shut off the Houston running attack and Ham intercepted a Dan Pastorini pass, and in the third quarter Russell intercepted and followed what appeared to be several dozen blockers 45 yards for a touchdown. "You got up so much speed, there, Andy, I thought we were going to be called for delay of game," said Ham. Russell was so excited to be scoring the first long-run touchdown of his nine-year career that he forgot to breathe while running, and could hardly stand on the sidelines afterward. Edwards returned another interception 86 yards beautifully for a score, and pretty soon it was 36–7 Pittsburgh. Franco ran a little bit but not too strongly.

Mansfield cut 6–8, 290-pound rookie John Matuszak, and Matuszak fell knee-down on Mansfield's back with all his weight (until he saw the films Mansfield thought it had been Sam Davis landing on him, and Sam was willing to take credit cheerfully), cracking one of the short ribs close to the backbone. For the first time in eleven years Mansfield had to be helped off the field. "It hurt so *bad,*" he said, half-holding his breath and slitting his eyes. "It must be the way you feel when you're wounded." But Clark couldn't snap very well with his broken hand and Mansfield played out the game. He said he would practice the next week too: "If I can suck it up a whole game I can suck it up a whole week." The body of Pastorini's wife, June Wilkinson the actress, caused sexist observers to grow dizzy when they saw her being interviewed before the game. An Oiler representative said of her body, "It may be why Pastorini is continually having abdominal pulls."

"Being fired up can only take you so far," said Noll of the Oilers' first-half spirit. "We want to stay on a level plane." A reasonably level plane bore the Steelers, hurting but riding high, back to Pittsburgh, where it is about time we took a look around the Three Rivers premises.

131

□ 12 □

THE PREMISES

Isn't this here a beautyful place?
—ART ROONEY

Before Three Rivers was built the Steelers played at Forbes Field or Pitt Stadium and their offices were in the Fort Pitt Hotel. For many years they were on the ground floor, and people would enter or leave by stepping through the window. All sorts of sporting and charitable activities were organized there, from prizefights to funerals for Irish paupers. For the latter, the Chief would send out his sons as pallbearers. Newspapermen, old ballplayers, pugs, horseplayers, people looking for a few bucks to tide them over, and politicos loafed there. When the operation expanded and the Chief and Fran Fogarty moved upstairs a few floors, the Chief asked Pie Traynor, the great old Pirate third baseman, why he didn't come up to visit him. "Sooner or later somebody is going to forget and step out the window up there," said Pie, "and it isn't going to be me."

The Rooney–Fogarty office of those days was filled almost completely by the two of them, their desks, and cigar smoke. It was next door to the men's room, and once while the Chief was being interviewed a man burst through the door pulling down his zipper. "Oops," the man said. "Next door," said the Chief, delighted. Fogarty, the business manager, was always punching an adding machine and writing in a yellow ledger. There were stuffed chairs with worn edges in the old offices, and pictures randomly hung, and an old air conditioner which made a loud noise when it worked.

Once a man came into the Fort Pitt offices and said he wanted to be the Steelers' p.a. announcer. He was told they already had one. "Yeah, but you need me because I can do it without a mike," the man said. "I just use a megaphone. I have the loudest voice in Pennsylvania." Okay, he was told, you can have a tryout, right here. The man went into the middle of the lobby and started announcing an imaginary game at the top of his lungs. Meanwhile the Rooneys called the police. They came in and grabbed the man, he said he was trying out to be the Steelers' announcer, and the Rooneys said they never saw him before.

The offices at Three Rivers have a different ambience, but maybe not as different as they appear to have at first glance. There are sweeping glass-topped

132

desks, fruitwood paneling, plenty of open space, thick carpets. In the reception area out front hangs a tapestry (sewn patches of corduroy and other material) depicting rather freely—it looks like what goes on in the air above a comic-strip brawl—the greatest planned play in Steeler history: a fake plunge up the middle by "Popcorn" Brandt and a 52-yard pass from Jimmy Finks to Elbie Nickel for a touchdown that beat the Eagles in 1954. It was a day when the Eagles had to be advised to wear their helmets on their way onto the field because bottles would be thrown at their heads.

The Chief's new office is four times as big as the one he shared with the late Fogarty, and he is in there alone. For a while after he moved in he tried to get staff members to share it with him. "I won't bother you," he said.

But all he has for immediate company are pictures of his friends. Pennsylvania political figures: Jimmy Coyne, David Lawrence, Joe Barr. Big figures of NFL history: Bert Bell, Tim Mara, Charley Bidwell, George Preston Marshall, George Halas, Joe Carr. The big figure of AFL history, Lamar Hunt, whom Rooney tried unsuccessfully to persuade the NFL to accept before he went off and founded the new league. And great old Steelers: Whizzer White, Lou Michaels, Bill Dudley, Ernie Stautner, Johnny Blood, Dick Hoak, Big Daddy. There's a picture of Coach Walter Kiesling, his shirttail out and fire in his eyes, being restrained by several people from attacking a referee whose call had cost him a game.

There isn't the same old crowd in the new offices but old Steelers come by, and political friends such as Iggy Borkowski, who used to be on the Con Squad of the police force—"He was the best man in the world on the pigeon drop. He made senators, too," someone told me. I think it was Iggy who told me about Monk somebody who "was a commander of county police. Before that he drove a cab. Some group said they wanted to go to a sporting house. He took them to Honus Wagner's Sporting Goods Store. Put 'em out, it was 11:30 on a Friday night, and said 'You can get anything you want there.' "

Dago Sam Leone used to hold the Chief's ring and money for him while he played ball, and he was a prominent figure on the North Side. He is eighty now—"and I lived hard. I lived a bad life, a lot of the time," he says with some satisfaction. Sam doesn't hold forth on the premises, but over at the 120 Bar a couple of blocks away he told me stories about the old days on the North Side. The Rooneys and their crowd were great ones for telling stories. When Vincent Rooney suffered a stroke and his son Tim hurried to his bedside in the intensive-care ward, not knowing how he would find him, Vince sat up in bed as Tim walked in and said, "There was this Jewish fella . . ."

The 120 Bar is on Federal Street. Baldy Regan, another friend of the Steelers, told me, "In the old days they said if Federal Street had a Ferris wheel, it would have everything. Then we found out that Ferris, the guy that invented it, was from Federal Street. There's a plaque over there if somebody didn't steal it. But it was made of metal. So somebody stole it," Baldy said. Now decay and urban renewal have reduced Federal Street's glories to a few modest ones. Across the street from the 120 Bar there is Ada's Lounge, "Go-Go Nitely, Friday and Saturday Exotic." There is an upstairs place nearby called the Greek Coffee Shop, "only you can't get a cup of coffee there, and they say 'm-f' worse than a colored person" says Dago Sam. A man named Shoes will play you illegal pinochle in the Greek Coffee Shop for any amount of money.

"This used to be a wonderful neighborhood," said Dago Sam in the 120 Bar. "Dan Rooney's saloon was where the stadium parking lot is now, and the old ball park was where the stadium is now, and gambling and sporting houses were all around. Nettie Gorman's, Big Elsie's, Lula Burdette's. Gradually they moved away from where the stadium is, and by the fifties they were all closed down. Lula Burdette's still alive, though."

The North Side is mostly black and poor now, and rough in a different way. "We never used to have trouble with colored people," says Sam. "It didn't start until ten, twelve years ago, after they got their freedom."

Milton Jaffe, now the manager of the Stardust in Las Vegas, used to have a gambling place over the bar that is now the 120, and his brother was in vaudeville in town and would bring the girls from his show over to Milton's place late and they would dance "and it would be nice," says Sam.

The 120 Bar is not a patch on the old North Side joints, but it is a companionable place, where the barmaid, Barb, whose husband's uncle used to catch for John McGraw's New York Giants, may be heard singing "My Wild Irish Rose" with two patrons in the three-part harmony. There is a big picture on one wall of Billy Conn, who would have been heavyweight champion if he'd used his head against Joe Louis and whose father was called Westinghouse Conn because he was a night watchman at the Westinghouse plant. Billy and his brothers and their father used to beat up surly types together, before Billy got into the big-time fight scene. The bartender in the 120 is named Ozzy.

"I was thirty-four," he told me. "I had $200,000 in the bank and my business—I had a pool room like nobody in the *country.*"

"How'd you lose it?"

"Just loony. But I have no regrets. I took care of everybody. How you like Pittsburgh?"

"I like it. It's got lots of color."

"Color," Ozzy laughed, shaking his head. A minute later he came back with a story.

"This drunk came in here, I said, 'I can't serve you.'"

"He said, 'No, just give me some scrambled eggs.'"

" 'Okay, I can do that,' so I said to Barb, 'scramble him some eggs.'"

"She said, 'I only got one back there.'"

"I said, 'He don't know the difference, give him anything.' So she threw in a pound of limburger, gave it to him, he ate it, called her over, said, 'Where you get your eggs?'"

134

" 'We have a hen out back that lays 'em,' Barb says.

" 'You got a rooster?' he says.

" 'No,' she says.

" 'Well you better get one,' he says, 'because a skunk's been fucking your hen.' "

Okay, well, that was just off the Three Rivers premises, with Dago Sam. Right there in the shiny new offices you have Uncle Jim Rooney, the Senator, holding forth.

Uncle Jim stands at an angle because of the drastic crook in his bad leg, in the reception area or in the hall, and when you come by and he knows you he starts telling you stories in a series of asides, in a soft voice, with little nudges, and the smile a man might have who is telling confidential friends about what it looked like twenty minutes ago when he saw the Supreme Court fall down a flight of stairs.

A lady's name came up. "She was as fine a lady as I ever knew. And she ran a tough joint, and nobody got out of line. Big," Uncle Jim spread his hands wide, "fine woman. Johnny Brown of New Orleens played piano in her place. He was a wonderful man . . . Sold his body for $120. To the University of Pennsylvania Medical School. All in ones. Came into the place countin' 'em out. Johnny Brown of New Orleens. Weighed 120 pounds. Dollar a pound. They brought in one these pianos that play themselves. It put Johnny out of work. He didn't have nothing to do. He got a rock and came in and put it through the piano. Johnny Brown of New Orleens."

"Where is he now?" someone asked.

Uncle Jim spread his arms and looked upward. "The University of Pennsylvania Medical School."

In either Kiely's or Joe Gordon's office during the season there would always be someone talking. Charley McSwigan, the director of stadium operations, might be telling about a friend who asks his big football player son, "What do you do when I knock you down?" and knocks him down, and the son gets up and says, "I get up," and the man says, "What do you do when I knock you down again?" and knocks him down again, and the son gets up again and says, "I have respect."

Or you could go down the hall to the scouts' offices and talk to them. Tim Rooney might be just back from a trip to Las Vegas. "Milton Jaffe's got a 6–5 security guard out there, he fills the door. We're bringing him in for a tryout. I don't know whether he can play or not, but he can fill the door." He went to that town, though, to look at prospects at the University of Nevada at Las Vegas. "Talk about the outlaw schools. There was this guy over on the sidelines, I asked the coach why isn't he playing. Coach said he's got a little problem.

" 'Oh,' I said.

" 'He knifed a girl in the girls' dorm the other day,' the coach says.

135

"I said, 'Oh. I can see he has got a problem.'

" 'No,' the coach says. 'He's got a *knee* problem. He'll be out there when his knee comes around.' "

I got to talking with Tim one day about how few Jewish players there were in the NFL, for some reason, and then I wandered over to Gordon's office. And who was in there but a big-bodied, great-nosed, bald-headed, elderly, animated man wearing a boldly striped shirt, a boldly striped tie, a stickpin, flip-up sunglasses, and a black cowboy hat.

He was named Dave Packard, he told me, and he was "the only Hebe who ever played for St. Bonaventure. I used to play for the Hope Harveys with Art. They used to tape my nose down and call me Cassidy, so St. Bonnie's wouldn't know it was me. I earned $3.50 and my mother thought I stole it. I was the only man ever knocked out in the hurdle, you know.

"Art and Dan were very religious. 'By Gad' was the worst thing either of them ever said. I was in the line and Dan was in the backfield and he told me to hit the guard. Somebody tackled him and he thought it was the guard. 'By Gad,' Dan said, 'Jewboy, I thought I told you to hit the guard.' I tried to explain but he swung and knocked me out. Right there in the huddle. 'Man hurt!' he yelled, and they came in and carried me off.

"Art hit Toots Sweeney one time—put his nose way over here. I spit tobacco in Sweeney's face and he said, 'You dirty Jew,' and Art hit him, Boom.' "

Packard had a watchchain going into each vest pocket. One had a Phi Beta Kappa key and a little gold football on it from when he played in the Rose Bowl. He started telling me about these mementos, bringing clippings and letters from college officials out of his pockets to document his stories. "Art was a godsend from heaven to me, because he said, 'Get an education and you'll be all right. I went to thirteen colleges playing ball, between 1928 and 1936. Here, this clipping is self-evident, here. I didn't have any money and I had to go where they'd pay me.

"One time Art said, 'Did you see that, that man kneed Jim.' He and Dan went over there, one of them held the man and the other one knocked him all the way down the steps. 'I don't know, the guy musta fainted,' Art said."

"What's that lapel pin?" I asked Packard.

"Oh, you get a hundred members for the Moose."

The Chief came in, saw Packard, and broke into a smile. "We used to play poker, and he was the only Jew and all the rest were Irish. They used to clip him every time!" The Chief began to laugh. "One day I saw him go in there with a saxophone." The Chief was laughing harder. "They even took him for his saxophone!" He was shaking now. "And they didn't even know what it was!"

Back beyond the administrative offices was a little kitchen—"Bless My Little Kitchen, Lord, and Warm It with Your Love," said a plaque on the wall—where you could freeload a good lunch of sandwiches and soup. The Chief was in there one day when he was reminded of the time he was eating breakfast with his college roommate and accidentally poured vinegar over his pancakes.

"Vinegar on your pancakes!" the roommate said.

"That's right, try it," said the Chief.

"I'm from Punxsutawney," said the roommate, "and we're not fancy with our food, but . . ."

After lunch we might walk back past the reception area, where perhaps, if it is still warm weather, Buff Boston is chasing local kids who keep slipping in through the front door to get in on the air-conditioning.

And then past the coaches' offices and the film rooms and the big meeting room and into trainer Ralph Berlin's office, where we see *Kinesthesiology, Professional Uses of Adhesive Tape,* a plastic novelty voodooish device which says on it "The Magic Authentic Sports Hex," and frequently Berlin smoking a cigar and playing gin.

His office leads into the training room, filled with whirlpool baths, an ultrasonic sound-treatment apparatus, all different kinds of tape (6,000 yards a week are used), jars of gooey balm (Cramergesic, Red Hot, Atomic) spray cans of "Skin-lube" which goes on beneath the tape to prevent it from cutting, little things called adhesive knucklets, salt tablets, and bottles and bottles of vitamin pills. One of the fringe benefits of being a pro football player is that you get to eat all the vitamin pills you want free—for instance, a daily handful of round amber vitamin-E-and-wheat-germ pills, which the players believed to be of sexual value. (As the old story goes about oysters, "I ate a dozen of them last night and only nine of them worked.") The body of even a Steeler can use only a certain amount of any vitamin per day, "so most of 'em are urinated out," said Berlin. "Americans have the richest urine in the world."

It was in an NFL training room that Lance Rentzel found a copy of *1984,* which, he said, so unsettled him that he began exposing himself to girls. I don't think anything that dramatic ever happened in the Steeler training room, but it was a good place for chatting. There would almost always be somebody in there lying on one of the steel tables, getting therapy: being massaged or soaking up heat or rubbing ice—frozen in a paper cup, so that you could hold on to the cup and tear it away as the ice melted down—over some pain or other. Or Berlin and his assistant Bob Milie would be taping ankles. Everybody's ankles had to be taped every day of practice, Tuesday through Saturday. Some players avoided it, but at the risk of a fine if they sprained an ankle untaped. Berlin and Milie always smoked cigars while taping. "All trainers smoke cigars," said Milie, "so they don't smell the feet."

The training room opens into the dressing room, a spacious carpeted area. The players' cubicles are against the wall all around in the order of the players' numbers. I don't know which were more remarkable, the rigors of the playing field or the comforts of the dressing room. The writing profession has many pros and cons, but one of the things I regret most, after a year with the Steelers, is that writers don't have dressing rooms. Maybe it's something that could be worked out. The staff of *Time* could have one, or the crowd at Elaine's. It wouldn't have to be a purely male-bonding thing; I could see having salty women in it.

The dressing room is the best clubhouse I've ever been in, with the best service: You come in there every day, dressed like Huck Finn or Sly Stone, and you go to your cubicle and there's your mail, possibly including a florid mash note from some strange woman who just might pan out, and there are your clean gold-and-black pants with the belt already threaded through the loops, and your clean jersey, and your ten or twelve pair of playing shoes, and your helmet with the gouges of service in it, and your "roll" containing clean white socks and T-shirt and jock, and maybe Iron City has dropped off a case of free beer, and there are two cursing men—Tony Parisi the equipment man and Jack Hart the field manager—and several devoted unobtrusive boys waiting on you hand and foot. If there's anything wrong with your equipment you take it to Hart or Parisi and he fixes it for you the way you want it. No coaches around—they have their own dressing room—except Noll on occasional brief visits. And the entertainment: Always somebody to play cards—gin or booray or tonk—or to throw Frisbee with, maybe competitively, to see who can scale it into a hamper three times first. Or you can catch John Kolb wearing bikini pants, which is remarkable because he is a member of the country, rather than the black or the geek, contingent, and you can yell anything vile at him that comes to mind, as Hanneman shouts, "And I got to sleep in the same room with him!"

If someone goes out without taking a shower you can mount an uproar, yelling things like "Pit check!" until he holds up his arm to prove that he doesn't offend.

There may be a game of Indian poker going on: Each player has one card plastered onto his forehead, face out, so that everybody but you knows what your card is, and you try to figure out whether you've got high card and bet accordingly—and Frenchy is trying to read his card in the reflection in Preston's eyeballs.

Hanneman and Greenwood are furthering their season-long gin game, probably with the score in tens of thousands of points on a long strip of tape on Hanneman's cubicle, and Hanneman may have just lost a hand so that he shouts, "Jesus fucking shitass!" or "I be go to fuck!" or some other imaginative oath.

Over on the other side of the room Parisi is doing his near-boogeying imitation of ex-Steeler Roy Jefferson's walk, and a nervous youth purportedly gathering information for a radio program comes up to Dwight White with a tape recorder and asks him what he is going to do with his playoff money. And Dwight goes into his exaggerated Kingfish voice to reply:

"Well, uh . . . Bein' a fella lak me, uh, whut nevuh had none of that kinda moneh befo, it kinda hahd to decide. But I prolly gonna give half of it to muh chuhch, and then I gonna use the rest of it to plant a row, uh, of collahd gree-uns, and a row, uh, of wawtuhmelons, and then I gonna lay out in the sun, and when they grow I gonna *eat* 'em"; and somebody yells loud enough to get it on the tape, "Dwight White's a faggot!" and Dwight starts over on his answer in a falsetto voice: "Wayull, uh, *bein'* a fella lak *mee* . . ."

Parisi runs up to Rowser with a sense of urgency in his voice: "Do you Believe?"

Rowser is willing to go along. "Yeah."

"Good," says Parisi. "Then I don't have to.

"We work seven days a week, sixty hours easy, during the season," says Parisi. "You have to really keep these guys happy. Being around it as long as I have, your mind's still gotta be working all the time." Parisi grew up in Canada and played ten years of hockey in Canada, England, Italy, Holland and Czechoslovakia, and then was trainer of the Pittsburgh Hornets, the hockey team, for four years before joining the Steelers. "The worst part was when we practiced on the grass at South Park and I had to clean forty or fifty pairs of shoes every day."

It is menial work that Parisi and Hart do—with the help of various ballboys, including North Side Freddy, a young black neighbor of the Chief's, and sometimes Noll's son or Dan Rooney's college-age son Art the third—but they act no more, or, they act less, like servants around the players than anybody in the front office. All the vice-presidents and the traveling secretary, after all, were jock sorters and belt-threaders for the Steelers as young men, and neither Dan nor Artie nor any of the coaches deal as relaxedly with the players as Parisi or Hart. They know what the players want: it was when Hart and Parisi came to accept my presence that I figured I must somehow or another fit into the dressing room.

Neither of them ever told me any of the personal things they knew about the players—the players took care of that—but they had plenty of talk to offer. "I was watching Parisi and Rooster Fleming in the equipment room the other day," said Tim Rooney, "and I was just sorry I was the only one around. I felt guilty the whole world wasn't watching." The thing Tim remembered most was that the minute Rooster walked into the room Parisi grabbed him by the wrists and told him to start clapping. Rooster clapped for a while, as Tony went about sorting things. "Why am I doing this?" Rooster said at length, and Parisi answered, "As long as you're doing that I know you're not stealing anything."

It was Hart who told me that Dan Rooney, the one that's a priest, was said to have had the job at one time of sitting in a gambling hall on the North Side—a big one where people would pay just to stand on a balcony and watch the action on the floor—with a machine gun in his lap, guarding against robbery.

I was reluctant to dress in players' guise, partly because I had the feeling that fierce linebacker Mike Curtis might run over from Baltimore and tackle me, the way he did a civilian who ran onto the field during a Colts game, and partly because it seemed like putting on airs; but finally Dockery nagged me into running with him and Bleier, and after that Parisi or Hart would readily round me up a roll and some sweat pants and a huge practice jersey and a pair of shoes, and I would borrow someone's rubberized jacket, to promote sweating (Mansfield would come in sometimes from practice, take off his jacket, and pour a good cupful of sweat from its sleeve), and I would dress in the cubicle with Mel's and my last name over it and go out and shag field goals and punts, or run a little bit, and fart around. Which included talking to a wide range of fellow marginal figures out on the field.

"There used to be a department store here, a warehouse, and a junkpile as high as the stadium," said Charley McSwigan one day. "Two junkyards. It took three years to tow the junk away." He pointed out the level high in the upper end zone seats from which a patron, perhaps seeking a closer place than the men's room to take a leak, once inadvertently slid seventy feet down a trash chute during the Steeler game. "To get into the chute he had to go through a door into a little room, then open the door to the chute, down low on the floor. It's the chute concessions guys drop trash down. He landed in a Dempster Dumpster on top of a layer of trash. We found him in there, bloody. He said 'I'll be all right, just help me out of here.' Then later he sued. A schoolteacher."

"The original design was to be completed in 1968," said Dan Rooney. "It would've been a great stadium—like looking into a bull ring. We actually got a lot of it from the bull ring in Mexico City. But a taxpayer's suit stopped that one. And the Pirates, who were the prime movers on building the stadium, just wanted to dress up Forbes Field and bring it over here. But we're co-tenants, our outlay of money was significant, and we wanted a real dual stadium. We demanded nothing less than the one in St. Louis. This one doesn't look like a bull ring, but it's still much steeper than St. Louis's, the back seats are higher and closer to the field."

For football the seats along the first base line swing around on tracks so that they're along the sidelines. And the dirt is taken out of the pitcher's mound and the sliding areas around the bases and replaced with plugs covered with Tartan Turf. Gerela liked to kick field goals from the pitcher's-mound plug because it bounced and gave him more spring. The field's markings are applied with special washable paint, and where the turf is painted it's almost as stiff as a wire brush. "That stuff be looking good," said Glen Edwards after his bare arms skidded over the white sidelines, "but it be burning my ass."

One afternoon McSwigan, Dan and Buff Boston started telling me about famous halftime shows in the Steelers' past. Bill Day, the half-time director, attends a meeting with the Steeler brass once a week, and they always ask him if anything special is coming up, and he holds up a printed sheet describing the forthcoming show and says, "No the sheet's right."

"Then maybe ten buses will show up from Alliance, Ohio, on Saturday afternoon, full of kids wanting to go on the field because they have to rehearse

140

for a special extravaganza, and the field's covered," says Buff, "and I have to tell them, 'You can go in and look at it, but you're not going on the field, because I'll throw you out.' Five hundred kids that weren't on the sheet."

Once Day arranged for howitzers to be shot off, and they shook the whole stadium. Another time an act was climaxed by the throwing up of hundreds of balloons, which went straight up and came straight back down onto the field. Buff with his great stomach and the officials in their stripes had to run out onto the field stomping at the balloons, trying to pop them, but they'd slip away and scatter when someone ran through them, so they finally had to be shooed and shoved and herded off, hundreds of gaily bouncing balloons, just in time for the second half.

"Then there was the time they had the children's zoo out here," said Buff. "All kinds of animals—ducks, geese . . ."

"Big things," said Dan. "Not deer, but animals like deer."

The children's zoo scattered too, like the balloons. Buff had to run around shoving them toward the door. "Then when we got them through the gate, they crapped all over the field. We ran the Zamboni, the sweeping machine, over it, but it didn't do too good of a job."

"We didn't tell the players," said Dan.

Dan was reminded, also, of the great fireworks show one halftime at night when they were still using Forbes Field. "It was tremendous. Everything you could want. Went on and on, flashing and booming, for twenty minutes. Then the lights came on and the field was full of smoke. You couldn't see a guy standing next to you on the field."

Also in evidence during practice was the ground crew, especially Steve "Dirt" Denardo. Dirt was round, bald-headed, fat, moustached and usually grimy, and wearing a red beret. He would roam around the field on the Zamboni, which is a vacuum cleaner you drive like a car, harassing Hart by running over balls with it. Whenever a new player joined the team Denardo would buttonhole him casually on the field and say, "Stop by my office before you go today," or even, "You better be making some plans, there is no way you can make this team." Before games Denardo would go up to the visiting coach and tell him where to get off. Sometimes he wore a Met cap. Once he came up behind Joe Greene in a San Diego hotel lobby as Greene was looking for his key amongst all the other players' spread out on a table. "You go to Tijuana, nigger," he said. Greene whirled and then saw it was just Dirt, and laughed.

"Yogi Berra wants to adopt him," explained McSwigan. One time Richie Allen of the White Sox, a native of nearby Wampum, arranged with Denardo to buy him a horse and deliver it to his Allentown farm. But Dirt didn't use a horse van to transport the horse in, he used a truck, and when he arrived the horse was all broken up from banging around in there loose. "They had to shoot 'im," said Dirt blithely. "But I seen running backs in worse shape." That story was enough to convince me not to adopt Dirt, but the Chief loved him and all the rest of the ground crew, one member of which the Steelers took along on each road trip. The ground crew got along a lot better with the Steeler organization than with that of the Pirates, headed by the relatively plutocratic John Galbreath. "Galbreath is in Africa shooting deer, or whatever they shoot over there," said the Chief one day at practice, and he and the crew chuckled over the folly of it all.

Then after practice if I had dressed out I would go take a shower and sit around NAKED IN AN NFL DRESSING ROOM WITH MEAN JOE AND RANGER AND HOLLYWOOD BAGS AND ALL THE GUYS! And maybe Ham is sitting playing boo-ray with Van Dyke and Clack and Mansfield and Rowser, and Walden, and somebody is shouting, "You booed him! You booed him!" and the stakes are up around fifty or sixty dollars and Ham's leg wrap is halfway on and halfway off, stretching out six or eight feet across the floor—he got it unrolled that far and then decided to start playing cards—and Bradshaw is hiding under the table with the balls-to-be-autographed on it, waiting for Dicus to come in so he can throw cold water on him, and somebody is warning Frenchy that there is a woman waiting at each of two exits for him, so he may have to go out over the center field fence again, and here comes a man *wearing a necktie.* Poor fool. Trying to sell the Steelers some bank-teller shoes. Oh, those are nice styles. They'd look good on you if you ever wanted to move on into a job checking people into a hotel or selling a line of stationery from store to store. L. C. is over there wearing red pants, a blue shirt open to the waist, sunglasses and a Steeler cap. When he's dressing *up* he might throw on a blue pullover sleeveless suit, brown pantyhose and a shoulder bag. Keating is wearing a shirt made out of a Nicaraguan flour sack. Man come in here with shoes like that.

"I'm not going to buy any," says Sam Davis loudly. "He don't even know which Davis I am. We all look alike."

"I'll buy a pair," says Henry Davis. "One to shit in and one to cover it up with. I'm sure they're, uh, some good quality boots, though."

"Good shoes," says the shoe man energetically. "They'll wear. Here," he says to J. T. Thomas. "These are the kind of shoes they wear in Florida."

"No they don't," says J. T. "I don't wear shoes in Florida. When I'm down there I go nudie." J. T. is wearing clogs, which cause him to shuffle rather like Step 'n Fetchit.

"Gimme some 'em Hush Puppies," said Dwight. "Had 'em in school. Call 'em Quiet Dogs. Here I come into class." (He takes a few steps bent over at the waist in the posture of a man making an entrance almost impossibly cool.) Then he forgets the shoe man and shouts, "I'm gonna go to the Colonel and get me a box of the *bird.* "

Joe Greene is explaining to the shoe man that he can't afford to buy any shoes just now, when Henry Davis explodes: "*Man!* Why don't you tell the man the truth? Why you fool the man? You don't talk to me like that. You told me you were looking for some shoes the other day. Why don't you tell him you wouldn't buy that shit?"

"What kind of talk is that?" says Greene, frowning at Davis. And then he remarks, looking as if into an imaginary camera, "He's right, though."

Oh, we're a tight bunch in here. We don't let just anybody wander in and set up shop. Now Hart, having loaded all the dirty clothes into the washing machine, is yelling at stragglers to clear out so he can finish cleaning and go home. He is flicking the dressing room lights off and on. He is pulling Ham's practice pants down, hurrying him along, as Ham talks on the phone. People are yelling, "Fuck you, Jack," and Hart runs into the toilet area and shouts at someone, "Take a shit on your own time!"

It's like having a mother nagging at you and taking care of you—a mother you can swear at. And I am sitting here in the dressing room thinking, Well, this is a fine, strange scene, and this is the way to cover a football team.

But then again three different Steelers, while discussing sensitive matters, have mentioned that they would kill or at least demolish somebody who, after people got to talking naturally around him, reported inside stuff to a callous world and got people in trouble. You can't thoroughly enjoy sitting in a big-time dressing room if you are forced to think of yourself at least partially as the agent of a jaded, vicariously voracious world.

When I went into the visitors' dressing room after the Denver game with other reporters to question Bronco quarterback Charley Johnson, and he was taking a drag off of a cigarette, and he said, "You didn't see me do that" (i.e., take a drag off a cigarette), I was annoyed. But after all a person should have some privacy in the place where he dresses, and there are political considerations as well.

In the movie *The Sea Wolf,* there is a writer character who is summoned to the captain's cabin to talk to Wolf Larsen as the crew is planning a mutiny. As the writer leaves the fo'c'sle his fellow crew members glare at him and he says, honorably, "I saw and heard nothing." Some of that kind of reticence is involved in the blandness of most sports reporting.

The Steeler organization was a relatively open and relaxed one, but the players still had a great sense of vulnerability—to the public, to their coaches and the front office, and to the league management. And to each other. They were paid to fling themselves through the air and fight each other tooth and nail. And they had to sit around naked, and fresh from a passionate session of flinging and fighting, being asked occasionally touchy questions by strangers from out of town with pads and pencils. And drunks taunted them in public places when they weren't playing up to par. And yet their careers could begin to seep away if they were ever revealed to have disobeyed a strong line of central authority or to have presented a less than suitably respectable image. They were heroes and invigoratingly wild lads, but kept ones. Like regular people.

143

* * *

As I sit in the dressing room I am reminded of a story about Bob Drum, the legendary former Pittsburgh sportswriter. Drum was in Troon, Scotland, for the British Open in 1973. He and an equally bulky and frog-voiced friend were in the dining room of the Robert Bruce Memorial Hotel in Troon, indulging in openly convivial talk and getting up from their table to do things like run through the Notre Dame shift, and a quiet Scottish couple were watching them, saying nothing. Drum and his party went on into the bar and the quiet Scottish couple followed them, took a table near theirs, and watched another long session of exuberant speech and heavy acrobatics. Toward the end of the evening Drum said loudly, "One thing about me, I'm welcome anywhere in the world."

And then the quiet Scottish couple spoke up for the only time, in the person of the lady, who said, "Once."

That story is not perfectly parallel to my situation, but my solidarity with the Steelers is a one-shot thing. What am I doing dressing in their dressing room anyway? I don't hit anybody. I don't have a hip pointer or a muscle tear. I don't know whether I, whose knees don't hurt all the time, or whose leg isn't permanently numb from midcalf to midthigh (as Dwight White's is from a knee operation), can tell what kind of time people with such legs are having. This is a very carnal scene here in the dressing room, and I am mostly eyes and ears. I don't even have a pad and pencil.

Recently Robert Mitchum was asked about journalists who hang around the actors and then go off to write cavalierly about them, and Mitchum replied, Frank Sinatra once explained it to me: "They jerk off and we buy yachts."

It seems to me that there must be some middle ground. Many of the players evince a powerful desire to tell, often luridly, about what their far-fetched profession is really like, as well as a desire to be protected from dangerous exposure. "I always wanted to be controversial," one Steeler told me. "Like Butkus. He says things and doesn't give a shit. But you got to have team unity. And when you don't the coach looks for the weak link and gets rid of him."

I finish dressing and go off to loaf with some Steelers away from work, perhaps at the Jamestown Inn, where at least I won't be sober.

□ **13** □

STEELERS AWAY FROM WORK

*A life is beautiful and ideal, or the reverse, only when we
have taken into our consideration the social as well as the
family relationship.*

—HAVELOCK ELLIS,
*LITTLE ESSAYS OF LOVE
AND VIRTUE*

The social ramble ain't restful.

—SATCHEL PAIGE

Whenever friends of mine would visit
me in Pittsburgh, some of them women for whom football had no charms, they
would come away surprised at how easy and friendly the Steelers and their
wives were. "What nice people," my friends would say.

"Nice people," I would say. "I introduce you to gladiators and their women
and you say they're nice people? You could have met nice people back home."
But they were, nice people. A Steeler wife of the not-too-distant past had been
known to go into the bathroom at parties—not at big parties, but at small
gatherings including her husband and teammates—and emerge naked and lie
down on the floor and say, "Okay, who's first?" But that got her husband
disposed of, and was by no means representative of Steeler wives. There was
also a fist fight between two Steelers' wives at a Halloween party during a
previous season, but nothing like that happened in '73, I believe. The closest
thing I observed was when a wife yelled something upstairs at one of the
players and he said, "Get down there at the bottom of the steps and spread
it and I'll be right down," and his wife, who was standing there with us, said,
"He's the only one who knows how to shut her up."

I mentioned earlier that Frosene Van Dyke, who made excellent lasagne,
persuaded me to interview her obstetrician one night when we met him in a
restaurant where my sister and brother-in-law and I and some other people
were dining with the Van Dykes and other Steeler couples. "These Steeler

wives lead glorious lives," the obstetrician said. But once when Frosene proposed that she write something about the pros and cons of the life of a pro football player's wife she said, "You'll have to make up the pros." But that was the way Frosene always talked. You couldn't generalize about the lives of Steeler wives, except to say that the wives were almost all very attractive and very physical—Janet Mansfield and Rosemary Hanratty arm-wrestled at the Russell's house on Thanksgiving day. One night at a party all the players' wives present took part in a weight-lifting contest with a barbell that happened to be on the floor. Janet, a refined, even delicate-looking woman, won with special coaching from Ray on how to get up under the bar and snap it up with her whole body. He seemed very proud of her.

I went to a meeting of wives with Ed Garvey, the Players' Association man. I was enjoined from reporting anything but general impressions, but I might say that the wives were extremely forthcoming about the need to make more money. When Garvey said players were very trusting people, one of the wives said, "Huh! I'd say naïve." "Gullible!" cried another.

"I wish I could negotiate his contract," said another.

"He won't push for more money because he's afraid they won't play him. I'd push for it. I don't care whether he plays or not."

One of the things many a Steeler's wife put up with was a husband who often stayed fairly late after practice drinking and talking at the Jamestown Inn, if he was white, or at the Name of the Game or the Black Magic if he was black. This social segregation, a contrast to the richly mixed socializing in the 19th Hole, was largely attributable to the fact that the white players mostly lived southward from the stadium and the blacks mostly eastward. But the best Jamestown session I sat in on was biracial—Greene, White and Ernie Holmes dropped by, as well as regulars Van Dyke, Mansfield, Russell and Mullins.

The Jamestown Inn advertised the Sensational Burt and Marty Nightly, but I was never around late enough for that entertainment. There was one drinking area identified by a sign over the bar as "Jimmy Breen's Roid Room," Breen being the proprietor and Roid being short for hemorrhoids—what you got, I guess, from sitting there too long. But the Steelers usually sat in the larger, dining area, and ate fried mushrooms, clam chowder, and bacon cheeseburgers along with their beers or Bloody Marys. Often there were non-Steeler habitués at the tables, like the fireman known as Lump, or Jonesy, who would come over to the Steeler table and start describing one of the players in a sportscaster's voice: "It's Mike Wagner, six foot one and a half out of Western Illinois, he cuts diagonally . . . *he picks up blockers, he . . .*" A former Steeler named Jimmy Bradshaw was often there, and a civilian named Joey Francis, who looked like Bobby Morse and when asked, "How's your wife?" would respond, "Pretty snappy, how's your pappy? Here's another: How's your mother? One more mister, how's your sister?" to which another regular named Jim Shanahan might answer, "Twice as nice as a mother's advice." One of the advantages of being a Steeler's business friend, like insurance men Sam

146

Zacharias and Chuck Puskar, was a place at the Steelers' table.

But there were only players at the table the time White and Greene and Holmes dropped by. The conversation therefore was more intimate. It turned to Franco, whose slowness to attain top playing form was attracting some worry. "There's a lot of pressure on that man," somebody said. "Outside pressure from the fans. He's been working *hard* to get ready."

Greene kept his family down in Texas. He was discussing real estate with Russell, with an eye toward buying a house in Pittsburgh for them. He turned to say of Franco's kind of intensity, more or less approvingly, "He's still a college player."

White said something and Greene said, "I may be rotten and self-centered, but one thing I do, I pull for dudes."

"We can't live together," said White to Greene, his apartment mate.

"I ain't selfish," said Greene. "But I am one thing; I am rotten." And he sort of leered.

"He eats a piece of chicken," said White, "and puts the bone down, on the floor, and it'll lay there for . . . It's infinite! Then call me nasty and funky."

Greene said, "That's why I respect Dwight, though. He tells it to you straight. Dwight is Dwight."

"You never going to be all-pro again," said Dwight to Greene. " 'Cause you're laxadaisical."

"I got to have some *meat,*" said Holmes.

"Got to get my jaws chompin'," agreed White. "I was down on Mel Blount's farm in Georgia. They got a hundred people down there, all of them related to Mel. I was down there and a different person had a birthday every night for a week. Mrs. Blount was driving back from Savannah and ran over a raccoon with her car. Picked it up and brought it home, *big* thing. Next morning I got up and they said, 'Come have breakfast. Get some coon meat.' Kids come in from school and get a coon sandwich. Sweet potatoes—got them all buried and the kids come home and that's their candy. They reach in and get them a sweet potato. And that's *good.*"

"I'm trying to get my mind right," Holmes told me. "I haven't wanted to talk to reporters much, since the incident . . . Trading for Keating—that gets me. Man don't think I can do the job.

"There isn't a moment," Holmes added, "from the time I got into that dressing room until the game is over, that I am not praying. People think I'm talking to myself, but I'm praying.

"With the mind," he added thoughtfully, "of a child, and the brains of a sixty-year-old-warrior."

Another time in the Jamestown Russell mentioned seeing Ray Nitschke, just retired from the Packers, so keyed up for one game that he dove, missed whoever he was diving at, and wound up head-first under a tarp along the sidelines. "You could see his feet kicking," Russell said, "and big bulges under the tarp where he was hitting out with his head and arms."

147

"Those days are gone," said Mansfield. "Iron men and wooden ships."

Another player told about a college teammate who used to lie in bed all day long, when he wasn't practicing, sticking boogers on the wall and grading them—marking the grade in pencil beside each one—on a scale of one to ten. "At parties he would barf on impulse," said the Steeler who remembered him. "To gross out people's dates. He'd barf and then pick out bits of it and eat them, saying, 'Hey, this is good!' "

Let me emphasize that that kind of thing did not go on at Steeler parties. I went to some very nice post-game parties at the home of Vaughn and Gerene Nixon in Mount Lebanon. Vaughn was an ear-nose-and-throat doctor who had befriended a number of the players. The Nixons' house had stained-glass (collected from demolished churches) in the ceiling over their pool table and autographed pictures of Steelers over the bar. The food was excellent and the conversation lively.

One night Gladys Davis, Sam's great-looking wife, said approvingly. "You hear a lot of 'Whiteys' and 'nigguhs' at these parties now. People used to stand around and then come up and say, 'Would you rather I call you 'colored' or 'black'?

" 'I'd rather you call me "Gladys," ' I'd say. Or I'd call *them* 'nigger.' Oh, they were shocked: She called *me* a nigger!"

Sandy Kolb, John's differently great-looking wife, approached. She was from Oklahoma and lived with Jon on a farm outside Pittsburgh and looked very homespun. "What if I called you a nigger?" Gladys asked her. "Nigger. Does that bother you? Or motherfucker?"

Sandy responded by telling a joke about a small black child who said "Mother" for the first time and whose mother exclaimed, "He just learned half a word!"

"See?" said Gladys, pleased.

Pamela Cash, wife of Pirate second baseman Dave Cash, often accompanied Gladys to the Nixons' parties. She said being a football wife was much better than being a baseball wife, because baseball players were away from home more. She was not high on being a baseball wife. After the Pirates traded Cash she said, "The photographer from the paper called to ask if he could come over to take pictures. I fixed the house all up, dressed up our little girl, and myself, and then he just took a picture of Dave. Nobody ever asked me how *I* felt about being traded. I was *born* in Pittsburgh. My *mama* lives here. Dave's just got to leave his friends. He can make new friends. I got to leave my *mama*. And our little five-year-old girl got hysterical when we told her Dave was traded. She thought he'd done something bad. People don't think athletes are human."

"I went on the radio," said Gladys, "and I said, 'Yes, I like being a football wife. Yes, it is good being a football wife.' " She said it between clenched teeth.

One night at the Nixons Warren Bankston, before he was traded to Oakland, was persuaded to do some of his imitations of Steelers. He had a real gift. He didn't just do people's voices, he took on their facial and bodily characteristics.

He did McMakin, invited to say something to someone who had called Bankston long distance, picking up the phone and saying, "Hey. Where you leeuv?" He did Rowser, engaging a listener intently and when the listener looked away grabbing him and saying, "Hey, listen to me." His wife pleaded with him to do Bleier, but for some reason he kept saying, "I don't do Bleier."

"Yes you do, you know you do," his wife said. Maybe he didn't like to think about Bleier coming on at running back after Bankston had been switched, himself, to tight end.

The Nixons' parties were attended by a wide range of Steelers, wives and girl friends. But although the black Steelers were all invited, the only ones I ever saw there were Preston Pearson, whose wife Linda was white, Franco, whose girl friend Dana was white, and Sam and Gladys Davis. Hanratty, who was often said to be significantly in solid with his black teammates, had given a teamwide party one year and was disappointed at how few blacks showed. Gladys said, "If blacks aren't doing a lot of chicken and wine, they don't think they're having fun."

On Thanksgiving Day a lot of us did a lot of turkey, goose, dressing, ham, pumpkin pie, baked beans, green beans, gravy, mashed potatoes, homemade bread, cranberry sauce, congealed salad, and raw milk from area cows, in the White County Center Building in Ninevah, Pennsylvania, near the Kolbs' farm. Hanneman was there, and Franco and the Van Dykes, the Meyers, the Bradleys, the Clacks, the Vaughn Nixons, the Sam Davises, relatives of the Clacks and the Kolbs' veterinarian's kids. Frenchy had signed up to come but characteristically he didn't make it.

"I'm so hungry I could eat the south end of a northbound skunk," said Hanneman to Van Dyke. "Couldn't you?"

"No," said Van Dyke.

The Kolbs, Bradleys and Meyers had prepared the repast, which was one of the high points of the season for me. "It's better than the time I stood in line outside the Salvation Army on Thanksgiving in college," said Hanneman. "We got some wine ahead of time and brown-bagged it down there."

"I thought you had to be hard up to eat at the Salvation Army," someone said.

"Our eyes were pretty beady by the time we got there," said Hanneman. "It's for anybody who doesn't have any place to eat on Thanksgiving."

"Did you have to pray or sing?"

"We got there a little late."

Sandy brought Franco some cold, foamy, creamy milk right out of a two-handed can. "That's far out," Franco said. "I could dig some of that stuff." Van Dyke's kids, who loved Franco, were clustering around him as he ate. "I one a monkey," said Jeff Van Dyke to Franco. "Say I two a monkey."

"I two a monkey."

"I three a monkey."

"I four a monkey," said Franco.

149

"I five a monkey," said Jeff.

"I six a monkey."

"I seven a monkey."

"Wup! Almost fell for the old 'I-ate-a-monkey' trick," said Franco.

Van Dyke and Hanneman both said that the one-room building, which doubled as a small gym, reminded them of the schools they'd gone to back home. "We had the biggest graduating class in the history of the school," said Hanneman. "Six."

"We had a guy sixteen in the fourth grade," said Van Dyke.

"Fourth grade," said Hanneman. "That *is* good. We had a guy to graduate at sixteen. Grammar school. He was in grammar school and he drove to school."

Becky Clack and I were eating everything but a monkey. "I've made myself sick," she said. "Isn't it fun?"

Hanneman decided he'd have some snuff for dessert. For delicacy's sake he put a napkin in the bottom of the cup he was spitting in. Becky was taken aback. "Want some?" he asked her.

"It smells like cow manure," she said.

"I babysat with a little girl," said Gladys Davis, "and when I got there she was asleep, and when she woke up she screamed. 'Cause she never had seen one of me. But her sister who was five explained it to her. She said, 'She's not dirty.' She got out the mustard and ketchup bottles and said, 'Some people are one color and some people are another.' But the little one couldn't leave it at that. As soon as their mother got home she said, 'Mama, is she dirty?' That's kids, they're honest. See somebody that's ugly, they say, 'Hey, you're ugly.' "

Meyer was wearing a DeKalb Feed cap, with a corncob emblem on it. Kolb had a big black eye, where a horse had bucked up into his face. "It would've broken my nose if I had anything left to break," he said. He mashed down his nose and it went completely flat.

As it grew dark a number of the company went off on a hayride, pulled by the Kolbs' tractor.

I also visited in a number of the players' homes. The Clacks' was the most impressive. It was a thirteen-room Victorian mansion in Washington, Pennsylvania, that they'd bought in bad condition for the absurd figure of $9,500 and then restored and furnished lavishly. Becky had gotten Jim interested in antiques, and now they went to auctions for pieces to sell as well as pieces to add to their furnishings. These included bird cages, teak-and-rosewood tables, a stained-glass window and a pink rug in the bathroom, washstands, Pears Soap ads, a Seeburg Select-o-Matic jukebox with "Dig Yourself," "Fingertips 1 and 2," "No Sugar Tonight," "Oogum Boogum," "Take Me Home, Country Road" and other tunes playable on it, Tiffany lamps, wallpaper with macaws and toucans on it, zebra-skin couch, Jim's battered Wake Forest helmet, gum machines, an eighteenth-century grandfather's clock, and an oak table with lions' feet. "When we were living in the Chatham West apartments, Becky found that on a trash pile, all in pieces," said Clack. "We put it together and there was only one toenail missing. One day I was driving home from practice with Preston and I looked out the window and yelled, 'Stop the car! I saw the toenail!' He said, 'Man . . . you're crazy.' "

Clack also showed me a portrait of one of the house's previous residents, a woman. "On the back it says she weighed 362 pounds and had thirty-six-inch knees," Clack said.

Clack himself had grown up tall and skinny and playing in the band until he was a sophomore in high school. "My father owned a grocery store and I always had to work with him in it, and I didn't have time for sports," he said. But after his father died he began to play football, was good, and got a college scholarship, but he was an awfully long shot to make it in the pros. The Steelers signed him as a free agent. "Noll called me up and said 'How much do you weigh?' I said, '228.' At the time I weighed 214. He said, 'That's great. I'd like you to report at 235. Seven pounds shouldn't be too much to gain.' " Clack ate a special weight-gaining diet and took steroids and lifted weights. "I'd lift two and a half hours at night. Three and a half. Jon Kolb and I—we'd work so hard we'd have each other crying. That's no lie. When I showed up Art Jr., who'd scouted me, didn't even recognize me. I'm up to 248 now." Becky, who was working on a master's in physical therapy, talked him into giving up steroids, which may cause such things as atrophy of the testes. "She says they don't do any good, but they do."

"No they don't," says Becky from the next room. At parties she screams, in an exuberant way. To set her off someone will say, "G-3," and she will say, "Bingo! *Eeeeee!*"

"But I just use Hoffman's High Protein now, and I eat a big snack before I go to bed." Some Steeler told me that whenever you were driving anywhere with Clack he was always trying to get you to stop the car so he could eat.

Clack was a self-made man in more ways than one. He had bought their home at such a good price through inside information, and he was also acquiring two more houses nearby as rental property. And they'd bought an apartment in Nag's Head, North Carolina, which brought in good rental income when they weren't using it themselves in the summer.

"If I were traded I would think seriously about not going, just quitting and staying here. Becky will be making good money with her degree pretty soon, and we'll have the real estate income. We'll be pretty well set. I'd like to get into politics around here. Besides, ball's no fun anymore. It's just a business."

The Kolbs had been much less lucky in life. They had bought a beautiful old house too, a farmhouse over 150 years old, but it had caught fire while Jon was building a show horse ring outside. His eighteen-month-old son Eric and three-year-old niece Cindy were sleeping inside. Kolb threw himself into his door three times before he was able to break into the house, and then he had to grope his way up a smoke-filled staircase to get the children. Since the smoke was too thick for him to go back down the stairs with them he climbed onto a porch roof and jumped from there, with his left hand in a cast and a child under each arm.

"How long did it take the volunteer fire department to get there?" I asked him.

"Not quite as long as it took the house to burn down," he said. It was lost, and for some reason his insurance didn't pay off very much. The Kolbs replaced the house with "the only trailer in Pennsylvania that's got a basement," as he put it, and they were hoping for a Super Bowl check so they could start building a new house. The trailer was decorated by Sandy Kolb's awards from the Firecracker Circuit of horse shows, in which her horse Sunshine had won five straight days. Kolb had lost all his football trophies, including his Steeler game ball, in the fire. He was represented by two uninscribed brass eggs which he and a twelve-year-old boy had won in egg-toss contests during the Firecracker Circuit. But Kolb would bring films home and the family would watch them together after supper. Sandy, who had learned a great deal about offensive line play in their years of marriage, would help him criticize his performance, and as they ran the plays back and forth, back and forth, little Eric would yell "Run, Daddy!" until he went to sleep. Once I saw Eric at a Steeler practice wearing his father's helmet. It covered his whole head and most of his shoulders, and when he tried to stand up under it he toppled over. Sandy and Eric and one of their nieces could often be seen in the Steeler offices' reception area waiting for Jon to finish lifting weights.

Iooss and I visited the Kolb farm for pictures one afternoon, rode in their jeep with them up the hill that used to overlook their big house, the jeep followed by three big bounding dogs, and then Jon stood under a big tree and looked out over his property and said that his biggest ambition in life had always been not to play pro football but to have his own prosperous farm. Whatever happened to them in football they planned to live out their lives here on their farm. Sandy tried to get us to go to Waterford Park for the races that night, as an inducement to Jon, who didn't much want to go.

After the season Sandy took Eric, left Kolb and his niece, and went to live in another trailer with a jockey who rode at Waterford Park. It was said that Kolb was doing a lot of drinking and breaking up bars.

One night after a game Iooss and I went to the Mansfields' house, a comfortable suburban home with the Ranger's by-the-numbers paintings on the wall. Iooss took pictures of their little boy Jim wallowing all over his father, and Ray explained why Janet had married him, back in Kennewick, Washington. "You saw me beat up the Schute brothers," he said.

"No, we weren't going together that summer," Janet said.

"Well you heard about it. The Schute brothers were named Dean and Laurel. They were supposed to be the toughest guys in Kennewick. I was in the car with some of my friends and when we drove by the Stop-and-Go we threw out a firecracker. When we came back around, the Schute brothers got out of their car outside the Stop-and-Go. 'Did you throw that firecracker?' they said. Then Dean Schute reached in through the window and hit my friend Winks, who was small. So we all got out, and I didn't want to fight, but then Dean threw me down and skinned up my elbow. Then I got mad, so I reached up and grabbed anything I could reach, which turned out to be Dean's mouth. I got a couple of fingers inside his cheek and pulled myself up that way. I commenced beating Dean up, and Winks came out of the car bleeding and said, 'Kick him,' so I drew back and kicked him in the ribs with the point of my toe like I was kicking off, and he went 'Uhhhh.'

"Then I turned around and all I saw was a big fist hitting me right here." In the middle of the face. "That was Laurel. I hit him once and knocked him rolling down a hill and all my friends, four or five little guys, chased him down it and jumped all over him, kicking, hitting, and jumping on his back. That was the fight in front of the Shell station."

The other famous fight Mansfield had had in Kennewick was in front of the Lutheran church. He and some friends waylaid some guys from another town who had jumped his younger brother and broken his glasses—"and he didn't have any money to buy new glasses." This story wound up with the Ranger banging the head of one of the out-of-towners against the side of the Lutheran church, leaving bloody splotches on the wall, and while he was telling it I kept looking over at his daughter, who was I believe seven, who had earlier entertained us with "Faith of Our Fathers" on the clarinet, and who was now reading *The Little House in the Big Wood,* by Laura Ingalls Wilder, behind the couch. I wondered how she was taking her father's story. After Mansfield finished the Lutheran church story she turned around and said, "Tell the one about . . ." There was another fight story she wanted to hear.

Janet said she used to fight too, as a girl. Once she was fighting with her best friend, because the friend had cheated her at a game they were playing, and Janet pulled out a fistful of her hair. "We watched her hair blow away in the wind," Janet said, "and then we took off in opposite directions home."

Well, let's see, a few more domestic scenes. I used to watch the Monday night TV game at Hanneman's apartment on Mount Washington. It was strange watching football under the influence of snuff. Hanneman said he would like to have "my own acreage somewhere, because then you can go out and scream at the top of your lungs and no one can bother you," but he was contenting himself with an efficiency apartment that offered a good view of the city. On his bookshelves there were *Roget's Thesaurus, Mother Earth News Almanac, The Day of the Jackal, Gambler's Digest, Population and the American Future, All About Stocks, The Hundred Yard War, The Greening of America, Future Shock, North Dallas Forty, The Closing Circle, American Government, Introduction to Psychology,* and *Motor Trend Basic Auto Repair Manual.* He had a color photograph of a logging truck driving past a Welcome to Oregon sign.

I helped Wagner and Mullins put together a huge aquarium one night at Mullins's apartment. Wagner had a fish that he said was "an Oscar. Grow to be ten inches long. Swallow a white mouse."

"I like fish that are really aggressive," said Moon. "My roommate and I had one of these, and it swallowed a goldfish in one bite, that was one-third its size. One bite, man."

I never visited Walden's farm in Climax, but he said he would use whatever playoff money he got to buy more cattle or land for it. He raised peanuts down there too. He and two other farmers were surrounded by a lumber company, which was trying to squeeze them out, he said. "They let hunters hunt on their property, adjoining mine—they have to let 'em, really, or the hunters will burn 'em out—and the hunters' dogs run over my land. I shoot 'em if I can. Or catch 'em. One time I caught three dogs and the man said, 'Those dogs cost me $300 each.' I said, 'I'm glad you told me that. It'll cost you $100 each to get 'em back.' Sheriff talked me into giving 'em back, finally. I want to keep 'em out because they disrupt the deer and turkey. It's hard to keep turkeys in an area."

One further note: Once in a bachelor Steeler's apartment I noticed that on the box in which he kept his mail someone had written in an elegantly decorative hand, "If the reach does not exceed the grasp, then what is Heaven for?"

"That's nice," I said. "Who wrote that on there for you?"

"Oh, some cunt," he said.

No, that's not a nice note to end on. It should not be assumed that the Steelers and their families were always comfortably at home with aggression. I asked Janet Mansfield how she felt watching Ray knocking heads with people. "When he's doing the hitting, you don't mind it," she said. "But when it's on that kamikaze thing, when he's on the wedge on the kickoff, and he gets it . . . then you get sick . . . and wish he'd quit football. You almost don't like to talk about it. The wives are quiet during the game. The fans around you handle the talking, and you can't talk back because that just makes it worse. Nancy Russell is like this [tense—wincing as Wagner said you must not do on contact] the whole game."

But that's not a *loose* enough note to end on. One Steeler wife revealed, though not directly to me, that she and her husband made love every day, "whether we're speaking to each other or not." How's that?

□ 14 □

GOOD-BYE, JOHNNY U.

I like to express myself through dance. I like to see people feel what I feel when they watch my movements. My message is mostly love.

　　　　　　　　　—DALLAS COWBOY
　　　　　　　　　CHEERLEADER VONCEIL
　　　　　　　　　BAKER

The San Diego game was not a love story, although the Steelers won it, 38 (their highest point total of the year, about three points shy of 41) to 21. It was Pittsburgh native Johnny Unitas's last game as a starter, most likely, and he was terrible in it.

Unitas played for a small Catholic high school in Mount Washington, St. Justin's, and as a junior quarterback he beat out Dan Rooney for the city all-Catholic team. "I don't know how he did it," said Dan. "I was a senior."

Unitas weighed only around 130 pounds leaving high school, so he went on to play for an obscure college team, at the University of Louisville. He was a star there, and because he was a local boy the Steelers drafted him. But they had Jim Finks, Ted Marchibroda (who was 5–9) and Vic Eaton (whose height or anything else about him very few people recall) at quarterback, and Coach Kiesling got it into his head that Unitas was dumb. Jack Butler, one of the best defensive backs who ever played and now head of BLESTO, the scouting organization, was a Steeler star when Unitas came to camp, in 1955. Butler says Unitas was so quiet and gangly that the veterans called him Clem, short for Clem Cadiddlehopper. But Butler also says you could tell that Unitas was quality. The only recognition he got in camp, however, was when a picture of him showing a football to two Chinese nuns appeared in one of the local papers. Pat and John Rooney, the twins, were kids helping out in camp that summer, and they wrote an impassioned twenty-two-page letter to the Chief, saying that Unitas was the best quarterback in camp but never got a chance to throw to anyone but them, the twins. The Chief left the matter to Kiesling, who cut Unitas. Later Kiesling, the Chief and a couple of the Rooney boys were riding somewhere and they came upon Unitas in his car. The Chief leaned across Kiesling and said to Unitas, "I hope you become the greatest quarterback in football."

155

He did. The Browns were going to pick him up—if they had he would have played with Jim Brown and Chuck Noll—but then Otto Graham decided to stay on for another season and the Browns told Unitas to wait until next year. So he had to play a season with the semipro Bloomfield Rams in Pittsburgh at $6 a game, while working as the monkey-man (the one who sits up top) on a piledriver rig. Then the Colts, with a $2 phone call, got in ahead of the Browns. The Colts' first-string quarterback was hurt the next season, 1956, and Unitas coolly slump-shouldered his way into history, the model of the unflappable, masterful field general and passer.

Musick of the *Press* used to play some kind of kids league ball on the same field, Dean's Field, the Bloomfield Rams performed on. "There was no grass and they put oil down to keep the dust down, and the field was uneven so pools of oil formed, so you'd get tackled and get a mouthful of oil and be throwing up oil for a week. The field was so hard it would rub all the hair off the outside of your legs. I didn't have any hair on the outside of my legs until I was twenty-two years old," Musick said. In the *Press,* anticipating Johnny U's homecoming, Musick wrote, "I hope he drills it straight and coppery through the autumn sunlight, and lofts it soft and sweet like a dove on the wing, and sails it long and true." That probably summed up local sentiment, even to some extent among the Steelers, though they primarily hoped he would lose.

Baldy Regan, the local justice of the peace and businessman who started out as a Steeler ballboy and still works in the Steeler press box, took me and his friend Jim McDonough on a wild trip through the darkest North Side one night hunting up former teammates of Unitas's. Baldy, a chunky bald Harp with a good open face, still operates on the North Side, and gives soul shakes and calls people "Brother." "Both gangs were there in the courtroom and I had my shit on and they knew it, and they had their shit on and I knew it," he says, telling of his efforts to settle a local dispute. He drives, up alleys even, as if he had a siren going when he doesn't. He would bring the car to a sudden stop halfway out into the middle of the street and we would go into bars where it appeared we would be shot before long, looking for a man named Big Head Mitchell, who had played with Unitas on the Bloomfield Rams. "I don't know whether you could fly an airplane off Big Head Mitchell's head or not, but I know you could lift a helicopter off it," Baldy said. "He has a big-ass head." Baldy told stories of the Chief's philanthropy over the last half-century. "I wish I had all the funerals he's paid for," he said. But we never found Big Head Mitchell. We did find Freddy Zangaro, who runs a pizza parlor now and played with Unitas at both Louisville and Bloomfield.

"He always had that stoop," Zangaro said. "In college we were playing Dayton, it's third and long, he's rushed and he switches hands and throws me a pass left-handed. He was always a great player. Kiesling told him the order to cut him came from the front office. The first game we played for the Rams, the coach, Bear Rogers, made John play defensive back because Bear was the quarterback. Bear was 5–6 and weighed 235 pounds, and he was wearing street shoes. Finally we were behind 41–0 and John went in at quarterback. That field had glass, rocks. It was hard like a piece of concrete. He wanted to quit football. His wife was always nagging him to quit." Freddy showed us a program from a '55 Bloomfield game. The second-string quarterback was listed as "J. Unites." The Chief pronounces his name "Unitees" to this day. Freddy and Unitas were still friendly, Freddy said, but when he went to visit Unitas in the Hilton before the Steeler game Unitas said to excuse him, he was tired, and he got in bed.

When I talked to Unitas the day before the game he looked like he was in severe pain. His shoulders seemed not only stooped but drawn in, as though he were holding back from the verge of a shudder. His legs were bad, his arm was bad, his back hurt so that he slept on a waterbed and his face was all cut up from a lick received the week before. At forty he looked like the football equivalent of a beaten-up old fighter; only he wasn't poor, he dressed in a nice blue suit and wingtip shoes among Chargers in wild colors and floppy hats; and he looked like a man none of whose words you would ever question in a huddle. But he had been retired against his will the year before by the Colts and he was playing with a sloppy team in a city where he'd been embittered by early rejection. Gossip among the Steeler wives was that before he'd left his first wife he lived downstairs in his rumpus room where his children brought all his meals. He told me briefly of working as a monkey-man, confirmed the story of the Chief's wishing him immortality from his car nineteen years before (" 'Unitees,' he always called me"), said to tell the Chief hello, and mentioned that when he'd been in camp with the Steelers they threw all the T-shirts in a big pile on the floor and if you got to the pile in time you got a clean one. He said he didn't get back to Pittsburgh much and tomorrow's game was just another game against just another team. He seemed only slightly more pleased to be where he was than the rookie Bernhardt had seemed in camp, but that little bit was deep-set, and enough to keep him going.

Russell told Fats Holmes that he had mentioned him to Unitas on the phone and Unitas had said, "Ernie who?" "That sort of disturbed Holmes," said Russell, who had just made it up. Holmes went to the Hilton and called Unitas to get his autograph, but Unitas wouldn't answer the call so Holmes got Deacon Jones's autograph instead. The day of the game Fats finally reached Unitas, who signed a ball for him: "To Fats Holmes, have a fine year, but take it easy today, Johnny Unitas."

Before the game Gilliam went up to him from behind and said, "Mr. Unitas, I've always wanted to meet you," and Unitas jumped. "I must've scared him to death," Gilliam said. "He turned around, and his face was all cut up. He looked sixty. He ought to get out, man. Not go out like Y. A., with his head all busted open." Y. A. Tittle's head was busted by a Steeler, incidentally. That was the only kind of achievement the Steelers used to be noted for. A famous photograph was taken of Tittle on his knees, looking at the ground, his career over and his bald head laced with blood.

Unitas had looked good to the Steelers in films of the Chargers' game with Cincinnati. But a combination of the Steelers' rush and the ineptitude of the Chargers' offense ("Putting him in there with the Chargers," said someone in the press box, "is like hanging the Mona Lisa in a garage") kept him in the hole, made him throw long passes, which fluttered like a quail on the wing, and he completed only two of nine. Once Hanneman hit him square in his bad back as he threw and Wagner intercepted. Blount intercepted another one. Dockery blocked a punt and Wagner recovered it in the end zone.

Hanneman and Russell hit a runner, who fumbled. Hanneman got the ball and rose to run with it but Unitas pushed him down. "That's embarrassing, when a forty-year-old fossil pushes down a defensive end with one hand," Hanneman said.

"Hanneman and I were lying there with the ball," said Russell. "I looked up and Unitas was standing literally right on top of us, a foot or so away. You would think this would be a very bleak period, after throwing two interceptions and this was the second fumble, but he looked down and winked at me. As if to say, 'These things happen, kid.' And I said to myself, 'Johnny Unitas, you're one cool cucumber.'"

When the score reached 31–0, Steelers, Unitas came out. Hanratty relieved a successful Bradshaw in the second quarter and threw another touchdown bomb to Shanklin, and at the half it was 38–0.

"I pray you, pass with your best violence; / I am afeared you make a wanton of me," said Hamlet to Laertes, reluctant with his poisoned sword, as the poison from the cup moved into the queen. The Steelers had little heart in the second half, which San Diego, with rookie quarterback Dan Fouts, won 21–0. At the half Noll had cautioned the Steelers not to lose their intensity. But he had to be realistic. "I'm not going to tell you the score's 7–0," he said soberly.

"Another one of Noll's statements," said a Steeler after the game, bemusedly. I don't know whether the Steelers had become vain, or whether they were becoming more honest with me, or whether Noll's remarks—which I had been given to understand were so consistently apt—were going downhill. The week before I had watched the Chuck Noll Show with two Steelers. Noll had resisted the notion of this TV show for some time, and he still seemed to be resisting it, on it. Once he made the co-host, local announcer Sam Nover, look foolish by staring blankly when Nover fed him a prearranged line which Noll was supposed to follow with a joke. "Doesn't the guy ever have any fun?" said one of the players, as we watched the show. "But that's what makes him so great," he added hastily, but not too heartily. "That total commitment to winning." Then Noll said on TV, "Pressure is what you feel when you don't know how to do your job," and the player said, "Don't print our reaction to that."

At any rate, after that first half of humiliating Johnny Unitas the Steelers never regained their best point-scoring momentum—all year. Noll used a number of substitutes in the second half and they let the lead dwindle to 17 points by the end of the game. Since the betting line had been the Steelers minus 18, there was considerable groaning and even booing in the stands, which hurt the players' feelings. Gamblers across the land had worse than their feelings hurt. "Thousands of guys were jumping off rooftops," said one in New York.

"I thought you were going to ask me what I told them at halftime," said Noll wryly to the press. He said he had "learned a lesson that you keep learning. This is about the thousandth time I've learned it. Don't let up."

Noll was asked whether he had felt any special compassion for Unitas. "When you're playing," he said, "as far as everybody on the other side . . . you don't really care."

"Is it that cold?"

"It has to be that cold. Or else you aren't successful at this game. I can't believe anybody's press clippings, even my own. It's hard—when you make me feel bad, like when you asked me that question."

"It's too late to salvage what he had," said Greene of Unitas. "You think of pro football, you think of Johnny Unitas. I hate to see the legend be tarnished. I think it is being tarnished."

Holmes said he had told the legend, "You always been my favorite man." Holmes reflected: "Playing football is like loving a beautiful woman. All of a sudden it's over."

In the other dressing room, Byron Yake of the AP asked Unitas, who looked battered and slack-bellied, what part sentiment played in a game like this, in his old home town. "The only thing I know about sentiment," said Unitas, "is that it comes in the dictionary between shit and syphilis." Which wasn't even true. For the rest of the season Unitas stayed on the sidelines, where the new starter, Fouts, would come to him for advice. "It's like going to the dictionary to look up a word," Fouts said.

159

□ 15 □

FANDOM

*I told him, that it [music] affected me to such a degree, as
often to agitate my nerves painfully, producing in my mind
alternate sensations of pathetick dejection, so that I was
ready to shed tears; and of daring resolution, so that I was
inclined to rush into the thickest part of a battle.*
*"Sir (said he,) I should never hear it, if it made me such
a fool."*

—BOSWELL, *LIFE OF
JOHNSON*

As Unitas was discounting sentiment,
Steeler fans on their way out of the stadium were expressing feelings of let-
down, and you couldn't blame them. The first half had been too easy to be
purgative and the second half had been a drag. Except for a 47-yard breakaway
by Preston Pearson and a 21-yard burst by Bradshaw, the Steelers' running
attack had been bottled up all day. I asked one exiting fan why he was
complaining so, when after all the Steelers were still unbeaten. He thought a
minute. "Put it this way," he said. "Last year they were a team of destiny.
Right?"

"Evidently," I said.

"You see any destiny out there today?"

The Steelers' Surrounding Fifty Thousand had been about as powerful as
their Front Four in '72, when by Russell's estimate the fans had made the
difference in two or three Pittsburgh wins. At the beginning of '73 the fans
were ripe to explode and thunder and fling themselves in a frenzy again. After
the Cleveland game Greg Pruitt of the Browns, formerly of Oklahoma U., said
playing in Three Rivers was like playing on either home field in the Nebraska-
Oklahoma game, which is an almost crazed annual expression of partisan
feeling. But when the Steeler offense would misfire early in games, an air of
petulance would take hold in the stands. The response of Burghers to the '72
Miracle had been, (a) the ecstasy of Cossacks in heat, and (b) the widely heard
remark "It's about time."

There were, of course, fans who went to great lengths to show their devotion in '73. Elmer Kiralli Jr.'s marriage to Loretta Augustine at St. Polinas's in Clairton was scheduled for the day of the 49er game in San Francisco, but there were to be television sets in the church and the wedding was to be held during halftime. As '73 went on, however, and the Steelers became somewhat less fantastic than they had seemed the year before, I got the feeling from people around town that they felt they were being rooked out of their rightful Super Bowl.

The prototypical Steeler fan was the mineworker, the millworker, who drank hard and fought hard and was violently resigned to losing out in life. The mythical hero of Pittsburgh was Joe Magarac, whose last act was to fling himself into a molten vat of steel, so that he would be of a piece with the fundament of the industry, or something like that. "Which is about the kind of hero Pittsburgh would have," one Burgher told me sourly. That was the kind of dubiously glorious body sacrifice the Steelers had been performing for thirty-nine years, and it made Steeler fans rugged but irritable.

"We thought the Steelers were assholes," I was told heatedly by a man who had grown up close to the organization. "We looked at the Steelers the same way we looked at Federal Street and the potholes. We figured if you lived in Pittsburgh, that was the kind of team you got." He said my story about the Rooneys, which had admired their low-key humanistic tone, had been saccharine. "The Rooneys were *assholes*," he insisted.

"Why?" I asked.

"Because they *lost* all the time."

Now at last the Steelers had become something, and the fans could blow off steam in some more positive way than by fighting each other—in struggles that flowed in ragged waves through the stands—in order to get close enough to the ramps to throw things at the players as they came on and off the field. In '72 the fans could bellow along with, lend to, ride upon the winds of change. In '73 they continued to surge—holding up games to rage at officials, for instance, until Joe Greene held up his hands to them to stop—and luxuriating in high moments, and showing up faithfully even after the new federal anti-blackout law required the Steelers to let local people watch sold-out home games on TV. When the new stadium was built, there was talk that corporations were getting blocks of the best seats and that "Joe Magarac is getting the shaft." Joe Magarac was still in weighty if not preponderant evidence in Three Rivers, but he was no doubt spread throughout the city's living rooms as well, and when there was no place for him to sit in the stadium it seemed reasonable that he be able to watch on TV. But the ultimate logic of sports television is for all games to be played in underground studios, videotaped, and shown on the tube with all but the highlights edited out and cheertracks added. May sports never become that hermetic. The Rooneys were worried about the effect of Congress's intervention in this matter—the Chief said *he* would probably stay home and watch on TV if he weren't treated like an owner in the Stadium—but the fans kept coming out. Pittsburgh had the second lowest no-show rate in the league, and the fans were ever a forceful presence, except when the game itself was not.

When the players' intensity appeared not to be as great as their own, the fans booed. Their enthusiasm would fade when the offense faded, and once the fans fell back they would hang back, waiting for the Steelers to show them a reason to cheer their best. They were ready to hate the Steelers again if it ever became clear that that would be more satisfying than loving them. Franco's Italian Army was subdued in '73, compared to '72, because Franco was. The crowd never seemed to identify much with Bradshaw. One fan in a bar complained that Bradshaw would never be the quarterback Bobby Layne had been because you never saw Bradshaw around town drinking.

Whenever I was around town drinking with the Steelers, however, fans' reactions seemed captious. One night I was standing with several players in Buddies, a singles' bar where one Steeler every Monday night was given $50 worth of credit (which he didn't have to drink up in one night) to come in and draw customers. A man who was about 5–6 slid by the players on his way to the men's room, looked up at their faces and said, "Huh. I thought you guys were supermen."

"Hoo hoo ho ho har. Fucker," said one of the players after the man got out of hearing, but the rest of them just shook their heads. My strongest impression of the interaction I saw between players and fans was that neither side knew what to make of the other. When Sam Davis was asked "Who are you?" on TV he said, "I'm a man. I want people to respect me as a man first and as a football player second." The players often said they wanted to be thought of as people, which was perhaps asking a great deal considering how unlikely it was for a given fan to know them as people and how readily the players accepted the perquisites of being regarded as superhuman. The fans tended either to stare at them openmouthed and become absurdly fluttery or to regard them as not superhuman *enough.* Or they would taunt the players for the pleasure of taunting someone whom they, the fans, had cracked up to be superhuman.

In bars drunks would yell at Steelers, "Why don't you guys go home?" as though the players were abusing a sacred trust by relaxing rather less nearly to the point of dissolution than their accusers were. After a losing game a cop stopped a Steeler who was speeding with liquor on his breath and said, "You guys are the shits."

The Steeler, in a difficult position, said yes, he guessed they were.

"It pisses me off to watch the way you guys play," said the cop.

The Steeler asked him how he would like to see the next game.

"How about two seats on the fifty?" the cop said.

Once at an after-hour place called the Brookline Young Men's Club, after a loss, a neighbor of the Van Dykes who ran a bar stopped Frosene on her way to the ladies' room and said, "When is your husband going to learn how to block?"

"When are you going to learn how to run a bar?" she replied.

Outright antagonism aside, there was an unreality about the way the Steelers' audience presented itself on a personal level that made player–fan relations a questionable proposition. Anyone who read and took to heart the letters that came in from fans would feel like a cross between Santa Claus, the Enemy of the People and Miss Lonelyhearts:

Dear Steelers,
I really like to whatch you're team play. Could you send me an atuagraphed picture of Terry Bradshaw and Franco Harris? Please do try to get it sighned? I think you have the greates team. I will be sending to you again to get things sighned. Could you please read this on TV.

Dear Franco Harris,
. . . I am part of Franco's Italian Army, and the biggest fan of your's. I know alot of kids probably say this but I don't think they like you enough to ask you write back like penpals sort of.
I read a article who did this with Rusty Staub, but I would rather do it with my Idle in Football which I hope to be in as a running back. You will be hearing from me again in about a month.

Dear Steelers,
I am a boy of 12 years of age and I love how good you all play. Please send all information and stickers.

Dear Steelers,
For Christmas I got a little Steeler man, a Steeler tablet, a Steeler pencil sharpener, a pennant, a Steeler towel, two Steeler shirts, a Steeler jacket and cap, and a Steeler football suit. Will you please send me some Steeler things?

Coach Chuck Noll,
I am turning my bedroom into a Pro Hall of Fame and I was wondering if you would send me a team Picture and maybe some other type of Nic-Naks. It would be greatly appreciated. If you have a spare Moment say hello to John (Frenchy) Fuqua AND FRANCO HARRIS.

Dear Steelers,
I hope you make it to the supper bowl, you are my favorite team and would you please send me a picture of any buddy on your team or a sticker. Tell Terry Bradshaw not to throw any more sideline passes, they get intercepted too easy. Your team are so good!

Dear Mr. Harris,
    . . . I hope nothing happens to you and Terry, because if you go to the hospital, I will not know which one you're in. So if you go to the hospital, would you write me a letter and tell me what hospital and when you are getting out so I won't send a letter to the wrong hospital. My brother likes the Jets and he said that Joe Nameth will send him his picture before you get yours here first but if you do I will also get $2.00 from my mother in this bet. Please hurry!

Dear Sirs,
    I have liked you ever since I was 5 years old! Please send me pictures of "Terri Hanratty" or any guys. Hurry!

Dear Joe Green, Franco Harris, Terry Bradshaw, Ron Shanklin, Terry Hanratty, L. C. Greenwood, Dwight White, Ray Mansfield, Frenchy Fuqua, Rocky Bligher, Barry Perreson, Glen Edwards, Mel Blount, I like you all equal. Could I have a small picture of all of you and one picture of the whole team. P.S. Could Franco Harris and Terri Bradshaw come to my house some day. Maybe on Saturday or Sunday. Please answer this letter to tell me when.

Dear Mr. Bradshaw:
    My husband and I watch you on TV, and we think you are degenerate . . .

Dear Mr. Gilliam:
    You black mother-fucker . . .

This last letter was signed by a woman, with a return address. She suggested that Gilliam go back to Africa. He wrote back suggesting what she could do.
    Occasionally players got mimeographed letters saying, "Dear _____, You are my favorite player, would you please send an autographed picture." Once a bunch of kids came over to Van Dyke's house for autographs and, just for variety, he signed one "Terry Bradshaw." "Hey!" the kid said, "Terry Bradshaw! Can you get me Franco Harris?" So Van Dyke signed "Franco Harris." "Hey!" the kid said to the others. "I got Franco Harris!" So Van Dyke signed various teammates' names for the other kids.
    To tell the truth I began to wonder whether watching football was a Jagov thing to do. The tones that arose from the fans, whether of adulation or of denigration, suggested sheer, indiscriminate escape. And critics of the game, after all, have been known to argue that watching it was no more than a cheap way to experience violence and dash, as watching dirty movies is a cheap way to experience sex, without personal risk. Was it for this that the Steelers sacrificed their bodies? Could football's redeeming social value be simply that if people couldn't watch Mike Wagner nail ball carriers they would go home and nail their wives or some stranger?

Fortunately I was saved from such cynicism, and from guilt about the pleasure I myself took from watching the game, by a letter, which came in response to an appeal for thoughts on the Steelers that I made on Myron Cope's show. This letter was from one Opal Lister of Wheeling, West Virginia. Pittsburgh is a near neighbor of West Virginia, which is one of the largely favorable ways in which it differs from Philadelphia. It is a lot countrier than Philadelphia. But Ms. Lister's letter did not smack of Appalachia. She wrote, "If you're looking for ideas, here is one about football which I wrote down in a notebook I keep. I am sorry, I did not write down who said it, but it expressed my feeling about the way Franco Harris runs with the ball. Here it is:

" 'Broken-field running is as fine, rich and witty an enactment of the solving of a maze as is found in our culture.' "

Yes!

Kick your feet up, take a snort, and lift your voice in praise
Of one of our best enactments of the solving of a maze.

I didn't go to graduate school for nothing. I was moved by Ms. Lister's quote to block out a defense of football on aesthetic grounds. (Such as one might make of a given dirty movie.)

Football is like improvisational theater. The running back trying to make it to and through the hole, a maze-door in space and time which exists for a moment and must be seized, not just discovered. A break-through; football is a conflict between stasis and the urge to break through. The blocker–runner combination or the passer–receiver combination breaking through the defensive structure; or the rusher breaking through the offensive structure. This is such a fundamental theme and football deals with it so repeatedly that its seriousness as an experiment in form and spirit is easy to overlook.

Football is like sculpture. What you can get out of watching a Franco Harris run surely resembles what you can get out of looking at a Brancusi bird; the tensions and the flow, the lines.

Football is like music. What do we want from football? Resonance, zing, dips and leaps, percussion, oomph, syncopation, overtones, unexpected bridges and hazardous connections.

Football is like poetry. Ordinary speech, said Robert Frost, is "only lovely when thrown and drawn and displayed," like the steps of a running back, "across spaces of the footed line."

A fan should not take too much to heart football coaches' or players' philosophies of life. Coaches' philosophies are designed to make people play a game intensely. Once players' years of playing the game are over they tend to be, at least for a while, at a loss about life. Generally speaking, people should no more emulate a great football player's life in any explicit way—even to the point of taking his advice on drugs or breakfast cereal—than they should emulate the lives of Edith Piaf or Thoreau. But the game itself when played intensely does make edifying statements about life.

See the ball carrier finding point after point in space and time where he will not be converged upon. Watch him turn the corner. Who cannot profit from a kinesthetic illustration of the concept "turning the corner"? The great thing about turning a corner in football, as in life, is that if you don't hurry, or if you hurry too much, there won't *be* a corner.

Okay, he has turned the corner; not been contained. Or he cuts through a hole: a narrow momentary door in a wall of battery. Then he intuits on the go a course negotiating the vectors of several different tacklers and several different blockers, always bearing in mind the imperative to advance downfield. A *bildungsroman*.

Then there is the spectacle of a quarterback and his receiver together finding and splitting "the seam of the zone"—actually the seam between zones, the place where defenders' effective responsibilities in space and time do not quite mesh. The very idea of a seam between individually patrolled zones implies a highly refined formal arrangement of persons; and it is an idea, moreover, which is not at all without application beyond football. Originality in anything is primarily a matter of finding the seams between zones. The zones were closing in on French painting in the 1890s, and then the Fauves found a seam. Some day some creative mind will similarly explode the zone defense as we know it, and there will be uproar and a new tradition.

Consider the action of defensive backs. They must stay tight enough in on the receiver to hit him if the pass is a quick one right into his arms or to cut in front of him if the ball is thrown short, but also loose enough off of him—"keeping a cushion" is what they call it—to prevent him from bursting suddenly beyond to catch a pass long. That is the defense's problem generally: rush the passer fiercely but with a caution ("a certain amount of abandon" is what I once heard a coach prescribe). After Frank Lewis caught a pass on the sideline against San Francisco, the cornerback's respect for Lewis's volatility was so great that he hung back for what seemed like half a minute waiting for Frank to commit himself, as Frank tauntingly juked back and forth. "He's not about to come up on Frank," a Steeler chortled. Again I am moved to reflect—and I think quite high-mindedly enough—on what it takes to be happy in life with, say, a woman.

You can be too anthropomorphic about football. Big time players are resistant and flexible enough, and padded enough, and high-keyed and reckless enough, physically momentous enough, *quick* enough, to become a medium that is nearly as different from flesh and blood as melody or stone. What the players as people have to do—including sacrifice their bodies—is demanded by the medium. They are in part artists, in part instruments, in part elements of the art object itself—football is hard on them in the way poetry is hard on poets, Beethoven I should think was hard on pianos, and *The Last Year at Marienbad* is hard on itself.

Football, as coaches and players realize, is less a matter of characters rising up and smiting each other on a personal level than it is a matter of vectors. Getting the right angle; bearing in mind whether the tight end releases—that is, disengages himself from the linebacker—to the inside or the outside. Maintaining, in the case of a defensive back, an "inside technique"—which is to say, always keeping himself between the potential receiver and the sideline. Of course the more you learn about, and are gifted at moving in terms of, these lines of force, the more your "personality" as a player emerges. But that personality may well be nothing like the player's social personality; Fran Tarkenton plays kinky and lives straight. Personality only becomes important among teammates; and even there it is mostly a secondary matter. The most effective quarterbacks currently—Griese, Staubach, Tarkenton—don't project much personality at all (Tarkenton does playing, but not talking) other than coolness. Both Bradshaw and Hanratty are interesting, in different ways, to talk to personally, but it could be said that each is most effective as a quarterback when his teammates in the huddle can *forget* about his personality, and everyone else's. That is to say, Bradshaw is best when his great natural gifts take over, making any kind of raw, lightning progress up the field seem possible. Hanratty's strength is best explained by the teammate who makes this comparison: "Bradshaw is liable to say '19 Power Right, uh, Left, uh Time Out.' Hanratty comes in and says, 'Okay boys, we're going downtown with this one.' And you know you are. So you go out and do your job, you don't worry about, 'Well I better not fake too hard on this because the tight end's liable not to block.' "

That last paragraph is only ideally true. One of the engaging things about the Steelers, one of the reasons they did things unpredictably on the field, was that individual personalities did emerge on the field. The idiosyncrasies of the Front Four, of the running backs, of the quarterbacks, had great effects on the outcome of the season. But football games tend to be written about too much as moral dramas, with the implication that the best people win. In that sense the games make very crude drama indeed, because they boil down to root hog or die, to the too-simple concept of "victory" and to people trying to hurt each other in order to gain selfish ends. However, if you think of the players not as people trying to bowl each other over but as symbols of people trying to close with each other, to stay in touch with each other, to figure out where each other is coming from, then football is full of subtle and telling points. (Though the game may be a scoreless tie.)

But the football public, me included, doesn't want ballet. It wants more in the way of characterization. It wants heroes and villains. It wants to say not only, "Nice pattern unfolding there," or "Nice move," but also, "Look at old Andy Russell, that scoundrel, he'll always think of something." This is an aspect of the game that coaches like to play down or eliminate. Often these days you hear from fans the criticism that pro football is overcoached. I think this is true, and that the NFL would do itself a favor by cutting down on the number of coaches a team can have, or requiring that each coach spend a year traveling with a circus—or by trying to ban the use of films, thereby making the game less of a science and more of an art. Taking still photographs of your opponents' formation is for that reason illegal now, and that rule is certainly not easy to enforce. (The Steelers claimed that Oakland had a man taking Polaroid snaps of their defenses during the first half of the first Raider–Steeler game.) The Steelers made such exhaustive use of films that by the time the coaches were through with them, as Mac the film man put it, "They look like they had them for lunch." The more thoroughly coaches study films and refine abstract strategies the more structured the game becomes, and the harder it becomes for quirky individual stars to emerge.

It could be that their reliance on films makes coaches lose track of the game as a form of live entertainment. After the films were analyzed and the resultant data programmed into the players, "The hay is in the barn," Noll said, and until he saw the films after the game he couldn't say for sure what had happened in it. Noll denounced ABC-TV's Monday night commentators for complaining that some of the games they were broadcasting were dull. The fashionable notion that pro football was becoming boring was "not the fault of the man in the street," Noll said. "It's the fault of the people programming him. These guys on Monday nights have done a lot to hurt the game. I watched the San Francisco–Green Bay game on television and I believed the commentators; I believed it was a bad game. Then when we got the films of it and broke them down I saw it was a good, hard-hitting game. Well executed."

But I watched that game too and thought it was dull, and although the ABC team got on my nerves for placing so much emphasis on itself, I resist the notion that they programmed me. I think that game *looked* dull, even if it wasn't. Watching the game carefully, systematically, with Noll as an expert commentator, would no doubt have been interesting to the serious fan. But Noll was not about to perform such a public service, even assuming that many fans were serious enough to demand it. Football is after all a popular diversion. What is the point of a popular diversion that only becomes interesting when the coaches study the films?

I must say that watching the films was edifying too from an inexpert perspective. I could not watch the Steelers' films, run backward and forward (*whurrr,* whurrr; *whurrr,* whurrr; a sound rather like that of cicadas) over and over again, blockers gaining leverage or failing to, without thinking of human relations.

Love may be giving, but you have to give tough. Marriage or an affair or raising children or even getting to know people is a problem of leverage— advancing so much, yielding so much, holding certain positions with various degrees of firmness, sympathizing so much, asserting so much. You ought to be liberal with folks but you must also be "strong at the point." (To use a scouting term. "Point" is short for "point of attack," which is the initial meeting of offensive and defensive linemen.) I would not want, however, to study human relations as methodically as the coaches studied blocking.

168

The trouble with football aesthetically is that the creative situation brings two different composers together in an attempt to whip each other's ass in a collaborative symphony. They don't care what kind of symphony it turns out to be, just who wins it. "Winning is the ethic of football," says Miami's Don Shula, the NFL's reigning coach. "You start with having to win, and you work back."

As far as that goes he is right, just as the writing teacher was right who told A. B. Guthrie that "credibility is the morality of fiction." Desire is the morality of sexual love, verbal coherence the morality of poetry. It doesn't matter how fine the sentiments or graceful the moves involved in fiction if the reader isn't taken in by it. Or in courtship if no one is aroused. It doesn't count. Oakland's Daryl Lamonica throws beautiful bombs but Oakland's Ken Stabler wins games. It is magnificent, but is it war?

But fiction must not *only* be credible. It needs a little magnificence. And art is not war, nor war art. If James Agee and Theodore White had ever tried to out-journalize each other head-to-head, White on grounds of soundness and resolution might well have won; but Agee is better because he takes more chances and is more surprising.

Football would be silly without a score, like pole vaulting without a crossbar, but football is also silly when it begins to look like peristalsis. Everybody knows that there is such a thing as a sensuously beautiful pass or run, and that such a thing is not what coaches are interested in. The coaches who hold sway in pro football believe, with empirical justice, that conservative football is winning football; therefore rather than take risks and make bold strokes, as even a conservative artist must do, coaches take the most reliable route between two points. There is something admirable in the idea of football played to win rather than to entertain (as there is, conversely, in a crusty old movie director's insistence that he is only interested in entertainment, not messages), but if a director is as singleminded as a football coach his movie will be either (a) if he is trying to come up with something moral, a tract, or (b) if he is trying to come up with something popular, trash. An individual player may do something crazy and, like a movie director, be considered brilliant (by me, at least), even if what he does doesn't turn out to make perfect strategic sense. But a coach, according to all accepted standards, must win in order to have coached well.

Would it be possible for some interesting movie director, say Robert Altman, to get hold of the Pro Bowl squads sometime and make a movie football game organized not as a battle but as a dance, with dialogue, in which defenders were matched up with attackers complementarily, so that there emerged not a sense of which players were best but of what great celebrations of the uses of the body and mind they could push each other to?

Probably not. However the game can be made livelier. I suggest the following four new rules:

1. Make the center eligible for a forward pass. This would give zone defenses

something else to worry about and would return a touch of amateurism to the game. I remember back in my youth how sometimes the center would be eligible and a lot of dramatic first downs, touchdowns even, were made that way, and the center himself, who figured not to be the flashiest player on the field, loved it. In baseball you have such things happening as Al Weis hitting a home run in the World Series; you don't have a comparably incongruous offensive possibility in football. Making the center eligible would also enable more white people to catch passes in the NFL. (All centers are white.) I like to see racial stereotypes broken up; I want to see more black people throwing passes and more white people catching them. It would be interesting to see how a center would spike the ball. Maybe between his legs.

2. If rule (1) would bring more amateurism into the game, rule (2) would mitigate that element of amateurism—the wrong kind, duller rather than sprightlier than professionalism—which already exists. As Alex Karras with his "I'm gon' to keek a touchdown" routine was perhaps the first to exclaim, placekickers' power over the score is out of proportion to their substance as players. So what you do is, you require a man, before he is eligible to kick a field goal, to have participated in at least one play from scrimmage per quarter elapsed. In other words, he can't try a field goal in the first quarter unless he's been in on one nonkicking play, in the second unless he's been in on two, and so forth. The Steelers' Gerela, who played as a defensive back in college and made several tackles on kickoffs during '73, could certainly handle this, and so could Minnesota's Fred Cox and Oakland's George Blanda. And the ones who couldn't handle it would be worth watching: after all, the most notable play, the one spark of humanity, in the last two Super Bowls was Garo Yepremian's pass for the Dolphins, intercepted by the Redskins some eighteen inches from his hand, in 1973. If you expect your opponent to sneak their kicker in at, say, wide receiver or safety, you could have a special defensive or offensive move ready to take advantage of that weak spot. Add another variable to the game.

3. The passer, on the other hand, I would make more of a specialist. As it is he is a sitting duck. It is just dumb that Joe Namath has been out of football for so much of his football career. Put a flag in the quarterback's belt and make pulling the flag out the only way to get him down unless he reaches the line of scrimmage, in which case he is running and fair game. Rushers could grab the quarterback and wrestle with him up to a certain point in attempting to get at his flag, but any contact reasonably sufficient to knock him down would constitute roughing the passer (as would, say, twisting his arm until he said "Okay! You can pull out my flag!"). A quarterback who fell down unnecessarily on being nudged, like a basketball defender trying to get a charging foul called, would be penalized for intentionally grounding himself. The old "I was in the act of throwing" argument would be brought in from sandlot games of touch, but then it already exists, in a different form, with respect to roughing the passer calls. With this rule the quarterback and his receivers would have

somewhat more time to work against the zone, and since quarterbacks' careers would be less likely to be cut short early, the old, seasoned, active quarterback—one of the most glamorous figures in the game—would become more prevalent. Of course he might not be so glamorous if, because of this rule, the general public came to think of him as a candyass. The general public's expectations may be too brave for this rule.

4. It is hard to get any real personal impression of football players from the stands. Everybody has his head encased in plastic. But there are a number of players who can make personal appearances that are markedly more interesting than, say, Curt Gowdy's or the average marching band's. Require one member of the forty-man squad to come out during halftime and do an act for two minutes. He could make a speech, tell a story, sing, dance, tumble, or do his imitation of a chicken (I say that because Rocky Bleier does an imitation of a chicken that is amazing, and yet he still looks like a football player doing it). And lest he just go through the motions, *give the team whose representative is more entertaining or enlightening one point on the game score.* Thus is color rewarded, and the rookie show in camp takes on a new significance. The problem arises, who will be the judges. You can't put an applause meter on the fans because they would go for their team's boy. You can't put it to a press box vote for the same reason. Political or entertainment-figure judges would be corruptible. The referees would seem logical choices, except that their taste would conform to the league's and therefore a player might have to read a tribute to Vince Lombardi or fly over the field in a fighter jet, or both, to be sure of making his point. After all, maybe the press would be the best judges, or at least would appreciate an imitation of a chicken most; and perhaps if an equal number of reporters from each city voted, and signed their votes, the thing could be kept honest. Maybe the two players could do their acts and then fight for the point. Somehow or another there must be a way that the concept of this rule can be refined into feasibility. If the Rules Committee could see Rocky Bleier's imitation of a chicken, they would appreciate the sense of urgency I bring to this proposal.

But these reflections have led us away from the question of *Pittsburgh* fandom. Go back to contact. "The tradition here was always Jock Sutherland rock 'em sock 'em coal miner football," said Artie Rooney. "In the old days Paul Brown beat us by throwing the ball—killed us. Our players went up to the Browns after the game and said, 'Why don't you join the Celtics?' " The Browns had won, in other words, but they hadn't been playing *football.* "That was a lot of b.s. But football is controlled violence, and the people around here were close to violence."

"Football was something you tried to play to get out of the mill," said Dan Rooney. And you figured the way to get out of a steel mill was to blast your way out. Dan recalled going to speak to fans in some millworkers' bar. "Somebody would ask a tough question, and before I'd get a chance to answer, somebody else would yell, 'What do you want to ask a question like that for?' and there'd be a fight." Afterwards he would be given a jar of pasta fazool as an honorarium. He sounded nostalgic.

"There's a new breed of fan now," said Artie. "They're one step beyond the real old violence. But only one generation beyond it." He said if you spoke to the Mount Lebanon Jaycees, pretty soon the questions and the tone of the rooms would get rowdy enough that you would think, they're getting back to what they came from.

If I wanted to get a feel for old-fashioned Steeler fans, suggested the Rooneys, I ought to go out to Chiodo Tavern in Homestead, the area where the historic Homestead Strike raged in 1892—strikebreakers were poisoned, strikers fought off barges full of Pinkertons and then let them land and ran them through a vicious gauntlet of kicks and blows, and authorities hung a man up by his thumbs for applauding the attempted assassination of the president of Carnegie Steel. Things were considerably quieter in Homestead now, but the mills were still turning out steel and Steeler fans there, and they drank at Chiodo's. "We were looking down from our box one time and Joe Chiodo had a guy around the neck, defending the Rooneys," Dan said.

"Well," Joe told me in his place, "a couple of boys were calling the Rooneys everything but white people, and I got between 'em. I took an elbow in the mouth. I saw the Rooney family watching from up above. I was defending their honor. I could tell they were ready to help me out."

"He was wrong there," Dan said later. "We were ready to call a cop, though."

Joe took a flashlight and shone it on each of a rich assortment of mementos over the bar: helmets and jerseys from the past; a pheasant ("Somebody's father shot that"); a pennant from Lake Chargoggagogmanchauggagogg-chaubunuagungamaug. On the side of the phone booth was a mounted deer's head.

Joe was the organizer of a group of about forty fans who paid a few bucks a week all year for a season ticket each and a trip or two to road games. They would go to all the home games in a bus from the Tavern, Joe wearing a Steeler cape and the bus sometimes hung with a Franco's Italian Army banner, and they were, as Dan Rooney put it, "great fans. Nobody wants to sit next to them, though," because they tended to get so demonstrative.

Well, let me say that I had a good time in Chiodo's Tavern. I sat there until 6 A.M. drinking the shots and beers that people kept buying me, and eating olives, cheese, green peppers and kielbasy. I think I had thirty-two of each.

"This year we took the boys to Cincinnati," Chiodo said. "For $65 look what they got: a bus ride there and back, a ticket to the game, all the refreshments they could drink, hotel room Saturday night, sandwiches, pop, we had a mass on Saturday night—I'm not talking religion now, but my brother that's a priest came in—and then the boys can go out and clown around.

"My mother passed away in June. This man Art Rooney, a millionaire, had time to come pay his respects to my mother. I had neighbors across the street who didn't come. I'm not talking religion now, but he sent mass cards—six mass cards.

"When the Steelers did nothing, if they won one game they had the fans. Now it seems like they should win every game."

There was a lady in Chiodo's who said, "My son is Joseph Pesolyar. Write that down. He says, 'Bradshaw is a stinker.' " She repeated that several times. I would have liked to hear from Opal Lister along about then.

Maybe I should have talked with the fan club which advertised itself in the Three Rivers stands as "Heads for Ham."

□ **16** □

THE BENGALS, THE JETS AND THE BENGALS

(In Which Franco Disappears, Returns and Runs Like a Saw, and the Fans Disgrace Themselves, and Han the Man Takes Charge, in Pain, and the Steelers Nearly Have to Play Without a Quarterback, "Like in Vietnam.")

You can bite steel but it won't break.
It'll just get spit on it.

—KIRVEN BLOUNT

After all that grumbling about conservative football let me say that the Steelers didn't play it. The offensive was supposed to, but it managed to be wayward. After the San Diego game I asked Ham how come his friend Wagner had scored before he had in '73. "I've given up that aspect of the game," said Ham airily. In Cincinnati it appeared that the Steeler offense had too.

Most teams are right-handed but the Steelers were left-handed. That is, teams generally line up with their tight end to the right, a strong-right formation, and run more often to that side. The Steelers usually lined up strong right, too, but they ran more often to their weak side, the left. Paul Brown's Bengals stacked up the 5 and 7 holes, the ones on the left, and the Cincinnati rush wouldn't give Bradshaw time to pass—he was sacked four times—and the offense never got anything going. The only time they scored was on a 67-yard pass from Bradshaw that happened to be tipped into Shanklin's hands by a defender. And the Steeler defense—the liberating force—never took the ball away from the Bengals. Final score, 19–7, Cincinnati.

The Bengals had a 245-pound rookie running back from Bethune Cookman,

174

a school in Florida which no one would have thought weighed 245 pounds itself, and he gained 112 yards against the Steelers. His name was Charles "Boobie" Clark, and Paul Brown said of him, "He's not very fancy, but he's a real armful." Whether Brown was punning on "handful," I don't know. "Bengals Impressed by Big Boobie," said a Cincinnati headline. "It appeared to me," said Andy Russell, who had to leave the game early with a severe charleyhorse (which might have been a good alternative nickname for Clark— "Severe Charley Horse"), "that Clark was getting a small hole and hitting it with a great deal of force, and falling forward."

And the Steelers were falling back. Noll's mouth after the game, as Musick put it in the *Press,* was "tightened to a bloodless scratch." "What the hell is there to say?" Noll said. "They beat our ass pretty bad. It's a quick drop from the penthouse to the shithouse."

"You don't mind if we use 'outhouse' do you?" asked a reporter.

"Use whatever you want," said Noll.

"He's writing a book," someone said of me. "He's liable to use 'shithouse.' " Noll gave me a level look.

"Your old teacher's done it to you twice in a row here," a Cincinnati writer said to Noll, in reference to Brown. There was no response from Noll.

"What happens to you guys here?" (The Steelers always seemed to lose in Cincinnati, as in Cleveland.)

"Nothing," said Noll. But in his weekly press luncheon back in Pittsburgh the next day he said, "Anytime you lose the battle of the hitting—anybody who hasn't played in a game won't understand. When you're the receiver and not the hitter, anything is possible against you. And all things *are* possible."

"There's a tendency for a team to get fat," said Noll. "Not physically fat, but emotionally fat."

"We were overflowing with confidence," Greene said. "Maybe we floated. Maybe this will bring us back to reality." Greene's wife had just had a baby girl, Joquel, before the game. "It's funny," Greene said. "I wanted a girl. It seems like I always get what I want. That's sort of scary."

"The Great God Tar-Tan," said Mansfield—invoking the resident turf divinity back home, whom Mansfield salaamed to at Three Rivers, who would not let them lose at home—"just rose up and heaved."

The biggest mystery of this game was that Noll didn't use Franco Harris at all. "Where's Franco?" people kept saying in the press box.

"There is one man who determines when and how much I play," said Franco. "That man, of course, is Chuck Noll. Today, he felt I wasn't ready— or at least, in good enough physical condition—to help the team, and I simply won't question his judgment."

"All I know is my trainer said he had a sore knee," said Noll. "Franco being in there wouldn't've made any difference today. It takes a whole team."

There was talk around town that Franco had a grave injury that the Steelers were hiding, though why they would do that was unclear. At the press luncheon Noll was peppered with questions about Franco. Noll had been saying in previous weeks that he was working Franco gradually back into the offense, because his hurting leg had set him back in training camp preparation. How was he ever going to reach form with no game work at all? "He was best last year when he was carrying the ball twenty times a game," Pat Livingston of the *Press* pointed out during the luncheon.

"You may be right, Pat," said Noll. His tone suggested that a scribe *may* be right about most anything, which doesn't mean that it ever matters whether he is or not.

"Look," said Noll finally. "There's nobody who wants Franco in the game, at the top of his game, more than me. Let's get that straight. There's nothing sinister going on." Then he loosened things up by saying, "I know everybody thinks, if I put Franco in, we'll have a miracle happen."

One Steeler, after pointing out Noll's opposition to the concept of stardom (he disapproved of all-star teams, for example), had a theory for why Noll didn't get Franco into the game. "I think he forgot about him," he said.

Against the Jets in Three Rivers he remembered him. Franco had declined to say much about his knee, but teammates said it was hurting him bad. "He's concerned about his legs, he's protecting them," said Noll. "He's worrying about his legs, about getting hit on them." A running back's knee is a system of gristle as profound to him as whatever it is in an artist's imagination that enables *him* to move in distinctive ways and to break into places where other people aren't. A running back can hardly help feeling dread when his knee feels wrong. But the cardinal sin of contact and reaction is thinking and holding back. Maybe Noll, by leaving him out of the Bengal game, was trying to make Franco feel desperate to run hard against the Jets.

It was a nice bizarre Steeler game, setting the trend for the rest of the year. The Steelers took the opening kickoff and drove nicely, but then Bradshaw threw two incompletions and Gerela's field goal attempt was blocked. The defense wouldn't let the Jets get anywhere. Third-string quarterback Bill Demory was playing because Joe Namath and his backup Al Woodall were both hurt. Steeler wives watched Namath on the sidelines (wearing, as I recall, a powder blue suit and crutches) and sighed at his looks. (The Steeler wives also sighed at Franco's looks.) But then the Jets recovered a Preston Pearson fumble and managed to drive 41 yards, thanks to *48* yards in Steeler penalties, for a touchdown. In other words, the Jets had scored on a drive in which their total offense was—7 yards.

Then Franco entered the game for the first time. Four straight plays he carried the ball, for 15 yards; the scoreboard flashed "LET'S GO FRANCO." The crowd didn't pick up the chant. The crowd was going to wait and see. Harris, Bradshaw and Fuqua, among them, advanced on the ground to the Jets' 14 before Bradshaw was sacked on third down. Gerela kicked a field goal.

On the next drive Steve Davis went 27 yards on a fake punt and Gerela kicked another field goal.

On the next drive Bradshaw threw an interception, with Shanklin wide open, and Demory followed with a touchdown pass. Steelers down, 6–14.

Then, with 35 seconds left in the half, the Steelers showed some magic. Harris went around left end for 8 yards, and then on second down he flashed what he could do uniquely. He took a pass in the right flat, all the way over by the right sideline, and cut back toward the other side. As tackler after tackler slanted into him he moved, fending them off, in a series of slues— looking for a gap to cut up through, never finding it, but always advancing somewhat on each hooked swoop, moving downfield gradually, gradually bevelly, bevelly, rhythmically, like a handsaw *ooo*-fah, *ooo*-fah, *ooo*-fah into hard wood—all the way across the field diagonally and out of bounds on the other side, to stop the clock. A 15-second 13-yard gain with a serrated edge. It was the best show of determined obliquity I ever saw. If there is any knee in the world that I hope is sound in '74, for the sake of what it can afford the observer, it is Franco Harris's.

Then P. B. Booker growled down the right sideline, pulled in a long pass, looked up at the clock and stepped out of bounds in front of a tackler with 7 seconds left. And Gerela kicked a 36-yard field goal.

Still the Steelers trailed 14–9 at the half. On their first possession in the second half the Steelers couldn't move. So Rowser intercepted to give them the ball back. And Bradshaw, passing to Barry Pearson and Shanklin, moved the ball to the Jets' 6. But once again the offense had to settle for a field goal. The crowd was restive, peeved. The Steelers were still trailing, at home, against a weak team using its third-string quarterback.

So the next time Pittsburgh got the ball, Noll sent in Hanratty, who had been wearing a baseball cap on the sidelines. A great cheer went up from the crowd. Hanratty went to what was becoming his trademark: downtown, a long pass to Shanklin, on the first play. It took a nice extra effort by the cornerback to break it up. The Steelers had to punt, but on the next drive they moved like the good Lord meant an offense to move. Harris swept left for 6 and burst off left tackle for 19, Fuqua went right for 5, Harris cut over left guard for 5 more, and then Hanratty went to his other trademark: the double-pump. The Steelers had been running a lot of pass plays on which the quarterback sets up quickly and throws as soon as he plants his foot, to a receiver cutting quickly out. Hanratty planted his foot and pumped the ball instead of throwing it, freezing cornerback Delles Howell, who had moved to cover the quick-out, and then Hanratty lofted the ball to Shanklin standing in the end zone alone. It was one of those rare football plays in which the fan has a clear leisurely view of the strategy unfolding, of a quarterback thinking, of a defender fooled. That was what I liked about both Hanratty and Harris: You could "read" over their shoulder. Now the Steelers were ahead.

177

And the defense took over for the rest of the game. As they had failed to do in Cincinnati, they had stopped the run and were forcing Demory to pass. Edwards intercepted. Demory dropped back, dropped the ball, picked it up, scrambled wildly for a long time, and the eager Steeler deep men came in on him, leaving Jerome Barkum open. But J. T. Thomas leapt high to break up what looked like a sure touchdown pass. Wagner intercepted a pass and ran the ball back to the Bengal 2. Harris took it in from there. Final score 26–14.

"My prayers work a little better on these Irish Catholics than they do on Southern Baptists," said Father Duggan, the Irish mascot, with regard to Hanratty and Bradshaw.

"The ball was slipping out of Bradshaw's hand," explained Noll, "so we went to the bullpen. They pay off on doing the job, not thinking you can do it. When you ask somebody and he says, 'I think I can get it in there,' . . . It has nothing to do with winning a job. Terry's our starting quarterback still, and we think we have adequate relief in Hanratty." Noll blamed the closeness of the game on Musick's pregame story which had low-rated the Jets. Of Franco he said, "He wasn't protecting himself today."

Bradshaw said the ball had stopped slipping out of hand (both he and Hanratty said the balls often seemed slippery that year); that wasn't why he was pulled. "I felt like I was coming. But he gave up on me. That hurts. But he's on the sidelines, he's getting totally pissed off. I tell you that Hanratty is dynamic, isn't he?" Then Bradshaw took a pull from his can of Fresca and discovered that someone had put out a cigarette in it. It was that kind of a day for him.

"Even writers have bad days," said Noll the next day at luncheon. "And you can't replace them."

"Writers don't have bad days," said Cope. "They have bad mornings."

I found out that besides running for 102 yards during the game Franco had saved the Steelers from a penalty. Clack had thrown a "collapse block" on a Jet defender. A "collapse block" is something you can resort to when a man is bending you backwards. You collapse and drag him down with you. It amounts to holding. Walt Sweeney of San Diego, said the Steelers, "is the collapse-block champion of the world." Clack did it right in front of an official, who was reaching in his pocket for his flag when Franco burst past with the ball and hit him. By the time the official pulled himself together he'd forgotten about the penalty.

"A knee's not something you fool around with," Franco said. "If you're hurt somewhere else . . . but a knee . . . especially if you're a running back. I need to run with more power. Although today I felt a surge at times."

The Cincinnati game in Pittsburgh was a hell of a game for surges. Noll called it "the hardest hitting game I can recall out here—where both teams really whacked each other." The crowd was hard-hitting too. In fact Paul Brown called the crowd "sickening."

"Bounce the Bengals' Boobie" read a banner. It was raining; but the fans were primed to ignite. As usual the Steelers won the toss, received, and their opening drive fizzled. Then Mel Blount recovered a fumble by Boobie on the Bengals' 22; but the offense could get only a field goal out of that break. The Bengals' Essex Johnson dropped a pass in the end zone and then caught a pass and fumbled on the Steeler 5, Rowser recovered, and another Steeler drive failed to get anywhere. The defense forced a Bengal punt, but Bradshaw passed too high, off Franco's fingertips, and Tommy Casanova intercepted for Cincinnati. Johnson providentially dropped a *second* end zone pass and the Bengals tied it 3–3. This score did not please the Pittsburgh fans.

Who soon showed their displeasure in a way which the Chief later said, sadly, "almost made me sick." Bradshaw, perhaps the toughest quarterback sneaker in the game, gained 4 yards sneaking. As he ground to a stop on the earth tackle Steve Chomyszak landed on him with a sound like that of his name, *Chomyszak!* It was not an unduly violent lick. "It was just waterlogged me falling on him," said Chomyszak, who was 6–6, 258 bone dry (and was married to someone named Debi). One of Noll's cold-blooded theories (bear in mind that "cold-blooded," or "cold," was a term of radical approval among the players, as in "this cheese is cold-blooded," or " 'Twilight Zone' is *cold*") is that you only get hurt bad enough to leave the game when you want to, when you need an excuse. Bradshaw was about due to be pulled, hurt or not. He was lying with the ball tucked under him, twisted a bit so that his posture was that of a wince, and the contact with Chomyszak slightly separated the shoulder of his throwing arm.

And as he came off the field, bent from the waist, his rifle arm winced in for sure and his left hand pressing his shoulder as if in an effort to hold it in place, the crowd got cold-blooded. A considerable portion of the fans cheered.

"You could hear it loud and clear," said Greene. "He hadn't taken two steps and he was holding his shoulder, obviously in pain, when that shit started. I'd be lying if I said he doesn't tick me off sometimes. But that was vicious. They don't know what it's like to bust your ass out there and take all that, and then hear people cheering when a guy has been hurt."

A caller on the Myron Cope show later in the week admitted that he was one of those cheering. "Down through the years," he explained, "the Steelers have always played the wrong guy."

"Would you cheer if they shot him?" asked Cope.

"Well, I wouldn't cheer if they *shot* him."

"You're saying it's fine to cheer when he's hurt, just to get him out of there?"

"How else you gonna get him out of there?" asked the caller; and then he asked a remarkable question. "How about his gray matter? If he's so smart, why didn't he go to LSU?"

"Sick, sick," said Hanratty later. But when he stood and threw off his black raincape to replace Bradshaw the fans had something positive to cheer, and they went wild. The Steelers had to punt, Cincinnati got close enough to kick

179

a field goal and go ahead 6–3, and then, after Steve Davis returned the kickoff all the way to midfield, Hanratty rose to the occasion. He planned to fake to Shanklin and pass to Barry Pearson, because the Bengal secondary had been rotating toward Shanklin, and he did look first to Shanklin, but when he saw safety Casanova moving back toward Pearson he faked to Pearson—as the offensive line gave him a luxurious 4.6 seconds to work with—and threw to Shanklin, 51 yards for a touchdown, Shanklin seizing the ball beautifully between two defenders. It was the third time in '73 that Hanratty's first pass in a game had worked for 6 points. "Adequate relief" indeed.

But things had just begun to perk. In the Steelers' first drive of the third quarter Hanratty hit Barry Pearson for 23 and Shanklin for 19, and just missed connecting with Shanklin in the end zone. He went back to pass again, Bengal linebacker Bill Bergey blitzed, and as Hanratty threw quickly, leaving his right ribs wide open, Bergey, diving, drove his forearm into them. Hanratty—not a man you would expect to throw a punch at a linebacker—started to go after Bergey with fire in his eye, but then he doubled up with fire in his ribs. After they watched the films the Steelers concluded that Bergey's shot had not been cheap, not culpably late, and I believe as a matter of fact he got the Steelers' vote in the Pro Bowl balloting at the end of the year, but Bradshaw said in his autobiography, "One of the few cheap shots that I've ever taken in the NFL came from Bill Bergey of the Bengals," and on the sidelines, as Hanratty left the field looking worse than Bradshaw had (did all of Noll's quarterbacks have an injury wish?), the Steelers were incensed.

"Get that sonofabitch," said Noll.

"I was going to hit him in the chops on an extra point," said Mansfield, "but then I got to thinking, he could hit me in *my* broken rib."

"I'm the cheap shot of all time," said Holmes after the game. "I'll hit a quarterback as long as he's standing on a dime. But not 30 seconds after he releases. I didn't hit his quarterback as dirty as he hit mine. Bergey, he actually tried to take Hanratty's ribs, I think."

Gerela kicked a field goal to make the score Steelers 13, Bengals 6. But the Steelers didn't have a healthy, eligible quarterback! Bradshaw was on his way to Divine Providence Hospital. Gilliam was on the deactivated list, standing on the sidelines in sweat pants and a yellow stocking cap. Hanratty was sitting on the bench with his eyes shut tight, having his ribs taped. Dockery, who'd stood in at quarterback some in practice with the Jets, offered to step in, but Noll looked at him noncommittally.

This was the kind of moment—a strange, interesting crisis—that brought out the best in the Steelers. Ham threw Essex Johnson for a 4-yard loss. Hanratty was still seated, fighting back the pain, but finally he rose, and as he tossed a tentative pass on the sidelines a great roar went up from the crowd, for him and for Ham, Greene and Greenwood, who had just descended upon Bengal quarterback Ken Anderson like an hundred-weight of bricks, sacking him for a 9-yard loss. They would have sacked Anderson at that moment if he'd been in Rome at her peak.

Little as I would like to admit it after the noises they made at Bradshaw, the fans probably deserved a game ball against Cincinnati. They'd been bored by the easy wins earlier in the year, but this was a situation they could sink their teeth into. Their roaring, thundering outrage and glee kept the Bengal offensive line from hearing their blocking signals on fourth down. Accordingly, no one came close to blocking Bleier as he rushed, and Bleier reached the punter at about the same time the snap did. The punter had to run for it, and Hanneman threw him at the Cincinnati 4.

And Hanratty came back in, standing straight. Fuqua from the 1 scored what turned out to be the winning touchdown. When the pile was untangled he sprang up and slammed the ball to the ground.

The rest of the game was a vortex of Steeler defense (Wagner won the NFL Defensive Player of the Week award for intercepting three passes, and he had a fourth interception disallowed because an official ruled wrongly that he'd come down out-of-bounds), audience tumult (the game had to be stopped seven times for the noise when Cincinnati had the ball—Franco finally waving a towel at the fans to get them to subside) and Hanratty grit (he even completed a pretty 34-yard pass to Shanklin over the middle, although throwing must have made his ribs feel like they'd been barbecued and gnawed).

Fuqua broke his collarbone. Rowser hurt his shoulder. A man's shoe flew up into the air from the end zone seats. With four minutes to go in the game the Steelers led 20–13 and had the ball on the Cincinnati 34, fourth and 1, and elected to go for the first down. (Noll, as a matter of fact, was a great one for going for it on fourth and 1. For all his steely exterior Noll was in many ways as madcap as his team. Hanratty, it was said, had to talk him into punting twice on fourth and 1 in the Jets game.) The Steelers and the Bengals both threw nearly everybody up front, lined up head-to-head, body on body, everyone leaning forward on his knuckles, ready to explode. The crowd was standing, quiet, hushed almost, in deference to the Steelers' signal-calling. But Pregnant! *Ready*—the air suffused with a fine mist of adrenaline like the coke smoke of yore—*ready* to blossom forth in a raw, red, open-hearth, molten sloshy oversurge of *noise*. And Larry Brown jumped offside.

Just as well; if the play had gone off, if the atmosphere had been positively discharged, it would have detonated a terrible fulminating criss-cross salvo of desire; there would have been people diving onto the field, I know it, chewing the artificial turf, tearing off their clothes and running naked (talk about jumping offside!), beating Bergey with liquor bottles, the players entering in, swearing horribly, breaking every rib and civilized sanction in sight—it would've been awful. Maybe the Great God Tar-Tan would have risen up in great folds of turf and borne the whole struggling mass away in a seething bundle to join Joe Magarac in Hell or wherever he was.

With two and a half minutes to go, after Wagner's last interception, it looked like the Steelers had things wrapped up, leading 20–13 with the ball well into Bengal territory. But Preston Pearson fumbled and the Bengals mounted a drive. Anderson hit Clark with a pass, a Steeler hit Clark with a helmet-prowed body, he fumbled, Johnson picked it up and *almost broke clear* but Russell ran him down. Then, on the last play of the game, the Bengals with no time-outs left, Anderson passed to Clark again on the Steeler 28. White and Thomas hit him a resounding corporate lick. White's helmet flew one way, his chin strap flew another, and Mad Dog himself pitched backwards and lay stretched out on the ground. As the last seconds ticked off, a Steeler tried to call time out so someone could attend to Dwight, but no one officially noticed him, fortunately, because that would have given the Bengals another chance. The Steelers let the clock move as Dwight lay there cold-cocked, and the game ended 20–13 Steelers. They led their division now by a game and a half over Cleveland and two games over Cincinnati.

"It used to be," said the Chief, "that time out would've been called. That's the way we used to lose games."

"There's Dwight White," cried Holmes in the dressing room. "Sacrifice his body for the team!"

"Ain't nothing wrong with going first class," said Dwight obscurely but radiantly, no longer stunned or anything like it. "Just don't go as often."

Bradshaw was out for four to six weeks, it was announced, and Hanratty's ribs were bruised. As a matter of fact, I learned that night at the Vaughn Nixons', Hanratty's ribs were broken, but that was going to be kept secret lest opponents concentrate on driving them into his lungs, which would probably incapacitate him.

The next day at lunch with the press Noll played down the drama of the quarterback situation. This was the fourth year of public controversy over who should be the starting quarterback, and Noll had been understandably tired of it for that long. And as exasperated as he got with Bradshaw, he was not what you would call a Hanratty booster. Somebody asked Noll if Hanratty hadn't handled being a backup awfully well.

"He's handled it as an adult," said Noll. "He's handled it admirably considering all the prompting he's had from outside. There's such a thing as being part of a team. He helps very much even when he's not playing. Quarterbacks on the sideline make suggestions, and many times they're used. They may get as much satisfaction—I'm sure they do—out of making a suggestion and having it used. Like a coach—seeing it work."

Why Noll felt called upon sometimes to be so pious, I don't know. Hanratty had certainly contributed from the sidelines, and it was true that every player had to think of the team's benefit, but anybody knows that a quarterback gets drastically less satisfaction out of suggesting plays for someone else than he does out of running them himself. When Hanratty let his hair down, especially

182

after a loss, he seethed at being behind Bradshaw. And Gilliam brooded, at least, over being behind both of them.

Noll said blandly that he didn't know just what he'd have done if both Bradshaw and Hanratty had been hurt too bad to continue. He said he might have had to call on a press box quarterback. "Or we'd punt and play defense, I guess. We'd play it like the Vietnam conflict."

"Now that Hanratty's number one," Noll pointed out, "the fans will be after him. They'll be yelling, 'Bring in Joey!' We may end up with Joe Gilliam as our starting quarterback."

And so they might.

□ 17 □

TERRY AND TERRY
AND JOE

Quarterbacks are just human people.
ART ROONEY

The Steelers as a matter of fact considered signing such a former pro quarterback as Mike Taliaffero or Kent Nix, and they might well have activated Parilli if a league rule had not prevented it; and Rocky Bleier was trained as the emergency snap-taker in case a no-quarterback situation arose (though Mansfield maintained he was the logical choice for the job; he knew all the plays and also how to take a snap, since he and Clack practiced their snaps on each other). But when the story came out that the Steelers might acquire Unitas from the Chargers (which wasn't true—the last thing Noll or Dan Rooney was likely to want around was a proud, pain-racked, legendary back-up quarterback with a tremendous salary), causing a big stir, they decided to stick with stove-in Hanratty and frail-looking Gilliam until Bradshaw, who was still assumed to be number one, was well.

Who should start for the Steelers at quarterback was at least as hot a political issue around town as "Liquorgate," a corruption scandal which I never understood but which the papers were full of and which involved booze, as did many things in Pittsburgh. Pittsburgh had always been a big politics town, appropriately enough for a place where you could have a smoke-filled room by just opening a window. Politics in the civil sense never seemed to be much of a topic around the Steeler players, though Clack and Mansfield campaigned for McGovern before the Democratic primary, but mostly, I gathered, for the sake of the contacts they got out of it. "The highlight of the whole thing was having lunch with Shirley MacLaine," said Clack. "She was the most dynamic speaker I ever heard." The Ranger smoked a huge cigar while campaigning, for atmosphere, but Clack said, "We didn't get involved in anything crooked." He accused Mansfield of jumping to Nixon after the primary "so he could take a banquet."

There was of course some political talk around the premises. When Keating heard the news that Agnew had been indicted he jumped into the air on the practice field and cried, "There is justice! There is justice!" The next day Bradshaw said, "That was something, what happened to my man Agnew, wasn't it? I couldn't sleep all night over it. He always had something to say."

"The bad thing about what happened to Agnew," said an Italian visitor to practice, "he's dragging Sinatra right down wid' 'im."

"If he don't go along, he'd have a grocery store in Baltimore right now," said Uncle Jim. "I had a friend, Max, whose nephew got elected to something. 'Is he on the take, Max?' I asked him. 'Mit' bot' fists,' he said. An honest guy can't get elected, Roy. Who would run him?" Come to think of it, Uncle Jim also said he had a friend in politics who said, "The sweetest words in the English language are 'Here is your end.' "

Around town, at any rate, tempers ran high about the quarterbacks. The *Pittsburgh Courier* boosted Gilliam; *Courier* columnist John Henry Johnson, the former great Steeler running back, supported Hanratty over Bradshaw. Most of the rest of the media devoted considerable space or time to debunking charges that Bradshaw was dumb. The man in the street was never likely to be satisfied by the quarterback situation.

It was a tribute to the Steelers' cohesion and Noll's control over them, then, that the quarterback situation was no more divisive an issue among the players than it was. One reason the team didn't split up into camps over the quarterbacks, probably, was that the virtues of the three were so various and pronounced, it was hard to be dogmatic about which man was best.

After the first Cincinnati game Mike Reid called Bradshaw the best quarterback in the NFL, and when Bradshaw was hot that was true. "Raw material," someone watching practice once said of Bradshaw. "America was built on raw material." Noll, it is true, was criticized by fans for not calling Bradshaw's plays for him. At Cleveland Noll had been a messenger guard, running plays in and out for Paul Brown, and maybe he resented that role. At any rate he said such a system "emasculates your quarterback. It's for coaches who want to be quarterbacks. Paul Brown's the oldest quarterback in the league." Still Noll seemed to prefer players he could deal with as raw material—whom he could ingrain, as he put it, with his thinking.

Bradshaw could throw as long and hard as you could ever ask a quarterback to do, and he was also a great threat to run. He loved contact too much if anything—once he tried to run right over Buck Buchanan of Kansas City, who is 6–7, 270. Bradshaw's wife Missy was a former Teenage Miss America. And Bradshaw was lively to talk with.

I brought my brother-in-law Gerald Duff into the dressing room one Saturday morning and Bradshaw asked him what he did. He said he taught college English. "*English?*" cried Bradshaw. "*Literature? I hated* that stuff. You write too?"

Gerald said he wrote some poetry. "Poetry! Behold, what light breaks from Camelot benow," said Bradshaw. "I write songs. My wife is always surprised in that I can be riding along and make up a song. I wrote one called 'What Is a Woman?' that I had recorded. It sounded good till they put the background music in and drowned me out. Hank Williams. He was a poet if anybody was. 'Kaw-liga.' Two wooden Indians side by side and couldn't kiss each other. Who'd ever have thought of that? But when it gets into all that symbolism, where that rug there means leaves, or something . . ." He shook his head.

We were sitting around talking with Mansfield and some other people, and the conversation turned to other subjects. All of a sudden Bradshaw, who'd been lounging on a stool musing more or less to himself about having to go autograph copies of his autobiography at a department store, spoke up.

"I could be happy just welding!" he said.

"Huh?" somebody said.

"Welding. I haven't got enough to do to fill my time." Back home in Grand Cane, Louisiana, he said, he had bought a welding apparatus and welded together an old tractor he'd found, then filed down the seams, made it look good, a nice solid job of handwork. "It passes the time so well," he said.

"Terry, you really come out with them, don't you?" said Mansfield.

Bradshaw had to go. "It is far better to be with thee, creative hearts," he said on his way out, poetizing, "then to plunge . . ." And he was gone.

Another time Bradshaw told me what went through his mind when he played quarterback.

"Relax. Confidence. Concentrate. Keeping a Cool. I say those four words to myself, and try to think about 'em, and they have an effect on me. I say 'em and stop letting people bother me. I'm totally committed to the football game. I can say the words right now and have a feeling come over me. My wife's a psych major, she's familiar with this. But you can't just say, 'Relax, confidence, concentrate, keeping a cool.' You've got to say 'em, think about 'em, let 'em take an effect.

"I always wondered what other quarterbacks think when they drop back to pass. If they really read defenses. Which according to the films I've seen a lot of them don't. Lot of times I can outthink myself. You take a pass you completed and you stay with it till they stop it. Too much thinking causes indecision.

"Last year there was, I guess the word's an aura. We gonna tear 'em up. This year we blew everybody out of the ballpark. Up until San Diego. Then we started evaluating our talent: Hey, maybe we don't have it after all.

"I may be too much of a kid out there. But I think football's a great kid sport—which it is, just a lot of kids out there, trying to modify it, trying to make it, what's the word, classier . . .

"When I throw a good pass I feel it all over. It's the most beautiful feeling. When you throw with a good whoosh, a good bjonng. Just turn it loose and a perfect spiral, just super pride, it fills you up inside, just thrills you to death. Even if it's intercepted. You drop back not worrying about a thing and see that

186

pattern and throw that thing and hear the crowd roar—that's a feeling nobody can have but yourself. Some of these technical quarterbacks feel the same way, if they'd be honest about it, if they didn't feel like they got to be all tightlipped and technical, intellectual.

"In college, you're dating Peggy Sue here whose father's vice-president of Domino Sugar and if you win he's going to give a big check to the university. If you lose, she'll start dating Butch Fletcher. So you just gotta win in college. For the glory of the school. You can't even think of losing in college. That'd be awful. And I had my Rydell XPs, shoes, you know, nobody wore 'em at Tech but me, they were a little fancier . . . You gotta win—you pass 600 yards, get that school record, you're gonna get that C. Maybe a B. Lot of dumb corny reasons. In college you got a whole group of people united for one cause.

"You don't have that feeling with the fans here. In college they feel sorry for you when you do bad. They support you. But I can't remember ever having a bad game in college. Maybe that's one of the reasons.

"Being from a Christian background, I always wanted to be nice to everybody, having everybody be for me, not hurting anybody's feelings. Pro football has a great way of destroying all that. Reporters. I call 'em two-faced. When a man's successful they're all around him, picking at him, asking questions. Where are they when things are bad? I don't see 'em writing pep talks for him. Just writing bad about him. And if you don't give 'em what you want, they'll run you out.

"So Relax, Confidence, Concentrate, Cool. I go about it like that. Because if I get to worrying about those people I'm done for. I've found myself being pretty rough with fans. At the Detroit game, some kid in the stands, he's yelling, 'Bradshaw. Hey Terry.' So I turned around. 'You stink,' he said. I'd like to throw the football right between his eyes.

"Or just—you go into the Sweet William to eat. They throw one of these things at you, placemats, food all over it, and say 'Sign this "For Julie and Arthur and David and . . ." What's your kid's name Walter? Oh yeah, "and Billy." ' What're they gonna do with those autographs? They're gonna lose 'em, burn 'em, kids going to tear 'em up. It's a make-believe world for some of these people."

Bradshaw was the team's most unabashed dreamer. Ever since a pole-vaulter told me he dreamed before a big meet that "the pole is a rope," I have been asking interviewees if they had interesting dreams. Most of them, in sports anyway, deny it. Andy Russell did admit dreaming sometimes that he was supposed to be at the stadium, and he was late, and the game was going to start without him. And his wife Nancy said that on the first Saturday night after the season—the first Saturday night in five months, then, that he hadn't slept with the Steelers—Andy woke up calling for his roommate, Gerela. "He dreamed he was sleeping with a football team," she said. "And if you don't know what that means," she said to Andy, "you're in trouble."

Henry Davis said he would dream that "the quarterback's going back, it's a pass—'cause that's the hardest thing I have to look out for—and the ball is up and I jump and *just* deflect it and I go *ooaugh!*"

The day before a game Kolb said, "I woke up this morning and I was sleeping on the stripes. Everything was off the bed. I'd been playing all night. Pass protection—setting up—over and over. Sometimes I'll wake up thinking I've played a game. Then I'll realize I was dreaming and I'll say, 'Oh no. I'm too tired to play another one.' If I'm about to get beat, though, I'll wake up. Got to stop it. Can't let myself get beat."

But Bradshaw was the only one who said, "My dreams have disclosed many things to me. Foreseeable things. Lots of times I've seen a face in a dream, and years later I'll see a guy and say, 'Where have I seen that face before?' I've dreamed about people dying, and then it's happened. I definitely believe I've got the power. I think I'm one of the few people. If somebody could psychoanalyze me, I'd open up a lot of things. It makes you feel good. But then sometimes it's not so good.

"I've had nightmares. I had a dream where I was loose on a long run, and I had the feeling I'm not going to make it. Nobody's around me, but I know I'm not fast enough. If I'd been awake I'd've made it, I know, but in the dream, it's tearing me up. Or dreamed that I had a guy wide open but couldn't get the ball to him. Couldn't get it out of my hand. You wake up, 'God A'mighty, why couldn't I get the ball to him?' It just tortures you.

"But I dreamed when I was a junior in college that I was going to go in and throw a touchdown and win a game, and I did, the next day. I've had that happen in the pros. If you can work on your subconscious mind—it rules over the conscious mind—and go to bed thinking about good things . . . Because if you think about bad things, bad things will happen. It's your subconscious mind overruling your conscious mind—which is a little devil at times. It can go either way."

So it was wrong to accuse Bradshaw of not having an interesting mind. But Hanratty was unquestionably a wilier field general, better at mixing plays, and by all accounts more confident in the huddle. Bradshaw, it was said, tended to make speeches in the huddle, whereas Hanratty came in with a gleam in his eye and fell to work.

"You want your quarterback to be a Bugs Bunny type," said one Steeler. "Or Daffy Duck. A guy who's got that sneakiness, who's always looking for that edge. That's Hanratty. Bradshaw's too much like Elmer Fudd."

Early in the season, as I stood among a group of scribes crowded around Bradshaw's cubicle after a game, I would often see something out of the corner of my eye that would be Hanratty, peering around from the adjoining cubicle with a villainous grin. Which is not to say that he was out to get Bradshaw. They roomed together and got along fine. "It was bad my rookie years," Hanratty said. "Dick Shiner was the other quarterback and his wife wouldn't speak to mine."

The person Hanratty didn't get along with was Noll. Bradshaw was the first draft choice after Hanratty's rookie year. "Noll called me after they drafted Terry and said, 'It's no indication of the way you played this year. We just drafted the best athlete.' Did I believe that? No. Terry turned out well, he's going to be good for them, but I don't think it ever entered Noll's mind from the first day I set foot here that I was going to be the quarterback. I don't think I've had a shot. I don't know why. There's definitely a personality conflict, but I don't know where."

But Hanratty said, "I think I've got a great future. I'm twenty-five years old. If I was thirty-five I'd be worried." After '73 he said he might play out his option and sign with New York of the World Football League, coached by Parilli, if he had to stay on the bench behind Bradshaw. Hanratty said he had talked the matter over with Bradshaw, but not with Noll. "He doesn't get tight with players," Hanratty explained.

The Steelers found this publicity embarrassing and dispatched a man to Denver with plenty of money, evidently, because Hanratty signed a two-year contract. I think he is probably angling to become so outspoken and expensive that the Steelers will trade him, but he may just have been angling to be expensive. Anyway he was angling.

Hanratty said football was fun "as long as you're winning—that's the only time it's fun." He agreed with Bradshaw about fans, though. "I'd like to walk right into somebody's office, throw open the door and say, 'You motherfucker, why'd you do that?' I'd throw $7 down on somebody's desk and chew his ass. I don't think the average person thinks you have a job. It's entertainment for them, so they think it's entertainment for you."

Not that it was an ordeal for him, ordinarily. "I've never been nervous in a game in my life," he said. "Lots of times you'll come off the bench and take the snap and read and in three seconds you throw, and afterwards you start thinking about how in hell were you able to do all that in three seconds. But it's amazing how many people you can look at, and pump. You're talking to yourself through your mind: 'Uh-oh, linebacker's swooping to the outside, I better throw inside . . . Dirty sonuvabitch fooled me—I thought he was going to be man and he rotates a zone on me—so better come back to the inside and see how the out-in looks . . .' You do all that talking in your mind in three seconds.

"In college you had more time to think. Once I had eight seconds to pass. I just dropped the ball to my side and stood there looking at my offensive line for two counts, like an orchestra leader looking to his orchestra to be applauded, they've done such a hell of a job, and then I brought the ball back up and threw it."

Hanratty was good at gestures of appreciation. If the Steelers had voted to see which quarterback would be first string I think Hanratty would have won. But then maybe Hanratty was too injury-prone. And think how well Bradshaw could deliver a football.

And don't forget the man with the quickest release of all. The Steeler scouts were making a film to illustrate the concept of quick release. They slowed down the films of Bradshaw, Hanratty and Gilliam releasing the ball. They all three released quick. But after they got the films as slow as they could possibly get them, Gilliam's hand was the only one that still remained a blur. Shanklin said that Hanratty's or Gilliam's ball was easier to catch than Bradshaw's because it was "less intense," it didn't spin as fiercely. And Gilliam's had more velocity than Hanratty's. So Gilliam probably threw the team's best passes per se.

And *loved* to. A *lot* of them. On the bus to the hotel in Cincinnati Bleier said to Gilliam, "Down there in Tennessee, what would you say to 'em in the huddle, Joe?"

"On the 5-yard line?" cried Gilliam. "On the 5-yard line?" He jumped up.

"I'd say to 'em: 'All right, dig it! Double clutch right on two!' " Then he did a little dance step: one-two, one-two. " 'Get it!' "

"Aw, *Tennessee,*" said White. "Do sumpin' *here!*"

"I'm goin' to. I'm goin' to. If they'll gimme a *suit!*" said Gilliam, restless on the taxi squad.

"They give you the ball," said Dwight. "Can't have the ball and a suit too."

"Go in there throwing," said Gilliam. "Last time I showed them I knew what I was doing. Next time, first play, skeleton pass! Better get ready!" He threw an imaginary bomb into the air.

"Hey," said White, "you be here for fifteen years, they have a ceremony, and they say, 'For long and dedicated service, we are . . . gonna give you . . . your *suit!*' "

Gilliam knocked on Holmes's wooden high heels. He didn't take to being third string. He was late to meetings from time to time, a practice pro football considers bad for team discipline, and once I noticed him hanging up his practice clothes singing bitterly, "Root, root, root for the home team . . ."

Gilliam had a solid background in soul-satisfying football as played by black colleges in the South. Once in the bus a number of the Steelers' graduates of this football were sitting around trading stories about what it was like to play on each other's home fields.

Gilliam mentioned the problem of a visiting team going into Florida A & M, coached by the venerable Jake Gaither. "They use everything down there—ultraviolet rays and shit. Got seven referees. Go into the huddle before the game, man says 'Captain Gilliam, this is Mr. So-and-So, the field judge,' on down the line. 'But hey, how about that seventh one? who's that?' Man say, 'Don't you mess with him, boy, that's *Jake's* referee.' "

And Edwards and Holmes talked of home team field goals falling on the 3-yard line and being signaled good, of "coming on the field in your nice gold and black uniform with white pants, and here they come: green *polka-dot* shoes! and their heads way back down low about the level of their feet, trucking in there, and all you could see was those polka-dot shoes."

There were also problems on your own campus: "Maybe you out walking with your woman. And maybe she be looking *good* and shit. Coach come up to you, 'Boy! What you doin' out? You better get on back and get ready for the game!' Then he says [oilily], 'Daughter, you need a walk to the dorm?' "

Whatever the hazards involved, however, that brand of football is a game in which the individual, especially if he is gifted at some aspect of throwing the ball a long way or running up under it after it has been thrown a long way, can flower. At Tennessee State Gilliam was the star of a powerful team whose defensive coach was his father. He was Jefferson Street Joe, who was known to put the ball in the air. "My style was the same as Namath's. Threw off-balance, all the time. I really felt comfortable throwing off-balance. Now I only do it if I have to. Then I had complete control of my offense. It was *mine.* If I was caught with the ball and took a good lick, I was going to get up and come back with the bomb. Consequently I threw a lot of touchdowns. Sixty-five in three years. Now I have to apply my talents to the system."

The system, speaking generally of pro football, was one which didn't believe in black quarterbacks. Black college quarterbacks of promise tended to be turned into wide receivers of defensive backs—positions in which they just had to be athletic, nobody had to take directions from them—in the pros. Gilliam purposely ran the 40 far slower than he could after he reported to the Steelers, because he didn't want them to use his speed as an excuse to take him away from his position. No further proof of the racism of pro football is necessary than that such a gifted passer as Gilliam—whose uncle is scouting director of the Minnesota Vikings—was the 271st prospect taken in the '72 draft. Noll, however, could dig a black quarterback if he fit Noll's system. Reports from the Steeler huddle were that Gilliam could have been a more commanding field general, but his arm and verve commanded respect, and he had won his spurs by relieving an injured Bradshaw against Houston the year before and helping to save the day by completing six of eight passes, some of them after his knee was smashed badly enough to require a subsequent, successful, operation.

Gilliam had a chance, then, to become the first established black pro quarterback, if he got a chance to play. He was intense, good-armed and nimble enough, and he had a way of coming through on emotional occasions.

Before the first Cincinnati game I was standing with Gilliam on the field watching the Kentucky State band practice. They were wearing sweatshirts with their individual nicknames on them: Frodie Rodie, Preacher, Meat, Winnie, Pacemaker of the Hole Gang. "My daddy was the coach at Kentucky State," Gilliam observed, "and there was a big beer bust and the president of the school got rid of the whole team, except for one guy who wasn't at the beer bust. My daddy had to use the freshman team. Then they fired my daddy.

"My sophomore year at Tennessee State, I was quarterback, and we were going to play against them, Kentucky State. My daddy got up and talked to us before the game, told us how much it meant to him. Tears running down my daddy's face. They ruined his football team and then they fired him. Well, we went out and beat 'em 83 to *nothin'.*

"Fire *my* daddy."

□ 18 □

THE CHIEF
AND FAMILY

You are the best influence in Pittsburgh.

—FATHER REARDON OF ST.
BERNARD CHURCH,
PITTSBURGH, IN A
LETTER TO ART ROONEY

"**T**ake a gas mask," said Noll, who hated cigar smoke.

"Take ten dollars," said Uncle Jim, who knew we were going to play the horses. "No more."

"You better take a can to pee in," said Richie Easton.

Richie, a chunky sanguine Syrian who drove a newspaper truck for a living and drove the Chief in his Imperial for recreation, and was one of the Chief's closest friends, was thinking of the Chief's disinclination to stop, for any reason, once he got rolling on the open road. The Chief, Richie and I were on a four-day trip to Liberty Bell Park in Philadelphia, Yonkers Raceway and Aqueduct in New York, Shamrock Farms in Maryland, and Shenandoah Downs in West Virginia. I kind of halfway hoped, professionally, to find out something disappointing about the Chief during this trip. It is a Jagov reporter who doesn't try to find out that people are different from the way they have been painted.

"Peezer Klingensmith," reminisced the Chief, after we had driven a ways. "Red Barr asked me to take Peezer up to St. Bonaventure, where the Steelers trained in those days. Peezer hadn't been feeling too well. He needed a rest. He was a friend of Red's. On the way to St. Bonny's, I thought we'd drive down to the farm. So we did, and spent the night there, and then we went to Delaware Park, and the next day to Garden State, then to New York, then back to Garden State for Saturday's racing. After the races we left for St. Bonaventure. We got as far as Scranton and went into a hotel, and here were these chicken fighters I knew from all over the country. So we went to the chicken fights. Right from the hotel. We didn't get nothing to eat. This is a

Sunday now. We checked into the hotel finally at 4 in the morning. I said, 'When is the first mass?' The man said '6:30.' 'Wake us at at 6,' I said. So we went to mass and drove on and dropped down out of the mountains into St. Bonny's.

"When we got there Peezer said, 'I been gone for four days. All I ate was apples and peaches. We never slept. He drives a hundred miles an hour up and down mountains.' Peezer was in the hospital after that for a couple of weeks." The Chief curled his mouth in merriment and looked closely at his cigar. All through the trip the three of us smoked excellent cigars the size of Joe Greene's fingers steadily, from a big stock in the glove compartment, and sometimes it was hard to make out objects inside the car. The Chief called these cigars "Tobies."

We talked about Bradshaw's injury and the fans' reaction, which the Chief deplored.

"Sunday Bradshaw was down. Before the game he was telling me, there's a new study going on now. In your body, there are certain times you're at a low ebb. There's three waves in you, say. When these waves get below a certain level you're in danger. I was saying that's all the bunk. I hoped he didn't believe in that low wave. I said I'd been in that wave forty years. But then I met this provincial of the Holy Ghost Order. He understood these waves thoroughly. He said, 'Oh, that's a study they're taking in the human being.' The minute I saw Bradshaw come off that field with that shoulder I thought, there's no way to convince him those waves are the bunk. His wife's studying them at Pitt."

The news came over the radio that the Steelers were underdogs in the upcoming game with the Redskins. The Chief seemed please. "We ought to be," he said. "All our athletes got their bones broke."

His thoughts turned lightly to final things. "I put in my will that my funeral can't cost more than a thousand dollars. Did my wife start to squawk. I said what am I gonna know? Oh, she screamed. 'I'm going to have to be dead too,' she said, 'because you can't get anything for a thousand dollars.' She's a McNulty, they worry about being sick. She says all the Rooneys ever say about being sick is, if a person dies, 'Well, he musta been sick.' that's still in my will about the thousand dollars.

"I put people in her box, you know. She has a big box in the stadium, and I put people there. Tuffy Hacker, the trainer. Bobby Layne's going to be up there Monday night with six people. She says to Johnny, the usher, 'Who are these people in our box?' He says, 'Mrs. Rooney, they've got tickets.' She says, 'I'm going to kill him.'

"I put a Greek archbishop in there once and she said, 'What am I going to say to him?' I said just the same as our bishop. They all believe in God. She liked him, though. Monday my cousin that's a nun will be in there and she don't wear her habit anymore. 'How can I tell?' my wife says. 'I don't know whether they're nuns or hoochie-coochie dancers.' Oh, she'll scream." The

Chief shook in the front seat with pleasure and started a fresh Toby.

Just outside Liberty Bell, on a road lined with motels, the Chief said, "Dan Parrish told me to buy all this land in here. But I was never big on land. I don't know about anything, only horses. And football. Sports. I didn't know you could go to the bank and borrow money. I thought you had to have it in your pocket."

"What you have to realize," the Chief's son Pat told me once, "is that my father is a great man. None of his sons are."

But the Chief never borrowed a dime in his life, and his sons, without any capital to speak of except their name and the Steeler franchise, have borrowed over $60 million. With the Chief they constitute ten different corporations that own or control the Steelers, Yonkers Raceway, the William Penn Racing Association at Liberty Bell, Green Mountain Race Track in Vermont and Palm Beach Kennel Club, a greyhound track in Florida. The Chief is sole owner of Shamrock Farms. The Rooneys used to own a soccer team. They have made an offer to buy Garden State Park in New Jersey and they are building a thoroughbred track outside Philadelphia. If the boys are not great, they are certainly doing well, and they all reflect their father in various ways.

For one thing they still do what he tells them. "The old man is policy," says a man who has been close to the family, and the boys readily agree that they all talk to him every day, by phone or in person, and that if he rules against something they won't do it.

They also take pride in being down-to-earth like their father. They were all brought up in a poor neighborhood with other Irish kids, not feeling any different from anybody else. They knew, of course, that very rough kids refrained from swearing in the Rooney yard and that their father owned a football team. But they also knew that the family drove to the games in a car that sometimes had to be backed up steep hills.

They knew, too, that most of the time their father was off playing the horses, arranging some kind of athletic affair or swapping stories with Toots Shor or Billy Conn. But the Chief always came home on the weekends, and if at the end of a day he found himself as nearby as, say Cleveland, he would always drive home.

The Chief was not one for heart-to-heart talks with his sons, but he kept their attention. When they put up a punching bag he would walk in and work out on it briefly in such a way as to leave the mouth of every kid present hanging open. He would also follow such unusual Christian procedures as bringing panhandlers in off the street for sandwiches. And when someone needed an authoritative opinion he would provide it, as when Artie complained that Timmy had just hit a kid over the head with a piece of sidewalk, which didn't seem fair. The Chief said, "When you fight, you fight with whatever you need."

The Rooney manse, an old Victorian house, had, and still has, white columns in front, 12 rooms inside, and a multipurpose backyard. The boys dug tunnels under it for war games, and in the winter they iced over the macadam-ized part for hockey, so they had plenty to do without hanging around pool halls. Their father told them never to hang around pool halls, and since he had hung around them enough as a boy to become a shark of some note, they figured he knew what he was talking about.

The Chief never had a harsh word for anybody else in the world, but he was inclined to call his sons "chumps" and "newly made." The old man says, "I always thought my coaches knew what they were doing. I *knew* the boys didn't."

The boys remember calling his hand only twice. One day he went to watch Tim, John and Pat play sandlot ball. Tim singled to the outfield and when he reached first he turned to the right. The Chief went up to him and said, "You're supposed to turn toward second."

"That's the way you old guys did it," said Tim, who was then about twelve.

"Give me those balls and bats!" shouted the Chief. "I don't want people to know you're a Rooney."

"I never watched them play ball again," he says today. "You'll have to ask them about their athletic abilities. For this reason: I never thought much of 'em."

The other moment of rebellion came more recently. Perhaps Tim was out of sorts after making the drive from Pittsburgh to Winfield, Maryland, the site of Shamrock Farms, the Rooney's thoroughbred stable. "My father would sit there in the car saying his rosary," Tim says. "He wouldn't talk to you, and he wouldn't let you turn on the radio, and he'd make you leave all the windows wide open in the middle of winter."

At any rate, when the Chief told Tim to take off his boots inside the house at Shamrock, Tim complained. So his father gave him a good shot to the head. "Then he turned to John, but John was on the track team, he ran," says Pat. At the time Tim was into his twenties, John was in college and the Chief was around sixty.

So if the resolution of the Oedipus complex requires the symbolic slaying of the father, the Rooneys will have to count on the Oedipus complex not applying to the Irish. It was only in the last few years that the boys dared to drink in front of the Chief, or even to appear in public with him dressed in anything but a dark suit, white shirt and tie, such as he most always wears. But if they can't overthrow their father, they can expand upon him.

Each of the boys would have liked to take the helm of the Steelers. The family heirloom fell, however, to Dan, the oldest. The Chief had in mind Dan's becoming an electrician, since he didn't want to be a doctor or a lawyer; the Chief had an in with the union. "But Danny just wanted to go up to the Steelers' training camp and work," he says, "and there's no point in making a fella do what he isn't interested in"—anyway not when it is a matter of his life's work, as opposed to his waking up at six in the morning on vacation in Canada to go to early mass.

As for Artie, the scout, when someone suggests that he may have inherited his father's handicapping gifts, in terms of ballplayers rather than horses, Artie looks pleased as Punch. But what Artie wanted to be when he finished college was an actor. The Chief says he is always running into old friends from among "Pittsburgh theatrical people," and he is proud enough that actress Anne Jackson is his cousin. But he was not eager to have an actor son. "I knew Artie was wasting his time," he said, "but I let him play the string out."

So Artie went off to New York to try his fortune. "Actually my type was pretty much in demand," he says. "I made everybody around me on the stage look like fruits." But after a year or so on the boards Artie turned back toward a role more like his father's.

When racing was legalized in Pennsylvania and the family bought into William Penn Raceway, Artie worked there for a while, it being his turn to get a chance to prepare himself for a managerial job. If he had stayed on he would have become president and general manager instead of John, but Artie wanted to return to the Steelers. "The other day after I got back from a trip to the coast," he says, "my wife heard me telling somebody, 'I saw Fido out there, and he said he's seen Bow-wow.' " Bow-wow and Fido are a couple of scouts. " 'When are you going to get a real job?' my wife asked." Artie smiles.

Most observers, however, feel that of all the boys Tim, thirty-five, is most like the Chief. They think he has the most spark. But Tim couldn't cling to his Pittsburgh roots because there was no more room for Rooneys in the Steeler setup, and after he had worked for a few years as a stockbroker he went down to West Palm Beach to help run the dog track. Then the brothers took on their biggest challenge: the purchase of Yonkers Raceway for some $48 million.

When Artie came to New York to be an actor he was warned by his brothers that if a man came up to speak to him on the subway it would be for the sake of making unnatural advances. So he nearly slugged the first man who asked him for directions. The Rooney boys are more sophisticated nowadays, but their venture into New York is a hazardous one. Off-track betting has cut into the attendance at Yonkers, the plant there is aged, Sonny Werblin is planning a big new harness track in New Jersey, and there are thirteen different unions to deal with.

The first night Yonkers opened under Rooney management there were pickets outside. Except for the 1968 NFL players strike, it was the only picket line the Rooneys had ever experienced. "If there was ever any trouble in Pittsburgh," Tim says, "there was no question whose side you were on; you were with the unions." But with Pittsburgh unions, he adds, "you were dealing with guys you grew up with."

There was no work for the twins, John and Pat, in sports when they finished college, so John taught high school for three years and Pat worked as a copper salesman. Then Liberty Bell opened and they worked their way up from punching tickets. Now John is president of William Penn, the nighttime har-

196

ness operation, and Pat is president of Green Mountain.

At least one man who has been close to the family for some time thinks that Pat is the twin with the most spark. Certainly Pat comes closest of all the brothers to making a pointed remark about the Chief's view of life. "My father just doesn't understand that when some people wake up in the morning and look at their face in the mirror, it's not the greatest thing in the world," Pat says. "He thinks being a good Catholic takes care of all that."

None of the young Rooneys will ever enjoy the geographical unities of their father's life. But the boys have advanced beyond their father in necessary ways. "He's a brilliant man," says Dougherty. "But he's a man of the handshake. He finds transition to tax lawyers and comptrollers uncomfortable."

So far, with their father behind them and with the help of an expert Philadelphia lawyer–loan arranger named John T. Macartney, who is secretary-treasurer of the Yonkers corporation, the brothers are making the transition with a looseness that Johnny Blood might appreciate.

"They can be agonizing in their casualness in coming to meetings late or leaving early or not accepting what the meeting is for," says Dougherty. "Like the Yale band, they like to march out of step. But they do it in a way that's probably as disciplined as the Yale band."

There are people in Pittsburgh, and not just snobs or Protestants, who find fault with the Rooneys' original sources of power. "Senator Coyne was Andy Mellon's nigger; the Mellons kept him in power," says one such critic, who goes on to point out that for all the Chief's philanthropy, modesty and residential loyalty to the North Side, he has never had anything like the quality of civic bravery shown by Jack O'Malley—a local boy who played basketball with the Detroit Pistons, became a priest, could have been the bishop of Pittsburgh but went to live in the North Side and organize the poor blacks politically. Irish cops drive by the ground-floor window of O'Malley's apartment at night and yell obscenities at him, and he jumps out the window onto the sidewalk and offers to fight.

"The worst thing anybody can do is go into Art's office and say, 'I won a lot of money on that game,' " says an old friend of the Chief's, criticizing him from another angle. "He doesn't want to hear anything about gambling around him. All that money, he's got too much responsibility. He can have all that money. He's not the guy he used to be."

The guy he used to be must have had rough edges, in fact a rough center. They say the Rooneys could be cold-blooded about getting where they wanted to be, about avoiding being thought of as rubes or stiffs or yokels. Certainly, though he has given away a lot of money, he has never given away an edge in business dealings. The Chief is a teetotaler now, and he has always gone to mass every day when humanly possible, but he raised hell in the old days. He used to loaf in the saloon of Owney MacManus, who said before he died, "Naturally I had to drink with the boys and, as the day wore on, the effects began to show, I suppose. I've always been a great talker, but I never thought

197

I was getting out of hand until my customers took it into their heads to throw me out one night. 'On what grounds?' I demanded to know. 'I own this place. On what grounds is the proprietor thrown out of his saloon?' They'd make some claim that I was guilty of monopolizing conversations. Pretty soon I was being thrown out of my own saloon every night. I even went to the extreme one day of refusing to drink anything at all. But did that stop Rooney and his gang? It did not. Cold sober, I was thrown out. That is man's final degredation—to be thrown out of his own place, sober."

That is the closest thing to a cold-blooded story about the Chief raising hell I have been able to turn up. Before he met his wife, Kathleen, a great woman in everyone's estimation, the Chief loafed with a lady who, according to an informed source, "was a rough one. When she got drunk she'd fight like a man." The Chief came up in politics at a time when North Side constituencies were poor and large sums of money came into political headquarters in cardboard boxes. Uncle Jim's advice to newly elected legislators is, "Get you an office with a high transom, so they can just throw the money in and you won't see 'em."

The Chief could be accused of dominating his brothers, except for Dan the priest, who probably could never have been dominated by anyone but God. The Chief was such a strong figure that it was perhaps easy for Jim and Vince to slip into drinking-uncle's roles, and for Jim to ruin the beer distributorship he and Vince went into, causing resentment on Vince's part. There is a family story that one afternoon while Jim, well into adulthood, was living with his mother, she said to him, "Jim, kill that fly for me," and he said, "I'll do it tonight." There is another story about Jim, that in his playboy days, when he was visiting New York frequently to patronize the Cotton Club in Harlem, he walked into his Follies girl's eighth-floor apartment and was confronted by a tiny dog that kept yapping and worrying at his feet. The Follies girl was in a back room, dressing. Jim picked up the little dog and dropped it out the window.

"Where's my little dog?" said the Follies girl, coming into the parlor.

"He's out taking a walk," said Jim. I guess that is a cold-blooded story.

I am trying to counteract some of the alleged saccharinity of my treatment of the Rooneys in *Sports Illustrated*. (I thought all that about his belting the boys was unsaccharine when it appeared in the story, but maybe not by Pittsburgh standards.) At the Super Bowl in Houston, when the Chief walked into a restaurant, a big table full of important TV people rose spontaneously and applauded. Norm Van Brocklin stopped his team's warm-ups before the Falcon–Steeler game to introduce all his players to the Chief. "There is no more beloved figure in the whole world of sports," says Edward Bennett Williams. It has been my experience that if you hang around a beloved figure long enough he will show a streak of meanness or fraudulence. Just like regular people. I was sincerely ready for such a streak to show up, hanging around with the Chief.

"My conscience is very elastic," said the Chief as we drove toward New York. "The way we came up . . . And some of this Watergate stuff has been going on since the beginning of time. Spies and that. But when you start forging telegrams and that, that's below the belt. And you use the security people you already have, legally. You don't go out and hire hoods.

"In this country, I don't think you would ever have the Nazis. The Jews, the Irish, Syrians, Italians, blacks. They wouldn't let them. It's not like there was all one kind of people, that could be fooled at once. But this here Erkleman, and Hardleman—it was like a fiction book. They had something on everybody. If someone hadn't got those guys, they would've been electing Presidents and senators for years.

"This Gray. I can see how a person can get involved in something. But the way he took those files, he hadda be either a rube or a weak sister. If anybody, I don't care if it's my brother, says 'Here, take these files and destroy 'em,' I'll say, 'You do it!' "

At Aqueduct the Chief apologized that he didn't know everybody the way he used to, but they recognized him right away at the gate, passed us all through, and people who looked like the tout on the Jack Benny radio show used to sound began to come up to him as soon as we got close to the windows. "Hello, Ott," they would say to him. "Were you in Florida? You know Ottie Siegel is very sick."

He played five races, using New York Racing Association vice-president Pat Lynch's "figures"—the kind of thing any serious horseplayer can work up, if he takes the time, from public information—and computed them out by his own formula, and he bet five or six hundred dollars altogether and came out close to $1000 ahead, hitting an exacta that paid $26.80. Not a bad day, but nothing like the killing he made in 1936 in two days at Empire City and Saratoga.

The Chief does not like to talk about the killing. I asked him about it in the car and he wouldn't say anything at all. It was probably the greatest individual performance in the history of American horseplaying. According to the story as it is usually printed, the Chief had $300 in his pockets and ran it to $21,000 one day at Empire City. He was planning to go back to Pittsburgh but he and a fighter named Buck Crouse dropped into a friend's sporting crowd restaurant and it wasn't long before the three of them were on their way to Saratoga. There the Chief bet $2000 eight-to-one on a horse named, portentously, Quel Jeu. The horse won, and so did several more during the day, by the end of which he had cleared $256,000.

Well, that is the kind of story which may well be inflated. In an attempt to get the truth of that story during my stay with the Steelers, I talked to six different people who were in a position to know, or to believe they knew. Here is what I found out.

Betting in those days was oral. You dealt personally, at the track, with established bookies, a class of people the Chief liked immensely. You could win bigger in those days because when you placed a bet at given odds it stayed at those odds, even if the bookie changed the price for subsequent bettors. When telephoning bets across state lines was made illegal, the Chief's large scale betting days were over. He doesn't see much percentage in betting under the parimutuel system, whereby the odds are continually recomputed on the basis of the handle and the state and the track take healthy cuts. He enjoys it fairly often, but he doesn't see much percentage in it.

When the Chief went up to New York for the races that weekend in 1936, he owed bookies money, I was told, and the Steeler franchise was in bad shape. The Chief was by no means a rich man. The killing established the Rooney fortunes.

The Chief's bets were based on Tim Mara's information, which was, as they say, good. There may have been eleven winners in a row. The Chief had to hire an armored car to get the money back to Pittsburgh. A good piece of it was somehow lost along the way. The Chief walked into brother Vince's house with currency spilling out of his pockets and said, "You don't ever have to worry about money again." He gave a nice chunk to Father Dan in China. (Who later paid him back with information on the soybean crop in China which enabled the Chief to make a nice commodities score. The Chief has been known since it is said to peel off $10,000 and hand it to a priest with a worthy project whom he has just met after a good day at the track.) I am forced to conclude, however, that the total was not really $256,000.

"He told me," said Milton D. Taylor, the director of racing at Yonkers— whom the Chief called "the Babe Ruth, Hans Wagner and Ty Cobb of this business"—"that he went to Saratoga with $10,000 and ran it to $380,000. And he would've gone to $700,000 if Frank Erickson had been there. Frank Erickson was a bookie who never scratched his prices."

Every time I talked to a new informed source, the figure got more confidential and higher. All I am at liberty to say is that it may have been a good deal more than $380,000—1936 dollars—and it may have been a *lot* more. You can talk about Man o' War and Arcaro all you want. The Chief for my money is the biggest figure in horse racing history.

We spent the night in son Tim Rooney's eleven-room house in Scarsdale. Tim has what he believes to be virtually every book written by or about the Kennedys. The next day he gave us a tour of Yonkers, where he informed us that "the mushroom people" take all the track's manure away. Farmers used to pay for it, but then manure became unfashionable and the track had to pay to have it hauled away, but now it is somewhat back in style and the mushroom people remove it for free. The previous ownership of Yonkers would probably not have known such details about the operation.

We left Yonkers and headed toward the farm, which is in Winfield, Maryland, down the road from the place Whittaker Chambers used to have. On the way the Chief said, "I brought the first Brahmans into this part of the country. They all had humps on their backs. People used to come look at them, they looked like elephants. I used to have all ex-horsepeople running the farm. Ex-grooms, ex-trainers, ex-jocks. They were all Irish. And they were all drunks. There'd be whiskey bottles under every tree. Seventy-seven cows died. I was on the train with this old guy and we got to talking, he said he was a farmer. I told him about the cows dying. He said it was probably from eating out of galvanized tubs. Some of the galvanized got in their stomachs. Then we talked a while longer and he found out I was a horseman and all, and he said, 'Your cattle didn't die of those tubs. Your cattle starved to death.' I started to laugh. I said, 'You know, I think you're right.' My guys were all horse guys, not cattle guys. And they'd drunk too much to go out in the sun. So I had to get rid of the cattle." He laughed again.

The farm is now run by Arnold and Roberta Shaw, a sober couple. Arn Shaw used to work as a brakeman with the Bangor and Aroostook Railroad. We viewed a Black Angus bull named Timmy Rooney who had delighted the Chief by jumping around and causing himself and his cage to go end over end—"doing a Brodie"—before the Chief's eyes at the Gaithersburg Fair. The mailman had told Arn that the bull did it because a lady had walked by with a poodle. The Chief was delighted by the idea of his having been at the Gaithersburg Fair in the first place. "You know, for a guy like me. A fair. And animals." He had the air of a slum kid at a petting zoo. Smoking a Toby.

We looked at some cows, which looked at us the way cows always do, as if they were saying, "Say what?" or "Uhr, excuse me?" The Chief seemed to like the cows almost as much as he used to like bookies.

As we were getting ready to leave for Shenandoah Downs to watch the Chief's horse Christopher R. run, the big locust tree out in front of the farmhouse was discovered to be on fire. It was a strange sight: smoke pouring from the top of an old tree, no flames. It looked like a cigar, with branches, being puffed hard. The Winfield Volunteer Fire Department was represented within a few minutes by twelve men, two fire trucks, one pickup truck and a boy.

"A tree fire," one fireman said.

"I be dog."

They poked around in the hollow part at the bottom of the tree and found it to be glowing. Somebody said to a fireman named Howard, "Here's your far, Hard."

"An owl used to roost up there," said Arn. "Sit up there looking at the cat."

"We'll be all right," the Chief assured an inquisitive fireman, "if Hanratty doesn't get hurt."

"Where were you when they called?" one fireman asked another.

"Down over back behind the house somewhere."

Smoke was still pouring from the tree. "Who's got the ax?"

"I don't know. Who had it last?"

"Weiner had it."

"Where's Weiner then?"

"It's funny," said Roberta, "that tree *looked* like it was smoking an hour ago."

The firemen were filling the tree—which was now perceived to be hollow all the way up and down the trunk—with water from a hose directed down from the top by a man standing on a ladder leaning against the smoking tree. It smoked on. An ax was laid unto the root of the tree and at the first cut black water rushed from it like blood.

The Chief looked as solemn as he had looked the whole trip. "You don't think it was the Toby I put in that hollow place at the bottom do you?" he asked.

The firemen took the ladder down and pulled the tree over with a rope. One fireman directed the hose all the way through the fallen carcass, which was still smoking and bleeding, and hit another fireman on the other end.

"Hey, Mr. Rooney," a fireman called as we left. "Them Redskins gonna burn out too."

"From the time I was a kid," the Chief said on the way to the track, "I was the manager of teams; running things, selling tickets. Kids don't have the opportunity to organize that I had then. I was like the coach of the Pittsburgh Collegians, the baseball team that traveled around. I was a kid, and they were young guys and old guys. We'd stay in places where you'd have to reach down with your hand and sweep the bedbugs out." This memory tickled him.

I asked him how he kept his teams together and under control. "Loafed with 'em. Never expected 'em to do anything I wouldn't do. If there were any fights I was right there. One time at a place called Cato, Ohio, at a Chautauqua, my brother that's a priest—he was a rough guy you know—he was the catcher and he took everybody on. That fight didn't end till the firemen came. All the clothes I had on at the end was my baseball pants."

At the track Christopher R. won the Tri-State Futurity—the biggest win for one of the Chief's horses in fifteen years. Tuffy Hacker, the horse's diminutive trainer, told the press in the winner's circle, "I'd rather not answer any questions. I just live from day to day and I just train from day to day." He chased everybody he didn't know out of the picture. The Chief allowed it to be Tuffy's moment.

The Chief had been a bit querulous with Richie and me when we missed a highway exit or got bogged down in the wrong lane of traffic: "My wife says don't go unless somebody's driving you. But look at you guys drive. I wish the football team was as good as I drive." Richie told me that the Chief could be a lot more critical than that of a person's driving. But what his irritation seemed to stem from was just his eagerness to get on as directly as possible to the next glad place. "I like my life because it's pleasant," said Jimmy Cannon of a sportswriter's life. "I function in glad places."

In four days we had visited four racetracks and a farm, in four different states, talking everywhere to dozens of people of high and low estate who came up to the Chief as if they saw him every day, and he had won enough betting at Aqueduct to pay for the trip several times over, and the whole four days had been an easy recreative glide through the cigar smoke Noll hated. At 5 A.M., when we reached Pittsburgh after driving straight from the track, the Chief didn't look any tireder than he ever did, which is to say he didn't look tired at all, and I was worn out from looking for a mean or fraudulent streak. He hadn't shown me one, and he never did.

A remiss streak, yes. There were those seventy-seven cows. And it *was* the Chief's Toby butt that set fire to the tree. Joe Williams (Edward Bennett Williams's son, who was working on the farm) and I saw the long Toby-shaped ash there at the roots. Arn hushed Joe when he started to say something about it.

But if those ex-horsepeople were even less suited to running a farm than Johnny Blood was to coaching a pro football team, I'll bet they were good company in many ways. And I would have paid admission to see that tree fire.

□ **19** □

BURNING OUT
THE REDSKINS

Boys got the muscles,
Teacher got the brains.
Girls got the sexy legs,
We won the game.

—CHEER BROUGHT HOME
FROM THE SECOND
GRADE BY ENNIS
BLOUNT

Before the Redskin game, which was a
Monday night TV game, Bobby Layne was in the Three Rivers press lounge
with two friends from Texas, a big black man named W. W. and a white dwarf
named Rooster. It was the same Bobby Layne of whose greatness at moving
the Steelers in closing moments Baldy Regan had said, "He could make two
minutes seem like an eternity."

I don't think it would be unreasonable to report that Layne and W. W. and
Rooster had been doing some drinking. Layne said W. W. used to be a great
high school running back, on a team that had three signals: W. W. to the left,
W. W. to the right, and W. W. up the middle. "Then tell 'em what happened
to you when you got to college ball, W. W.," said Layne.

"I couldn't understand them audubons," said W. W.

Layne said he had found disfavor as a scout for the Cowboys because he'd
insisted (rightly, it turned out) that UCLA's Gary Began was too short to play
pro quarterback. "Hail," Layne said, "I wadn't tellin' 'em anything but the
truth. Hail, he was shorter'n Rooster here. And *he* couldn't *sing*. You'd want
Rooster on your team for his *singin'* ability."

Somebody asked Layne if he could do something in town the next day. He
said well, he thought they had to go back to Texas. "Don't we, Rooster?" he
said.

"We don't *haf* to do innything, rilly," said Rooster.

Earlier Layne had been on Myron Cope's radio show. "A lot of these modern players don't seem to have as much fun as you guys did," Cope said.

Layne sighed. "I know one thing," he said wearily. "I've had all the fun *I* want."

So did the Steelers and the Three Rivers crowd of 49,220 that night. On the first play from scrimmage Redskin quarterback Billy Kilmer fumbled and Greene recovered on the Redskin 19. But, here we go again, the Steelers couldn't score. Franco was thrown for a 6-yard loss and Gerela missed a 26-yard field goal. Then before long Hanratty threw an interception which set the Redskins up on the Steeler 23. Ham threw Washington's Larry Brown for a big loss and the Redskins settled for a field goal.

How well and for how long was Hanratty going to be able to pass with broken ribs? He was wearing a big thick pad like a mustard plaster taped over them, but Washington led the league in sacks. The day before, George Perles had said to Hanratty, "You know, I look at you a little differently now. Have the endorsements started coming in? Good cripe! No wonder the game's sold out. Everybody who ever went to Notre Dame! All the Irish! All the former quarterbacks! Johnny Lujack will be watching! I don't think the other guy, Hornung, was the Golden Boy after all. You are. You gonna cut your hair?"

"No, George."

"Aw, come on."

"It's just another game, George." Then Hanratty rolled his eyes and made his hands, holding a sandwich, tremble.

Now Diron Talbert of the Skins with a chance to cream Hanratty, just ran in, yelled "Terry," and grabbed him gently. They waltzed a half-turn around. Hanratty was grateful and a little puzzled; they had never met personally before. Soon Hanratty hit Shanklin for 6 and Harris went 35 yards over left end and Hanratty threw 7 yards to Preston Pearson, who leapt and speared the ball in the end zone.

In the second quarter Hanratty was hit and thrown by 275-pound Verlon Biggs, but he pulled himself up, and after a Washington field goal he took the Steelers on a 64-yard drive which ended in a beautiful 24-yard pass between him with smooth spiral and Shanklin in full stride for a touchdown. Steelers 14–6.

In the second half Hanratty threw another interception. Mel Blount's pass coverage held the Redskins to a field goal.

Then the Steelers pulled one of those *sauve qui peut* plays that they did so well: Harris fumbled a handoff on the Steeler 15, Van Dyke and Washington's Ron McDole dove for the skidding ball, McDole got it, ran 3 yards, Harris returned to stick McDole, McDole fumbled almost into the Steeler end zone, Mullins picked up the ball and ran it back to the Steeler 10. Whoops. It was a lively bit of give-and-take, and Franco's quick role switch from fumbler to fumbler-causer was a nice touch, but there was a better loose-and-loose-and-loose-again-ball play coming up.

Not to mention more quarterback drama. This game was the first one I had watched from the sidelines. (I visited the press box only long enough to notice a magazine up there called *Touchdown,* "the best American football magazine for specialist in Japan," which was mostly in Japanese but had a clothing ad with the slogan "Round and Round, Run and Run, with Your Duffle Coat On! Joe," and seemed to attribute the statement "Winning Isn't Everything, It's the Only Thing" to a man named Jim Hisa.) The sideline area was a strange new place, with people running in from the field with slightly glazed eyes to stand next to me like characters stepping down off a movie screen, and television cables and earphone wires snaking and whipping in coils all around our feet, and recurrent great surrounding roars bursting on us as though we were caught in a tiger's throat. I only remember two things clearly from down there that night. One was that I spotted a man in the stands in a purple fur coat and told Frenchy that someone in the crowd had outdressed him, had on a purple fur coat, and he said, "Yes. That's Henderson, my tailor." (Wearing his sequined arm sling, he had earlier complained that anything he wore—such as his multicolored tasseled Serbian yarmulke—"might look *attractive,* but I can't win any dressoffs with my arm like this.")

The other thing I remember was the sight of Hanratty suffering after being hit for the fourth time and leaving the game. He sat on the bench huddled under the cowl of his bad weather cape (it was just over freezing), his head down, only his nose and moustache showing from the side, and TV and still cameramen all over him with lenses. We don't get to see much actual live on-the-scene suffering on television. This was a clear-cut case of it and Hanratty portrayed it with great dignity. He looks a little like the *Esquire* man, the one with the big eyes, only in his case it's a combination of eyes and bags, but he has a great face for roguishness and also for pain. Hanratty sat fixed, alone except for the visual people. It would have been a strange sight from directly overhead: a frenetic game on behind the backs of two dozen cameramen who were focusing on one still bowed, seated figure in black.

On the field, meanwhile, a Redskin fumble was recovered by Wagner and fumbled by Wagner and recovered by Edwards. And a quick black figure in black and gold, Joe Willie Gillie, started leading the Steelers downfield. He hit McMakin twice, and Franco picked up two tough first downs, and then Gilliam decided he'd just put it up there again to buzz through the night air like a huge brown hell-for-leather bee and somebody intercepted it.

And Wagner intercepted right back, fumbled, and recovered his own fumble. A great night for loose balls (the big one still to come). And also for loose Joe: he threw two incompletions, scrambled and ran for 10 yards, and then hit Barry Pearson—striding between linebacker and safety like a man slipping by dint of great timing through swinging doors untouched—for a 54-yard touchdown. Wagner, who had as Gilliam put it "saved my ass" with his just-previous interception, ran onto the field and hugged Gilliam, and it made an even better picture than Hanratty had: black man and white man, both with full smiles and good moustaches, in each other's arms with no reservations.

206

It was carried by both the *Pittsburgh Courier* and the *New York Times.*

Joe Gillie, it was clear, was not afraid to walk out there in front of the world and Howard Cosell on skinny black legs and put the ball in the *air.* As a matter of fact he threw a pass again the next chance he had, from his own 22, and it was intercepted. The Steelers had now caught three of Gilliam's passes and the Redskins two. The Redskins soon scored to make it 21–16 Steelers.

On the sidelines two Steelers were resting, waiting to go back in, and talking. They had each given tickets to two different women, and all four of these women were sitting close together. The players kept looking back over their shoulders at the stands, hoping the women would not get to talking among themselves. One player used the word "sluts."

The other player thought for a moment. "You know," he said, "somebody might call *us* sluts."

The ball went over. The crowd roared, screeched, shook its myriad fists, importuned the fates. Jumped up and yelled and got jostled for standing in front of somebody and yelled back at the jostler and sat down, still yelling in all directions.

The first player looked around at the tumult and mused. "I'll bet," he said, "we're the only two people in this stadium talking about pussy."

And they pulled on their helmets and reentered the fray.

The Steelers had to punt and the Redskins were about to score the touch-down that might well have won the game for them when the Steelers pulled out their secret weapon: the hot-potato turnover. The Redskins' tight end slipped and fell at the line of scrimmage, so Wagner, who would have been covering him, moved over to help out against Larry Brown, and as Brown caught a pass on the goal line Wagner smacked him so hard the ball squirted away and Edwards caught it, and when Edwards went on to fumble it Wagner fell on it, and when Wagner lost it Greene recovered it. The ball bounced like that all night and the Steelers kept coming down on it. Why wouldn't it keep on bouncing like that as long as their hearts were pure?

Gilliam refrained from throwing any more passes for the last two minutes, Franco picked up two more tough first downs, and the Steelers had rolled up another strange victory on God's rough tumbling ground.

A scribe asked Gilliam why he quarterbacked the way he did.

"Put it on my zodiac," he said. "I'm a Capricorn."

The next morning at the Hilton I saw Howard Cosell, who was hoarse, and he said, "I never saw a game with so many errors."

I don't know whether Bobby Layne went back to Texas that day or not. The last time I saw him he was walking along a Three Rivers walkway (*toward Mrs. Rooney's box?* And what were his other four friends like?) with his arm around his former teammate Jack Butler—quarterback and defensive back, like Gilliam and Wagner—saying, "Jack . . . you liked to *hit,* din't you?"

□ **20** □

RACE

*Please stop my subscription. I have had just about all the
colored people stuffed down my throat I can stand.*
                    —LETTER TO *SPORTS
                    ILLUSTRATED*

"**I** never judge a person on the color of
his skin," said Bradshaw. "I have a black man working for me who doesn't
have any fingers. But I hire him, 'cause I trust him. Black kids come over and
throw the football with me. To me, the color issue's not an issue at all. There's
an old saying, you're sitting under a skunk but can't smell him; maybe that's
the way it is. But I don't see it."

"Ralph!" exclaimed Dwight White one day in the training room, when
Berlin betrayed an ignorance of a WAMO (the local soul station) disk jockey
named Superman whom Dwight had been praising. "I thought you was socially artickilate!"

Dwight shook his head. "But that's awright," he said as sententiously as
possible. "Ralph and I gonna work out the problem. As long as people of good
will can get together . . . Hooo!"

In fact Dwight ate Thanksgiving dinner at Berlin's house. Bruce Van Dyke
and Gladys Davis once walked into a banquet together to see what the assem-
bled Burghers would say. "They weren't *ready* for it," said Gladys.

The Steeler organization could point to several signs of nonracism: A black
first-string middle linebacker. A black quarterback who got chances to do his
thing. Two black offensive guards, one of them first string and the offensive
captain. (Those three positions require cogitation and have been predomi-
nately reserved to white people around the NFL.) A black assistant coach. A
regular defensive eleven of which eight were black. Five black first-round draft
choices in the six years beginning in '69. An owner who lived catercorner from
an establishment known as the Islam Grotto.

Still, there were differences between being a black Steeler and being a
white one. One afternoon there were steaks in front of the lockers of several
white Steelers—honoraria for their appearance at the Duquesne Club to chat
with the members. "No steaks for anybody with black skin, I see," said a

black Steeler. Frenchy, Franco and Joe Greene were in demand for public appearances, but most of the other blacks were overlooked. In four years, Mel Blount had had one autograph session. Hardly any of the blacks made the business contacts that the whites who wanted to did. The blacks were more likely than the whites to be preyed on by people who, as Gilliam put it, "seem sincere and all the time they're planning to fuck your mama and blow you up too."

In '73 there were 26 head coaches in the NFL and none were black, 160 or so assistant coaches and five were black. Pro football executives and fans are predominantly white. Once in a scouts' meeting Artie Rooney mentioned that a certain prospect represented a rare chance to get a good white defensive back. I asked him why whiteness was a positive value in a defensive back.

"We're not racists," he said undefensively, "and Noll certainly isn't, but, you know . . . some people are." On all white-run professional sports teams there is a prevailing, even unconscious, assumption that for the sake of fan empathy and ethnic balance it is always good to get hold of a white player with enough ability to play with blacks. Dave Williams, who played only a few downs for the Steelers, was one of their highest-paid players, because he'd built up a premium value with San Diego as that rarity, a quality white wide receiver.

The various black athletes' revolts of a few years back made an impression. White coaches now must at least make an effort not to show prejudice. One Steeler assistant told Musick, when he was writing a story about Gilliam in '72, "They're all the same . . . lazy. No, damn, I don't meant that . . . but some of them are." When that quote appeared the front office knew right away who the coach in question was and he was called on the carpet. But football coaches don't like people who are skeptical of authority, and black players in general have more reason to be skeptical of NFL authority, or of American authority, than white ones do. Three players have been dumped by the Steelers under Noll because they were considered insubordinate: Roy Jefferson, Dave Smith and John Rowser. All three are black. "No room on this team for anybody that talks," Rowser said.

Rowser had been in disfavor since having a shouting match with Bud Carson on the practice field. When he was traded to Denver Carson said, "Let's don't tell him. Let's make him read about it in the papers."

Bill Nunn was offended when Dave Smith said Pittsburgh blacks were Uncle Toms, but in general Nunn pointed out, "When scouts are talking they'll say, 'He's a little bit militant.' Hey, they don't ever say that about white kids."

Pro football is a bubbling pot from which TV and ticket owners can ladle out a hot stew of redneck grit, immigrant drives, European kicking and Afro-American oomph. Eight of the Steelers' defensive starters and half of the whole first 22 were black and from my part of the country, the South and Southwest.

I went on a scouting trip with Bill Nunn to watch black college ball in Mississippi.

A receiver would dive for a catch, hit the ground and roll. A second man would come flying up, sail over the first one's body, hit the ground and roll. Then an official would come flying up, sail over the second man's body, hit the ground and roll. Officials in black college football are not detached. Rosey Brown, the Giants' scout, says he once saw an official throw his flag, detect another infraction, get excited, reach for his pocket, find the flag gone, run over and pick it up and throw it again. I saw a fight between the full squads of Jackson State and Grambling that ranged over the whole field. A bunch of Gramblings would chase a Jackson State 30 yards before he swung back around into the general melee, and then a bunch of Jackson States would isolate a Grambling and chase him a long way. It went on and on. I heard of times when the fans would get so involved that they not only started encroaching on the sidelines but would cover one end of the field to the thirty. And I heard about the time everyone stood for the national anthem and saw the afternoon's two head coaches come rolling out onto the field, tearing each other's shirts to ribbons, over the question of whether the ball would be striped or not.

At one festive point during that trip—all the points I recall were festive—Garcia, a black representative of the SEPO scouting organization, said, "You never been around so many black people for so long, have you? You never heard so many *motherfuckers* and *niggers* before, have you?" To be honest I had to reply, "Well, I never heard so many *motherfuckers.*"

And I never had any better time socially than I did the night Nunn and I went over to the house of Coach W. C. Gordon of Jackson State. We had boiled chitlins with hot sauce and crackers and bourbon and then we went on to an after-hours club where we had bourbon and slapped hands every 30 seconds for good reason over something that had just been said and at one point people were talking about the ways various friends smelled and someone cried, "You talk about a nigger that's *fonky!*" I wondered, "Should I be here?" and about then I fell flat on my back on the floor, as a result of tipping my chair too far back and one thing and another. If I'd been a black person in the Duquesne Club and that had happened to me, I would have been made to feel uncomfortable. But in this place no one even called me a Jagov.

Black athletes look and move better than white ones on the average. I don't see anything invidious about the belief that black people have longer Achilles tendons than whites (which means, as a friend of mine once pointed out, that Ethel Waters can jump higher than Kate Smith). Everybody knows that black athletes tend to be faster than white athletes. "Couldn't a white boy catch me," said the Pirates' Richie Zisk of his speed as a schoolboy receiver.

But when fleet black receivers threaten to blow pro football open, white coaches don't go with the blow the way black college coaches do—they devise zone defenses to neutralize the flash. When black defensive linemen (most of the great ones recently have been black; it used to be they were Italian) dominate the game, white coaches devise boring short-pass and junk-blocking strategies to muffle them. Pro football would be a more exciting game if it appreciated black influence as much as American music has. I wish a black concern—such as Stax, the record company that has considered buying the Memphis basketball franchise—would buy a team in the NFL, or the WFL, and hire Gilliam as its quarterback and go for broke.

The black Steelers were proud, but experience had proved that you got by best in football by keeping your own counsel and going with the system. Gilliam had been at Tennessee State when Stokely Carmichael came in and stimulated a campus riot. "Stokely said kill whites and then left before the trouble," Gilliam said. "He appealed to people's emotions. Violence isn't the answer. Education and money are. Money talks. Bullshit walks."

As for white people's attitudes toward a black quarterback: "They still think he'll never do it. I can't begin to know why. I think that comes from deep within each man. I don't even give it that much thought."

Al Young, the gifted receiver who came down with the blood disease in camp, was in the crowd of students fired on by white National Guardsmen at Orangeburg, S.C. He hit the dirt. Two of his teammates were shot in the back. One died and the other was paralyzed for a while "and was never the same person. I was bitter," said Young. "But I had to live. And this [football] was real."

Dwight White often turned to the recorded rapping of John Kassandra, a.k.a. Moses, "when I fall off into my funky moods. Moses brings me on back." One of the things Moses said was, "Maybe we ought to quit crying and laying on black. All black people aren't poor, all poor people aren't black."

And Dwight had his sense of humor. "I was moving into my house in a new subdivision in Dallas," he said. "You know how you are when you're moving, hair all over my head, cigarette hanging out of my mouth. The doorbell rings. It's this man and his wife and little kid. White. I open the door and their mouths fall open. I tell 'em, 'Come in,' and they say 'Anything we can do to help . . .' But next thing I know they got a big white fence around their house, and something back there, every time I drive up, goes 'WOO WOO WOO!' I don't know what it is, but they got something back there, goes 'WOO WOO WOO.'"

Still things happened that were too dumb to laugh off. Dwight and I were eating Mexican food in the hotel at Palm Springs when a small pink man sitting with two white-haired ladies came over and said, "Excuse me. Those two boys that stuck their heads in the door a minute ago. Those two black boys. Were they basketball players?"

Dwight said he didn't know.

"Because they were so tall," persisted the man.

"Maybe they were with the free love convention," I said.

"Oh," said the man. "You with the free love convention?" he asked Dwight.

"Yes," said Dwight.

As a matter of fact the two tall people had been Dwight and Webster. The pink man went back to the two ladies. "He's with a free love convention," he reported.

"Now that man," said Dwight gravely, "is a fool."

□ **21** □

MAD DOG

Americans have a special horror of giving up control, of letting things happen in their own way without interference. They would like to jump down into their stomachs and digest the food.

—WILLIAM BURROUGHS

Dwight White was into letting things happen. As a rusher he was headstrong, in spite of the way he knocked out or broke several teeth in college: "The quarterback was scrambling so I was after the cat. He goes like he's bracing for the blow. But this cat's like a coward—he crumples to miss the lick. I dive, he goes on the ground, and I keep right on going over his head. I'd just got a new helmet and it was half on and half off. I went right into the ground with my mouth."

As an announcer of himself to hotel desk clerks he was expansive: "That's me. The man who walked the water and tied the wind, come to bring good to your neighborhood. You can see me free till Sunday."

As a writer, he had been more into flow than control: "In English class I coulda been a Hemingway, a Edgar POE. I laid a *verbal avalanche* on that woman. A theme this long!" He stretched his hands out as a man might in telling a fish story, only vertically, and smiled with pride. "But I'd have all these comma splices. She'd give me a B plus or a A for expression, slash, a F minus for grammar. Point out a sentence fragment up here. That's what I wanted up there! Leave 'em hangin'! Lookin' for more! Cut it off right there!"

"Did you ever pass?" asked Gilliam.

"No," said Dwight. "I never did." They slapped hands.

But as Dwight said himself, "I'm not unintelligent by any stretch of the imagination." And, "Football isn't enough. It doesn't contest me. I don't want to be a star in one thing and a turd in everything else."

So he reflected. "I always been one of them old rough awkward dudes. I am a hateful old—I can be as hateful . . . I'm sick. I'm really sick up here in the head. Sometimes I could spit in the Pope's eye. I can be arrogant and nasty and it's just me. I think the road to recovery is knowing you're sick. I know it's me.

213

"To be as considerate as I am. Like this black and white thing. I'm just off into *people*. I think I'm real considerate. If I don't know you, I'd rather for you to offend me than me to offend you.

"I'm just crazy. I haven't figured myself out yet. Lot of things are too easy for me to figure out. Some things rest very heavy on my mind. I see so much stuff that through some physiological or metabolic way—it gets inside me and I take it out on football. But after the game, it don't go away. I'm aware of too much.

"Back home in Dallas, my little brother eight years old, he sees dudes driving up and down the street cursing, old drunks, broads selling pussy. Dick Gregory said he saw all that, everybody getting along fine—he had no interest reading about some little broad Jane, going up on the hilltop with little dog Skip and some dumb jive broad Sally . . . He sees hos selling themselves on the street. That's more interesting to him.

"I want to inspire the kids. It's an illusion about pro football, that we're supermen. I'm just like you, man. I'm just like everybody. But I'm something the black kids can identify with.

"I see this broad standing on the corner. Broads like that are just sick. It's a long, long history why broads get into that. But I talk to her, like I talk to other people. The broad collapses. I know immediately she OD'd. I have learned, coming up in the black community, there are some things you don't fool with.

"Am I going to let her die, or what? If I call an ambulance they just going to put her in the joint to get her off heroin, and that means she wont' be in the street for that pimp she's working for, who's not going to like that at all. People are going by just letting her lie there.

"So I called an ambulance.

"Her pimp comes then. Wants me to pick her up and take her to his place. Says all he's got to do is pack her in ice, she done this before. He swear down on me: 'You ain't going to help me, man?'

"I said I really wish he'd wait for the ambulance to take her to the hospital. But he calls his friend to pick her up. This cat—he didn't care anything about her. Didn't care whether she lived or died. All he cared was that she make money for him. That's just ignorant; being a low-down person.

"And that's my own people, man! I had no personal attraction to her. She was just a plain broad. Pimp says, 'Hey, that's the way you got to do them broads.'

"I'm aware of these things, man, and it just fucks me up. I'm sick. I know about too many sick things. It makes me sick.

"I like to break a quarterback's, you know, spirit. Give him a good body blow or slam him to the ground. I'll be just as vicious and brutal as I have to be. Football's not hard to me. It's the thing right at hand to do. And you can use it. It's giving you a couple of giant steps before you get off into the race, into the world.

"Last year, offenses did obvious things to us and we did obvious things back. This year they're playing all kinds of games with us, and it's funky. You can figure out too much shit. But if it's third down and twenty, I don't care if you know exactly what I'm going to do. I don't care what you're going to do. I'm going to jack my tail way up, get that sprinter's start and you know I'm *coming.*"

□ 22 □

OAKLAND AND DENVER

Rapture's great, but you can get hung up on it.
—TIMOTHY LEARY

Football language is very sexual. Rushes are said to "put their ears back and come"; before a game someone may walk around the dressing room crying, "Get it up! Get it up! Get it up!" Against the Oakland Raiders in game 8 the Steeler Front Four got it way up and came and came. Clever Ken Stabler was knocked out of the game early by L. C. ("Attaway Bags, fuck him up!" a Steeler cried on the sidelines), and Stabler's replacement at quarterback, Daryle Lamonica, liked to drop back and throw the long one, which made him the Front Four's meat.

The World Series had been played on the same field just the week before and turf had been laid down over the infield and rained on. "Once my head slid under a piece of turf," said Greene. "I thought I was playing baseball and my head had slid under second base." The Steeler defense behind the hurting Hanratty wasn't much—194 yards to Oakland's 395—but Wagner recovered a key fumble, Hanneman helped provoke two bad snaps by belting the Oakland center in the head, Blount and Edwards intercepted and White picked off two passes—one that Greene tipped into the air and another that Dwight swept right out of Lamonica's hands. Asked on the sidelines how he managed to catch the second ball, he gave the sort of answer which, if postgame interviews were more truthful, would often appear in sports sections: "I did my hands like this," he said, waving them gleefully, "and the muffucker stuck." The Steelers won 17–9.

"The Lord has his hand on our shoulder; I hope He don't take it off," said the Chief. The Lord may have had it on the Raiders' and it slipped off; several Oakland blockers, the Steelers maintained, had their shoulders smeared with Vaseline. "It's like you gonna wrestle a greased pig," said Greene. One of his most terrible charges, featuring his feared forearm uppercut, came after he complained fruitlessly to an official about the gunk on the guard opposite him, George Buehler. (After the Pro Bowl Russell reported that the Oakland trainer had confided to him there that Buehler had admonished him, since there was a rule against foreign substances on the jersey, to "make sure that Vaseline's made in the United States.") Mansfield also reported that he'd been handed a partially deflated ball to snap. This was certainly possible, because, as Jackie Hart pointed out, balls are inspected before the game by officials, but after that the home team has every opportunity to doctor them. Hart said in the exhibition game in New York the Giants had made little marks on the balls, which would have made it possible for them to slip special ones to the Steeler offense. Mansfield looked down at another ball he was about to snap in Oakland and saw that "FUCK YOU" had been written on the laces.

The sky was gray-black. Birds reeled overhead. They would settle in the stands and then rush out into the sky over the field again and then resettle. I couldn't figure out what made them take off. It didn't seem related to the surges in crowd noise. I couldn't trace any pattern.

I thought I could, though, in the Steelers' recoveries. They should have been beaten but they kept coming up with the big play. I said to Wagner, "It's destiny."

"Determination," Wagner corrected me.

"*Pre*determination," I insisted.

But I was probably wrong. Fate probably doesn't care who wins football games. The next week against Denver, at home, the Steelers lost 23–13.

"In fairness to Pittsburgh," said Denver coach John Ralston, "we caught them at an ideal time. They just had three emotional games. We were in the right spot on their schedule."

In their entire history, actually. The Broncos caught the Steelers on the one weekend in 40 and 10/14 seasons when the team was sitting pretty. "This game will be an interesting test," Hanratty had said. "We never had a cushion before." The Steelers had a cosy division lead and a 13-game regular-season home-field winning streak.

The Broncos pawed the great god Tar-Tan, galloped over him and ate him up. Denver running back Floyd Little managed in the dressing room to confuse the metaphor as well as he had the Steelers' defenses. "The hungry dog," he said, "hunts best."

Noll was advised of Little's remark. "That's said well," he said. "We were either tired or fat."

The Steelers, after all those years, suddenly found fat! Reminded that they put their pants on one leg at a time, more or less like everybody else. (Cus D'Amato, the fight manager, used to hold his pants low and jump into them with both feet.) The Steelers' greatest strength, moreover, had been used against them. "They have the best defensive line we've seen," said Little. "We didn't want them flying in the backfield. We made them commit themselves, and then ran away from them."

"You're always supposed to stop the run first and make them pass," said

Keating. "We started out rushing the passer." And the rush's wave, which had reached such a crest the week before, broke.

Traps, draws and 13 passes whose combined length was only 86 yards left the Steelers in a mighty but misdirected lurch. Hanratty passed for 217 yards and hit Shanklin for a 42-yard touchdown bomb to tie the game early in the fourth quarter—okay, the Steelers were going to pull it out after all. The fans were calling for Joe Greene, who'd been sitting the game out with a bad back. He came in, moving his great thighs. The fans roared and stomped the concrete. The defense was going to rise up again!

But it didn't. And the offense was not nearly strong enough to compensate for the defense's failure to take the ball away from Denver once. The closest the Steelers came to one of their madcap turnarounds was when Wagner so nearly intercepted a pass that he obstructed Edward's view of the ball, and Edwards dropped it.

"They didn't have any pep," said Uncle Jim Rooney. He looked hurt.

□ 23 □

THE BODY

Ah yes; beanbag. Becomes very exciting at times. I saw the world championships in Paris. Several people were killed.
—W. C. FIELDS

I got to talking to one of the Steelers about the people—press, executives, attendants, hangers-on—around the team. The player pointed out that these people were skinny, bulbous, stooped, listing or minuscule, nearly every one of them. "It's the most cataclysmic collection of fucked-up bodies I ever saw," the player said. I had been pretty much discounting the bodies of all these people and dealing with what they had to say. I was brought to realize how much more a player, whose professional medium is largely body, must relate to people in bodily terms.

Few of the Steelers looked ogreish out of uniform. All-pros Wagner and Ham were normal-sized people who claimed to have spent their adolescence as indifferent, overlooked athletes. Dockery in his moustache and cloth cap looked like a schoolteacher who might do slippery moonlight work for the IRA. Mansfield said people often told him he looked more like a professor than a jock (though a friend said, "Well, a professor, or a brick shithouse"). Fuqua looked a couple of inches shorter than his claimed 5–11, and Shanklin might have been a young congressman.

At six feet tall and 200 pounds I felt physically diminished in the Steelers' company, but not in terms of size so much as consistency. A player once grabbed my forearm to illustrate some anatomical point, looked at it for a moment, and then put it down and grabbed a player's arm, which was substantial enough to signify. My thews were as Reddi-Whip to the Steelers' hand-packed French ice cream.

It was true, too, that a given Steeler might occasionally talk to a scribe whose self, wife and first child together the Steeler not only could have lifted easily but also outweighed. And yet the Steeler could nip through a narrow, brief gap between people more readily than scribe, wife or child. The biggest Steelers were incomprehensible compounds of heft and twinkle.

So it was not surprising that even though most of the Steeler bodies could pass for fairly normal, they had strange characteristics. For instance, one Steeler frequently wet his uniform pants. And the bottoms of White's, Shan-

219

klin's and others' feet had to be shaved. "I'm a little too tall," explained Shanklin, as he wielded his safety razor, but the case was actually that running on artificial turf loosened the skin on his soles so that it ruffled and flaked. There was also a condition known as "Astro-toe." To get a good feel of artificial turf the players wore shoes so flexible that toes were often bent drastically in various directions, causing severe sprains.

Bobby Walden once had to have the end joint of his little toe amputated. "When will it grow back?" he asked the doctor. Gerela, the other kicker, had virtually no toenails. Gilliam's feet were so bad that he said, "I wish just one morning I could set my feet down and they wouldn't hurt."

Then there were the hearts. "Their electrocardiograms often look abnormal," said Dr. David S. Huber, one of the two Steeler physicians. "Some of them, if they weren't players you'd rush them straight to intensive care." They say that when Buffalo Bill guard Joe DeLamielleure's heart was tested it blew up the machine.

A part of the body that attracts considerable private speculation, but hardly any public, is the old boy. That was the name one Steeler had for his. I was in his motel room drinking with some people one evening on the road when this Steeler's voice issued from the bathroom. "Look at that face!" he was saying to the mirror. "No wonder they all love me. M-m! And then," he said after a moment, his voice choked, "when I look at my old boy . . ."

"I've seen all of them," said a scout I met on the road. "The biggest in sports was _____'s." And he named a former Steeler, a black one. "People used to come over from the other dressing room to look at it." I mentioned this to a white Steeler who'd been around in _____'s day and he said, "Oh I don't know. It'd been a tossup between his and _____ _____'s" (an interesting image), and he named another Steeler who was white.

I got a friend of mine into the Steeler dressing room and the next time we were out in company together he said, "They aren't much. I mean based on mine, I'd say they were about normal." This struck me as a none too subtle form of self-aggrandizement.

"Who is that guy?" one Steeler asked me about another stranger. "Come in here and wander around looking at our dicks." One media figure was said to keep his tietack at a distance from his tie knot equal to the length of a certain Pirate's old boy. A Steeler claimed he knew someone back home whose old boy was so big "the *veins* in it are like your little finger." The question why some people might loaf with football players as much as they do was answered in part for me one night when one such person said to a Steeler, "Tell him about that night in . . . You don't want to tell him about that, do you?" It turned out this man and the Steeler had once been with two girls in the same motel room, one couple on each bed. The girl under the Steeler was quiet, while the one under the friend was crying, "It's so big!"

A college teammate and professional opponent of a certain retired great said

220

he was once asked what he and the great had said to each other, as opponents, on the field. "He'll tackle me and I'll be dragging him across the goal line," my informant replied, "and I'll say, 'My young son's dick is bigger than your young son's.' "

Then there was the question of overall bigness. "I read somewhere in a magazine, a psychiatrist said life is more difficult for two groups of people," said White. "Fat people and ugly people. They're not accepted in a lot of circles. If I could add one to that it would be big people.

"I want a sportscar so bad, but what would I look like in a sportscar? If I went to buy a suit, I'd probably be a 50, 52 extra long. Shoes, I'm 12, 13, 13½. When you find 'em they cost you. And little old inobvious things like—I go to somebody's house. He has a little benchlike chair. I break the damn thing. You can't just flop yourself about like everybody else. You tear things up. It's embarrassing."

No matter how big you were, you also, on the field, tore parts of yourself up. In college Dwight had a knee injury and subsequent infection which almost cost him his leg. The same kind of thing killed a player the next year, he said. In '73 he played hurt all year, and so did Ham and Russell. Bradshaw, Hanratty, Fuqua, Lewis, Harris, Gravelle, Clack, Mansfield, Mullins, Sam Davis, Keating, Webster, Bleier, Greene, Holmes and Shanklin all missed considerable playing time because of injuries. As for Greenwood, he said "I have never played football in a completely healed position. I always wondered how I'd be able to perform that way."

Russell was the team playing-hurt champion. In '73 he missed a substantial portion of only one game, although he had the following injuries: a pulled hamstring, a pinched nerve and back spasms which bothered him enough that he tried acupuncture, a broken finger, a badly sprained big toe, a shoulder hurt severely enough to require three shots of cortisone, a pulled stomach muscle, a pulled groin muscle, a bruised thigh with a pinched nerve, a slight dislocation of the previously hurt shoulder, a bruised knee, a bad bruise of the other leg, and a tear of the groin muscle that had been pulled. "There you have a realistic picture," he said a little modestly, "of what most players feel like toward the end of the year."

So did the Steelers need a chemical lift? Russell maintained that modern-day ones eschewed amphetamines. "In the old days, some of those old Steelers would stay up all night drinking and then pop bennies like they were popcorn," he said. "These days players are better prepared and in better shape, and they don't need pills." But after the Redskins' George Burman publicly estimated that a third of his teammates were taking pills to get themselves up for games (and as a result Coach George Allen said of Burman, "I'm through with him"), a Steeler let on to me that the one-third estimate would probably be low for the Steelers. He showed me a bottle of capsules. "These are what gave _____ that great game against the _____s," he said. (After that game an opponent said of _____, "He was full of fire.")

Now what I should have done was ask for one of those pills, pop it before a game, and report on what it was like to watch a game bennied-up. But I have had an abhorrence of pills ever since I took a Dexedrine to study for a college exam, learned a whole Introduction to Philosophy course in one night (and forgot it right after the exam), and lay awake for thirty-six hours expecting to see Mephistopheles any minute. A pill strikes me as a bad limb to go out on. I have taken one to make a deadline, though, and so have a lot of other scribes.

As the Colts' Mike Curtis says, "Look, how often does a player take pills? Fourteen times a year? No, make that twenty games a year. That's small in comparison to what some housewives or business executives take." Not to mention some people in other fields of vivid entertainment. It is good that pills are no longer dispensed by NFL trainers. But playing pro football under the influence of speed can hardly be much more hazardous to one's health than playing it straight. "If anybody were thrown out of the game for taking bennies," said one Steeler, "it'd be like getting arrested for doing 70 in a 65." Only "90 in an 85" would be more like it.

Another drug the NFL is officially down on is marijuana. I might say that there were Steelers who resented not being able to smoke it on the team plane after a game, when beer was handed out by a representative of the airline. I know of at least one sports team which is fairly open about referring to reefer; when this team is rallying a player will yell from the bench, "We're smoking that *good* shit now!" But the Steelers were highly cautious about mentioning it. Chuck Dicus was quoted as saying that the Chargers were divided into two camps: smoking and nonsmoking. Pete Rozelle subsequently, and rather summarily, fined several Chargers for "drugs." I guess the idea is that the players' private lives ought to be model, or at least legal, so that they will be a proper influence on their fans. This is at least a little bit like requiring Christians and lions to keep their whiskers trimmed so as not to encourage hairiness among patrons of the Colosseum.

There was at least one area of the Pittsburg stands which regularly smelled of pot, and just before the season Three Rivers hosted a Led Zeppelin concert during which, according to an official source, "There was this thick cloud of marijuana smoke over the whole stadium. They loosed some doves and they hit that cloud and fluttered back down and just stood around in the stands blinking. People wee picking them up and taking them home." But I would hate football *fans* to start popping pills before a game. I can see them now, diving onto the field and grabbing players around the ankles, slobbering, raving. Fans are intense enough unbennied.

One of the most intense things about the Steelers was all the swelling going on, or trying to. Ralph Berlin was always trying to keep the swelling down so they could play. He himself ran like M. Hulot because of terrible college-ball injuries to both his knees. Such severe hurts were treated by the team orthopedist, Dr. John Best. A tall, great-bellied, white-haired man with a Russian wife, Doc Best wore a rumpled hat like the Chief's and once hailed a cab from a

moving ferryboat. The kind of thing characteristic of Doc Best was for someone to say to him, "Doc, I got a cold," and for him to muse for a moment and
then say in a rusty baritone, "So do I."

When part of the body was hurt, Berlin explained, blood and fluid rushed
into it, causing a loss of mobility. You had to resist that by ice, compression
(tape) and elevation. Then after a while you started using heat to *draw* blood
toward the area, to facilitate healing. This alternation of ice and fire Berlin
referred to as "a milking process." Systole and diastole, always going on, all
year.

Which is not to say that the whole thing was down to a science. I sprained
my ankle while throwing the ball around with Dockery and Meyer. Ralph
kindly taped it up for me. After a less than perfectly restful night of waiting
for my ankle to explode I cut the tape off. Ralph was put out: he had wanted
me to leave it on for several days. My ankle felt much better untaped but I
felt guilty, innerly untough. Russell reassured me: "Oh, you always take the
tape off," he said.

In practice Van Dyke asked Berlin what the hard knot in the back of his
leg was and Berlin said scar tissue. Then one of the doctors came up and said
it was a clot, and sometimes those things never go away. Then Van Dyke ran
a play and when he came back the doctor was gone. "He said it was a clot,"
Van Dyke said to Berlin. Berlin said, "Yeah, well, it'll go away." Van Dyke
said, "He said sometimes they never go away." Berlin said, "Yeah, well
. . ." And then Van Dyke ran another play. "If I die," he said, "I've told my
wife to sue."

Once Bradley got blindsided and his whole leg turned purple from the groin
to the toe. Keating had a lump half the size of a baseball come up in the small
of his back, for the first time in his career. If a football medical person took
every such anatomical event to heart, he'd go crazy. The players would have
liked for their cases to be considered more nearly unique than they were.
"Sometimes Ralph treats you like a body," said one Steeler. "I don't want to
be treated like a body by that asshole."

□ 24 □

SCOUTING

A productive kid, though I don't much like his feet.
—FROM A SCOUTING
REPORT

I liked scouts. They had not too much officiousness and a lot of stories. For instance, about the 40-yard dash: the Cowboys once mistakenly timed a prospect in the 35, and drafted him second, he seemed so fast; 49er scout Joe Perry wangled his son, who had one eye, a tryout and then beat him in the 40 in camp, breaking his confidence ("Maybe I shouldn't have done that," Perry said); a scout once timed a prospect over 40 yards down an airport corridor; a scout once reported a prospect's time as "4.9, but he had one leg in a cast."

Bill Nunn, the Steelers' black scout, a Pittsburgh native, told of running out of gas in a little town in Mississippi. A local white man drove up with his wife in the car, stopped, asked Bill if he could help. Bill said he'd appreciate a ride to the gas station, the man said sure, jump in, he was just as friendly and helpful as he could be, and Bill told a local black man that the white man had certainly been nice. "Yep," said the black man. "And the thing about it, it was his brother killed Emmett Till."

There were legendary scouts. Lloyd Wells of Kansas City, one of the first full-time black scouts, drove about in a big El Dorado, hobnobbed with Muhammad Ali, called himself and everybody else "Judge," and might sum up a prospect as follows: "6–3, bowlegged, 240, waist 32, big old blacksmith arms, big old legs, *beautiful.* Most muscular man I ever saw. Whoo! Muscles all *over* his body. He's like a *washboard.* And courage. He'll knock your dick out." Or, on the other hand: "Cush-footed. Walk on his heels. Look at him. Look at his legs. Look at his general makeup. Raggedy. Ass in the air. See his ass over everybody's. He couldn't play *dead.*"

Then there was Will Walls of BLESTO, who was Sammy Baugh's receiver at Texas Christian and had a bit part in *Thirty Seconds over Tokyo.* Now he drives 50,000 miles a year at high speeds even though he has been through a few head-ons such as the one when "I tore this ear off, knocked my teeth out, I heard somebody say 'He's dead,' they put me in an ambulance and I said,

'That's your ass,' and fought like hell to get out and then I woke up and they were boring two holes in my head and I jumped around and said, 'That's your ass,' and they tied me down, God damn that upset me, then I woke up and they said, 'You'll be here a year,' and I said, 'That's your ass,' and they said, 'Well, six months then,' and I said, 'That's your ass,' and got out of there as soon as I could." Wherever he drives, Wells carries a pistol, his own light bulb, because motel light bulbs are too small, and his own good-sized bar of soap, because he can't stand "those little fart bars" you get in motels. He is liable to say of a prospect, "He's fat as the town dog," or, in writing, "Has a very poor stance as his feet are right underneath his buttocks."

I enjoyed watching films of college games with scouts and listening to them discussing the figures on the screen:

"He's the guy, they had another guy scored a touchdown and wouldn't dance in the end zone, so this guy went down and danced for him."

"He the one that stole the desks?"

"Yeah."

"Why'd he steal desks?"

"I asked them that. They said. ' 'Cause that's all there was.' "

"He's got the quickest head I've ever seen. Look at him look around to see if anybody's going to hit him."

"He's a complete coward. But look, he put a good move on there."

"The trouble was, there was no one there to put it on."

"Now this guy's physical, but he doesn't have any movement."

"He even falls slow."

"Can he see, you think?"

"At Villanova we had a one-eyed center. He blocked the ref on one sweep. One game he played against a one-eyed middle guard and the whole game they were saying, 'What's your bad eye?' 'I'm not telling.' "

"He's got the best-looking body in the U.S. But he doesn't do anything."

"Cuticle tackler. He's a reacher and grabber."

"They're all outlaws over there. This other guy hit a policeman in the face with a brick." (The golden mean was somewhere between this and cuticle-tackling.)

"This guy gets in some of the most unfootball-like postures I've ever seen. Lying on his head with his feet up. But where you going to get a guy who runs like this and weighs 235?"

"This kid shows you some real vibration, but he gets fat through the stomach all the way down into his legs."

"When this guy gets inside, he gathers in his body, and doesn't move his hips. I'm not saying he's looking for a place to hide, but . . ."

"You know he had that terrible accident, where he crushed his hips."

In general coaches will tell you that scouts are just guys who can't coach. (But then, so are brain surgeons.) The Steeler coaches tended to make the

Steeler scouts feel like Jagovs. "They throw those Xs and Os at you," said Artie. "It's like a white person who just assumes that a black person's inferior, talking to a black person."

The coaches—that is to say, Noll—had the last word on the draft; but sometimes the scouts prevailed. For instance, in the case of Franco Harris. Artie and his scouts wanted to draft Franco first in '72, but Noll liked Robert Newhouse, a short running back, on the theory that a good little man was better than a good big man. Noll could argue this theory, whatever the strength of its premise, forcefully. The scouts held out for Franco. One day before the draft Artie was working on his charts on the floor of his office. Noll was talking to Haley about how much better Newhouse was. He knew Artie was listening. Noll put his foot on the corner of one of Artie's charts. "You've stepped on my chart!" Artie cried. Noll went hopping around among the charts, saying, "I'm not stepping on your fucking charts!"

However, Noll went along with the scouts and they took Harris. Then Harris called up, unsigned, and said he wasn't going to show for the first day of training camp. Noll threw the phone at the wall. "What a mistake!" he yelled. He never withdrew that statement until after the '72 season. Noll and the scouts were watching the films of Chuck Foreman, another big running back Noll had said wasn't as good as a little one. Foreman was impressive. "I guess I'm wrong," Noll said. "Just like I was wrong about that fullback last year."

Noll left the film room. The lights came on and all the scouts cheered. Then the lights went back off and they returned to their search for good heart, good upper body strength, good feet.

□ 25 □

LOOSING TWO BARELY

*Dead? I, C. Ellsworth Stubbins, dead? Madam, a Stubbins
may sleep much, but he seldom dies.*
—W. C. FIELDS

The Steelers had not won in Cleveland
since 1964. This would have seemed to be the year to do it, they had beaten
the Browns so badly in Pittsburg a few weeks before, but Cleveland coach Nick
Skorich was quoted as saying, "We're not intimidated by the Steelers anymore."

How did Sam Davis feel about Skorich's statement? "Can't listen to that
stuff," he said. "If you get too psyched up, you can't do shit. It's like getting
so mad in an argument you can't convince the other guy. If you don't get
psyched up at all you can't do shit. You have to stay in between."

Gilliam had talked to a man about a possible vending-machine and car-
leasing business using the man's connections and Gilliam's name. "I might
make some *money,*" he said. "If I get to play too, I'm liable to snap out. Be
too happy."

Before the Washington and Oakland games the Chief had told Babe Parilli
he "had a feeling" the Steelers would win, and sure enough. Parilli asked him
if he had a feeling this week. The Chief put him off for a couple of days. Then
he said, "No, Babe, I haven't got it. You're on your own."

The Steelers read in the Cleveland papers about how mean and crazy,
respectively, Joe Greene and Dwight White were. One story said Dwight had
spent much of his time as a youth watching the Three Stooges on TV, and
when he learned that they weren't really hitting each other he got so mad he
went outside and set a cat afire. I went to lunch shaking my head at what an
outrageous bit of apocrypha, and when I came back to the dressing room
Dwight was telling Keating and Van Dyke, "Cat went 'Waaaah!' " He said the
Three Stooges part wasn't true though. "Where'd they get that?"

In Cleveland it was wet and the wind was high. Early on, Franco swept wide
and was knocked into a sideline puddle. He remained muddy-colored and
ineffective, except faking, the rest of the day. And after hitting McMakin on
a pretty neatly timed 27-yard pass between two defenders Hanratty was hit.

He fell backward onto his throwing wrist, spraining it badly, and once again Joe Willie Gillie stepped in.

Several things happened in this game. Gerela kicked a field goal while falling on his back on the wet ground. Greg Pruitt broke loose for the Browns a couple of times when Steeler defenders gambled, went after him too aggressively, "failed to contain." And Joe Willie Gillie almost created of himself a whole new kind of mythical figure: a skinny black good-armed Bobby Layne. He took over from Hanratty and hit Shanklin for a 9-yard touchdown in the midst of a crowd, and the next time the Steelers had the ball he threw it, while leaning backwards off balance, into the wind, way up into the air 50 solid yards right into the hands of Frank Lewis, who, however, dropped it. The Brown's Nick Roman ran into the backfield and belted Gilliam after a penalty whistle had stopped the play (when the Steelers told Roman to watch that stuff, he said, "Fuck all you guys"), and indeed rushers were flailing at Gilliam's thin limbs the whole game; but he did a cool, vivid job, with advice at times from Mansfield in the huddle.

"That's what helps make us go," said Gilliam. "Relaxing in the huddle. Some of these other clubs, people probably not allowed to say anything. Ranger said, 'P-action, P-action.' I faked to Franco and three guys, four guys hit him. They ate his ass up! Then I give it to Preston and psshong!" On one play he savored the fake so long he was late with the handoff, but he dived full length to get the ball into Pearson's belly, and Preston went 39 yards.

In the third quarter, trailing 14–13, on fourth and an inch on the Brown 9, the Steelers went for it. The play was a 13 trap, Franco up the middle, and would have probably gone all the way for a touchdown: "We haven't run any middle action since Hanratty broke his ribs," Mansfield pointed out. "They were plugging up the outside. We were going to trap the tackle but we didn't have to; he ran himself right out of the play. Sam hit the linebacker." But somehow Gilliam flashed "12-trap" instead of "13-trap"; "It's like drawing a 'P' backwards when you're a kid," Mansfield said. Gilliam turned the wrong way, bumped into Franco before he could get the ball to him, and the play aborted. "We made the fucking inch anyway," Mansfield claimed. "Franco hit me in the back and I had Walter Johnson stood up two yards downfield. But then they pushed us back and they placed the ball where Franco was lying."

Then the Browns took over and quarterback Mike Phipps scrambled, and scrambled, and shook off several tacklers, and ducked to let Pine Edwards fly over his head, and after nearly a minute of scrambling he passed, just as Russell hit him, to Pruitt for a long gain that set up the game-winning touchdown. The crowd leapt to its feet except for Donald J. Tanner, forty-seven, who slumped down with a heart attack. People around him called for help, tried to massage his chest and give him mouth-to-mouth resuscitation. He was carried out over rows and rows of seats. Cheers went up again and again. Tanner slipped out of the wheelchair he'd been placed in. A man handed Tanner's wife an overshoe that had fallen off. She flung it away. The people who had been trying to save Tanner turned their energies right back to roaring at the game. Tanner was dead when he reached the hospital.

The Browns were ahead 21–16 but the Steelers kept coming at the end, with the ball on the Steeler 19 and a good 57 seconds to go. "I felt good," said Gilliam. "Right down to the end I felt good." He hit Shanklin for 34. He hit Lewis for 19. He hit Shanklin for 13.

Here we go. All of 29 seconds left and the ball on the Browns' 15. And Lewis was open in the end zone! He'd slipped just a bit going out but he was there and Gilliam was rushed hard and instead of hanging it up for Frank he had to drill it—quarterback being rushed is like a man shooting a charging rhino, only he knows that even if his shot is on the money the rhino is going to hit him anyway—and it went just beyond all but the diving Lewis' very fingerprints. Three more passes were incomplete and that was that.

"Seems like suitable surroundings," said Noll, receiving the press in the dank john area of the visitors' dressing room. "We could've beat their ass with our third-string quarterback," he said. "I wonder if they could say that."

On the plane Mel Blount said, "I feel like we blew it for you, Gillie. Letting Phipps scramble like that."

"Naw," said Gilliam. "They're just punks. Of all the teams we play, they're punks. I don't know, I know they're dudes just like us, but . . ."

The Steelers led Cleveland now by only half a game, and they had to go to Miami and try to beat the world champions in a Monday night TV game with their third-string quarterback. There were interviewers all over Gilliam during the week and he parried: "As to the amount of confidence I display, that's not for me to say. To me, it's just doing my job." And, "You're not going to get me to say I want to leave Pittsburgh."

In the first half the Dolphins "showed us what championship intensity was," said Noll. "We were kind of in awe." Gilliam threw seven passes, completed none, had three intercepted. "He wasn't the same guy he'd been in Cleveland," said one Steeler. "In Cleveland he was like a man jumping up out of a foxhole and charging into the bullets. Tonight he was like a man who'd been waiting all week for his execution."

On the sidelines it was amazing, the noise and the . . . suspension. The sound filled up the atmosphere all around, so that I felt it was holding me just lightly off the ground. Shanklin got lumps in his calves that were moving up into his thighs. Lewis had them too but his lumps were smaller, or moving slower, so he stayed in. About all you could hear players saying were things like "Those linebackers are dropping right off" and "Take away the I cut." Perles jumped way up in the air with his fists clenched and his knees up almost under his chin and yelled "Oh, SHIT!" at a development, but mostly the Steelers seemed frozen by being so overrun and outintensed.

Bradshaw's shoulder was still tender but he took over from Gilliam. "It was really weird," he said. "I couldn't see anybody or anything out there. It was like a total kind of wow! feeling." He threw two interceptions himself. At the half the Dolphins led 30–3.

"Look at Joe!" cried Perles in the second half, as Greene ran a man out of bounds on the other side of the field from his position. "Is he playing his ass off! We all are!"

Yes sir. The Dolphins had let up a bit and the Steelers were coming back. Bradshaw, dynamic, hit Preston and Barry Pearson for touchdowns and Franco ran again and again for 7, 5, 11, 14. He swept for a one-yard touchdown and was shaken with dry heaves.

"It took getting the shit kicked out of us to wake us up," said Greene. But one Steeler drive was stopped on the Miami eight, and then with a little over a minute left and the score 30–24 the Dolphins did a trick.

Walden had punted from the Steeler 48 out of bounds on the Miami 1. On third down L. C. stopped Larry Csonka a yard short. On fourth down the Dolphins took a delay-of-game penalty. Then surely they were going to punt. But no. They lined up as though they were going for it. "What's the matter with you guys?" Greene said to Miami's Larry Little. "Man, you don't want to run the ball." Griese started his count. "What the hell is going on?" Greene demanded.

Noll maintained later that he knew what the Dolphins were doing. "I wish he'd told *us,* then," said a Steeler. "I wondered what the hell we were doing too," said Miami's Dick Anderson.

What they were doing was taking a safety—giving the Steelers two points in return for a free kick from the 20. Griese ran out of the end zone, pursued by Greene. There was confusion on the Steeler sideline as to whether the punt-return or the kick-off-return team should go out for a free kick. And Larry Seiple, who had beaten the Steelers in the playoffs the year before with his run off a fake punt (causing Perles to yell at his image on the TV screen one Monday night early in the season, "We're going to get a piece of your ass!") kicked the ball 70 yards. Then Jake Scott (who'd suggested the safety to Miami head coach Don Shula, causing Shula to be acclaimed a genius in the TV booth) intercepted a Bradshaw pass with half a minute to play. That was it.

When Miami's Manny Fernandez was asked if the safety wasn't a sneaky way to win, he said, "When they bombed Pearl Harbor, that wasn't traditional either. But it worked."

□ 26 □

FRANCO, FRENCHY AND PRESTON: DANCING AND BLOWING

How beautiful are the retired flowers! how would they lose their beauty were they to throng into the highway crying out, admire me I am a violet! dote upon me I am a primrose!

—JOHN KEATS, LETTERS

God doesn't like ugly.

—JOHN FUQUA,
CONVERSATION

During the doldrums of the regular season's last couple of weeks, as Cleveland won the division title and the Steelers settled for a wild-card playoff berth, a special players-only meeting was called to get everybody on the right track. The only jarring note was struck by Preston Pearson, who said, "You guys got to get meaner. I don't mean this personally, Sam," he said to Davis, "but I know you're not mean enough." He also said Franco was going to have to stop dancing.

Now Bill Nunn will tell you, "That's a good touch on a kid, if you can see him dance. John Henry Johnson, Roy Jefferson, Otis Taylor, Sam Davis—they get on the dance floor and they're *good.* You know. Tim Brown, I was over at his apartment and he got up and imitated James Brown. Said when he came into pro football he couldn't dance one bit. Said he practiced six and seven hours a day. And he got it *down.*"

But the kind of dancing Preston was criticizing was jitterbugging, or pussyfooting, when you're a running back charged to hit a certain hole. Franco was

231

never a plow-ahead Csonka-type fullback. Bradshaw said, "He don't pop the hole, but he has a knack of getting there in good time. Once he's in the secondary he can generate. And he puts on some pretty good moves." Sometimes he would take one step into a hole, pull out, find a better one, and then blow through that one and knock somebody down with his forearm on the other end. Van Dyke said this improvisation made it harder to block for Franco—you might block somebody into him by mistake—but it worked and was great to watch. It required, however, knees of steel. In '73, according to the doctors, Franco was bothered, oddly enough, by the ripping out of adhesions dating back to a college operation. Adhesions are scar tissue you are suppose to let rip, but that is easier said than done. The gradual tearing of Franco's caused his knee to swell way up. At times in the dressing room during the week he could hardly put his weight on his foot; he hobbled like Uncle Jim, only less serenely.

And when he tried to pick his holes in '73, too often—except in his good games like the Miami one, when he pushed himself to the point of dry heaves—they all closed before he could cut into one. Frenchy was a strange wild twisting runner—something about the way he carried his shoulders high and pointed his trunk one way and his hips another made him look like a frantic old lady holding her skirts high and fleeing a bull while trying to avoid mud puddles—but he could also be a hard-nosed plunger through a hole or into a man. One of the things about Preston's criticism that irritated other Steelers was that Preston was not regarded as a head-knocker himself. He was at his best slithering, finding daylight, and turning on speed. "That's all right for me," Preston said. "But Franco weighs 230. He ought to *blow.*" Preston complained in the press that he didn't get to play enough, but many of his teammates felt Frenchy was the soldier back—a better blocker for Franco, for one thing—and that Noll actually showed Preston favoritism. After Preston spoke out, though, Noll tried to trade him.

Appropriately enough for men of their position, all three of them were hard to come to grips with. Franco was quiet and Frenchy was full of talk but still elusive. Frenchy wore such things as a multicolored tasseled Serbian yarmulke, a sequined arm sling, a lavender jumpsuit, a "mod Mexican outfit" with sombrero and serape. He kept saying he was going to wear shoes with glass heels with goldfish in them. "Won't the fish die?" I asked.

"No problem with that—I'll run a little tube right up through my socks and through my pants and right up into my purse, for air." He and a friend were supposed to have showed up in a Pittsburgh nitery one night with twenty girls between them. (The most I ever saw him with though was two, and one of them looked annoyed.) When a clothier called the Steelers trying to collect on a year-old bill, Frenchy said airily, "With the Frenchman the statute of limitations is three months." He kept his autobiography cloudy: "The thing that gets me the most when I'm telling people shit is the way their smiles turn serious looks. When I see that it makes me even more sincere. And I *really* start running it over. I have to check *myself* sometimes. I'll be making out a credit application and they'll say, 'Where you from, John,' and being French I'll find myself saying, 'Quebec.' "

Franco didn't like to talk about being black-Italian. He considered himself black and enjoyed Italian food. Outside the stadium after a game once, he was surrounded by what looked like equal numbers of little black cousins and little white cousins. He played in the Steelers' heavy poker games, dressed uninterestingly, bought an old house to restore on the North Side, and was seen with unflashily offbeat-looking people. After a '72 home game in which Franco had gained over a hundred yards, the Hanrattys, driving home, saw two hitchhikers outside the stadium, one of whom was a teen-age kid and the other of whom looked like Franco. It was Franco. The same fans who had been cheering themselves to a frenzy over him a few minutes before were driving right past him now. Hanratty stopped and offered him a ride. "You sure it won't be too much out of your way?" Franco asked. He made Ford commercials which were downright touching. He would talk to a little cartoon car: "Don't cry, talking car. The Ford end-of-the-year sale will make a lot of people happier." You could tell he *liked* that little car.

□ **27** □

MEAN JOE

Noooo.
—TINY TOW-HEADED BOY
AT THE END OF A
TRAINING CAMP
PRACTICE, ON BEING
ASKED BY HIS FATHER
WHETHER HE WOULD
LIKE TO MEET THE
ONCOMING JOE GREENE.

The Steelers made the playoffs by beating the Oilers 33–7 and the 49ers 37–14, in two ragged games. In the Houston game, at home, Ron Shanklin had a man land on the back of his neck and "when I tried to get up, nothing happened. I thought I was pushing off the ground with my hands, but when I looked around I discovered I was still lying on the ground and my arm was back behind my head. I couldn't tell where my arms were or my legs were until I looked at them." He began to get his movement back on the way to the hospital, but he was out for the season. In the San Francisco game, there, Hanratty on the sidelines was so vexed by the plump appearance of 49er middle linebacker Frank Nunley that he yelled, "Nice body, Nunley! Way to have a good body!" and when the governor of Nevada came into the dressing room after the game Keating said, "Oh, sure, the governor of Nevada has no connection with gambling."

But what was most notable about the Oiler and 49er games was that Joe Greene took himself out of the first and had fun in the second.

No other Steeler could get away with removing himself from a game because he didn't feel like playing, he wasn't playing well, nobody was playing well. In fact it didn't set well with some of his teammates. "My stock in Greene went way down," said one. Keating said, "That's the way football is. You hardly ever feel like playing. Sometimes you think, maybe I'll get sick, and won't have to play. But you play anyway. I wouldn've mothered somebody who did that at Oakland, but I haven't been here long enough." (When a player speaks of mothering someone, of course, he means calling him a mother.)

Greene had a special position on the Steelers. Gilliam would say to him,

"You better watch it. I'm gonna give yo big ass a flip," and Mullins would push him and call him "Bitch." It was like teasing an indulgent big brother. Greene's college coach called him "a fort on foot." He was anomalously built—no definition, loosely and rather oddly jointed, a trunk that came in at the shortribs and flared back out again, a huge head and a wolfish clever face. In a film once I saw him knock down a tackle with his forearm—change the whole flow of the blocking with that forearm—and then grab a guard up in one arm and the ball carrier in the other. "There's a whole lot of things we can do on the line because he's Joe Greene," said Greenwood. "There are certain plays the offense just won't run because that's his spot. And he comes off the ball so quick. Normally you react off the snap or the man in front of you, but I don't even watch the ball. I react off Joe."

And Joe was an inner-directed man. He freelanced on the line and he played for his own reasons. Aesthetically he was probably right to leave the Houston game. It was a drag from everyone's standpoint. And maybe the Steelers should have reacted by saying, "Hey, we better come to life. We're so listless Joe won't play with us."

"I used to get a great deal more pleasure out of the game than I do now," Greene said. "I've gotten maybe smarter, I don't play as loose and reckless as I used to. The game gets more conservative, a little dull. When you've been winning for a while, the pressure to keep on winning builds. You don't want to make mistakes."

This was what Noll preached against. "A big theme in Noll's coaching," said Mansfield, "is that caution creates mistakes." But maybe the kind of pressure Noll had started exuding had made the Steelers cautious. On the other hand it may have been their opponents who did it to them.

"I just play my game," Greene maintained. "You got to reckon with me, I don't have to reckon with you." But opponents were reckoning with him to the point that he had to change his style. Paul Brown said, "We outfinessed him with junk-blocking—a series of alternating line blocks that varied with changing movement of the defense." This made things easier for the rest of the Steeler Front Four, but it caused Greene to spend most of his time thrashing blockers instead of chasing quarterbacks.

"Guys who tell you they're playing for that twenty-five grand are playing for the wrong reason," he said. "It's for the sake of doing what you do good." What he did best was not bang into opposing linemen, though he had the tools for that too, but "beat a man quick. Those first two steps like snapping your finger. Fool a guy—that's the fun part of it. Lot of times I'd get the quarterback and never touch the guard. I'd take off in a direction, he'd take off after me, I wouldn't be there. Now they play way back off me and just ride me back. Lot of people think football's a physical game—beat 'em up. Well, that's the game they're *making* me play, now."

He didn't like a lot of grappling. "*Holding.* You never get used to that. Against Philadelphia my second year a guy was holding me, just obvious, he didn't care. I tried to take his head off. Tried to grab his head and face mask and twist it. Sometimes I feel like I could kill a man out there. And that's not a good feeling."

It also made him feel bad to be thought of as an animal. "Parents tell their kid to come up to me for an autograph: 'Go ahead, he's not going to eat you.' I hate to be typed. I go to Lincoln, Nebraska, nobody knows me there, first thing anybody says is, 'You a football player, aren't you?' Why I got to be a football player? Lot of big people aren't. I find myself always on the defensive. 'You the biggest person I ever saw in my life.' I want to say, 'So what, runt.' It's not that the comment's so bad. It's just that I hear it so many times. When I fly commercially people stare. Woo, I hate that. 'Who are you?' they say. Well, who are *they*? I don't like the person I've become because of all that."

Against the 49ers, though, he had such a good time he tried to put himself back in the game when Noll rested him. Once he jumped the quarterback, took the ball away, ran into the end zone, tossed the ball over his head, caught it behind his back and handed it to a cheerleader. A quick whistle had downed the ball before he grabbed it, but on the sidelines Hanneman said, "Guy for the Globetrotters wants to sign you up." Russell said, "You're something." Ham said, in a rare tongue-out-of-cheek remark, "That was a cool move." It was the kind of thing pro football needs more of. "That's what the game's about," Greene said. "Winning and having fun."

□ 28 □

MONEY, AND SUPE

Next to money, I like life.

—FRENCHY FUQUA

"Our problem," said Players' Association exec Ed Garvey in considering why the public tends to have little sympathy with players' bargaining demands, "starts with the word 'player.'" Most of the Steelers agreed more or less with Mel Blount: "Football is all work. You wouldn't play football if you could do somepn'-rother else and make some money. 'Cause every time you get on the field you put your health in danger." The players have just a few years to make football money and if I had to take sides between them and the owners it would not be with the latter, some of whom were capable of such statements as, "You'll play on concrete if we tell you to." Keating told the story of a player–owner meeting during the '70 strike when Tex Schramm of the Cowboys suddenly raised the issue of players' running around in velvet jumpsuits. He didn't like it. John Mackey, then of the Colts, happened to be wearing one during this meeting. "Some of us may not like you wearing white socks with a suit, either," he said to Schramm.

The players expected to strike in '74 not only for money but for "freedom issues." Pete Rozelle used to be the only sports commissioner in the world who wasn't an absurd figure, but the notion of him has begun to pall too. Where does he get off fining Minnesota's Bud Grant for complaining about the terrible dressing room assigned the Vikings for Super Bowl practice? And it seems un-American, after all, for a player to be owned, unable to work where he chooses. I don't know, however, that many players realize what difficulties are involved in freedom for most people. Civilians are at liberty to shop around for jobs, but on the other hand vast scouting systems aren't searching them out, and after they take a job they are not waited on the way pro football players are. "I've had players come up to me in hotels and ask, 'Where's the bus?'" said Dan Rooney. "Where'd they think it was? On the third floor?" It was right outside the front door, where it always is. Everything is handy for the players on the road, except that they have to be in bed by eleven. You wonder what players would be like if they were freer *and* less coddled.

As for pay, the Steelers' average salary was around $25,000 or a little higher, and the highest-paid player, who was probably Joe Greene, made less than $100,000. Of course, as one Pittsburgh bartender put it, concerning even

237

$25,000, "I'd have to suck 90 dicks a day to make that kind of money." "In Pittsburgh," someone else said, "180." "You know what I mean?" said the bartender.

And even Garvey conceded it was hard to feel like Cratchetts around the Rooneys. They had never been known for paying big money—with the single exception of Whizzer White's $15,800 in 1938—but they had been known for straight, warm, man-to-man dealing and for paying injured players everything due them.

Andy Russell did say that, when negotiating salary with Dan Rooney, "it's like he's got a gun to your head." I asked Dan how he felt negotiating with people who could give away 100, 120 pounds. He said, "Shaking hands—my hand's not really a small hand, with the normal person, but when I shake hands with a defensive end it gets lost, my hand. I've stood up and yelled at them, and they've yelled at me, we were toe to toe that way. But that's an exception. And I've never had any fear that I'd get slugged. There's no correlation," he added, "between how aggressively people play and how they negotiate. Defensive backs and outside receivers are the toughest. Maybe that's because they're the smallest." Being able to tell that player that if he doesn't play ball with you next year he won't play ball at all, at any rate, adds a good deal to any owner's negotiating stature.

Garvey claimed that the Steelers must have made $1 million profit the year before. Dan said they wouldn't have broken even had it not been for the $600,000 they were still getting annually from the league for going over to the AFC. The players wanted to believe Garvey but many of them felt that Dan wouldn't lie. Garvey told the players that the owners could afford to pay everybody $100,000. "Figures don't lie," said one of the more conservative Steelers, "but liars figure."

One night I went to dinner with Dan and player rep Andy Russell for the purpose of getting down to brass tacks figure-wise. Here they are, as Dan revealed them under Andy's probing and I wrote them down at the table:

Approximate Income, '73

$1,500,000—TV
1,200,000—Home box office (team's share)
800,000—Road box office
250,000—Two home exhibition games
600,000—Four road exhibition games
100,000—Radio
50,000—Concessions
15,000—NFL films
600,000—Transfer to AFC
30,000—League entrance-fee money from
            past expansion teams
_____
$4,145,000

Approximate Expenses, '73

$1,600,000—Total pay to players (including exhibition
games, bonuses, per diem)
400,000—Scouting
60,000—Camp
165,000—Travel
150,000—Pension fund
1,000,000—Administration and overhead (secretaries,
coaches and front office salaries, office expenses)
300,000—To Stadium Authority for operations
35,000—Equipment
50,000—Medical
50,000—Legal and accounting
_____
$4,115,000

"You guys don't make *any* money," said Russell. "What are you in this business for?"

"We added it up together, right?" said Dan.

The trouble was that we added both columns wrong. The figures actually add up to $5,145,000 income and $3,810,000 expenses. (Another figure that might have been added into the expenses was a $10,000 fine for "hiding" Lee Nystrom—keeping him around after he was cut from the roster. The Steelers hid several people.) Discovering these discrepancies after leaving Pittsburgh, I checked with Dan. "You got the training camp expenses wrong," he said. "They should be $260,000. And our player salary estimate was low. It should be $2 million, including pensions. That should make expenses $4,650,000." But that wasn't quite right either. With the $150,000 pension figure included in the $2 million, the absolute firm corrected bottom-line figure must come to this:

Income $5,145,000
Expenses   4,260,000
_____
Profit $ 885,000

At any rate there is not much point in trying to get a man's profit picture, however honest he is, from figures that you have to take his word for. I daresay NFL owners will be paying higher salaries as long as the new World Football League offers competition—which proves that they could have paid higher salaries before. And I daresay it would be interesting to see how pro football might work as a loose open-market setup.

On the other hand, I think it is possible to adopt a legitimately nonrevolutionary economic attitude toward being owned. It helps to be country, like Supe Blount.

Supe valued himself thoroughly, even though he was losing hair. "I think

239

it's distinctive. Everybody's got an Afro, but not many got a bald spot in theirs. I'll look young when I'm a hundred." As for football, "I've always been a quality athlete. And I think I have proved to the Rooney's the man in me. A man is not made of things he possesses. A man is what comes from inside a person. The family farm—I have brought it a long ways. My grandfather, back during the Depression he held twenty-five hundred acres of land. This was a black man, in the Depression. Charley Sharp." The farmlands had been divided between a number of descendants, and Mel was working to pull it all together, stock it, and make it more productive.

I asked him if he'd been tempted to blow his money on big cars. "I was never *tempted* to buy big cars," he said. "But I always *bought* big cars. I got a Continental." He also had a beautifully preserved '48 Chrysler and a couple of other cars, but none of them gave him more satisfaction than "the old truck I've got down on the farm. I painted it maroon, and I drive it through the city of Vidalia. And everybody know who it is.

"Farm life is a clean, independent life. The North is not the place for black people in my experience. People think you're freer, but I'm not talking about racial freedom, I'm talking about freedom of mind. Freedom to walk and see the fields and the horses play. Up here, instead of being trees, they're buildings. Instead of being crossroads, they're red lights."

Supe thought the Steelers got his services too cheaply. "And they know what we're worth. If I got a bull and he breeds twenty-five cows, I know what he's worth. Come spring, going to have twenty-five calves hit the ground. We're collateral. We're stock to these people."

That was right. Whether or not there was more loose cash the Rooneys could be distributing, they were certainly building a financial empire on the Steelers' body sacrifice. And that part was all right with Supe, because in the process he was building an empire of his own.

"If you're brought up in the city, you don't want to leave it. You ain't got nothing to do but stay here and deal with it and try to make changes. But I can quit and get my money and take it home.

"If I'm going to be making changes, it's going to be on the field. Coming up with turnovers. After football I'll go back to the farm and do the same things I did in high school. I can just dream about the life I'm going to live. Get up early and saddle my horse and ride across the field and see my cattle, man. Watch my horse run across the meadow, man. 'Cause that's *money.*"

If cattle ever organize, though, Supe may have to rethink his position.

□ **29** □

HANDS

Sometimes, when talking, he will move his fingers, gradu-
ally close them into a fist, and then, suddenly opening them,
utter a good, full-weight word.
                                    —GORKY ON TOLSTOY

"I'm as sure," his uncle said, "as I am that this here," and
he held up his hand, every short thick finger stretched rigid
in front of Tarwater's face, "is my hand and not yours."
There was something final in this that always made the
boy's impudence subside.
                                    —FLANNERY O'CONNOR,
                                    THE VIOLENT BEAR IT
                                    AWAY

Asked to describe his feelings on dancing with the cobra,
Ricker, gasping for breath, smiling, replied "I wasn't even
there."
                                    —NEWSPAPER ACCOUNT
                                    OF RELIGIOUS
                                    SNAKEHANDLING IN
                                    NEWPORT, TENNESSEE

One afternoon during practice I was watching the linemen pound away at each other, wump, clack. Van Dyke paused to say, "What are you doing?"

"Trying to get a feel for this," I said.

"If you really want to get a feel for it you should put on some pads and get out here and get blocked," he said.

I answered him in much the same terms Groucho Marx uses in the role of an attorney in *A Day at the Races,* when Eve Arden, in the role of an acrobat, asks him to put on her suction-cup shoes and walk on the ceiling, so that some money she wants will fall out of his pocket: "No, I have an agreement with the horseflies. The flies don't practice law and I don't walk on the ceiling."

"Actually," I went on, "I thought I would get a feel for it by asking you how it feels."

"I try not to notice how it feels," he said. "If you felt it, you wouldn't do it."

I admired Noll's response when a reporter came up to him after the Steelers' loss to Cincinnati and asked, "How do you feel?"

"It hasn't changed," said Noll. "I still feel with my hands." Often, you had to hand it to Noll.

So I thought I might try treating the question of how pro football feels by asking players about their hands. One conclusion I was led to by that line of questioning was that pro football feels terrible.

On the backs of their hands and on their knuckles many of the players had wounds of a kind I have never seen on anyone else: fairly deep digs and gouges which were not scabbed over so much as dried. They looked a little like old sores on horses. The body must have given up trying to refill these gouges and just rinded them over and accepted them. During the year, at Noll's suggestion, the offensive line did the backs of their hands a favor by adopting the thick black leather gloves that fighters use for punching a heavy bag. Before he started wearing these gloves, Van Dyke said, the backs of his hands were so sore all season from banging into defensive linemen's ribs that he hated to shake hands with people. And probably the defensive linemen he banged didn't like people tickling them in the ribs.

Different Steelers taped their hands all different ways: the middle two fingers together, the last two together, or just one or more jammed fingers taped singly for support. For some reason, and not just because the movement is restricted, a jammed finger hurts less after it is taped. Hanneman boasted that he and Joe Greene were the only two defensive linemen on the Steelers who didn't tape and pad their hands and forearms heavily. I asked Hanneman why he didn't. "Just to be tough," he said in a self-deprecating way. But he taped each of his fingers, because they were always jammed or broken from catching on opponents' helmets. Lloyd Voss, who retired as a Steeler defensive end in '72, used to tape all his fingertips, because otherwise he was prone to get his nails jerked out. (He also used to bring his small daughter into the dressing room, causing some consternation.)

As for Greene, the reason he used very little tape might have been that, as one teammate put it, "each one of his fingers is the size of a grown man's turd."

"Joe told me he was afraid of that little white ball," said Pirate slugger Stargell. "Huh. I told him he could use his hand as a bat."

"I've never broken a finger," said Greene. "Had 'em stepped on, twisted, but not broken. One time I grabbed at Jim Plunkett and my little finger caught in a twist of his jersey and he ran for a ways dragging me that way, by my little finger. That turned my little finger around, but it didn't break it."

Most of the defensive linemen had broken many fingers. "You can't play football, I don't care what position, without hands," said Dwight White. "I use 'em to pull, knock down, grab. Hands are as important as eyes."

He looked down at his. "Look at some players' hands," he said, "you can tell that they have been used. See this finger. I got it jammed five years ago, and it's just started to straighten out. See that finger. Can't wear a ring on it. I got some of the uggliest fingers in the world. They get bloodshot from licks. Come in with the whole end of it brown from hitting."

In '72 L. C. looked down at his left hand in the midst of a play to see that the upper two-thirds of the middle finger was completely twisted around backwards and crossed over the ring finger. "I couldn't figure out what had happened to it. So I fixed it right there in the middle of the play and went on." He had it splinted and then played with the splint on, and now that finger sticks out at a grotesque angle. He said he would get it straightened out after he got out of football, no point doing it until then. It hurt in cold weather, he said.

Fats Holmes pounded the insides of his wrists, where the veins and tendons that suicides slit are, in sand to toughen them up.

Wagner said he broke three fingers his first year in the pros, from grabbing at receivers, so now he tried to keep his hands out of his tackles. It was good tackling technique in the open field to use your shoulder and body instead of your hands anyway, he pointed out.

Receivers, running backs and quarterbacks could hardly keep their hands out of play, and they had to use them too subtly to be able to tape their fingers. "My fingers stay jammed," said Gilliam. "Stepped on. Pop 'em on helmets. Holding on to the ball while people are trying to pull it away. Every time one gets jammed you have to alter your grip, throwing the ball, and that makes you anticipate your throw. Makes you think about it. That's bad. My two little fingers never will be the same. I jammed the right one in camp last year and it's still bothering me. The other one I got a compound fracture in when I slid up under a fence on the side of the field in high school. Up to my senior year in college I could just move the top part of it. My left hand, I can crack all my knuckles. My right hand, none of them. Imagine what somebody like Brodie or Jurgensen's hands are like, who's been playing so long."

Here is the kind of thing, speaking of hands, that used to happen to the Steelers: One year Larry Wilson of the Cardinals intercepted two passes against them with both of his hands in a cast.

All the skin peeled off Rocky Bleier's hands at one point during the year. He didn't know why.

"I don't hold," maintained Sam Davis. "If I know a guy's going to beat me and get the quarterback, then I'll hold. Otherwise I use my fists. A lot of. push-offs. Hit him with my fists—catch him on the side, uppercut him in the ribs. Make contact with your shoulder and then come up with your hands, and it's like a second man coming in to hit him. You ball your hands up, so you have a firm type fist situation." But Sam got called for holding a number of times during the year. Noll put together a film to send to the league office, showing Sam getting called for clean licks and other linemen holding blatantly, without getting called. I suggested to Sam that he caught officials' eyes because he had the only black fingers in the offensive line, but he didn't think so.

243

"You can hold their jersey a little bit with your hands in close," said Mullins, "but a lot of times defensive ends will come up with one of their arms under yours, between yours and your body, and you'll get called for holding on that."

"There isn't a play run," maintained Walden one afternoon in the Jamestown, "when holding couldn't be called."

"That's an old wives' tale," said Mansfield. "But if I'm holding on purpose, there's no way I'm going to be caught at it."

Things fall apart, if the center cannot hold.

"Hands are all in your head," said Scolnik of the concept "good hands" in receivers. "Your hands themselves are important, of course. When you're catching facing the ball you have to squeeze it and snap it at once. When you're facing away from the quarterback you cradle it and go with it. But a great receiver is totally relaxed from the waist up. His face is not all tight. He relaxes so his jowls hang, he eases, and he takes it real soft."

There were other tricks to receiving, Scolnik pointed out. "Shanklin—when he runs his patterns he growls. Just to fuck up their heads, the guys covering him. Give them one more thing to worry about. They got to worry about why he's growling. They say Lance Rentzel used to pluck at his jersey like he had minute hands—like he could pick a fly up by its wings. Give them something to think about."

Some of the receivers worked putty in their hands to keep them strong, or squeezed rubber balls, or just spent a lot of time carrying a football around and tossing it from hand to hand, to stay in touch. Steeler receivers had to have better than ordinary hands (coaches and scouts tend to grade players' qualities, such as hands or quickness or toughness or feet, as "good," "ordinary," or "no") because Bradshaw and Gilliam threw so hard.

"The main thing," said Shanklin, a great man for getting *at* the ball as well as for hauling it in, "is just think of nothing but that spiraling ball. But in the off-season I spend ten minutes a day with each hand dropping the ball and catching it."

That is not easy, holding a ball out in front of you in one hand, releasing it and then catching it with the same hand. Barry Pearson, the Steeler you would think of first if you thought "sure-handed," said his hands weren't big enough to do that. They were broad but stubby. He relied on concentration. "I watch the ball all the way in. You can't let the point hit either one of your hands; it should come in between them." Preston Pearson had the biggest hands on the team. His fingers were as long as Little Lulu's ringlets. He had broken five of them playing ball and dislocated one in camp catching a pass. He said the only important fingers in catching a football, as in shooting a basketball, were the forefinger, middle finger, and thumb.

"Lots of guys have good hands and nobody knows about it," said receiver coach Lionel Taylor, "because they don't have the concentration." He put the

Steeler receivers through a number of entertaining drills to make them concentrate on the ball.

He would throw them knuckleballs, floaters, end-over-ends. "In an AFL All-Star game Cotton Davidson said he was going to throw me a knuckleball. I never had seen one. 'I can catch anything,' I said. I didn't catch it! I wouldn't let him throw me another one. But I learned it. I also learned a lot of hard-catch drills from Mac Speedie. You'd go out for a pass and he'd wave a towel at you, even throw weeds at you. Big handful of brush! You'd say, 'What was *that*!' But then in a game you're used to distractions and you don't flinch. After receivers come here from other teams they flinch when I throw my hat at them or something for about two weeks, then they're all right."

It was not just the mental and strategic aspects of hands that Lionel concerned himself with. It had been five years since he retired as the man with the third highest number of lifetime pass receptions in pro football history, but he still put lotion on his hands every day.

"That's right. My hands are a tool. Got to take care of 'em. Hey, a race car driver tunes his engine, I got to tune my hands. Listen, hand lotion—that's it. Hands are supposed to be soft! Some days before a game my hands would feel fat. I was worried then. I'd soak 'em in salty water. Some days your fingers feel stubby. That's right. Today, now, they feel long and thin. You put your ring on your finger sometimes and it goes on real good, and other days it feels fat? That's what I'm talking about. That may sound silly but that's a stone fact. I would never do push-ups. Or if they made me, when I was playing, I'd do 'em on my knuckles. Got to keep that touch soft. If I'd known then what I know now, I'd a gone in the steam bath before a game. When my fingers felt fat. That's it.

"I always liked to catch with my thumbs together. You know, facing the passer. Some guys would rather catch everything with their hands around the other way. I could never catch diving. Some people can. I liked to catch with my hands out in front. Then I had two chances at the ball. But I couldn't react, lot of times. The ball would get through my hands, and it'd be slipping down my body, and I could see it, but I *couldn't get it*. Never *could* get it when it was slipping down like that.

"Another thing about receivers, is when they get hit by somebody when they're coming over the middle. Oh, they come through the middle next time, they're *short*arming it then. They don't *want* to catch it. I always thought about two things when the ball was coming. Getting hit, and catching the football. Always expect to get hit when I caught the football. Expect somebody to tear my head off. Then I wasn't surprised."

You never get far from contact in discussing any aspect of football. But the contact of ball on good hands is a special kind, an especially fine kind, a miracle of withness, firmness and tact. A ball is hummed 40 yards and its sticks in a web less than half its size. I saw a football cartoon once in which a pair of hands reached out from the ball to catch the receiver's, as if the reception were a transaction between aerialists.

The ball is hard. I once asked Mansfield if it were possible for a man to explode a football by squeezing it with his hands, as Ben Davidson of the Raiders appears to do in his bouncer's role in the noted dirty movie *Behind the Green Door.* Mansfield said I wouldn't ask that if I had ever fallen on a loose ball, point up, and had several people land on my back, driving the ball into my solar plexus. However regularly lotioned they are, the receiver's hands are also hard. But a pass goes *snk* at the end, or even *sk* or, more softly, *ft,* or *p,* or *pth*—instead of splack—when the right touch gets hold of it. "You don't fight the football," someone said. Iron hands in velvet gloves.

"See those hands," said Kansas City scout Lloyd Wells as we watched a Jackson State College receiver go out for a practice pass in Mississippi. "Those are board hands. You be scouting long enough you can tell. The sound of 'em—ball bounced off before he caught it. Plus the fact that the ball made him waver, it made him stride, it made him start to go raggledy-dedaggledy.

"See Otis Taylor suck it in some time."

Wells said Jimmy Hines, the track star drafted by the Chiefs, "could fly on a pattern. Thought he was going to be another Bob Hayes. Run fast, fast, *fast.* But he could not catch the ball. Not with a basket could he catch the ball. Hank Stram did everything he could to make him a wide receiver. Used to take him out and throw him 200 and 300 passes. And write every one of them down. Made him walk around with the ball. He could not catch it."

So prehensility must in large part be a gift. But adjustments can be made to improve it. Elbert Dubenion, the Buffalo Bills scout, said he had trouble developing good hands as a player himself because when he ran out for a pass he would always run a half stride too far. He'd stick up his hands and be looking over his shoulder and the ball would hit him on the helmet. When his coach made it clear that if the ball kept on landing on his head he would land on the street, however, he learned to run a little shorter. (When the Falcons signed a speedster Norm Van Brocklin said, "We'll have to start diagramming our plays on longer paper.")

Consider the ball. People who handle it frequently develop a connoisseur's hands. The Steelers went through forty dozen official Wilsons a year. You could see one in practice for a week on artificial turf before the pebble grain was worn down too far. Hart said he could spin a ball up in the air and tell whether it was balanced. Some of them weren't. Referees would reject a game ball if it had a little bulge around the laces or if the black stitching around the laces didn't follow exactly the black line around them. "Guys claim the night ball is fatter, because the white stripes make it look that way," said Hart, "so we use those in practice a few days before a night game. The old Duke balls, when they got wet you could put them in your car and let the heater dry them out. But these balls you have to deflate and dry out overnight, or they'll lose their shape. If you get a dark ball, it's better to grip. A lighter-toned ball is

246

slippery." A game ball cost $13.95, a practice ball $12.95.

"We ought to have brand-new balls every day in practice," said Hanratty. "When you can get a good ball, you just want to stay with it. Some are slick and some are fatter than others. Noll will look at it and say no, that ball's not fatter, but unless you've thrown the ball as long as a quarterback has you can't tell. That's one of my pet peeves. Another one is that damn stickum some of the receivers and defensive backs use on their hands. It gets on the ball and you can't throw it. It ought to be illegal. It is in basketball."

Ham and Wagner were among the Steelers' stickum-users. There was a spray can kind but they preferred an amber gunk that they kept smeared on their game socks at calf level, so they could reach down and get tacky whenever they needed to. Wagner said a defensive back needed it because often he had to reach out suddenly to snatch at a ball and he needed an instant fixative. When the stickum got wet, though, it got slippery.

"One of the worst things you can do to a receiver who doesn't use stickum,' said Lionel, "is tackle him and get some on his hands."

"I hit 'em in the ear," said Rowser, who was playing poker nearby. "Can't hear the audibles."

"Hey, my whole game is hands," said George Webster. "I use hands more than strength." And he did a little move in the aisle of the airplane we were talking in, playing off an imaginary blocker, and the move began in his hands and traveled through the rest of his body. The Steelers had a device with artificial hands on it—a big frame set up in front of the passer when he wasn't being rushed, with feelerlike things sticking up from it to stimulate rushers' hands, so he would be sure to throw high enough. The height of the rushers' hands these days is the reason a number of gifted quarterbacks shorter than 6–1 aren't signed by the pros. Blockers are supposed to hit low on pass plays, so rushers will keep their hands down trying to fend them off.

Bradshaw and Gilliam both had big hands, like most quarterbacks and baseball pitchers—Dizzy Dean and his brother Paul used to pull on Paul's boy's fingers all the time when the boy was growing up, so he'd have long fingers like Sandy Koufax. It didn't work.

I told Bradshaw I'd seen a picture of him and President Nixon comparing hands, palm to palm, in some White House ceremony, and it looked like their fingertips matched exactly. "Nixon must have big hands," I said.

Bradshaw said well, Nixon had cheated up on him a little bit from the bottom.

Chuck Dicus said he'd had to stop working on cars, which he loved to do, because it cut up his hands too much and it was bad for a receiver's hands to hurt. I asked him, "Can you do anything special with them because they're a receiver's hands?"

"I can do this," he said, and he crossed his middle finger over his forefinger and his ring finger over his little finger at the same time, without using any of his other fingers to help them into place.

247

Now that, I thought, is a good little index to a receiver's hands, maybe. I was talking to one of the linemen about hands and I said, "Dicus can do this." And I did it.

Oddly enough I could only do it with my left hand. Still, it must not be much of a hallmark of receiver's hands. Unless . . . Unless . . .

One afternoon during practice when I was all dressed up in sweat pants and a yellow jersey and shoes with lots of short plastic cleats for artificial turf on the bottoms, Gerela started lofting me passes and I looked marvelous. I don't think any other part of my body could *conceivably* make it in the NFL. Once I scrambled down a gravelly hill in Knoxville, Tennessee, in front of Scout Tim Rooney, and at the bottom I said, "Pretty good feet, hunh?" and he said, "Yeah. If you had one more of 'em you might be a player." Once in the dressing room Ralph Berlin came up behind me and kneaded me at the base of the neck, at the point where the trapezii slope away into the shoulders, the seat of the upper-body strength which is so essential. He acted as though I didn't have any trapezii. "We don't get many in here like you," he said. That made me feel wonderful.

But my hands were nearly as big as Bradshaw's (about the size, then, of Nixon's). I am a third baseman in Central Park softball, and playing third base requires quick hands. I was catching passes from Gerela and a wave of competence came over me. Not only was I catching the ball neatly with my fingers, *ft, pth,* but I actually felt I was *moving* well. I was catching the ball at the sidelines and putting both feet down deftly in bounds.

"Hm, *Sports Illustrated,* eh?" said Gerela, and it sounded vaguely like an acknowledgment. I trotted off the field and Dan Rooney said, "You looked like you knew what you were doing out there." The man who directed the club! I think I may have told him as modestly as possible that I caught the only forward pass completed all season by my dorm floor in freshman intramurals in college.

Still I had a great reticence about asking the quarterbacks to throw to me. I don't like people bothering me when I work. Once when Bradshaw was working his arm back into shape I ran out and he *underthrew* me. I may be the only person of my speed ever to be underthrown by Terry Bradshaw. I think he was afraid I would fly apart if he hit me. Or maybe I looked even slower than I was. At any rate I knew it wasn't doing his timing any good, throwing to me. It would be like me trying to write dialogue for Gerald Ford. So I never asked him to throw to me again. (Iooss did, though, and he barely got his hands up in time. "All of a sudden the ball was just *there,*" he reported. "The ball came in a *line.*")

In Palm Springs preparing for the playoff game with Oakland, though, the Steelers were very loose. They were usually loose, but in Palm Springs there was a lassitude, almost, in the air. Which Noll, as you can imagine, did not approve of. When Mullins pulled too slowly for his taste, though the rest of the offensive line thought Moon was pulling hard, Noll said in a very hard voice, *"If you can't run any faster than that, maybe we've got the wrong people out here."*

But generally the tone of things was very relaxed in Palm Springs, and I was spending even more time than usual with the players since they didn't have homes to go to. One afternoon in practice I found myself catching up for Bradshaw. When quarterbacks were warming up they had someone else catch the ball when it was thrown back, so as not to take a chance on hurting their fingers. Bradshaw was throwing to someone standing next to Hanratty and Hanratty was throwing to me.

One problem was that I was wearing street clothes, including a shoe whose crepe sole was loose and flapped. Another problem was that I had thrown my arm out the week before, throwing Gerela's field goals back to him in cold weather. And I have never been able to throw a football very well. I have a good arm in softball. Ask anybody. But I tend to snap my wrist, as you do throwing a softball, when I'm throwing a football. That produces a wobbly pass. It was after my performance in Palm Springs that I told Russell that a wobbly pass is embarrassingly like a limp penis.

So when I tossed the ball to Bradshaw after Hanratty threw it to me, I looked bad from the beginning. I admit that. And the fans got on me for that right away.

There were fans watching. Local people who had nothing better to do on a weekday afternoon (I don't think anybody in Palm Springs has much to do; everybody looks rich; I hate Palm Springs) were clustered around the field watching practice.

But hey, I was catching the ball. I would run a little pattern in the end zone and Hanratty would pop it to me and I would catch it with just my hands. "Great hands, terrible arm," Hanratty joked once. I disdained the use of my arms and body. (In part perhaps because I was mindful that Chris Speier, the San Francisco Giants' shortstop, had caught passes from the Steeler quarterbacks one afternoon and the next day the insides of his arms were black and blue.) I wasn't going to wrap the ball up desperately, I was going to flick my hands out there like magnetized rags and just *snk* that ball. I did that. Twice. That pebble grain feels good, like living skin, on the whorls of your fingers. I recall the best fingertips passage ever written—by James Agee in *Let Us Now Praise Famous Men,* with regard to coal oil: "This 'oil' is not at all oleaginous, but thin, brittle, rusty feeling, and sharp; taken and rubbed between forefinger and thumb, it so cleanses their grain that it sharpens their mutual touch to a new coin edge, or the russet nipple of a breast erected in cold . . ."

Twice. Or maybe three times. Then my hands gave out on me. I may have been *noticing* too much, and therefore becoming self-conscious. But it was also true that my hands got numb and leathery. I would put them out like before and there would be a sort of splutter, or splatter, as the ball struggled in them as though frightened and squirted through. Once, trying not to tighten up, I overeased and the ball just tipped my fingers and went zooming way beyond

249

me. "How did I ever catch something like that?" I began to think.

Bradshaw was taking part by coming up heavily behind me like a defender. Footsteps. Like a crowd I would shy away, and reach out at the ball awkwardly. Now I am not thoroughly frightened of running into big strong people. If there had been any chance of Pine Edwards's helmet driving into my face as I turned with the ball (assuming I ever turned with the ball again) I would have have packed my bag and flown back to Pittsburgh, but I wasn't afraid of bumping into Bradshaw. I was a blocking back in college intramurals, and although I could never get in front of anybody who tried to juke around me—and although I did once, trying to position myself optimally, give enough ground that I blocked with my coccyx my own team's extra point—I liked collisions within reason. It was just that I didn't feel I belonged there anyway and if Bradshaw wanted to be somewhere my instinct was to get out of his way. I didn't want to change the Steelers' course, I wanted to sense its nature. You can't work negative capability and defend your right to real estate at the same time.

But I should have flung my body at the ball if I couldn't get my hands to perform. Stop it *some* way. The ball, though, is hard. Hanratty does not throw as hard as Bradshaw but he hums it. And it has that blunt point like an unsharpened stake. For the first time in my life I had balls coming at my face which if I missed them would smash my face. It is one thing flinging yourself at a ball if you are wearing a helmet with a faceguard on it . . .

"Sacrifice your body!" cried a still small voice in my head.

"How about my pride?" cried a louder, more vibrant one.

And the fans' voices did me no good at all. They were groaning and yelling and hooting; especially when I tripped over the pitcher's mound deep in the end zone and went sprawling, tearing the knee of my pants. "Here! Let *me* do it! He can't do it!" several adolescent boys cried out. If there were critics watching and jeering every time I put down a tentative line (there are, but they are internal and I can work with them) I would have a hard time writing. "Oh, God!" some witness cried in perverse delight.

"Now you know what we have to put up with," Bradshaw said softly behind me.

I persisted raggedly and finally Hanratty and Bradshaw were through warming up. I took a nice soft one from Hanratty over my shoulder, spiked the ball to spite the crowd, and trotted hang-dog to the sidelines. Dan Rooney looked away.

There was an eighteen-year-old girl around the pool at the Gene Autry Hotel where we were staying who was so wonderful-looking it made you mad. She was amazing. I'm not even going to try to describe her. She wore a terry-cloth bikini which you could not have dried off a little mouse with. She would wade out into the pool occasionally and get wet and then go back and lie down again in the sun. I think she was why the Steelers lost, if she bothered them as much as she did me. She was there with her mother. McMakin went out with her chastely one night, with a teammate and her mother, and the next morning a non-player said, "She's nice-looking all right, but the way McMakin's hands have been going he'd probably drop her tits."

That remark seems indelicate in print, I know, but in the context of locker room talk it is suitable—certainly it was the kind of thing a teammate would have loved saying to McMakin. I relayed it to Russell shortly before my receiving experience began. He didn't really laugh. "That's cold-blooded, as the guys say," he said. As I came to the sidelines in disgrace Russell was standing there. I was filled, as I approached him, with the realization that as tight as I might be with the Steelers, for a scribe, I didn't have the license to exchange cold-blooded talk with them concerning on-the-field matters. I shifted the focus of my cold-bloodedness. "The fans hate me," I said. "I hate the fans."

"You loved that, didn't you?" said Russell, smiling.

Loved it? I was startled. I felt terrible about it. I had *dropped* all those passes . . .

"Journalistically," I conceded.

□ **30** □

THE PLAYOV

I like to watch football for the falls. In every game there are hundreds of falls. And every fall is different.
—PITTSBURGH
GYMNASTICS TEACHER
JEANNETTE JAY

As I was getting some faint measure of feel for the game, the Steelers were losing theirs: it is hard to be intense in Palm Springs.

Some interesting things did happen there. The Chief used the term "bikinkies"—as in bikinky bathing suits; Joe Greene ate hot sauce until, according to some observers, steam rose from his head; a Steeler got a free massage at a local parlor by telling his masseuse she was under arrest; Van Dyke exemplified cold-blooded football humor by saying companionably to Walden, who'd been having a highly uneven season punting and was getting up in years, "Well, this is about it for you, huh, Bo?"

Van Dyke also confessed doubts on the part of the offense: "When we get down close to the goal, we're wondering if we can score. You're not just doing your job; you're asking yourself if you can score."

A sobbing anonymous father called the hotel from a Pittsburgh hospital to ask whether Greene and Ham would talk to his dying young son. They strained to hear the boy's weak voice. "We're going after those Raiders," Ham told him. "Are you going to watch the game?" The boy said he didn't know whether he would live long enough to. "Joe and I will come and watch you play football when you get better," Ham said. The boy's answer was inaudible. Ham and Greene were shaken.

"The Raiders are just like any other bunch of kids who like to beat up another bunch of kids," said their great receiver Fred Biletnikoff. But they were also the kids on whom the Steelers had perpetrated The Immaculate Reception. And Oakland was where things had been so favorably wild for the Steelers six weeks before. On the way out onto the field Bradshaw slung his golden arm over my shoulder and sang a country song: "Hello trouble . . . Come on in . . . Ain't had no trouble since you know when . . ." Whatever the sideline equivalent of being on the edge of your seat is, the Steelers were. I found myself sort of bouncing in place like the players, and stopped, feeling silly. The fans were primed. They were holding signs that said "Murder Franco," "Mean? Joe Greene Wears Panty Hose" and "Keating Doesn't Know Tomato Juice From Vin Rosé."

"If that doesn't get you up nothing will," I said to Keating the oenologist just before the toss. Earlier he had said of the fans: "If they only knew! Madden once called them rats leaving a sinking ship." Now he said "Yeah" and didn't smile.

On the first play from scrimmage Mansfield gained 5 yards by snapping the ball quick while a Raider was leaning offsides, and on the next play Franco ran hard for 8 yards. "Look at this game!" cried White. "This is gonna be a *good* game!"

But it wasn't. Stabler didn't get knocked out this time and he completed 14 of 17 short passes, and Marv Hubbard completed a lot of 5- and 6-yard runs, and the Steeler defense never took the ball away. No Cinderella things happened.

Just before the half Bradshaw did hit Barry Pearson for a 4-yard touchdown pass to make the score Oakland 10, Pittsburgh 7, and Van Dyke exclaimed "We've got them now! And they know it. Oh, they may make it look good for the fans, but they know it. It's like that cigar commercial. 'We're gonna getcha!' " Surely the God who looks after drunks and little children would save the Steelers. Or the Steelers' winning nature would assert itself. Or the Raiders would choke. Somehow things would fit together.

They fit together for Oakland. During the halftime Bradshaw nodded his head, "Yeah, yeah, yeah," as Noll tried to tell him what to do. In the third quarter as the Raiders kicked two quick field goals the Steeler offense didn't move. "We're trying to *lose* this game!" said Barry Pearson, as if he were a fan. "No sense in that!"

"We're getting beat across the board," said Furness. "Offense and defense." The defense had been saving the offense all year; finally they had both gone flat.

And then Bradshaw threw a sideline pass right into the Oakland secondary's rotation. Hello trouble. Willie Brown intercepted and went 54 yards for a touchdown and the game was a shambles. The fans were happy as hepatitic clams. "P-U-S-S-Y," they chanted behind the Steeler bench. "Hey Keating!" cried a young man with a contorted face, "how does it feel to be a *loser!*" He said that word hard: *"lewser."* A drunken kid in a Woodstock T-shirt was crowing and leering, and flipping back and forth a sign which said "Hurt Bradshaw" on one side and "Blood" on the other.

"Could be a sad ending to your book," said Hanneman.

"It isn't over yet," I said absurdly. Hanneman shot a bird at the fans, some of whom were trying to get one of us, even me, to come over the fence and fight.

Franco was pacing back and forth like a zoo lion whose knee was throbbing. L. C. was sitting on the bench with his hands and arms swathed in thick, peeling, stained bandages like those on besieged marines at Dak To in pictures in *Life*. His head was down. A sideline attendant wearing a chartreuse sweater, a red shirt and a green bowtie in the shape of two holly leaves with a red berry in the middle asked him if he could do anything for him. L. C. said no.

Loren Toews got in a fight on the field, came off, and was hit with a chocolate ice cream cone from the stands. Ice cream was all over the back of his head, mingling with sweat and grass and dirt and running down the cords of his neck. The fans whooped and laughed. Toews was disgusted. Franco got him a towel.

The birds were wheeling and dashing in and out of the stands again in a way that I still could not relate to the rhythms of the crowd and the game. Probably it was unrelated.

Bradshaw hit Lewis with a touchdown pass, but he threw three interceptions in all and the final score was 33–14. Bradshaw dressed hurriedly, shunned the press, and left. He didn't go back to Pittsburgh, where Missy, to whom he had dedicated his autobiography a few months before, was waiting for him. He went straight to Louisiana, having decided his marriage was over.

(Hanratty also took a separate plane, home to Denver with Rosemary. Hanratty was angry because though his wrist had healed he had not been reactivated; Gilliam had remained Bradshaw's backup. Some of the white Steelers thought Noll kept Gilliam up to avoid being accused of discrimination. "Of all the things that could've happened in the airport," Hanratty said later, "the worst did. He grimaced. "I saw Bob Hope."

("We hate Bob Hope," said Rosemary.)

Joe Greene sat in the dressing room. On the field after the game he had said to the formerly slippery Buehler, "You guys don't need all that shit you used before. You're a *winning* team." On the floor around his feet now were scattered jockstraps, dirty towels and battered empty tape-husks that had been cut away from hands and still looked grasping. "We're one of the best teams in the country with one of the best coaching staffs," he said. "But something was missing. We didn't have that kind of frenzy Miami put on us. That's the way Pittsburgh plays football . . . But today, that special ingredient was missing.

"Now I'm gonna be home with my little boys and girl," he said.

"What are they getting for Christmas?"

He opened wide his arms and said with authority, "Me."

But then he sagged. "Now I got to go out and probly fight. 'Cause somebody's going to say something I don't agree with. You gonna help me?" he asked me.

I told him I'd be somewhere behind him. But all the bellicose fans seemed to have gone home. There was a man who looked like Fred Mertz who said, "Hi Joe. Heh-heh. Hi Joe. Heh-heh. Wish I had my camera. Heh-heh."

On the plane back, Ham and Wagner jocularly blamed various teammates: "It was *your* fault."

"It's a game of inches," Ham said.

"Sometimes it's a game of feet," said Wagner.

Bleier did his chicken imitation. It was much better than the game. He brushed his hair up like a comb and hunched down with his chest out huge and walked like a hen and clucked. Maurice Sendak might have drawn him.

Sam Davis looked pent up and desolate. I asked him a dumb scribe's question: How did he feel now compared to the way he felt after the last game in '72?

"Same," he said.

"Does it always feel the same after you lose the last one?"

"It does. To me."

Someone brought word that Greene wanted Sam to come up to first class and lose some money at poker. Sam winced.

"What you want me to tell him? Go fuck himself?"

"Yeah," said Sam.

"It's over," said L. C. "Too many people thinking about tomorrow. Or yesterday. It can be today, if you just let it happen. It'll come." I told him he'd played a good game anyway, as he had. If he'd known the game as a whole was going to turn out the way it did, he might not have gone to the trouble, he implied. A few months later he became the first Steeler to sign with the WFL.

The Chief was playing gin with George Perles, in apparent equanimity. "Wait till next year," he said.

"A guy like me," said Meyer, meaning a marginal recklessly-disregard-your-small-body guy, "I don't know whether I'll have a next year."

"I'd call it a predictable ending," said Rowser. "With our offense anything we got was a bonus." Several other defensive men agreed. They grumbled about Bradshaw's thinking, and Noll's.

"The terrible thing," said Mansfield later, "is that the defense didn't die on the beaches with their bayonets. They ran into the water and drowned. I think that's basic to the success of humanity—don't quit. What if the United States laid down in World War II?

"I don't know how many more years I have to play. I don't know whether we'll get this close again." Close that is to the Super Bowl. To the only season that ends upbeat.

"My eyes look like two sheep turds in a bucket of blood," said Hanneman. "I'm hotter than a freshly fucked fox in a forest fire." How did he feel about the playoff? "It's like what Adlai Stevenson said after Eisenhower beat him so bad. It hurts too much to laugh but I'm too old to cry."

People were taking hits out of various things to augment the two free beers.

"Watch out for Noll," someone said. "He won't venture back into the pit," said someone else.

In the dressing room after the game, in his last '73 address to the team, Noll had been brief: "We're too good a team to be losing. We're going to take a long concentrated look at the season. We're going to find out where the mistakes came and why. All I can say is Merry Christmas." He didn't smile. "Merry Christmas," he said. Now he sat wordless up front staring straight ahead. He had lost. He could be criticized by Jagovs like fans and scouts and scribes.

When we reached Pittsburgh it was very early in the morning of Sunday, December 23. I said good-bye to people as though it were high school graduation. "I can't drive back to Oregon in time for Christmas. Can't buy gas on Sunday," Hanneman said blearily, solemnly. He was afraid his defection two years before—going back to Oregon over that girl he'd since given up on—had left him so marginal in the coaches' eyes that he'd be cast off after their long concentrated look.

"You know what I said about Stevenson . . . not crying. I say that, but I will. I'll break down, before I take off back to Oregon in the car."

What kind of end was this for a year with hard-rolling men of contact? Something missing. Something missing. In a plane crowded with 250-pound people, not one image of fullness. Nothing like The Immaculate Reception, or the blazing tree the Chief lit, or the polka-dot shoes that came trucking up in memories of black college ball. In the picture in your mind there's a hole that life runs through. "Football is a game of attrition" was one of the coaching clichés Wagner and Ham had recited for me in Palm Springs, along with "It's a jungle out there" and "You can't suck blood out of a dead squirrel."

"Anything you feel like a piece of shit after is not a sport," Keating had said, exuberantly. And Bleier who had been in combat said "You don't want to play. It's not fun. You could do something that would cause you to be put down or traded, or released outright."

> Released outright:
> Hurled from the world
> To endless night.

Alternative—not to say grab-ass—versions of the game were what made the players feel sportive. The weekly tough football game amongst the linemen: "I made a catch in that game the other day that people said was the greatest catch they'd ever seen," said Mansfield.

"Sometimes," said Bradshaw, "you'd like to go out there and really give them something to boo: have 20 interceptions, hand off to the wrong people, lose 100 to 0. Come off the field and the coach is laughing, everybody's hugging everybody, just having a good time."

Russell enjoyed the Pro Bowl, in which all the stars futzed around and told each other stories: there was the time a linebacker bought a sandwich from a

256

vendor behind the bench, at a small-town exhibition game, and then was sent back in to play. He carried the sandwich into the game and handed it to the man next to him in the defensive huddle, who passed it to the man next to him, who thought, What is a sandwich doing in the defensive huddle? and passed it on. Just before the play went off the strong safety handed it, less several bites, to an official. In Pro Bowl practice when his man got behind him and caught a pass Russell stopped, watched the man run downfield for a while, and then pointed his finger like a pistol and shot him.

Jagov notions! Jagov notions! As if to imply that fun is what is missing from this game! That this game is *only* onerous!

A couple of weeks after the season was over Mansfield ate his eggs, and then some of my eggs, in a late-night hashhouse in Pittsburgh and told me this: "In college, when we were running, they'd say, 'Mansfield you're fat and last.' I'd hang back and beat everybody in the last minute. They wanted me to run hard all the way. They had guys built like Greek gods who couldn't block their ass, and I got stomach hanging over my belt and I knock shit out of people. I didn't get the MVP my senior year—a guy who was nice did. That's what I like about myself: coaches don't like me. I like to have a good time. But I do the job anyway.

"I'm getting at the stage now where I have to worry about losing my physical ability. My neck hurts so bad sometimes I think about killing myself. I know I'll be a cripple by the time I'm fifty. But if that's what it takes, fuck it. When I was growing up my family never had anything. I want to enjoy life. Next to loving, football is the thing I like most."

And right after the playoff loss, in the dressing room before his sweat was dry, I talked to Russell. Russell who used to be one of the game's great hunch-playing blitzers, but who had sacrificed much of his abandon to Noll's disciplined team-play system. Russell who can't be playing purely for money, because he makes twice as much in business as in football. Russell who told every pro team that asked him in college that he didn't want to play pro ball, but was drafted by the Steelers because they didn't ask. Russell whose snappy wife Nancy believes in women's lib, and also Big Business. Russell who plays with stomach tears and groin pulls and sprained toes. Russell who on a football players' tour of Vietnam, finding himself in a barracks vulnerable to attack, spent the night on the steps with a rifle, a martini and a candle, while Buck Buchanon of Kansas City hid in the bathroom.

That was the Russell who after the ignominious play-off spoke to me literally of ecstasy: "I was into that game. There was no other world outside it. There was nothing. That's the thrill."

"Does that make it hard to lose?"

"No, easier. You know you gave it all you had. Some games you're distracted, by an injury or something, and you get down on yourself, question your character. This game I was away; into the *game*. We lost. But all I could think afterwards was 'God damn, I had fun.' "

And so I guess did all of those frothing fans, and even the wheeling birds maybe (who knows?) and maybe even Noll, and so journalistically and personally did I the detached scribe, who had thrown my arm around Russell's shoulder pads on the sidelines there as defeat loomed; the closest I ever came to tackling a Steeler; and so did the fan back home in Pittsburgh who later wrote:

> Dear PittsBurgh
> I like your team. I watched all of your games. pittsBurgh when you lost to Oklalang I think it was are right and Because you Bet them 3 times so what well pittsBurgh I am very glad that I am a fan of your team well pittsBurgh I am glad I wrote this letter well I guess Id, Better go well Bye. Bye.
>
> love your fan
Steve
>
> (PS) I love your team.

"It's some game," Russell went on. "It's a great game. It's not like going to play a game of squash."

·TWO·

...AND
THE LOAD
FILLED UP

■ ■ ■

□ 1 □

SUPERBOWL, 1975: "YOU'RE A PART OF ALL THIS"

I backed off, took a little run and butted Mean Joe Greene right in the numbers. Really. I had sneaked down onto the Steelers' sideline during the last two minutes of their Super Bowl victory, which I felt a part of. I had spent the whole 1973 season hanging around with the Steelers, to write a book called *About Three Bricks Shy of a Load . . . The Year the Pittsburgh Steelers Were Super but Missed the Bowl.* Now, with the clock ticking down, the Steelers were about to consign my title to ancient history. I had more or less taken the position in my book that being humane, or something, was better than winning. Now that my friends had the Bowl all but sewed up, I could see that ultimate victory did have a certain charm, and I was doing my best to join aptly in the exultation. From up in the stands it may look easy, the exultation. But I was burdened by a little red-and-blue bag I had been given in the auxiliary press box. Inside the bag were wadded-up mimeographed play-by-plays and the remains of my press lunch: strange sandwiches called "muffelettes" and some other things, chicken fingers, I think. It is complicated to tote muffelette scraps and embrace Ernie (Arrowhead) Holmes at the same time.

Holmes is the only person I know who is 6–3, weighs 260, has a big gold tooth and wears his hair shaved off except for what forms the head of an arrow pointed at you. Later that night at the Steeler party I was reminded of how unsettling Holmes looks when I said to two different people, "That's Ernie Holmes over there, you want to meet him?" and each of them said, "Oh my God." Two years before the Super Bowl, in a serious emotional crisis, he had shot at a policeman in a helicopter. During the Super Bowl he was largely responsible for reducing the Vikings' offensive line to quivering jelly. Two weeks before the Super Bowl he had been telling me to "get away" in an ominous tone. Now, I just shut the muffelettes, and to some extent the jelly, out of my mind and grabbed Holmes and bounced around with him. And beat on L. C. Greenwood, who off the field wears a gold medallion given him by

261

a lady, which has "TFTEISYF" on it, which stands for "The First Time Ever I Saw Your Face." And did the grip with Mel Blount—under whose picture in the local paper my name had appeared once that week—and tried to outglow Dwight White and yelled, "Moon! Moon! Moon!" at Moon Mullins and slapped the shoulder pads of Andy Russell, who slapped my shoulders (another problem: no pads) and cried, "You're a part of all this!" I guess I would have felt better if I had been celebrating the signing of an eternal amity pact among all the nations of the world, but I don't know.

Greene and Terry Bradshaw hugged each other. During these last minutes Bradshaw and his quarterback rivals Terry Hanratty and Joe Gilliam and their hard coach Chuck Noll and six cameras all had their noses or lenses within inches of each other, figuring the next play or recording the figuring, and they were all grinning, even the cameras. Greene and Holmes bent way over from the waist and bumped their heads together triumphantly.

The Steelers had the game wrapped up, and I wasn't feeling objective at all. The final gun went off and we all roiled around like an invading army that had just started to whoop after taking a castle, and Greene and Franco Harris picked Noll up on their shoulders and—behold, the winning smile on Noll's face. I had never seen Noll's mouth so wide open. It was as though the Dragon Lady had gone all soft around the eyes and said, "Oh, baby." Glorying, I headed off the field with the players and got nearly crushed between Greene and the Vikings' Carl Eller, who were being crowded by yelping, snatching fans, but who said to each other, emotionally, respectfully, something profound, which in retrospect I believe was "Good game." I looked for Ray Mansfield, the Steelers' newly famous center, so I could pound on him, but I didn't see him until afterward in the press interview tent, which looked alarmingly like a sideshow—Steelers in blood-spotted white-and-gold suits, standing on platforms above milling, curious reporters. "How does it feel?" "What do you weigh?" Right after the gun, Mansfield told me later, he had been busy retrieving the ball, which was lying on the field unnoticed. "Players were running right past it. Even fans," he said. "All of us had been fighting for it so long, and now it was just lying there. It looked kind of sad." He gave it to Russell, who presented it to Art Rooney, who had been wanting it for forty-two years.

Up in the stands Julie Marx, twelve, a friend of mine who had never seen a football game before but had been yelling "Deee-fense!" at the top of her lungs, also noticed the ball lying free and then Mansfield carrying it away. "Do you think," she asked her mother, "they would give it to me?"

Everybody wants to get into the act. I was into it because of my book, copies of which had reached the players at about the time—early this past December—when the team, which had been on-again, off-again, suddenly became a juggernaut. I feel that some, if not most, of the credit for this transformation should go to the players and the coaches, and perhaps to Radio Rich, who has thirty-four radios in his room at the Pittsburgh Y and has been hanging around the Steelers longer than I have; but on the afternoon before the Super Bowl, Greene did offer an unsolicited testimonial. I had brought Reggie Jackson of the Oakland A's into a small room-shaking festivity involving Greene, Holmes and Dwight (Mad Dog) White, who had a viral infection. "This guy's book had something to do with us being here," Greene told Jackson. "He raised some shit that we dug."

I don't know what specific shit I could pinpoint as helpful, but the great thing was that I had been acknowledged as . . . a factor. Me, a factor. Like the wind and the turf and the cartilage in the running backs' knees. Like all the other press during the week leading up to Super Bowl IX, I had often felt the urge to mutter "IX, SCHMIX," or when some player or coach said, "It's only another game," to rise up and shout, "It certainly is!" But when you see yourself as a factor, your attitude changes.

"PROFESSOR STUDIES SUPER BOWL, SAYS HAS MYTH QUAL-ITY," read the headline in the *New Orleans Times-Picayune* on Thursday morning before the game. Andy Russell was reading the story aloud at breakfast. "Sociologically speaking," said the lead, "the Super Bowl is a 'propaganda vehicle' which strengthens the American social structure."

"I can't stand that shit!" Greene shouted.

"More than a game, it is a spectacle of mythical proportions which becomes a 'ritualized mass activity,' says Michael R. Real, assistant professor of communications at the University of California at . . ."

"Shit," Greene cried. He seized the paper and tore it to shreds. "I'd like to run into that guy," he said of Michael R. Real.

The Steelers have a number of stars and leaders of various kinds, but Greene is their sun. The main strength of the team is the defense, of the defense, the Front Four, of the Front Four, Greene. There may well never have been a lineman at once so smart, strong, fiery and, especially, quick as Greene when he is inspired. People who watched the films of the Steelers' playoff victory over Oakland said that on one play Greene began his rush a millisecond after the snap and hit the quarterback half a millisecond after the ball did (he was penalized for being offside and thought himself that he must have been, but the films showed that he wasn't). And that he once went straight *through* Oakland Center Jim Otto, like a 275-pound chill through a man with no coat. They kept slowing down and stopping the film to see exactly how he went through Otto—between the two *T*s, maybe, or headfirst through one of the *O*s. They could never figure it out. One moment Greene and Otto were head to head, and then they formed a blur together, and then Otto was more or less where he had been, only lying down (and perhaps spelled "Toot"), and Greene was entangled with the Oakland backfield in a pile. The only lineman to compare Greene with, says Steeler Defensive Line Coach George Perles, is the

263

great end, retired, of the Colts, Gino Marchetti. "Alan Page," said Perles, when the distinguished Viking tackle was mentioned. "Joe could whip Alan Page and stand on him."

Throughout their closing surge this season, as they blew New England, Cincinnati, Buffalo, Oakland and Minnesota off the field, the Steelers relied more and more heavily upon a unique Stunt 4–3 defense, designed by Perles around Greene. Greene and the intimidating Holmes would smash a hole in the middle of the line; the nimble White and Greenwood would pinch in from the sides; All-Pro Linebackers Russell and Jack Ham would stick to the short-passing targets (Minnesota's Fran Tarkenton said they did it "maybe as well as anybody in history"); and everybody in the secondary meanwhile was (1) liable to break a receiver's back and (2) drooling for interceptions. That was basically the defense last year, too, when the Steelers failed, but toward the end of this season it eschewed fancy variations and revolved around Greene, and nobody did anything against it, except Oakland's estimable Ken Stabler with his long passes that were not enough. The Steeler defense was a guerrilla operation, featuring vicious, opportunistic hitting, hell-for-leather pursuit and the repeated generation of loose balls—balls bounding free, popping up, squirting out and rolling around. The game ball Mansfield picked up was probably not much more baffled, lying there, than it had been all afternoon. My favorite turnover of the day was when Minnesota's Chuck Foreman ran into the middle of the line at the Steelers' five. He fumbled in the midst of a huge seething pileup, and Greene, standing beside the tangle, appeared to reach into it and slap the ball up into his arms like a bear scooping a fish out of a stream. What actually happened, said Holmes, was "I hit Foreman. . . ."

"What did you hit him with?" I asked.

"Stuck my head in there," he said sort of modestly. "And the ball got loose and squirted back through Ticklehoff's legs"—Holmes called Viking Center Mick Tingelhoff "Ticklehoff," not meaning any offense, I think—"and Joe picked it up." It was almost as though the Vikings had snapped it to Greene, which seemed appropriate.

There were other factors in the Steelers' improvement this year. Competition among the three quarterbacks produced a much steadier Bradshaw. "He got rattled a couple of times in the huddle," said Rocky Bleier after the Oakland game, "but now we're not getting uptight about it. We settle him down and he comes through." Last year Bradshaw threw key interceptions that deflated the team. This year, after winning the job back, he kept coming up with spirit-lifting third-down completions. That is the difference, or difference enough, between a dumb quarterback and a smart one. I had quoted a Steeler saying last year, "You want your quarterback to be tricky, wily, like Bugs Bunny, or Daffy Duck. Bradshaw's too much like Elmer Fudd." When that came out, Bradshaw called his attorney and asked, "Who is Elmer Food?" But knowing how to pronounce Fudd is not essential. Johnny Unitas last year said, "All I know about sentiment is it comes between 'shit' and 'syphilis' in the dictionary," which wasn't true, and when I asked Fran Tarkenton before the Super Bowl about peripheral vision, he said, "Periphial vision is bullshit." Which is also, Tarkenton's pronunciation aside, untrue. Hanratty is the Bugs Bunniest of the Steelers' three quarterbacks, and Gilliam is the most exciting, the one you'd go for if you were building your team around the quarterback. (And he is the one some other team is likely to go for soon—he is too restless to be your ideal No. 2 man, and he has told teammates that he asked Vice-President Dan Rooney for "one point five over five," which is to say, a five-year, $1.5 million contract, and got his feelings hurt when Dan seemed amused.) But the Steelers believe in Bradshaw now, hence Greene's hug.

Also this year Harris ran hard again, suppressing his leg pains and ceasing to "dance." Wounded vet Bleier became the solid, good-blocking halfback needed to complement Franco. The offensive line improved. Tackle Gordy Gravelle "arrived." Jim Clack switched from center to guard, and he and Mullins pulled so vigorously ahead of the 230-pound Harris that by the end of the season they weighed less than he did. The new offensive line coach, Dan (Bad Rad) Radakovich, was regarded with no warmth by his charges, who were fond of his predecessor, Bob Fry, whom Noll fired. Radakovich told Mansfield after the Oakland game, "Good work, Ranger, but remember, I've got the young guy [rookie Mike Webster] waiting in the wings." But Radako-vich drilled them exhaustingly in new techniques that opened big holes for Harris and allowed the quarterbacks to be sacked only 21 times in 17 games. Rookie Receivers Lynn Swann and John Stallworth added dash to the offense, and Jack Lambert, another rookie, mastered middle linebacking in one year. Bleier talked Russell into lifting weights, and Russell for the first time in his career went uninjured. Russell talked Bleier *out* of lifting weights late in the season, and Bleier was less tired toward the end.

Usually it is only after you see how the season ends up that you can figure out what the factors were, or which ones were good. For instance, it now appears that having your reserve quarterback's wife shot at in the off-season could be a good omen. That happened to Rosemary Hanratty (by accident, since it was someone else the man was angry with). But a more reliable indicator of the Steelers' fortunes is Joe Greene's behavior each year during and after the second Houston game.

In '72, when half the team was hurt or sick for that game, Greene rose up and beat the Oilers almost single-handedly, sacking the quarterback five times. The Steelers went on to win their first division championship. In '73 Greene was so disgusted with the Steelers' lack of spark against Houston that he took himself out of the game, an action many of his teammates resented. The Steelers fizzled badly in the playoffs. In '74 the Steelers lost the second Oiler game, 13–10, on December 1, which looked bad. "After that we just about packed it in," says Art Rooney Jr. "We were getting ready for next season.

People were saying, 'That Paul Brown, he's a genius. Doesn't have half the talent Noll does and he still wins.' " But Greene was saying something different, and Noll was on top of things.

Greene has been heard to complain that Noll is not emotional enough. A good deal of the time Noll is what you would have to call grim. Early this season, not long after the players' strike was settled, Safety Mike Wagner was walking through the Steeler offices with a check for something like $4.17 that he had been issued because earlier he had been slightly underpaid during the exhibition season. "Look here, Coach," he said lightly to Noll. "This is all they paid me."

"If you're just in the game for money," Noll said stiffly, "you'd better get out of it." Once, during the Steelers' dark losing days, Cornerback Lee Calland came into the dressing room at halftime weeping. He rose tearfully, dramatically, and began making a heart-rending appeal for a better second-half effort. "Shut up, Lee," said Noll, and Calland sat down and Noll fell to diagramming plays on the blackboard.

So Noll didn't feel called upon to whip up his troops after the Houston game this season. Greene did. He went to certain members of the offense and told them bluntly that they had better shape up. He said if the Steelers didn't make the Super Bowl, he was going to quit them.

"If you do," Russell told him semijocularly later, "you better not come back and play against us, because we'll kick your ass." But Greene had established his own intensity, at least, for the rest of the year. He is a proud, emotional player, who demands that his context be worthy of and responsive to his fiercest and most acrobatic efforts.

A week or so after that came copies of my book, which raised the stuff Greene approved of, and as the Steelers were picking up steam and moving toward the playoff game with Oakland, Noll tossed in a little provocation of his own. He came into a team meeting with his lips compressed even more tightly than they usually are when his back is up. Before Oakland's first-round game with Miami, Raider Coach John Madden had said of the Raiders and the Dolphins, "When the two best teams in football get together, anything can happen."

"I'll tell you what *anything* is," Noll told the Steelers. "*Anything* is that Oakland isn't getting into the Super Bowl." The room was charged. Greene jumped up and began waving his fists and yelling. The fat was in the fire.

The Steelers soundly whipped Oakland. They felt better about that than they did about beating Minnesota in the big one. The year before, in the first playoff round, Oakland had made them look bad. "I never thought I'd see a team of yours embarrassed like that," Art Rooney Jr. told Noll in the Steelers' first draft meeting after that game. Although Noll's instinct for talent and Artie's scouting operation have, by means of the draft, built the Steelers' material up from almost nothing to a young abundance—three Rookies of the Year in six seasons—the partnership has been abrasive, and those words must have galled Noll. He had been tense then, goading people the week before that '73 loss. He was loose this time, before the '74 win, the win that got them into the Super Bowl. He even cracked jokes about the locker room horseplay in which Kicker Roy Gerela gashed Lambert's ear with a tossed Coke can. The Steelers went into the game happy and came out happier. When I went into the cramped visitors' dressing room at the Oakland Coliseum after the 24–13 win—into the room where the Steelers' season had ended in defeat the year before—Stallworth yelled, "No more bricks!" and we slapped hands, and White said, "Now you got to write: *A Full Load.*" "*A Load and a Half,*" said Gilliam. "*Bricks to Throw Away!*" said While.

I sat down next to Holmes expecting a friendly talk, and he said, in a suppressed furious growl, "What'd you put that shit in your book for?"

Now, if there is one person on the Steelers, or the earth, you don't want to have furious at you, it is Holmes. His given first and middle names are Earnest Lee, and that is the way he likes people and the way he beats on people. He does things earnestly enough to seem vulnerable as well as formidable, and I hated for him to think I had sold him short. Things had been very vague while I was with the Steelers the year before, as to what they were saying for publication and what they weren't. In general, it was up to me to decide. While I was with them they had tended to forget I was a writer because I was always drinking with them and eating chowder and playing liar's poker instead of taking notes. Several of them told me they assumed I would never actually write anything for that reason. I knew that what I had written had hurt the feelings of three or four players I liked, and that made me feel bad. But I hadn't expected Holmes to be one of those players. "*What* shit?" I asked him.

"Said I had the mind of a 6-year-old child," he replied in a low tone that caused a tremor in the stool I was sitting on.

"Oh," I thought, "my God." What I had in fact done was quote Holmes as saying, one afternoon when we were drinking martinis and eating chowder, "I'm trying to get my mind right. I haven't wanted to talk to reporters much since the incident." He was referring to that time after the '72 season when he broke down under the pressure of personal problems and started shooting from his car at trucks and wound up in the woods firing, accurately, at a police helicopter flying overhead. "There isn't a moment," I had quoted him as adding, "from the time I go into the dressing room until the game is over that I'm not praying. People think I'm talking to myself, but I'm praying. With the mind of a child and the brains of a sixty-year-old warrior."

That had struck me as such a poetic statement, I felt he would be proud to have it repeated. Nobody with a small mind could have expressed such a thing. Now I felt as though I had quoted Wordsworth as saying, "*I wandered lonely as a cloud,*" and he had chewed me out for accusing him of not having any friends.

"But *you* said that," I said. "And it was about your state of mind when you were praying. And it was a *great*—"

"Get away," he said, and that's more or less what he said on the plane back to Pittsburgh whenever I tried again to explain. "Stay away from him," people said, but I didn't want to leave it at that.

Otherwise, it was a pleasant trip. "Last year on the plane back from Oakland," said Mansfield, "Ham kept asking me, 'When did you know you had it lost?' This time, it's like he's in a daze. I know he's in a daze because he says he doesn't want to play gin."

Ham was not to bedazzled to advise me that my title should have been *One Year Shy of a Book.* Tony Parisi, the equipment man, said, "I'm giving you an exclusive. I knew they were going to win this one. You know why? Because before we left for Oakland nobody asked me for a box."

"A box?"

"To ship their stuff home in. Last year before Oakland, a lot of guys asked for boxes."

White said on the P.A. phone, "Mr. Rooney has something to say in the jubilance of what we've done," and Art Rooney, the Chief, the Steelers' founder and owner forever, said something that nobody remembered.

"The first time my father brought Johnny Blood home," Art Jr. said later, "us kids expected him to jump up on the table and take off his clothes or something. But he was very polite, we had dinner, he talked about, you know, pertinent things of the day, and at 9:30 he and my father left. I can't tell you how disappointed I was. Here was this legendary guy, and that's all he did. And that's the way it's been with my father. He hasn't said anything much. Mainly, he's worried about making sure he gets a Super Bowl ticket for every policeman and fireman in Pittsburgh."

The Chief, however, doesn't have to say anything dramatic in order to be a powerful presence on a victory-over-the-Raiders flight home (though personally I would rather make a remember-the-terrible-old-days drive to the racetrack with him), and when we got into the airport there were 10,000 Pittsburghers waiting, at 1:15 A.M. Later, several of the Steelers said they were glad when they got out of that crowd. "I got more beat up by them than I did in the game," said Greenwood. "When I got in the car finally, I just sat there for a minute. People were banging on my windows: 'Open up, we're your fans!' I said, 'Yeah . . .' "

But I loved it. I was congratulated by Frenchy Fuqua, who had been back in Pittsburgh with two broken wrists; and kissed by Ham's fiancée, Joanne Fell, who looks better than anybody else in the world; and for a distance of what must have been a mile, all the way from the gate down the long corridor and through the baggage area and way on out into the parking lot, I proceeded like a loaded blood cell along a narrow artery through hungry tissues of people, who were jammed into every inch of space on both sides of us, and they were all cheering. They were reaching out hands to shake. I shook them all. Women sitting on friends' shoulders were bending down to kiss my head. People were yelling, "Great game!" at me, or "Great cigar!" (since I was smoking an Art Rooney stogie of great size). It was like heaven, everybody happy, everybody loving you. Holmes bared his chest and raised his arms in triumph, and the crowd thundered, "ARROWHEAD!" It went on and on, through the warm, bright airport out into the cold, dark lot, as though it were going to go on forever, through day and night and all the seasons, and one person toward the end even recognized me for what I was and (rather than snorting "You're no player") cried out, "Great book!"

I went away from Pittsburgh for a few days then, after the Oakland win, and dreamed two Ernie Holmes–related dreams. Once he was reaching to shake my hand, I guess, but then maybe not, and I was in some kind of craft—a team plane—a helicopter? The other time my head was shaved completely, no arrowhead even, and I looked silly, exposed.

I rejoined the team in Pittsburgh, then flew with them to New Orleans. During the ten days leading up to the Final Reckoning I headed toward Holmes a couple of times but ran into someone else on the way. Then, on the day before the Bowl, I entered the room where Holmes, White, Greene, Mrs. Greene and some friends were drinking bourbon and Coke and beer and Mateus and dancing and rejoicing over the coming victory, and the first person I walked head-on into was Arrowhead, who said, "Hello, Archenemy."

The Steelers were loose all during Super Week. They enjoyed the attention of the press. "Centers are totally overlooked people in this world," Mansfield told an interviewer grandly, "and things like the Super Bowl are good to bring the personalities of people like me out." After the first two nights, which were no-curfew nights—from which I retain an image of Mansfield standing for some reason on top of Russell's rental car—they faithfully returned to their rooms at the Fontainebleau by 11 P.M. But within the fold there was considerable shouting and running around in the halls and drinking and entertaining of guests. One of the diminutive "security men" posted in the players' hall was scandalized. "If the Vikings' coaches impose more discipline on them," he told a Steelers in a tone of deep concern, "you guys are going to be in trouble." Noll, unlike Minnesota's Bud Grant, permitted the Steelers' wives to stay with them on Friday and Saturday nights, although he had never allowed cohabitation on the night before a game even at home during the regular season. "Yes, there will be a bed check," said Russell. "He wants to see our wives in their nighties." Kidding. Kidding.

And Holmes was loose when he called me archenemy. "I'm not your enemy," I said, "I'm a good man. And so are you." I suppose that sounds kind of silly. You had to be there. We shook hands, and then he took my picture. A good many of the Steelers have recently gotten enthusiastically into photography. In this party in a small room of the Fontainebleau, Holmes, White, Greene and several of the friends present all had cameras, and they were all taking pictures of each other. A wrestling match between an Oriental and a Latin was proceeding unattended on the TV set. Flashbulbs were popping. Rosé was flowing. Music was playing. "Of all the writers here, writing all those words all week," said Greene, whose shirttail was out, "nobody has reached it. Nobody has said what it means. We're *happy* to be here. We're feeling *good.*" Holmes was dancing the Bump with Greene's tiny, self-possessed wife, Agnes, whom people were calling "Texas." "Get *down,* Texas," people yelled, and Holmes started bumping her hip with his head. Greene hurriedly focused his camera. "Shows what kind of a photographer I am," he said. "I missed it." Holmes started to bump with his head some more, for the picture, but Texas made some slight indication that she'd rather dance the Bump in a serious normal way, thank you. "I'm sorry," Holmes said politely.

White was there, with his viral infection. I had visited him in the hospital a couple of days before. He'd been lying there losing eighteen pounds because he hurt too much to be hungry. In the rooms around him were old ladies with complicated wire-and-tape apparatus in their noses and mouths, lying there silent as Dwight. An old lady turned over in her bed and said, "Oh!" vexedly to no one. An old man was helped off the toilet and into a wheelchair by a nurse—"Now sit," she said. Dwight was morose; at least seventy-five percent certain, the doctors said, not to play. Now, in the motel on Super Eve, he was still sick, but out bouncing around anyway. The room seemed about to burst. White was saying, "Doc Huber sat down on the bed and put his arm around me and said, 'I know how you feel.' I was crying like a little punk. I said, 'Know how I *feel*? You don't know how I *feel*! I'm gonna be in there. I may fall out, but I'm gonna fall out *in* the Super Bowl.' They rolled aside the rock," he proclaimed with arms flung wide, "and I came walking out, *standing up*!"

"You're ready! You're ready! I can tell you're ready," Greene told me as Reggie Jackson and I left the party. Jackson is a good-sized person himself and usually at least as expansive as anybody in the room. "I have never seen people so *physical,*" he said.

And as the world knows, they were physical on the field the next day. Before the game Glen (Knotty Pine) Edwards, the rough-as-a-good-bark-covered-stick free safety, sat in the dressing room and noticed that his teammates were unaccountably sitting around like zombies. That was the first time they had been subdued all week. "Where the hell am I, anyway?" he said, and everybody broke up. Pine, whom the Steelers elected as their most valuable player this season but who attracted widespread notice only when he hurled himself egregiously at the head of Cincinnati Quarterback Ken Anderson as Anderson went out of bounds on TV, was in the press interview room one day during Super Week and nobody was interviewing him. "Nobody wants to talk to a muffucker like me," Pine said. But in the Bowl itself he came up with one of the biggest plays, nailing Viking Receiver John Gilliam so viciously that an all-but-completed pass deep in Steeler territory bounced high out of Gilliam's arms and into Blount's. Edwards wasn't invited into the interview tent after the game either. In the dressing room he said he'd probably spend his championship money on a new house. He bought one last year, but he thought he'd get a different one. And he'd take a vacation. He didn't know where. He went to the Bahamas last year and didn't much like them. Edwards once told somebody that when he went places in Dallas with Greene and White, people made a big fuss over them, all of them, including him. When he went back home to Florida, however, people said, "Hey, Pine. Hey, Pine. You still up there?" "Hey, Pine. They cut you yet?"

In the victorious dressing room the Chief entertained a bunch of reporters by telling them that he never showed emotion at ball games. "Even in my betting days at the track, when I was betting a fortune, a guy standing beside me would never know it." Once during training camp last summer a teamster official at a party tried to introduce James Michener, the novelist, to the Chief. "Oh, he's with me," the Chief said. Michener was in town gathering material for a sports book. The Chief hadn't heard of him as a writer, but since Michener had once run for Congress in Bucks County, Pennsylvania, he knew of him as a politician, and they had come to the party together.

The teamster official was impressed. "Whoever you're with," he told the Chief, "it's always a top guy. If it's a politician, or a hood, or a union man, or a gambler, it's always a top one." Now the Chief was with the top football team, but he didn't look any more distinguished or any less rumpled than usual. I told him it had been an honor to be associated with him. I felt almost tearful in the back of my eyes. He looked embarrassed.

"Ohhh," he said, "you fit in like a glove."

Everything seemed sort of washed out in the dressing room and in the interview tent, where Greene was saying mildly that his thoughts turned to the Vikings, in sympathy. There was something disconcerting about the Steelers becoming winners. The Rooney regime's charm always had something to do with rising above defeat. Now that the Steelers are kings of the mountain, would they stiffen up? When Tex Schramm of the Cowboys phoned the Chief a few days later and expressed hope that the two teams could do some friendly trading, the Chief reminded him of the kinds of trades Schramm used to try to foist upon the old irregular Steelers. "One time they sent us a player with a broken arm," the Chief recalled fondly after hanging up. "I called up Schramm and said, 'We've got just two days till the season starts, and you send us a man with a broken arm!' 'Well,' Schramm said, 'he has an Irish name, doesn't he?' "

The Chief seemed happier over that story than he did over winning the Super Bowl. I wonder whether such stories will collect around the new Steelers. Kathy Kiely, college sophomore daughter of the Steelers' public relations director, said on the plane back to Pittsburgh after the Super win, "This is the first and last hurrah."

The welcome-home parade in Pittsburgh the day after the Super Bowl wasn't as good as I expected either, not as good as the one after Oakland. The Super reception was nice along the highway in from the airport, where people had been standing in the cold for four hours waiting—a nicely dressed middle-aged lady standing alone waving her sweater, two kids banging potlids together, a new fan club holding a sign identifying itself as "Bradshaw's Brains." But when we got into downtown Pittsburgh, people beat so hard on the top of the convertible I was in that their blows reached my head, and they leered unhingedly in through the car windows. It was unnerving. I hope nobody ever looks at me that way again.

So I guess the climax of the Super Bowl for me was back there on the sidelines, jumping around like a fool, or maybe in the bus after the game when Holmes said, "I don't know. This thing has got me off into something that I don't hardly know how to express. It's just . . . too much. After the game I wanted to start slapping reporters."

I said maybe I'd better get on another bus, but he said no. He looked at his ring finger's middle knuckle, which was as big as a golf ball. He was trying to decide where to wear his Super Bowl ring. "I think I'll put it behind the knob," he said.

Holmes's eyes looked glazed, he was so fulfilled. "Them guards was in there *quivering,*" he said of the Vikings. "It was like they were little kids. Joe was down there saying, 'You fucking faggots!' I think they were terrified."

Greene got on the bus. "How'm I look-in' *now!*" he cried.

White was regretting that his illness, despite which he had played almost the whole game, was going to keep him from partying that night. "That's half the Super Bowl," he said.

"No," said Greene. "No. This is it. This is all of it. Right here." I looked around the bus. I *felt* like I knew what he meant, but I'm not sure. Greene has a certain mystery about him. Tarkenton told Russell that a man from Greene's home town told him Greene was born thirty-three years ago. He is listed as twenty-eight now. At that little party the day before the game Greene said something about being twenty-eight, and White said, "On the books, anyway," and Greene grinned. Can Joe Greene have hidden five years away somewhere? I don't know. I didn't ask. I didn't care. I wasn't feeling like a reporter. I had been sucked into the Super Bowl and I felt good. We were all factors on that bus. Eat your heart out, Michael R. Real.

□ **2** □

SUPER BOWL, 1975, P.S.

Before the opening kickoff, Pittsburgh's starting defense and Minnesota's starting offense lined up along the same corridor under the stands waiting to be introduced to 80 million people. But Edwards lined up with the Viking offense! Had he defected? Taken leave of his senses? No. He had stepped over to chat with a Viking he'd known in college. Who would not acknowledge his presence. The Vikings had apparently been instructed to remain silent. None of them would utter a syllable to the bouncy, scrubby Steeler who had infiltrated their file.

"What's wrong with you guys!" demanded Edwards, looking them all over and getting exercised. What kind of jive Vikings were they? he wanted to know. They remained mute, towering over Edwards, who sighed. "You guys," he said, "better buckle up!" Then he rejoined the Steelers, having taken perhaps a bit of the snap out of the Viking attack.

Steeler Head Coach Chuck Noll is not one of your emotional halftime rousers. But with Pittsburgh leading the Vikings only 2–0 after the half in '75, he did want to make one important point. "Make sure," he told his squad, "to start off with a good deep kick." The person to whom that injunction applied directly, of course, was kicker Roy Gerela. Gerela took it to heart. He concentrated, ran up to the ball, swung his foot and fell on his back. As he went down he managed to nudge out a little dribbler, which the Vikings fumbled and the Steelers recovered to set up their first touchdown. It was one of the biggest plays of the game. "Well," said Gerela later, "I did try to give it a little extra."

An unsung stalwart in the '75 game was Steeler Ed Bradley (now with Seattle), who took over as middle linebacker when then rookie sensation Jack Lambert was injured early in the second half. Bradley played so well that hardly anyone noticed that Lambert was out, which meant that hardly anyone noticed that Bradley was in. After laboring in obscurity and on suicide squads for two years, Bradley was still lost in the crowd; but he could be proud of having risen to the Super occasion.

There was one man prouder, though. For an hour during the Steeler victory party that man stood outside looking in and crying. All sorts of hangers-on found their way into the party, but the crying man couldn't convince anyone that he belonged there. Until finally his son caught sight of him, brought him

273

into the party, embraced him and started crying too. The man was Ed Bradley Sr., who played for two years with the Chicago Bears in the early fifties before returning to ordinary life. On another occasion Ed Jr. had said, "These days my father's working somewhere with his hands out in the weather, the cold and everything. Which he likes . . . I have a football he gave me the day I was born. Signed by Johnny Lujack, Bulldog Turner, Ed Sprinkle, all the Bears. I don't know. Football's been my life."

A Steeler official who'd noticed the weeping man outside the party felt bad when he realized who he was. "I've met Ed Bradley's father before," he said. "But he was crying so hard I didn't recognize him."

□ **3** □

JOE GREENE:
"HE DOES WHAT HE
WANTS OUT THERE"

September, 1975

"**I** am not a dirty player," says Charles Edward (Mean Joe) Greene. "I have at certain times had violent urges, but I don't think I ever have hurt anybody. Tried to a couple times, but I don't think I have. Yeah, guess I have. In high school. I was dirty then. Kick 'em.

"I do play football no-holds-barred. Any edge I can get, I'll take. I'd grab a face mask only in a fit of anger. Uncontrolled anger is damn near insane."

Greene once shattered three or four of Cleveland Guard Bob DeMarco's teeth, and they were big teeth way back deep in the jaw. Once, Greene admits, he tried to twist the head off a fellow professional who was holding him. Is it because deep down inside they are so relieved that he is not going to twist their heads off—is that why people who spend time with him are proud to say that Joe Greene is a nice, warm, thoughtful, sensitive man?

Certainly there are other men who are nice and don't get the credit for it that Greene does. He's famous, that's part of it. And he has such *bearing*. He can look as grave around the eyes as James Mason, but stronger, of course. His head may be as big as James Mason's chest. Art Rooney Jr. says that Greene is the only man in whose mouth one of Steeler patriarch Art Rooney's huge billy-stick cigars looks normal.

No one would take Greene for a sweet/terrifying child of nature, the way they took the late Big Daddy Lipscomb. Greene has this *discerning* look. When Steeler Quarterback Terry Bradshaw tells a joke to the team, one observer notes, he looks to Greene to see if it has gone over. If it's a good joke, it probably has. With teammates or friends, though not with fans, Greene is usually comfortable to be around. He doesn't dominate a table.

275

But there is that big head. And hands about the size of shovel blades. And there is a molten quality about Greene's limbs. He is no Apollo (Zeus, maybe). He is jointed oddly, and moves at once more smoothly and more floppily than other strong big men. His physical presence suggests that he could shift— *flick*—any loglike portion of himself in any direction at any moment. His college coach called him "a fort on foot." And sometimes, on the field, he goes damn near insane.

Wearing a loose T-shirt and swim suit, Greene sits back in a soft chair in his comfortable home in a suburb south of Dallas, with his two-year-old daughter Jo Quel drowsing on his chest. He has an air of profoundly edgy repose, like a mountain that would like to ramble but is not about to slide. He muses, "I'm always nervous like I got to do something, something other than what I'm doing. I don't know what it is. Except playing. When you get into that game, you haven't got time to think about what you ought to be doing. That game, that's it. I feel I've got some helluva games in me. I'm just waiting for 'em to come. That's what I keep pushing for—waiting."

Lord preserve our sense of reality if whatever consummation Greene awaits comes to him. The ground may open and he will descend to a place more intense, where he can chase Beelzebub around kicking at him, or a chariot may come down and bear Greene off to a better place where he can make all the tackles and also run back punts. As it is, he once threw the other team's ball away. Once he spit on Dick Butkus in front of everybody. Once he rushed the quarterback, stole the ball from him, rumbled into the end zone with it, tossed it over his head, caught it behind his back and handed it to a cheerleader.

Greene is so daringly self-defined and outrageously responsible that it is said of him, as of very few other sports figures, "He does what he wants to out there." He plays—or, sometimes, refuses to play—the conservative, regimented, technology-ridden game of pro football as if it were a combat poem he is writing, and gets away with it, and yet fits himself well enough into the prevailing system to be the warmly accepted spearhead and bulwark of a winning organization. There is no ballad of Mean Joe Greene, but there was a TV commercial in which Greene took a seat in a United Airlines plane, shifted his loosely put-together frame around to test the seat's comfort, then looked coldly, perhaps grimly, into the camera's eye and said, "I almost like it."

Greene loves football. He quit it the first time he went out for it and was still threatening to quit it for good as late as last season. If his gifts had not been so blatantly extraordinary, he would never have gone so far in his militaristic profession, for he has never taken to what is generally considered discipline; he tended to run amok in high school ball, and when an older group of Steeler scouts, since departed, watched him play for North Texas State, they deplored his attitude. "Puts on weight, tendency to loaf," said one. "Physically this boy has all of it," said another. "Mentally he is disappointing in that he only uses his ability in spurts. Will need a heavy hand, but he can play." Where

276

anybody was going to find a hand heavy enough, the scout did not say.

The last entry in the Steelers' scouting file on Greene says: "I would question taking a boy like this in the first round as he could turn out to be a big dog."

Art Rooney Jr., the Steelers' vice-president in charge of scouting, was not put off by the unevenness of Greene's college play. "He was a third-down player, all right," Rooney says, "but that was the only down he had to play. He was a guy who just completely dominated guys when he wanted to." Still there were quibbles over Greene when members of the BLESTO scouting combine got to looking at figures. Someone had measured him at just under 6–3, which is short for a tackle. Officially Greene is 6–4 (and 270 pounds), but maybe he didn't want to be the day this scout took the tape to him. The inch in question was a gnat on which several BLESTO people choked, until one of them, Don Joyce, who had been a chunky standout tackle with the Colts, declared that he was only 6–2¾, and allowed himself to be measured against the conference room wall to prove it. Thus are geniuses calibrated in our society.

In the end Greene was rated among the top prospects in the country, and Coach Chuck Noll, going into his first draft with the Steelers, was especially high on him. When the Steelers made Greene their first pick in '69 they laid the first and biggest building block of a six-year program that brought them up from perennial failure. That primacy is one aspect of Greene's eminence on the team; another is the assumption among the Steelers that Greene can whip any man, if not indeed any team, when he wants to. Wanting to, though, the way Greene wants to, is not something you can turn off and on routinely.

Greene held out for a long time before signing his first Steeler contract, then showed up in camp fat and late. Center Ray Mansfield, now a ten-year veteran, recalls looking forward to teaching the presumptuous rookie some lessons with the help of Guard Bruce Van Dyke, now a Packer. "After a couple of days," says Mansfield, "we wished we'd never seen him." Greene took on the offensive linemen one by one, quickly learned to deal with a couple of moves he hadn't seen, and then proved too strong to be overpowered, too elusive to be hobbled and too smart to be fooled. Nobody had seen a player so quick and strong at once. He was something new, like aluminum when it first came out. Nobody wanted to fight him. The coaches wisely kept anything resembling a heavy hand off him. "Play your game, Joe," they said.

Still he had the frustration, during his first three years with the Steelers, of playing on losing teams. "That's bound to make you ugly," he says. Greene's nickname derives from that of his college team, the Mean Green (thought up, incidentally, by a lady named Sidney Sue), but in the pros Greene has done a number of things to deserve it. In his rookie year he was ejected from two games. Once he threw his helmet so hard at a goalpost that pieces of helmet went flying. Another time, after an opposing guard had hit him a good clean block, he seized the offender with one hand on each shoulder pad and kicked him flush between the legs. One day he was glaringly outplaying a good

277

Cincinnati guard named Pat Matson, a 245-pound ball of muscle, until at last Matson developed a bad leg and began limping off the field. Greene ran over and grabbed him before he reached the sideline and tried to coax him back into play, crying, "Come on, I want you out there." "I'll never forget the look on Matson's face," says Steeler Defensive Captain Andy Russell. There is even a story that once after being thrown out of a game, Greene returned to the bench in such a rage that he opened up the equipment manager's tool chest and pulled out a screwdriver. Whatever he intended doing, he had second thoughts and threw it down.

Then there was the time he spit on Butkus. The Bears were humiliating the Steelers. Butkus was blitzing at will, taking long running starts and smashing into the Steeler center just as he snapped the ball, and Greene couldn't stand it any longer. The Steeler offense was on the field. Greene had no business out there, but when Butkus passed within ten feet of the Steeler bench, Greene bolted out at him, yelling challenges, and drew back and spit full in Butkus's face.

"Butkus didn't look intimidated," says Russell, "but there was Greene obviously wanting to fight him, and fully capable of it, and you could see Butkus thinking, 'This wouldn't be the intelligent thing to do.' " So Butkus turned and walked back into the security of the carnage on the field. When Russell ran into Butkus in the off-season and asked him how he could let a guy spit in his face without retaliating, Butkus said, "I was too busy making All-Pro." Greene—who was himself named All-Pro for the fourth time, and NFL Defensive Player of the Year for the second time, last season—is perhaps the only man alive who could make Butkus come off sounding rather prim.

"Joe's first year," says Russell, "I didn't see how all that emotionalism could be real. It looked like showboating. But I realize now that he's that way. When I get beat I just think, 'Well, I was out of position, I made a mistake, I'll do this to correct it.' With Joe, it's in his psyche. It's like it's war, and the other side is winning because they're more violent. And he's the only guy I know, he can be playing a great game himself, but if the team's losing, he gets into a terrible depression. It could be an exhibition game!"

The other thing that gets Greene's goat, or rather his mountain lion, is being held. He says he realizes that if the rules against offensive holding were strictly enforced, offenses would never get any plays off, either because offensive linemen would keep on holding and flags would be thrown all day or because they would quit holding and the quarterback would be smothered all day. Greene lives in an age in which defensive lines dominate pro football. But sometimes he feels guards cling too much. He likes to think of his game as one of quickness and finesse, of avoiding blockers, rather than one of violent contact. "It's that thing in me that I want to be a running back," he says.

"You want to be a running back?"

"Sure. Don't you?"

278

When he feels dragged down by contact with blockers he reacts, even now in his more statesmanlike years. Houston has a young guard named Brian Goodman whom Greene credits with pertinacity—"I kick the shit out of him and he keeps on"—but whom he can't stand to oppose because Goodman "doesn't know how to play, he just wrestles me. I feel like I'm worthy of a better person across from me than that."

"When we saw the films of the second Houston game last year," says Art Rooney Jr. with a shudder, "we sat by the phone waiting for the league office to call up and say they were going to put Joe in jail. He just *beat* on the poor guy. Goodman's younger brother came through the draft last winter and we joked about drafting him for Joe."

Greene has a firm sense, then, of how the game ought to be played. One time in Philadelphia during the Steelers' dark years, they were getting beat, and Greene was being held, and the referees weren't calling it, and finally, before the Eagle center could snap the ball for another play, Greene reached over, grabbed the ball and threw it into the second tier of the stands. Then he stomped off the field.

Russell remembers the moment with awe. "Everybody looked at him. 'He can't be doing this,' we thought. We watched the ball spiral into the seats. It seemed like it took forever. The crowd was dead silent. And the players—there we were, we didn't have a ball, we didn't have a left tackle. It was like he was saying, 'OK, if you won't play right, we won't play at all.' Nobody else would do such a thing. In the NFL! Anybody else would get in trouble with the league, with the coaches. Joe did it. In a moment the crowd exploded. They loved it."

And the Steelers loved Greene. One afternoon when Dwight White, who was living with him in Pittsburgh, was discussing Greene's sprawling funkiness as a roommate, Greene smiled. "I may be rotten," he conceded, "but I pull for dudes." When, during Greene's second year, the Steelers cut a former North Texas State teammate of his, Greene, in tears, declared he was going to quit. "Joe," said his friend, "I was just glad to come to camp," but Greene had to be talked out of an early retirement. When Craig Hanneman, a reserve Steeler defensive end, was traded to New England last year, Hanneman's coach never said a word to him, but Greene took the time to commiserate and tell him good-bye.

To reporters, with whom he deals very well, Greene persuasively deprecates his own performances, and praises, quite aptly, the work of the other defensive players. Only on such a strong defensive team would Greene get away with taking as many instinctive chances as he does, free-lancing perhaps more than any other player in the league. But the Steeler defense would never have developed its terrific thrust without Greene. L. C. Greenwood may be the league's fastest, slipperiest defensive lineman, and he plays his own graceful game while Greene's intensity helps psych up the highly mobile White and the terrifying Holmes. But as quick as L. C. is, he can't match Greene's initial burst. The films are likely to show Greenwood taking one step by the time Greene is past the line of scrimmage.

"He has the courage of his convictions," says Russell. "He doesn't wait and read, he just does it." He used to get trapped, and that hurt his pride, so now he has more discipline, but he reads on the run. Even if he's made a mistake, he's penetrated so quickly, it may not matter. And he rises to the occasion. When half the team was out sick or hurt against Houston in '72, he tore the Oilers apart almost single-handedly, sacking the quarterback five times, most of them at key moments. He's a great hand for recovering fumbles; last year against Cleveland he picked one up and lateraled off to J. T. Thomas for the winning touchdown. You don't see many defensive linemen winning games with laterals.

Still, Greene feels he gives up a great deal to the system. Noll insists on his defenders' meeting blocks instead of dodging them. Greene is usually double-teamed, and he has to fill certain gaps against a possible run before he can go after the quarterback. He is more likely to cause the initial derailment of a play than to make the tackle, which is what he likes.

"The kind of role I play is like an offensive lineman; doing a good job but not being noticed," he maintains. "I feel sorry for myself sometimes. But as long as the end result is there, I can dig it." Greene has never been at odds with coaches or management. His first two years he staunchly backed boat-rocking player representative Roy Jefferson—going so far during the '70 players' strike as to spit in the face of Pittsburgh sportswriter Pat Livingston when Livingston adverted to the Steelers' poor won–lost record during an argument with Jefferson over the strike. But after that incident Greene was taken aside by Guard John Brown, now a successful black banker in Pittsburgh, and Bill Nunn, the Steelers' black front office man. "They made me realize that I wasn't as mature as I thought I was," says Greene, "and that the coach had to run the team." Jefferson was traded, and Greene, though he was to be an unwavering supporter of the '74 strike, turned away from Jeffersonian militance to consolidate his power on the field.

As a matter of fact, a good many Steelers will tell you that Greene now runs the team. No one questions the administrative or strategic authority of Noll, a man so unemotional that when his wife excitedly greeted him after the Super Bowl victory, he held out his hand to be shaken and said, "Well, we did it." Neither does Noll question Greene's sense of fitness, which caused him to withdraw himself from a game in '73 and to walk out of a team meeting— crying, according to one account—last year. In both cases Greene was put off by what struck him as a lack of fervor among his teammates.

"When we're losing, Joe will get to stalking around out there," says Russell. "Last year we were beating New Orleans, but they were moving the ball and Joe yelled in the huddle, 'Andy, what're you going to do?' I got mad. 'I'm just going to play football,' I said." When Henry Davis was middle linebacker and ran the huddle, he threatened to come to blows with Greene to shut him up. "Joe's such a great player," says Russell, "maybe he thinks everybody else can play better if they try harder. He doesn't seem to realize that other positions require more restraint, that you can make mistakes if you get too hyper. I don't think it works to keep making emotional pitches.

"In team meetings last year, I felt we should stress the positive, talk about how we're going to improve. Joe thought we ought to be more honest and bad-mouth the negative. As it turned out, he figured his approach worked."

What Greene did last year, before the Steelers suddenly went into high gear, was criticize the Steeler offense to the press, exhort his teammates in general and insult opponents at the line of scrimmage. Some of the Steelers found it all a bit excessive, but many of them were doubtless lifted. They knew at least that Greene wasn't posturing. "It was after the playoff game we lost to Miami in '72 that I really got to know Joe as a friend," says Mel Blount. "He and his wife came over to the house and sat around with me and my wife and we talked about it. And a few tears were shed. That's when I got to know Joe as a true person."

On the other hand, Greene is not the only person on the team. Shortly after training camp opened this summer, Receivers Lynn Swann and John Stallworth and Defensive Back Jim Allen, all second-year men, were sitting together in the 19th Hole, an almost cellar-dark bar to which many Steelers repair after practice. Swann, Stallworth and Allen wanted to make the point that Greene was "no big brother or daddy" to them.

"I think he's a great player," said Stallworth, "but I think I am, too."

"He'd stick out like a sore thumb without the rest of the front four," said Swann. "And he gets so excited on the sidelines. He'll go up to Chuck saying, 'What's the quarterback doing!' He'll go up to Lionel [Receiver Coach Taylor] and say, 'What're the receivers doing!' He gets so excited he's got us playing conservative, while he's taking chances.

"He gets such respect! Last year somebody clipped him and he stomped on the guy's head. The referee ran up to him, says, 'Mr. Greene!' Not 'Mr. 75,' like he'd say to anybody else. 'Mr. Greene! I saw it,' the referee says about the clip. 'He won't do it again!' " Swann shook his head.

"I give him all kinds of trouble," added Swann about his non-big-brother. "I'll yell at him, and he's so strong he might kill me. So I got him where he can't do anything."

Over at another table, a quorum of the offensive line was drinking Lite beer in big glasses of ice and building a pyramid out of the cans. That afternoon there had been an Oklahoma drill, known on other teams as the Nutcracker, in which an offensive lineman tries to stop a defensive lineman, one-on-one, from getting to a tackling dummy held by Dan Radakovich, the offensive line coach. Greene had beaten a couple of guys, rested a while, then stepped up to Gordy Gravelle, who had earlier won raves by putting Greenwood on his back—the first time anybody could remember that happening. Gravelle had worked against a couple of rushers with success, was psyched up and sweating. Greene made a move to step in. "You want to rest?" Greene asked playfully. Gravelle glared at him. "You too tired?" asked a coach, more seriously.

"For *him*?" Gravelle snapped with what seemed like real feeling. Greene came on; Gravelle, straining, held him out, held him out, held him out. Greene let up, as though beaten. Then, in a lightsome way that seemed out of keeping with the grunting and groaning that had gone on before, he spun around a relaxed Gravelle and, too late to count, tagged Radakovich's actual person.

Except in terms of who could be more whimsical, it seemed that Gravelle had won. "Gordy handled Joe pretty well, huh?" I asked the offensive linemen at the table. The offensive line blinked. "Because Joe didn't try," they said.

"He does what he wants," said Guard Gerry Mullins, who is white and was Greene's roommate on the road last year. "His hand is so big—the heel of it hits the front of your shoulder pad and you think he's pushing you back, then his fingertips grab under the back of your pad and he pulls you forward."

The offensive-line table reflected upon Greene as a gathering of mariners might reflect upon the sea. The Steeler offensive line was effective last year in large part because it felt so relieved, in games, to be blocking against defensive lines other than the Steelers'.

"Isn't that infuriating," I asked, "to have a guy beat you at his pleasure?"

"Infuriating?" said Mansfield, who won an NFL Blocker of the Year award last year and says there is nobody he can't handle one-on-one except Greene. "When Joe Greene stomps you, it's not infuriating. It's more like frightening. If Joe really wants to shuck a guy . . . Did you ever see a dog get hold of a snake?"

Then Greene entered. He sat at a table by himself. He was wearing a sort of misshapen big-brimmed golf hat, and in the darkness it was hard to make out much of him except eyes and teeth, both of which flashed fitfully. I joined him.

For some reason he began to talk about getting beat. "A black man—I say a black man, we got no corner on the market, but every day in some form or fashion you got to prove you're a man," he said. "But you want to keep the life-and-death situations down. I can get beat. But there's getting beat and there's getting stomped. When I start getting stomped, then I get . . ." Here he acted out, in subdued and semihumorous form, his reaction to getting stomped. It was sort of a wild-eyed, spread-armed hopping around in his chair which threatened to propel the table and me across the room.

But Greene was in anything but a stomped mood. He looked fondly at the other Steelers. "These guys," he said of the offensive linemen. "We gave them hell. Called them sissies. Called them girls. But they did a job.

"Looking in the guys' faces," he said, "I see the happiness, I see the peace of mind, I see what winning that Super Bowl means for the first time.

"The whole. That's what's important. The whole." He glowed in the dark.

He threw his empty beer can. Whango! It exploded the offensive line's carefully constructed three-foot-high pyramid of cans. Cans bounded all over the floor and the offensive line. "Time to go to supper anyway," said Greene. No one took offense.

Greene was born twenty-eight years ago in Temple, Texas. He looks older—not aged, but just not boyish at all. He was always big for his age, and always will be. The rumor began some time ago that he was actually six years older than his official age, as if he had been found unknown in the fields somewhere and passed off by his high school as an adolescent. Art Rooney Jr. checked the records and found the rumor to be untrue. Greene was raised by his mother, who lives with him and who always called him Joe, which is a good thing because Mean Charles Greene sounds silly.

He grew up without a father. What if he'd had one around? "Maybe it would've made me stronger in some ways in which I'm weak," he says. "Given me some stability. I often wonder. But I always knew my mother loved me. No matter how hard it was, she always took care of us. I chopped cotton some, picked cotton, but all the kids did that. When I was twelve I told myself I'd never go back in the fields. I had a burning desire to be a success at *something*. Not necessarily football. I often sit around and reminisce. I don't want to get away too far from hustling money for a pair of shoes, and being into everyday black situations. Times were—I guess they were tough; I miss 'em. It's been a long time—since high school, early college days—since I've felt at ease. I feel anxieties, pressures, feel that people are going to ask me for an autograph even when they don't. Sometimes I feel good about giving autographs, when people are really nice and it means something to them. But people come up to you when you're out to dinner. 'How much you make?' Out of the clear blue! 'What you doing out this late?' 'When they gonna put you to work?' What you mean *they*? If I'm gonna work, I'm gonna put myself to it."

Greene is bothered by fans all the more because he has a genuine dread of hurting people's feelings. Strangers come up to him as if he's known them all their lives and he racks his brain, thinking he ought to remember their names. Then they say something like, "Wooo, you're big," and Greene wants to say, "*Yeah* I'm big, runt." He says, "It's hard for me to hide my emotions. I come off as being mean, ugly. Sometimes I get the feeling I am that way."

But now he is thinking back to what he was. "I never got into trouble when I was a kid, but it's strange, I got the reputation of being a bully. I didn't deserve it. Before I started playing football, I was getting my butt kicked constantly. It was always some old, little guy. At one point I was more round than tall. I was a bit timid, shy. I still am a bit. Then I started playing football and I guess that all kinda went away. I started taking my aggressions out on other people.

"But all through high school, guys would tease me. As late as my senior year some nut drew a picture of me on the board. A picture of some kind of beast. I guess they didn't know it hurt my feelings. All of a sudden one day I'd say 'Hey' and pop them on the side of the head."

Greene's wife, Agnes, stays in the Texas house while Joe is in Pittsburgh half the year. For that reason it might be suspected that she is a negligible figure, but in fact, though diminutive, she is not only very good-looking but smart, lively and, as Andy Russell puts it, "very powerful."

"When I first went out with Joe in college," Agnes says, "I went to some of his home girls from Temple and asked about him. They said, 'Yeah, we know him. But girl, he is *meannnnnn.*' I guess I just don't bring it out in him." They got married in college and now have three kids.

"In the eighth grade," recalls Greene, "I weighed 158. But they didn't even give me a full uniform. I quit. The next year I weighed 203 and started getting what you might call confidence. My sophomore year I weighed 235. By my senior year I weighed 250. From my sophomore year on, I was a middle linebacker, and I love that position. If there was a tackle being made somewhere, I was on it. We didn't win, though. I got a reputation for being the dirtiest ballplayer that ever came out of that area. When we were losing I'd act the fool.

"My sophomore year in high school I got kicked out of nine games. No, I got kicked out of all of 'em. My junior year it was nine. I ran over a few officials. Sometimes intentionally.

"I'll tell you how crazy I used to be. A team came to Temple and beat us, and afterwards—we had this little dinner in town. I came in there and the other team was eating. Their quarterback had an ice cream cone. I took it away from him and smeared it all over his face. He didn't do anything. He went back to the team bus. Then I heard somebody call my name. I turned around and a soda bottle hit my chest, and the guy I'd done that way ducked back into the bus. Like a damn fool, I went at the bus. In the front door. They all went out the back door.

"But I'm not a brawler. I can't imagine getting hit in the face with a fist being any fun. I was standing in a bar in Pittsburgh. A guy came in, he was fairly good-sized, he walked straight at me. I moved, assumed he didn't see me. He came back. I moved again. He bumped me. I had the feeling this guy wanted to try me. I thought, 'Uh, oh.' I stay out of those situations. They do get into life or death literally. I couldn't conceive of myself doing any harm to anybody fatally. But there's that old saying, 'Better he than me.' If you do jump into something like that, it's got to be final."

Flick. Greene makes a grabbing motion from his armchair. Then he makes a throwing motion. A dead fly bounces off the wall. "Did I get him?" he says.

"It's a hell of a thing to realize you can't do anything but play football. I'm capable of other things, but that's the only thing I know now. In college they tried to get me to go to a lot of classes and things, but I kind of lost interest.

I couldn't write. Because I didn't have anything to say. You can't be descriptive about nothing."

Greene has prospered. With a friend, he has started a janitorial company. He's appeared in a few quickie films—in one of which, *The Bad Black Six,* he picked white motorcycle hoods up over his head and threw them. He seems a bit defensive about his movie career, though he shows up well enough on the screen. This summer he turned down a chance to star in a movie as a washed-up ballplayer. Like most ballplayers, he has no taste for the rough give-and-take of business.

"Business is dirty. All of it I've been into—seems like it's unethical. They call it leverage. People are always going under the table trying to outflank you. I try to be straightforward and right."

He has trusted several agents who he feels cheated him. "When you make a lot of money fast, that's when the buzzards are thickest," he says. He is suffering currently over his estrangement from several college friends who had gone on to play pro ball. He had been involved with them in a firm that planned to represent other players and invest in real estate. Greene withdrew from the group. "They thought I deserted them. But we just didn't have the vehicle. We'd have wound up ripping people off, too. I'm not gonna let the snake bite me if I know it's there."

Greene is settling down. "I'm more into practice, and working out," he says. "I didn't used to have the patience for those things. This off-season I did something every day, or every other day, or every chance I got. Jog, play basketball." Steeler Strength Coach Lou Riecke brought him a set of weights in February. "I used to just life when Lou or Chuck was looking. When they turned their heads I'd stop. But then some of the guys I used to throw around a little bit, I couldn't anymore. I'd have to spend too much energy doing it. I'm basically lazy."

This season Greene looks different. His upper body is more conventionally muscular, his distinctive spare tire is gone. He has a championship to defend. Does all this mean he will be even better?

"When I dream at night," he says, "I visualize techniques. Some of 'em are just ungodly. It's just cat quickness; run over a guy, hurdle him, jump 6 feet, put three or four moves on him so he freezes. No flaws in those moves. Perfect push and pull on the guard, jump over the center. Another blocker, slap him aside. Block the ball when the quarterback throws it, catch it and run 99 yards. 'Cause I don't want it to be over quick! The only thing that ever matched the dreams I had was the Super Bowl."

Greene and Art Rooney seemed to enjoy the Super Bowl more than anybody. Rooney, the Chief, was in camp one afternoon this summer, standing beside the practice field. A kid asked him for his autograph. "I'm not one of the players," said the Chief, who is 74. The kid said that was all right. "Where do you come from?" asked the Chief. The kid named a town. The Chief asked,

"You know Doctor Weaver there? He had a sign in his office: 'I'M NOT A DOCTOR. WHAT I HAVE IS A GIFT FROM GOD.' But he could do more for your muscles than anybody." The Chief went on about others of his wide range of friends, Tip O'Neill, Sargent Shriver, Mean Joe Greene.

"I knew we were going all the way last year before the playoff game with Oakland when Joe came up to me. He grabbed my hand and said, 'We're gonna get 'em.' That was an emotional moment. I never had a moment like that."

Greene comes over and greets the Chief. They chat for a moment and then Greene moves away, saying, "Enjoy yourself now." It seems an odd thing, but a friendly thing, to say to one's owner.

"That Joe Greene," says the Chief. "He *takes* you. I've never seen a player lift a team like he does. I just hope he plays out his full years. He's the type of player who wouldn't want to be associated with a team that didn't play all-out."

There was a time when the Chief voiced doubts about Joe Greene. That was when the Steelers had drafted him No. 1 and he was holding out. "Who is he anyway?" the Chief grumbled. "I don't know that he's so good."

A few years later, Art Jr. would gesture at the photographs of old Steeler greats—Ernie Stautner, Whizzer White, Bullet Bill Dudley—covering the walls of his father's office and say, "Someday you'll have to take all these down and throw them away and put up one of Joe Greene."

But he didn't say that when the Chief questioned how good Greene might be. "Joe Greene is as good," Art Jr. told his father, "as you can imagine."

□ **4** □

RAY MANSFIELD: HOW TO RAISE YOUR BOY TO PLAY PRO BALL

October, 1976

Since I have done a good deal of work in the sportswriting field, people ask me, "Where did you get that unusual tan?" (I go to a nearby tannery every spring, lay out twenty-eight dollars and a little something for the attendant, and have myself dipped.) "What is the right grip for squash?" (Grasp the squash firmly by the neck with your left hand, then take a knife with the right hand and bring it down in short, crisp strokes on the part of the squash not covered by the left hand.) But most of all they ask me, "How do I raise my boy to be a professional football player?" This last question I answer by saying, "Set an example. Lay and finish nine sets of steps in one day."

And then I speak of concrete grit, pride of workmanship and what Ray Mansfield's father, the man who laid the steps, called "that preservation meanness."

Mansfield still sells his millions of insurance in Pittsburgh, but he has finished out his career on the gridiron, where, he once told me, he felt like a knight in armor. For over a decade, through 1976, he was the Steelers' starting center, emergency placekicker, and stalwart of beer and stories. His father, Owen Mansfield, was proof that you can be legendary in your work even if your work isn't something glamorous like bowling people over so that somebody can run a leather-covered bladder past them.

In '75 I went with Ray to visit Owen in Kennewick, Washington. Owen was a tall, well-preserved-looking man of sixty-five who had finally given up heavy labor because of his heart. He puttered around his small house, picked and sang Jimmie Rodgers songs and reminisced about working and fighting.

287

Owen grew up on an Arkansas farm. When he was no more than a sprout himself, he was "putting sprouts in the new ground. Start plowing and the plow would hit me in the stomach. Plow'd run into a root right under the ground, the mules would stop, the end of the plow would come around and hit me in the shin." But he had the example of *his* father before him. "My dad. That was the workingest old man you ever saw. And he was a Christian, believed in living right. I remember one day my dad was getting the best of Uncle Port, and Uncle Port's dog run up and bit him. He turned around and held Uncle Port and hollered, 'Somebody kill that godd . . . that dog.' He thought better of himself, you see. Uncle Port was the meanest man that ever hit that country down there."

Since he couldn't be the meanest or the most industrious man in Arkansas, in the late twenties Owen rode the rails west. He'd stop off and scratch around for work or live off the land. "I remember if somebody had eaten a lot of bananas, I'd pick up them banana peelings and eat 'em. They was good. I could eat a tree, I believe." He dodged the railroad cops. "Texas Slim. He lined up forty of us one time and said, 'All right. First one that catches the train, I'm going to shoot him.' He wore a nice suit, a big white hat, two guns. He was a *nice*-looking guy. But a *mean* son of a gun. I just patted my hands when I heard he was killed. I wish I'd a been a fast draw, *I'd* a killed him.

"I was 'Slim,' too, all my life nearly, working. Had the longest neck of anybody in the country."

His first job as a married man was splitting logs for rails. He and Mrs. Mansfield eventually had nine kids. When Ray was born, the family was living in a tent in a farm labor camp outside Bakersfield, California, and Owen was in the hospital with a rattlesnake bite. "They gave me a shot of some stuff and I started trembling all over, got quivery all through my body. I said, 'Dag burn it, I guess I'm going to die in this little old place.'

"Then, when I got well, our first daughter, Merelene, got pneumonia. They took Merelene to the same room I'd been in. Wasn't long till she died. I tell you, it was hard times. She was seven and a half. Merelene. A name I studied out myself, to get something there wasn't anything like."

"We all took Merelene back to Missouri," Ray says. "Like the marines never leave their dead behind, my parents didn't want to leave their child out there in California on the road. This was in '41. Dad put Merelene and all the rest of us except Gene, my oldest brother, on the train, and then he put a mattress on the backseat of the car and put Gene on it and just took off. I don't know whether he got to Missouri before the train or just after it. Driving a broken-down 1929 Chevy. Mother said she saw my dad the whole day, off and on, when the road came close to the tracks."

Owen told me, "The car broke down once and I was fixing it and that train passed. Made me so lonesome I couldn't sit still."

When they got Merelene buried back home, they headed back out looking for a place to settle. A few years later, living in Arizona, Owen flipped a coin to decide whether to go just to Joplin, Missouri, or all the way to the state of Washington. And Washington won. That's where Ray grew up, in Kennewick, where Owen got into concrete. "One of the hardest jobs in America," Ray says.

"Dad was always top hand on the job," says Ray's younger brother Bill, who played football at Washington State and now is back in Kennewick, in concrete himself. "It's a good thing he's not working today. It'd kill him to see the way people work these days. He wasn't any college professor, but he was as good as there was at what he did. Guys like him are gone forever. We'd lay a floor, I'd think it was finished—it would be, today—and he'd say, 'Son, we can't leave until you can dance on it.'

"You talk to Dad's old foreman and he says, 'That Owen was the finest-working man I ever knew.' When we'd work with him, he'd grab a shovel and all you'd see was sand. A forty-eight-year-old man outworking our ass. When he was fifty-nine years old, he was going full speed. My brother Gene kept saying, 'Dad, cool it a little bit.' He'd say, 'Ah, let's get the job done.' Now it's: make money and get by if you can. He never learned. . . ."

Ray says, "We grew up expecting to work. It came with breathing air. He hired us out when I was in the second or third grade. Me and my sister and older brother, we'd be out at four in the morning cutting asparagus until eight, go right from work to school.

"When I got older, I'd sell papers on the streets. I just loved being on the streets. Even though there wasn't but one main street in Kennewick. I was afraid I would miss something.

"I worked all one morning to get fifteen cents to go to the movie. I ran all the way to the movie and found out it was twenty cents. I ran all the way home, pissed off, kicking things. I told my father what was wrong. (He was home in between his work in concrete. He had to lay it in the morning, wait for it to set, and then go back late to finish it up.) He reached in his pocket, pulled out a handful of sand, and came up with a nickel. His fingers all dry and split open from the concrete. He gave me the nickel. It was probably the only nickel in the house. I ran all the way back to the movie: James Mason as Rommel in *The Desert Fox*.

"When I came home, my father was back at work. I lay awake until one in the morning, when he came home. I sneaked downstairs and watched him get undressed and go to bed. I never thanked him. I just wanted to look at him and think what kind of dad I had.

"There was so much warmth around the house," Ray says. "We didn't have any mean kids in our family. Everybody was loving of each other and tolerant of other people. I got into a lot of fights, but I didn't like it especially. If you ever want to get a Mansfield mad, pick on another Mansfield. We've got almost too much family pride. I remember there was a big kid around Campbell's Cabins, where we lived for a while. I did everything I could to avoid him. But he picked on my little brother Odie, and I went after him and nearly cold-cocked him. I had no fear when one of my brothers was being picked on. But even after I whipped that big kid, I was still scared of him."

Bill tells an old family story: "This guy, thirty-five, got into an altercation with our grandfather, Pa, when Pa was sixty-five years old. Our Uncle Granville was seventeen, and he goes flying through the air, kicks the guy's ass through the dusty streets till the guy whimpers like a dog and gets out of there. My dad's eyes gleam when he tells about it. That's why it was good having Moynihan in the UN. You can't take too much shit."

Ray and Bill Mansfield and I were drinking and getting profound in this place in Kennewick, and Bill said to Ray, "Remember when we were working out—I was just getting ready to go to Washington State—and you said, 'Bill, don't ever, ever accept getting beat. Don't ever let a guy beat you and walk away and say, "Well, he beat me." You have to fight and scratch and bite. If you're bleeding and crying and scratching and shitting, keep on fighting and that guy will quit. As long as *you* don't.' "

Not many occupations today bring together fighting and working the way football does. But working was a kind of fighting for Owen. And both working and fighting were kinds of sports. "I'd get a kick out of troweling cement with other trowelers," he said. "Out of staying about the length of this table ahead of the other fella. That would tickle me to death." The story about their father that made Ray's and Bill's eyes light up the brightest—Bill almost boiled up out of his chair telling it—was the one about the steps.

"He laid and finished *nine sets of steps in one day.* Did a Cool Hand Luke shot. Then two thousand, three thousand square feet of concrete. It was superhuman. How it happened: It was a Monday, and the man told him it had to be done by Wednesday. My dad said, 'Don't worry.' The man said, 'Well, you better get it done.'

"That made my dad mad. So he said, 'I'll show you.' And he did it all in eight hours. Edged it, everything. He was running the whole time, and he was forty-five. When he finished, there was smoke coming off his body, but there were the nine sets of steps. All those assholes were scratching their heads and saying, How did he do it? It's still a legend around here."

Right after Ray's last season, Owen was talking to Gene and Odie, and they told him he'd better do something about his hair—he'd let it grow awfully long. "I'm not going to get a haircut," Owen said. "I'm going to go buy a dress." And he rocked back laughing and suddenly died.

Afterward, Ray's brother told him Owen had been glad that Ray was retiring from football. Owen had said he'd always thought of Ray as a boy, of course, but that Ray was getting too old to play a kid's game.

□ 5 □

SUPER BOWL, 1976:
"YOU CAN'T COVER IT"

I don't know who he was or what out-
fit he represented, but the man in the maroon pants in the Konover Hotel on
Miami Beach last Super Sunday morning said it for us all. His eyes were slits
or wished they were, his moustache looked as if he had passed out on it wrong,
and his sport coat was sort of bent out of whack. He was carrying from the
media buffet table a plate full of eggs, sausages, toast, marmalade and canta-
loupe, along with a glass of tomato juice, his commemorative Naugahyde
briefcase and a handful of press releases. He wavered for a minute and everything started to slide. Eggs and tomato juice spilled all down his pants leg and
in among the laces of his shoes. Press releases and sausages were mingled on
the floor.

"Sh . . . it fire," he said. "There ain't no *way* to cover the Super Bowl."

A lot of people try, though, and here it is almost suck-it-up-for-Super-Week
time again. Pasadena this year. I guess Graham Greene and Solzhenitsyn will
be there, snubbing each other across the press lounge, and maybe a specialty
act, like Irving Berle, the sports-minded superintendent of some editor's apartment building, sent out to do a Super Berle Looks at the Super Bowl sidebar.

People just go on ahead and write about the World Series. The Super Bowl
they have to get an *angle* on. Try to blindside the sucker. Find the seam in
its zone. Usually, after a week of free liquor and promotion, they wind up just
scoffing at the $2.8 million Bowl-eve party, because they had to stand in line
for the stone crabs behind Tony Orlando's go-fer, and file a hung-over game
account that runs under the head "SUPER BOWL NOT SO SUPER". Two
years ago in New Orleans, Milton Richman of UPI did get sent to the leper
colony outside of Baton Rouge to do the leper angle. "Not a bad little story,
actually," his colleague Joe Carnicelli told me one bleary morning during
Super Week IX. "Turned out one of the lepers was a high school teacher of
Bud Grant."

I don't know why nobody ever gives me those great leads. But last year, X,
in Miami, I figured I would get some kind of fresh perspective. Reporters
untold were there in the Orange Bowl packed into press boxes, and I was "Free
To Rove."

Those were the words handwritten on my Special Photo Not Good on Field or in Press Box credential. Since I had been assigned to cover not the game itself but only the making of the movie *Black Sunday,* which is about someone trying to blow up the Super Bowl and was filmed partly during the game, it was the best I could scrape up.

By most standards it was a pretty rotten credential, but I figured it would enable me to watch the movie making, and the game, from all sides. As I approached the stadium and saw a low metal enclosure with a sign on it saying "BEWARE. BAD DOGS", I felt a certain twinge, but shrugged it off. Two nights before, after all, I had been tap-dancing (no room to explain here) with a Steeler called *Mad* Dog. Let dogs stalk me. I would stalk the Bowl. In the round.

As soon as I hit the stands, a security man challenged me. I showed him my credential. He said, "Well, you can't rove here." He meant I couldn't rove in his section, but I interpreted his remark literally and snuck (I'm not telling how) down onto the field.

I love being on the field. You can't see the game down there, but you can *feel* it. I stood next to the Steelers' sideline and soaked up the old pregame heavy. Makes you want to holler "Hi-de-ho." The players warming up, shaking their fingers in the air and hunching around. That old scratchy carpet stuff beneath your feet. Surely that pseudoterrain was pregnant this afternoon. I could feel that TV audience out yonder tossing fitfully and hear those warm-up passes clacking into those shoulder pads and sense that stadium filling. I thought that Poly-Turf might split open and a big golden bird fly up out of it and swallow the sky. I was *up.*

I tend to forget I'm a scribe, or try to. As a scribe you are supposed to get behind the scenes, but generally you just see different scenes: a lot of people standing around naked being interviewed by people in leisure suits, for instance. I keep wanting to know how it *feels* out there, *in the game.* Andy Russell backed up the Steeler line all one year with a broken fat pad in his knee. The fat pad is not fat but a web of cartilage that cushions the knee joint. Running on a flat fat pad, says Russell's teammate Ray Mansfield, "is like driving on a flat tire." Russell also played that year with a stomach tear. Running and hitting while you have a blown-out knee and a torn stomach is as incomprehensible to me as working *eight hours* or finding your way into town *by yourself* used to be when I was six.

"A very physical game," players are always saying about bloodbaths they have just emerged from. I was standing on the Super grid working on the physical angle when a security man demanded to see my credential.

I was going to reason with him. But then I saw one of the bad dogs. It was a German shepherd, walking the sideline with a cop, and it looked glassy-eyed. I did not want my story to be a first-person account of how it feels to become the first sportswriter ever eaten by a dog at the Super Bowl. I roved on, back among the spectators; try the crowd angle.

But when a tangle of seat seekers forced me to stop moving for a few seconds, another security man told me I was "out of place."

"I can't be out of place," I said. "I'm free to rove."

"I don't care who you are," he said, "you can't stand here."

"I'm trying to cooperate," I said.

"I don't care what you're trying to do," he said, "you can't do it here."

So I beat on against the current, and the game began, and I had to circulate pretty briskly because people kept yelling "Down in front"—*at me*. It is hard to watch a game and the filming of a movie while picking your way through a hostile crowd. I sat down in a no-show's seat.

To my left was a large, rawboned youth wearing a black leather jacket and an orange T-shirt that said ZINGO. To his left was a plump, conservatively dressed couple. The youth was sprawling and the husband kept telling him to stop crowding his wife or he would call a cop. "I might have to knock you around a little," he added.

"You're bad, huh?" the youth said remotely. I couldn't root for either guy. When the husband wasn't threatening to defend his wife, he was hollering insults at players. That was his right, of course, but he would yell things like "GERELA YOU DUMB CANUCK YOU AND WALDEN WILL BE THE FIRST PEOPLE THEY DON'T PROTECT IN THE EXPANSION DRAFT." There is nothing more boring than a fan who tries to yell complete complex sentences. By the time he finished one insult, he was half a play behind. At least that's what I thought. It was hard to see from our seats—on the 45-yard line, but low.

In the first place, the Steelers on the sidelines were standing in front of us.

We couldn't see the game for the players.

In the second place, a huge mounted sideline TV camera kept moving in front of us.

We couldn't see the game for a great medium of communication.

I did see Lynn Swann make his first great catch. That is, I saw his hands come up out of a lady's hat and pull the ball down. I heard the rawboned youth say, "Super Bowl, huh?" I went back into my rove.

At every opportunity I stole a look at the game. As luck would have it, I got a good view of Swann's second great catch, which was such a sensational catch that everybody in front of and around me leapt and whopped. Except the Steelers' Jack Ham. He was looking right at the catch, 15 feet away, and he never changed expression. Doubtless he was thinking ahead to what he was going to do on defense.

He couldn't see the game because he was too much into the game.

As I roved, ever angling, the game did not seem physical or, anyway, very concrete. It zoomed in and panned away, pivoted now slowly, now abruptly, as I peregrinated from the south stands through the west end zone through

293

the north stands and into the northeast corner, where the glare of the sun blotted the game out entirely.

By now it was the fourth quarter, the *Black Sunday* people had finished their filming and were slapping each other's hands as if the game were over (few people realized that Robert Shaw had just saved them from a deranged blimp pilot) and the Steelers had finally gone ahead. I squinted and forced myself to look into indescribable solar blots and auras.

I couldn't see the game for the broad daylight.

I was standing next to a railing. "You can't stand there," said an usher. I said, "I'm . . ." and waved my credential.

"You'll have to get on the other side of the railing," he said.

Well, on the other side of the railing was the field. "Right," I said, and I eased my unauthorized person back onto the green carpet. Back to the ground-zero angle! And the first face I saw was a German shepherd's.

I didn't want that dog to get a close look at my credential. I sought a haven. There on the turf right behind the end zone sat several dozen clean-cut young people of every human hue. They were the Up with People halftime performers. All of America's ethnic strains were represented harmoniously in this group. I didn't see how a dog, even an Aryan dog, could eat me in the midst of such melting pot purity. I sat down among them.

Now at least I had an angle. The sun was not in my eyes and I could watch, and feel, the horrible whacking and grinding on the field.

For that is what it was, if you looked closely, which you could because the action was bearing right down on us. The Steelers were advancing to within one yard of our end zone. The battle of the trenches was right in our lap.

I'll tell you what it reminded me of. There is a brief, arrestingly undynamic moment in *Birth of a Nation*. In the middle distance a Confederate soldier is sitting in a trench hitting a partially fallen Union attacker with his rifle, thud thud thud. Leadenly beating a man with an iron-and-wood rifle, with resignation, fear and distaste.

The Steelers hit the Dallas line three times, thud thud thud. There was one flash of personality, when Franco Harris (who emerges from a game, reasonably enough, with the expression of a sensitive person who has just been beaten and pursued by vicious assailants) plunged, took a hit, fumbled up into the air, looked up at the ball as an unusually collected man might look up at his arm just blown away, and snatched it back. Then several bodies buried him. The rest of it looked like a lot of cows falling off a truck.

I had lost my pregame high. Here was an angle—the Super Bowl as a bunch of people thumping and wallowing and acting like they were trying to squeeze through a subway door. But what kind of angle was that? After the NFL had gone to so much trouble. There I was amid all those still radiant Upwiths, feeling down and against. I watched as the game lurched and sprawled way off down to the other end of the field. I had to get a new fix.

294

And suddenly it came. Rocketing right back toward me. In the form of the aerial pigskin. The lofted spiraling ball. As the philosophizing coal miner in *Beyond the Fringe* says when he picks up the lump of coal, "The very thing we're looking for." Fifty-four yards on the fly.

The ball got bigger and bigger until it was close enough so that I could see its tip wobbling just slightly out of true, moving from side to side. It might fly over the Super Bowl forever.

But here came Swann again. He sped toward us a step ahead of the defensive back and *whack,* his shoulder pad met the ball, and he clasped it and bore it into pay dirt, ran right up to us, bringing us into 29 million homes.

I might have gone down in the highlight films of history in a small, irritating way by running out and congratulating Swann. But no. That would have been like a critic dancing down the aisle at the opera. You could tell by the look on his face—transported, number but near-frisky—that Swann and we out-of-the-end-zone people were not in the same physical world.

After the game, Dallas tackle Rayfield Wright complained that the Steelers—a couple of whom are social friends of his—played like meanspirited bullies. Intimidation was the Steelers' game, groused the Cowboys. The Steelers answered, Sure.

"I really hate Dallas," said Pittsburgh's Glen Edwards. "They try to fool folks, instead of outphysicaling them, the way football should be played." The Steelers had beaten receiver Golden Richards half to death—as Oakland had done to Swann in the previous playoff game (and did again this year, causing Steeler head coach Chuck Noll to suggest that there was "a criminal element" at work in the NFL. The NFL fined Oakland's George Atkinson $1,500 for assaulting Swann, and Noll $1,200 for saying such an awful thing).

Here was a grim angle indeed. *Winning Through Intimidation* was the title of a current noxious bestseller. My tender young son had been watching the Super Bowl back home on TV, no doubt wearing his Steeler jacket, hat and button. If teams of big, fast, highly motivated guys went out burning down other teams' houses once a week, would I go along with them to record how arsonists really talk, thinking to myself as homes went up in smoke, "I'm getting some good stuff here"?

But who wants to read a sportswriter's soul-searching? That night at the Steeler victory party, I still needed an angle. I noticed that L. C. Greenwood did not seem festive.

Greenwood is a terrific defensive end, 6–6 and very lanky, who has said he wished he'd been a medical student in college. Quickness, not brutality, insofar as possible, is his game.

I asked him why he wasn't up dancing with Ethel Kennedy, who was at the party. He said he hurt too bad—a pinched nerve, a screwed-up ankle. . . .

"I'll trade bodies with you," he said.

I said something about how he wouldn't have wanted to do that during the game, and started to rove on. But then I stopped. Talk about an angle! We made the deal. I threw in an optometrist to be named later. Leaving L. C. sitting there looking more comfortable but diminished, I moved out tentatively, in greatly elongated and more resilient strides, with neural outrage thudding all through my limbs. Thrilled, exhilarated, apprehensive, amazed, as if I were on a strange new motorcycle powerful beyond my sense of scale, revving it a little, trying to get the feel of it, wondering what it would do.

But then I couldn't find a typewriter big, strong, quick enough to handle me. There ain't no way to cover the Super Bowl.

□ **6** □

SUPER BOWL, 1976, P.S.

Baseball's Oakland A's have proved that intrasquad squabbling needn't hold a team back. But harmony is a nice championship virtue too. During Super Week '76 a TV crew was at the Steeler hotel filming interviews with the Steelers' celebrated Front Four—Joe Greene, L. C. Greenwood, Ernie Holmes and Dwight White. Suddenly Steeler reserve Reggie Harrison hollered across the pool to the TV people, "Why don't you talk to the *MVP* of the Front Four? And he pointed to Steve Furness, who had played outstandingly in relief of the injured Greene and hadn't gotten much credit for it. Harrison's remark was notable because the assumption is that football players stick up for each other along racial lines, and Furness is white while Harrison and the famous Four are black. During the Bowl itself, Greene realized he was holding the Four back and stepped aside for Furness. Greene is intensely proud; didn't he feel frustrated at having to leave the game? "No," he maintained calmly in the dressing room. "I try to be a man in all things."

Veteran Pittsburgh center Ray Mansfield got a shock when he took the field for Super Bowl X. A Cowboy came up to him and said, "Hi, Mr. Mansfield."
The Cowboy turned out to be Ron Howard, who had been a high school sophomore in Pasco, Washington, in 1968, when Mansfield was doing his student teaching there in order to finish up his education degree from the University of Washington. Mansfield had lost track of the lad since, and didn't realize that they were due to meet again on the field of battle.
"You never expect to see a kid you had in class out there trying to knock your head off," said Mansfield. How did it make him feel? "Old."

Roy Gerela's kicking in X was subpar for two reasons. On the opening kickoff, he threw his ribcage in front of Dallas's Thomas Henderson at the Pittsburgh 44, thereby preventing a touchdown but also getting himself shaken up. And before the opening kickoff, he didn't get to take as many practice kicks as usual because all his warmup balls went into the stands. Unaccountably, someone had taken down the net that had been put up to catch the practice kicks at the Steelers' end of the field, although the Cowboys' net remained at the other end. Spectators who caught the balls—though that end zone section was full of Pittsburgh supporters—refused to return them unless they were given the miniature souvenir balls someone had told them they would receive in exchange. So after snitching one of the Cowboys' practice balls and kicking that, Gerela went into the stands—stepping on a customer's ankle in the process—and dragged a man out of his fourth-row seat in order to retrieve a ball for one more kick. Several fans shoved Gerela. A security guard and several Miami cops had to escort him back down onto the field. "Our fans hit him harder than the Cowboy players did," marveled a Steeler. After the game at least one of those fans sued, to boot.

Some of the most heartfelt contact in the Super Bowl has not been what you would strictly call blocking or tackling. In '76 Dallas's Cliff Harris, whose smasher instinct is so uninhibited that his own teammates have spoken of being afraid he would hit them, warned before the big game that Lynn Swann had better watch his head. That may sound physically impossible, but Swann, just recovering from a concussion, knew what he meant. Swann was not intimidated, however, so Harris tried getting under Roy Gerela's skin. When the Steeler kicker missed a field goal, Harris told him "Nice going" and gave him a little slap on the helmet.

"He just kind of tapped me," said Gerela, but middle linebacker Jack Lambert—who earlier in the week had said of Roger Staubach, "I hope a shark bites his arms off"—felt his kicker was being pushed around.

"Harris jumped up in his face," said Lambert, "and slapped his helmet a couple of times. He laughed in Gerela's face. When I see injustice, I try to do something about it. I didn't say anything. I just threw him on the ground."

Several seconds after the whistle, Lambert grabbed the Dallas safety by the shoulder pads and threw him down flat, the way John Wayne might have dealt with a bad guy who was bothering a lady. Later in the game Harris blitzed and knocked Terry Bradshaw cold, but not until a split second after the Steeler quarterback released a touchdown bomb to Swann. As for Lambert, who says, "I happen to be a man who yells a lot," he got so worked up during the game that he flung off the forearm pads he wears customarily. "I want to hurt some people," he explained to Steeler field manager Jackie Hart.

□ 7 □

THE SHORT, HAPPY LIFE OF JOE GILLIAM

December, 1976

[*The following piece, most of which appeared in* 2Esquire *in December 1976, turned out to be mistaken. Gilliam, it turned out, was hooked on heroin. By the time he got off that stuff and returned to real life, he had spent years bouncing around in semipro ball and criminal courts. He was arrested for drug possession, weapons possession and robbery. He never played in the National Football League again. So you could say that drugs were the devil after all. Certainly I am less inclined now to believe simplistically that drugs don't mess people up, people mess people up (if I may paraphrase the National Rifle Association on guns), than I was when I wrote this critique of football solidarity. Still, I think this critique has its point. Toward the end of his time as a Steeler, Gilliam would disappear to a toilet stall before a game, and his mates drew away from him (cocaine was what they suspected). The people who run professional sports now make earnest efforts to help addicted athletes, and someone with Gilliam's problems today might be reformed, as Dwight Gooden has been in baseball and Lawrence Taylor in football. At any rate, the person who does heroin is responsible for what heroin does to him. But I still say that football players could be more significant heroes if they had more freedom to shine in their own screwy lights, more freedom to be as volatile and brilliant as Gilliam was when he and the team, heterogeneously together, were hooked on aerial magic.*]

Billy Dee Williams in *The Bingo Long Traveling All-Stars & Motor Kings,* the movie about preintegration baseball, reminds me of Joe Gilliam: skinny, springy, with a lot of frustrated zest in him. But that movie was too trivial and soft to show the way frustrated zest marks you. Joe Gilliam's looks are more bothersome than Billy Dee Williams's. Gilliam is a gaunt twenty-five-year-old.

After practice sometimes you used to see Gilliam hanging silently by his hands from a goalpost crossbar, his minimal body forming a Y in the air, nobody paying him any mind. He looked sort of ethereal up there, suspending his weight from his arms more lightly than most people stand on their feet, though his expression was grave. As a matter of fact, he told me once, he had terrible feet; they hurt him so bad that some mornings he hated to set them on the floor. Maybe that had something to do with his missing 6:45 breakfast one morning this July, which was the last straw for him with the New Orleans Saints, who waived him "out of football."

For Gilliam to be out of football makes about as much sense as it did for young director Orson Welles to be kept out of movie making. Less sense, because athletes have fewer years to work in. Welles, incidentally, didn't learn discipline while out of action.

By the time this column appears, Gilliam *might* be doing what he should be doing: quarterbacking a National Football League team, jumping around in the pocket like Jiminy Cricket and hitting people's hands with off-balance forty-yard passes. But that is unlikely. The New Orleans Saints say they won't consider inviting him back to their camp until next year, and every other NFL team passed him up this summer before the Saints bought him for one hundred dollars from the Steelers. Gilliam's father has told people that Joe will probably sit out this season in Nashville, where he can "get his feet on the ground."

At this writing, anyway, Gilliam is in limbo and not speaking to the press. Doubtless he would prefer no more publicity, following those newspaper stories about his arrest for possessing drugs, possessing a pistol and recklessly fleeing police. But what he has been through during the past three years needs looking at from a nonofficial point of view.

He was wonderful to watch, from any point of view, during the six exhibition and six regular-season games in '74 when he was winning, reveling in and losing the Steeler starting-quarterback job. Often he seemed to be throwing off the wrong foot or with both of them in the air—Blanton Collier, the old Cleveland Brown coach who took an interest in Gilliam when he was in college, "told me off-balance was a matter of opinion," Gilliam said. But once the ball left his hand, people were reminded of classical drop-back heroes like Norm Van Brocklin. Usually he held the ball unclassically down low before he threw, instead of up by his ear. But they used to say Cassius Clay held his hands too low, too. Gilliam's delivery was so quick—no matter how slow Steeler film analysts ran footage of him throwing, his arm was still a blur—he could hold his hands where he pleased.

And wouldn't he hang the ball up there. He would throw eight or nine incompletions and keep on throwing, and hit the next eight or nine in a row. During the exhibition season one opposing coach said he might have given "the finest performance I've ever seen by a quarterback." In leading the Steelers over the Colts in their regular-season opener, he hit 9 of 11 for 151 yards in the second quarter alone. In a terrific, rowdy 35–35 overtime tie with Denver the next week, he completed 31 of 50 passes for 348 yards. Most contemporary

300

pro quarterbacks' personalities are masked by armor, caution, zone defenses and real or simulated sangfroid. But Gilliam, when a big play clicked, would beam and bounce around with both hands in the air. Once he openly waved off a play sent in by head coach Chuck Noll. Another time he doubled up laughing when one of his offensive linemen flattened a rusher.

He threw too much, though. He kept on throwing even into the teeth of complicated defenses rigged up with his proclivities in mind. He had a couple of bad games. To win it all in the NFL these days, it appears, you have to play a carefully controlled offense founded on the run. (And count on your defense to kick the shit out of the other guys.) The Steelers were about to come to a head as a team and didn't want to take any chances. Noll went back to the quarterback whom Gilliam had supplanted, Terry Bradshaw, and after a couple of bad games of his own, Bradshaw worked his own great, though less flamboyant, talents into Noll's system so well that the Steelers went on to win two straight Super Bowls. Gilliam was once again an understudy. Then a black sheep. Then an outcast.

You can't say the Steelers didn't want a black quarterback, unless a black quarterback is defined as one who can't stand to get bogged down in all that grinding-it-out mess. They gave Gilliam a good shot. Everybody in football seems to feel that Gilliam's being out of it is his fault, that he blew it, that he let himself down. "He let *us* down," says a Steeler who is black. The Steelers couldn't even get a good player in return for Gilliam when they gave up on him. "That's the real tragedy of the thing," says Steeler vice-president Art Rooney Jr. "He could have been making $100,000 a year here, counting pension and playoff money. He lost all that." And his market value.

But wait a minute. On another team, one that was building, Gilliam could have had a much better chance to use and develop his gifts. Why is it necessarily right to take a lot of money in return for not doing what you most want to do in life? What if actually getting out there on the field and playing quarterback regularly was so important to Gilliam that he'd rather leave the world champion Steelers and join a team that he could hope to start for?

Well, in pro football, unlike in America, you can't just up and quit one company and go to work for another. It would have taken Gilliam all the way through the '77 season to finish his long-term contract (which, like all pro football contracts, bound him to the team, but not the team to him) and play out his option year. The only way for Gilliam to get another chance like he had in '74, short of serious injury to the robust young Bradshaw, was for him to force a trade.

That is what many people assume Gilliam was trying to do last year, however consciously or unconsciously: force the Steelers to trade him. That is like trying to be so obnoxious to your landlord that he will let you out of your lease. Joe had been known to be late to team meetings before—a serious sin in pro football. Last season he was late to a lot of them, missed whole practices, was out way, way after curfew one night on the road, and seemed

301

to be detached from things. "He would drift off somewhere," says Art Rooney Jr. Joe Greene asked team captain Andy Russell to talk to Gilliam, ask him why he was the only one who seemed to get caught in tunnels on his way to practice.

"I guess I've just got buzzard's luck," Gilliam told Russell. "But I can't get down on myself."

Everybody else could get down on him, though. Russell, who loves to blitz and made a name for himself that way, largely eschews blitzing so as to conform with the new disciplined Steeler defense. Other Steelers who might well be starting for other teams are accepting loyal-backup roles. Why couldn't Gilliam be a good citizen?

If you're on the bench and grumbling, you've usually got plenty of fellow sufferers. But what if you're on an essentially harmonious team that's winning a lot of money and corporate glory and greatly wants you for quarterback insurance, and you have a desperate desire to *play*? You are supposed to keep that desire burning, of course, but what if you want to take it off to some other team where you can use it—against, quite possibly, the team you're on now? Then nobody's on your side. It must be hard to be surrounded by a tightly knit team that's not on your side.

Your wife and kids' interests, financial ones at least, are against yours, too. And your parents'—well, Gilliam's father is a highly respected but self-deprecatory defensive coach at Tennessee State College, where the colorful head coach, John Merritt, gets the acclaim.

I have met Joe's parents and they are very nice people, and I'm sure they've stuck with Joe through his difficulties. But they can hardly have rallied behind him in his contrariness. "His father has more Wasp-type attitudes than you'd think a black man would have," says Art Rooney Jr. in his Pittsburgh Irishness. "Very puritanical and middle-class."

So when he stopped getting along by going along, Joe was pretty much alone. His nadir as a Steeler, as a quarterback, was the last game of the '75 season, against the Rams, a game the Steelers coasted through and lost, having already won their division title. Gilliam was scheduled to play the second half. "During halftime everyone was looking for Joe to go over the defenses," a Steeler says, "and nobody could find him. Finally we found him in the furthest toilet stall." When he took the field, Gilliam was not sharp. And one of the Steeler offensive linemen had heard that Gilliam had said he was no good. The Ram that offensive lineman was supposed to block shot straight in and creamed Gilliam twice. Joe had to leave the game. He was the only Steeler who didn't play in the Super Bowl.

The Steelers were trying to trade him by then, but no one wanted a "problem" quarterback. Certainly not—racism can't be discounted—a problem black one. Finally, when he slept through one practice and was late for another during the Steelers' early rookies-and-quarterbacks camp this year, he was put on waivers. If more than one team had claimed him, the Steelers would have taken him back off waivers and tried to make a deal, but only the Saints spoke up.

The Saints' starting quarterback, Archie Manning, had had a bad year followed by arm surgery. It was a good team for Gilliam to make it on. Then, a couple of weeks before he was to report, he and a friend were arrested in Nashville after a high-speed chase, Gilliam driving. Police found marijuana and a firearm in the car and recovered some cocaine that had been thrown out the window.

So that was hanging over his head when he reported early, July 4, to the Saints' camp. On the sixth he borrowed another player's car and disappeared from camp for four days. When he returned he apologized to the team, accepted a $1,000 fine, and then in Saturday scrimmage he completed sixteen of the nineteen passes he threw, and two of the other three were dropped. Joe Willie *Gillie*!

But Monday he had the flu, and when he returned to practice Wednesday he wasn't impressive, and on Thursday he *missed breakfast.* "We don't have an overabundance of rules and regulations, but the ones we have will be followed to the letter," said Saint head coach Hank Stram. "If I don't enforce them, I'm doing a bad job as a coach." All meals in the Saints' camp are mandatory. Gilliam was cut loose.

He got a better deal in court. All the charges will be wiped away if he does sixty days of public service work in the next nine months. He passed a lie detector test saying the coke wasn't his. If every NFL player who's had pot on him had to go to jail, it would look more ragged than the WFL out there. And a lot of players carry guns in their cars. I remember a former Steeler who weighed some 280 pounds reflecting with relish on how the person who'd just stolen his car was going to react when he started looking at what was inside it. "First he's going to find my gun, and say 'Uh-oh,' " he chuckled, "and then he's going to see the size of my *clothes.*"

But if Gilliam was trying to get traded, why didn't he straighten up for the Saints? Well, becoming a pariah isn't the most stabilizing exercise in the world. "Some who have known Gilliam speculate that his emotions had finally reached a breaking point," says *Jet.* That makes sense, and it doesn't seem disgraceful.

People—players as well as management—also mention drugs. This factor seems to have been figured into his official profile already, or I wouldn't mention it. "We felt he was enjoying some funny stuff," says Art Rooney Jr. "And we don't think this was an all-American boy who got into this only after something was taken away from him. Our understanding was that he had experience with something like that before."

Well. That would not have made him unique in pro football, certainly. And there are plenty of players who win approval for their performances on speed. And the Steelers were long famous for their *drinking* quarterbacks. And I was just reading in the New York *Daily News* that people are working stoned in *banks.* "Drugs" seem a dubious devil theory to me.

Now, I don't deny that the Steelers and Saints have grounds for exasperation. Clearly Gilliam is going to have to act more middle-class, or something, if he is going to be allowed to wear another NFL suit. But people might consider that during the last two years he took the only course his need to play allowed him to take, maybe a more admirable course—I'm talking human spirit, now, not prudence or teamsmanship—than sitting there stifling his instincts, being punctual and keeping his nose clean.

Duane Thomas was such a beautiful runner, but once he got wiggy, the game stiffed him. He did get very wiggy, of course, but things like being rude to sportswriters and going after hecklers in the stands are not what you could call entirely unreasonable, and things like refusing to take a three-point stance strike me as comparable to an inspired two-finger-typing sportswriter's refusing to learn the touch system. There would be less in the way of disruptive dissidence in sports if all dissidence weren't automatically considered disruptive. And I'll be damned if I don't think pro football would be more interesting on Sunday if rules required all key players to miss at least one practice every week.

"I had such *desires*," says baseball's troubled, splendid Richie Allen, "and then they wanted me to go to *meetings.*" At one point Allen was so upset by his clashes with standard off-the-field procedure that when a kid came up to him for an autograph he cried, "Get away! I can't stand it!"

"You can't let them [the powers that be] kill the little boy in you," says Reggie Jackson, who has managed to flout the system to some extent and yet stay on top of things. Jackson's sport, baseball, is somewhat more tolerant than football, but each sport perpetuates the childhood of players, complains about their childishness, and crushes them when they try to take any aspect of the game more threatening than balls and bats into their own hands.

Football's image of Joe Gilliam now, presumably, is: trouble. My image is of what he was like when he was doing what he loved to do, turning pro football into something more than grim head-knocking—romping around out there like a young dog with a stick in his mouth. Talk about enjoying funny stuff! Football is supposed to be something fans can get off on, isn't it? Off-balance is a matter of opinion.

[*I would like to say one other thing about Gilliam, by way of apology. In '74 training camp, after the "Terry, Terry and Joe" chapter of* About Three Bricks Shy of a Load *appeared in* Sports Illustrated *as a prepublication excerpt, Joe expressed delight that I had used his anecdote about vindicating his father 83–0. I was delighted that he was delighted, as I'd thought he would be: I wished I'd had an opportunity to stand up for my father so resoundingly. (My father died the same day I turned in the nearly finished manuscript of* Bricks *to the publisher, and my first thought when my mother told me on the phone was "At least he'll be spared the dirty words in my book.") But a few weeks later, after the whole book had come out, and Gilliam was riding high as the Steelers' starting quarterback, and I interviewed him for an SI cover story, he was distant. I decided he was just under a lot of pressure, with the starting job. Then in that story, in what I suppose was my Southern-liberal way, I waxed so enthusiastic about the ascendancy of a black quarterback (Gilliam became the first black quarterback to start and win an NFL opening-day game, throwing for 151 yards in the second quarter alone and breaking up in midfield laughter over a beautiful Jim Clack block) that an editor took it upon himself to tack something onto the end of the story's last paragraph. The last paragraph as published was:*

> *It is also not classic for a quarterback to smile and bounce around with both hands in the air after a successful play. But that too is Joe Gillie. So what.*

The last two words were what the editor, in his peculiar wisdom, tacked on.]

□ **8** □

HOLDING OUT
WITH BLOUNT

Summer, 1977

I t has been established earlier in this book that Mel Blount was wrong when he said to me in 1973, "Your great-grandfather probably owned my great-grandfather." ("No," my father assured me, "your great-grandfather didn't own Mel's great-grandaddy, because your great-grandaddy didn't own anything.") But as a football player, Mel himself *was* owned by the Steelers. When training camp opened in 1977, however, he was withholding his services. And demanding to be traded. And suing Steeler head coach Chuck Noll for $5 million.

The suit alleged slander. Last year Noll accused Oakland Raider defensive back George Atkinson of being part of "a criminal element in football" because Atkinson had belted Steeler receiver Lynn Swann in the head when Swann didn't even have the ball. It was brave of Noll to apply moral judgment to an act of football, and brave of Atkinson to acknowledge the gravity of the matter by suing Noll and the Steelers for defamation of character, and brave of Noll and the Steelers to refuse to settle out of court. It is good to establish that there is such a thing as a vicious tackle, in the strict, or nonsporting, sense of the term. Fortunately no NFL defensive line or backfield had taken "The Criminal Element" as its nickname, so that term was able to carry some force of disapproval.

When Atkinson's suit went to court in July, the jury decided against him. But that wasn't the end of it. During the trial, Noll managed to say something that got him sued *again.* Under cross-examination, Noll was brought to concede that films shown by Atkinson's lawyers revealed some of Noll's own players striking blows as nasty as Atkinson's. It must be said for Noll that few NFL coaches entertain enough humanistic pretensions, pieties aside, to get themselves into such a fix. He was led to acknowledge that Steelers occasionally could be included in his concept of the criminal element (the definition of which seemed to expand as rapidly as Andy Young's definition of racism—although it never included anyone white). Nettled, falling back on sarcasm and betraying a certain flappability, Noll went so far as to say that Blount's belting of Raider receiver Cliff Branch when Branch didn't even have the ball was a "dastardly" act. That looked bad in the papers.

"I always got along fine with Chuck," Blount said when I called him. "But how can I play for him after that?" In pro football, however, you can't change teams just because you don't think you'll be at your best playing for someone whom you're suing for slander. "Jimmy Carter keeps talking about human rights in Russia," Blount said. "He ought to take a look right here in the NFL."

I doubted that the President would get involved, although Blount had accompanied him through Pittsburgh steel mills before the Pennsylvania primary ("I got more attention than he did," Blount said), but I wanted to see what it was like to hold out. The field is where a player proves himself as an athlete, but it is by contract demands that he makes his way in the world. Football is art. Holding out is life.

For three days I joined Blount in the Eden Isles development on Lake Pontchartrain in Slidell, Louisiana, where he has a nice house bursting with paintings of himself and honorary-deputy-sheriff proclamations and Steeler team pictures and many of the balls he has intercepted in the NFL. And here is what we did.

We got the dryer fixed. The man came out right away, on a Saturday, when he realized who Blount was. "I love this little town, man," Blount said. "There ain't nothing I can ask for that I don't get." The only thing wrong with the repairman's visit was that he said, "You know, the way that story was printed, it looked like you were suing Noll for $5 million. We got a big laugh out of that." Blount didn't say anything at the time, but later he said, "People are strange, man."

We ate a lot of wonderful gumbo and red beans and rice. We took a dip in the canal behind the house. We went to Blount's small farm nearby and looked at two of his quarter horses. We drove around in his wife's new Mercedes and his '48 Chrysler ("This car is the same age as me"). I watched TV (there were usually two going, a big one and a little one) while he ran two and a half miles in the noonday sun. I watched him squeeze Silly Putty to keep up the strength in his hands. At one point he looked at the living room lamp, whose base is a Steeler helmet and said, unemotionally, "I guess I won't ever wear one of those again."

He called a friend of his in Pittsburgh. "I just want to find out if they've started throwing niggers off the bridges," he said. The friend reported that Middle Linebacker Jack Lambert was also holding out and several other Steelers were expressing dissatisfaction. Blount felt a distant solidarity. "Players never talk to each other about what they make, though," he said.

We stopped in at former NFL star Rosey Taylor's New Orleans disco, the Big Apple, where the then resident disc jockey, Emo, said things like "Mel Blount over there. Great God!" between records. I asked Taylor, a former defensive back, what he thought about Atkinson's hit on Swann. "What was it?" Rosey asked.

"He clotheslined him," said Blount.

"Well, you got to expect to be hit," said Taylor.

"Yeah," said Blount. "I was talking to Ed Bradley, the TV newscaster. He said, 'What do they think it is, flag football?' "

"As long as he's carrying the ball," Taylor said.

"He wasn't, though," I said.

"Oh," said Taylor. "Well, I hate to see that."

"Yeah," said Blount. "Well, it was a terrible hit."

Blount played "Time Is on My Side" and "The Price Ain't Right" on the jukebox. "That's some terrible music," he said, moving with it.

We went to see Richard Pryor in *Greased Lightning*. At one point in that movie a white racetrack owner says he wants the hero, a black stockcar driver, to race at his track "because the whites will come out to see a nigger get killed, and the niggers will just come out."

"That's what they want me for in Pittsburgh," Blount said.

We both wanted to take off and go to Blount's big ancestral farm in South Georgia where he grew up, where any number of his relatives live and where he likes to harvest crops and run through the fields with his horses. His agent told him to stay put because something might break. But nothing did. The Steelers were waiting Blount out. His wife, Leslie, went to a beauty product demonstration. Blount and I twirled a jump rope for his eight-year-old daughter, Tanisia. Blount showed her how to jump properly and said, "Don't ever learn something the wrong way." Sunday morning before church we ate grits and eggs and watched Rex Humbard, the evangelist, on TV, and Blount said, "God is right where he ought to be. In the center of my life. That's why all this don't trouble me."

If he wasn't troubled, though, he was alienated from the team he had served for seven years and in two Super Bowls. The cause, it became clear, was not simply inadvertent calumny in court. "I might as well tell you the whole story," Blount said.

He made something like seventeen, eighteen and twenty-one thou his first three years with the Steelers. His salary had not grown by leaps and bounds as of 1975, when he was named the Steelers' Most Valuable Player and the NFL Defensive Player of the Year. Although his contract still had another year to run, he told the Steelers he felt his '75 performance entitled him to more money. They agreed to give him a $50,000 signing bonus up front and $50,000 a year if he would commit himself all the way through 1979. This he did.

Then last year, before the Steelers' first game with Houston, which they had to win to make the playoffs, Blount sprained his ankle in practice. "It swelled up like a ball," he said. Terror swept the organization because Blount's backup, Jimmy Allen, was in California recuperating from an appendectomy. Allen was flown back hurriedly, but, Blount said, "I went to work on my ankle with horse liniment, man, and went ahead and played on it." He covered Ken Burrough, one of the league's best receivers, on a sprained ankle, "and everybody was saying what a great thing I'd done for the team." Blount figured such a great thing ought to be worth something tangible, so he went to team president Dan Rooney, who, Blount says, "said maybe they could work something out that would be good for me and help them with their taxes, too."

Blount suggested they lend him some money. He wanted to put it into the Georgia farm and into the employment agency he is opening in New Orleans. Rooney asked him how big a loan he wanted, and Blount said $168,000. Rooney said that was way too much, but they'd figure something out.

However, according to Blount, Rooney and Jim "Buff" Boston, the Steelers' traveling secretary and negotiator, kept putting him off. Finally they said they would sit down with him in New Orleans the week of the Pro Bowl game (of which Blount was the MVP), but they didn't. Blount says he kept phoning them, but they wouldn't return his calls. "And here I am one of their superstars."

Blount retained an agent, Reg Foster of New Orleans, who had been introduced to him by the president of his local bank, and who will get five percent of anything Blount signs for beyond what he has coming already. They wrote a letter advising the Steelers to draft a defensive back because Blount would not play with them again. The Steelers ignored this notice. A couple of days before Noll's testimony in the Atkinson trial, Buff Boston came to New Orleans to try to straighten things out. Foster said Blount was worth $250,000 a year. Boston said that was out of the question. Foster said okay, Blount didn't want to go back to Pittsburgh anyway. Boston responded, according to Foster's report to Blount, "He'll starve, then, because we're not going to trade him."

"Then the next thing I hear is that Chuck is saying I'm a member of the criminal element," Blount told me. "I don't know if Buff might have told him something and that was in the back of his mind. . . ."

Dan Rooney called Blount to express his regrets and to say that Noll had been pushed into his statements. Steeler tackle Joe Greene and retired Steeler captain Andy Russell called to tell Blount they'd hate to see him play for another team. But, essentially, it was neither mollification nor appeals to team spirit nor even money that Blount was holding out for. Nor did he expect his lawsuit to come to anything. What he wanted was for football to fit his life better.

"That's not bad money they are paying me," Blount said, "if I could get it in the South." What he wanted was to be traded to the New Orleans Saints. It would be an easy commute, and he could come home in the evening and sit out on the canal. Blount likes warm weather and large bodies of water, so if he can't play in New Orleans, then he wouldn't mind Miami or Tampa Bay. And becoming a sports hero in the area he has roots in would be to his business advantage. Pittsburgh, whose tone is set by white ethnics, is not an ideal town economically for black athletes.

If Blount and I had gone to his Georgia farm, we would have flown into Atlanta, where my kids were visiting their grandmother. When I advised my eight-year-old son of this possibility, he began to warm audibly over the phone. "Tell him to bring his helmet!" he said.

But holding out deepened my sense that wherever a given player's head may be at, it is not bounded by his team's helmet. "My son will be disappointed if you play for somebody else," I told Blount. "He loves drawing pictures of you and other Steelers in black and gold felt-tip pens."

"Unh," said Blount.

Blount said he owes some money, but no more than a businessman should, and a lot less than Bert Lance. The Georgia farm, in which he has an interest, nets some $80,000 a year from tobacco alone, and it also produces corn and peas and peanuts and cattle. He and his brothers have converted an old barn on the property into a nighclub that has been known to do $1,400 in a weekend.

"There's a chance I won't play football again," he said. "But I'll go on living. Starve to death! We grow enough food on the farm to feed everybody in Pittsburgh."

□ **9** □

SWANN'S WAY

November 27, 1978
January 15, 1979

I keep watching for some really new departure on a football field. Say a referee were to intercept a pass. There he goes, streaking downfield: no one is sure whether to tackle him. Now we *know* there is something funny about the officiating.

In the meantime I enjoy watching Lynn Swann dance with the ball.

Whenever I see Swann hang and twist inimitably in the air to snatch a pass away from glowering, jealous defenders, I think of W. C. Fields stomping away from a Charlie Chaplin movie, growling, "The son of a bitch is a ballet dancer."

Swann began to take dancing lessons when he was in the fourth grade, at his mother's insistence. His mother had always wanted a girl, so she made him dance, after naming him Lynn.

What a name to play football under! Lynn Swann. First name girlish, last name not only birdlike but Proustian; and all those extra *n*'s trailing around. Why do wide receivers get stuck with names like Lynn Swann and Golden Richards?

"The first day of school, every year, there I was listening to them call the boys' names," says Swann. "And every time, they'd call all the boys, and I'd think, 'Oh, God, I'm on the girls' list again.'"

Fortunately, Lynn's older brother Calvin "was a year ahead of me, but then he had mononucleosis real bad, and one day he was showing off in front of his class and swallowed a straight pin, which they never did find, so altogether he was sick in the hospital ten months. So from then on we were in the same class. And when people got on me about my name or dancing, Calvin beat up a couple of people, and everything was cool."

However, in 1975 when he was a rookie, Swann decried the notion, advanced by an older Steeler, that Mean Joe Greene was a "big brother" who whipped on opponents so that other Steelers could do their thing. It was true that in those days the Steelers overpowered the rest of the league primarily by defensive intimidation, and Greene was the head intimidator.

Greene on the field was in some ways Fieldsian: irascible, unaccountably deft for his bulk, and generally overbearing. The Steeler defense, still featuring

Greene but now better typified by the fuming, slashing middle linebacker Jack Lambert, remains crucial, but the team's most spectacular element this year has been its passing attack, of which Swann is both the steadiest and the niftiest element.

And Swann on the field is Chaplinesque: small, frequently pummeled, bouncing, poignant but uncrushable, a tough little nut sometimes lighter than air.

Swann is also one of the few people in the NFL who can be identified in any significant way with freedom of expression. In 1976 he had the temerity to complain about the fact that, even when he was nowhere near the ball, defensive backs were belting him viciously in the head and giving him concussions. "The game is tough enough within the rules," he said, and if the cheap shots continued, he would quit the game.

The subsequent uproar involved fines, lawsuits, rules changes and widespread denunciations of Swann (even sometimes, privately, by his teammates) not only as a prima donna California big shot who appeared on television too often but also as a sissy, a punk, a tattletale and a crybaby. Fortunately a boy named Lynn gets inured to that kind of talk.

Furthermore, his receiving style is so distinctive that he doesn't have to do posttouchdown gyrations. He makes over three-fourths of his catches over the middle, where small, fleet receivers have traditionally been less than avid to tread. And he excels at such unobtrusive aspects of his position as running correct patterns and blocking.

On the other hand, at the University of Southern California he majored in public relations. He wants to be on camera, isolated, doing amazing things with the ball. When his somewhat less acrobatic but equally effective receiving mate John Stallworth catches a touchdown pass and Swann appears on the screen empty-handed, Swann does not always appear to be a hundred percent pleased. When Stallworth was catching ten passes against Denver in the playoffs, Swann's thought, he says, was "That's supposed to be me doing that."

He also wishes that pass receivers weren't so dependent on the passer.

"Before this year," he observes, "people were saying, 'Lynn Swann is making such great catches, he's making Bradshaw look good.' All of a sudden Terry has a great year, and people go back to the typical attitude, that the quarterback is the guy who completes the pass.

"That's why receivers tend to be such loners. In high school, in San Mateo, Jesse Freitas and I were a big passing combination. My senior year he went to Stanford. When I graduated, people wanted me to go there so we could team up again, but I went to USC because he wasn't there. You don't want to go on not knowing whether it's you being that good, or the quarterback."

Perhaps most receivers are too sensitive about being regarded as "little guys hanging out there on the end," as Swann puts it, to risk complaining about being illegally mauled. After Swann had spoken out, the retired great receiver

Lance Alworth declared that he always considered cheap shots to the head a compliment to his ability.

"I don't want a compliment," says Swann sensibly, "that could end my career." His protests led to rules limiting defenders' jostling of receivers, and to the league's practice of scrutinizing game films and fining people whom the films revealed to be behaving too savagely.

"I think if you do a study of well-known cheap-shot artists," Swann says, "you'll find that a number of them this year are sitting on the bench, or they're out of the league." Certainly pass receivers are flourishing. The game has become somewhat less grinding and more buoyant. And none too soon.

Swann has flouted conventional wisdom and other forms of repression before. At first he was mortified to be taking dancing lessons, but then he came to like them. He continued taking them all the way through high school and college, and even now, "every once in a while on the field when I'm twisting, jumping, doing a crossover, I think back to dancing."

Off the field, he seeks release in something even more dandified. He writes poetry. One of his shorter verses was, at first, as follows:

> *Why say it?*
> *Why write it?*
> *Open up and feel it, it will last longer.*

By way of a gloss on those lines, he comments: "There were a lot of things I felt and there was no young lady there that I could share everything with, all my insides. So I told myself, 'Open up and feel it, let it out.' I did that, and somebody betrayed my openness, and I was hurt."

So he added two more lines:

> *But until you find the heart to listen,*
> *Write.*

Here is another example of Swann's way with words:

> *Like flowers,*
> *Friends and lovers need care.*
> *To be held when they are lost,*
> *Touched when they are lonely.*
> *When all ears seem to be closed,*
> *Yours must be open.*

That's a wide receiver's theme. Getting open.

□ 10 □

SUPER BOWL, 1979: SPOTS AND WATER AND ROCK

Miami
January 20

The Pittsburgh hotel was the Marriott, out by the airport. That's where the Steelers were staying, and that's where half the population of Pittsburgh was loafing. In other parts of the country you call it "hanging out." In Pittsburgh you call it "loafing," as in, "Oh, yeah, I used to loaf with that guy." Around the pool at the Marriott was half the population of Pittsburgh, loafing and wearing shorts—wearing Steeler shirts, Steeler hats and, since there is no such thing as Steeler shorts, just plain shorts that they bought somewhere, when they got to Florida probably, because people in Pittsburgh don't wear shorts. They had come to Florida and bought some shorts, and there they were, white-legged, loafing and yelling "Pittsburgh!"

Mean Joe Greene was there. The mayor of Pittsburgh was there. Father Duggan, the Steelers' priest, was there, having made the Steelers promise to fly him in from Ireland. Lynn Swann came out of his room wearing a cowboy hat, carrying a tape deck and looking as if he were getting ready to do something incredibly stylish, and half of Pittsburgh yelled:

"Swanny! Hey, Swanny! Hey, Swanny, save it for the game!"

"Psycho income," said Art Rooney Jr. "Or psychic income, whatever you call it. That's what the Super Bowl is, psychic income. You're hiring a guy, and you tell him either you'll give him $25,000 a year, or $20,000 a year and send him to the Super Bowl, and he'll take the $20,000. The Super Bowl. Whether it's Hollywood Henderson or some guy from the Aliquippa Open Hearth, everybody wants his own little piece of it."

My piece of it is a chance to talk to Art's father, Art Rooney Sr., known as the Chief. The Chief is a real Pittsburgh guy. I would venture to say that he has never worn shorts in his life. Even at a Super Bowl, the Chief will bring

314

you down to earth. So here is a story from the Chief that doesn't having anything to do with Super Week, except insofar as Super Week is defined by liquor, insularity, bigness, boyishness, seafood and excess.

The Chief was eating spots, which is a nice little flavorful fish. He smiled. "The first time I ever had spots," he said, "it was one of the funniest things that ever happened to me." He was already laughing. "The outdoors writer for one of the papers in Pittsburgh took me fishing to Cape Hatteras. We took along this fellow Quinlan. He was a big Irish fellow. He told stories and sang a lot of songs. He worked for one of the breweries in Pittsburgh. And there were a couple of other fellows along."

On the way to Cape Hatteras the car became stuck in the sand, and the group had various other misadventures. "Finally we got to this little island. The man who lived there—I'll never forget it—was named Rance Odom. We took along some whisky, and Rance's wife started cooking these spots.

"Rance," the Chief said. You could tell he loved the name Rance.

"Well, Quinlan was singing Irish songs and eating these spots. And Rance Odom said, 'There's three things never been on this island: a colored, a Catholic, a Jew.'

"I said: 'Well, Rance, you just broke your maiden. Three of us here are Catholic, and he's a Jew.'

"Rance couldn't get over it. He kept shaking his head. He couldn't understand it. He said, 'But you're just like regular people!'

"And Quinlan kept eating these spots. And singing. And Mrs. Odom was calling him Big Boy and saying: 'I can see who's got the appetite. I can see who's the real eater in this bunch.' And Quinlan ate so many spots he got sick.

"The next morning I saw him in bed, and, oh, was he sick." The Chief was shaking, laughing.

"So I went up to Rance's wife and said: 'You know, the thing Big Boy likes most of all for breakfast is a plate of spots. And what he likes with it is a bottle of whisky.' So she came into the kitchen and cooked up some of those spots and went into the bedroom with some of those spots and a bottle of bourbon on a tray—singing a song!

"Oh!" said the Chief, his crumpled face aglow. "You should have seen her. Running out of there with those spots!"

January 21

Two minutes twenty-three seconds left, and you would think the Pittsburgh Steelers are not about to become the winningest team in Super Bowl history. "Why do we do this? Why do we always do this?" cries Gerry Mullins, the guard, sitting slumped and dirty on the bench. "We had the game on ice, and now we're in trouble. Why do we always have to make it hard?"

The Dallas Cowboys, who were down 35–17, have suddenly started scoring points. "We can't play easy games," says John Banszak, the defensive end. "We can make it every way but easy."

Up in the press box Super Bowl XIII looked wild enough, but down here on the sideline it is crazy. Coaches are yelling, players are pacing, balloons from the halftime show are drifting about, everybody is filthy, and the sweat is running down faces as if the players had shower heads inside their helmets.

"Unnnnhgh," or rather a sound even less pleasant than that, is what Steve Furness is saying as he comes lurching off the field with the support of two teammates. A lot of bumping and pushing and scrabbling goes on as people clear out of his way. Clump! He lands on the bench. "Unnnnhgh." He has what will later be diagnosed as a "probably broken ankle."

The Steelers fumble an onside kick, and the coaches are fit to be tied. All this work to get here, and it could be slipping away. How can the players be doing this to them? Sam Davis, the guard, won't speak to anybody. He is glaring at the ground beneath his feet as if it were an enemy.

"Water!" cries someone, and everybody takes up the cry. "Water! Water!" Nobody seems to know who wants water, but somebody does. And at any rate, yelling, "They're yelling for water!" passes the time. Pittsburgh wants time to pass. But Roger Staubach is passing too, for the Cowboys.

Jack Hart, the Steeler equipment man, is casting about for water, but then he sees Jack Lambert coming off the field. "It's for him? Water for Lambert? I'm not getting water for Lambert. Forty-one seconds to go, and Lambert has to have water!" Lambert and Hart bicker a lot. So Hart hasn't lost his cool. He has the presence of mind to get in a few shots at Lambert.

Dirt Winston, the linebacker, is composed as well. He is chatting with Rocky Bleier, the running back, about the dog that is staring at them. The dog is on a leash being held by a security man. Bleier is telling Winston that the dog is meaner than Winston.

"That dog?" says Winston, as if astounded. "That dog? I would kick that dog. Paralyze his body."

But most of the people on the sideline are tense, pacing, looking dead tired—saying "whoo!" and wiping their faces like a farmer in his field at noon in July. And the possibility exists, however remote it may seem to everyone else, that thirty football seconds from now they are going to have to say, "I'm beat."

The Cowboys score again. It is 35–31. The Cowboys try another onside kick. "Get the football, everybody!"

"Everybody! Hold the ball!"

It is, of course, impossible for everybody to hold the ball, but for a moment everybody seems to be trying. On the field, a great clattering and banging. And on the sideline, a hush.

Then:

"Rock fell on it!"

"Rock!"

Bleier. The old reliable Nam vet. Who just a few seconds ago was right here talking to a man about a dog.

"Rock."

"Yeah, Rock."

The near-elemental word goes around the way "water" was going around earlier, only in a different tone of voice. Old Rock. Just a handful more seconds to go, and the Steelers have the ball.

"We got the ring!" somebody cries. Mel Blount and Ron Johnson, cornerbacks, hug each other; flashes go off all around.

But there's not a lot of delirious whoopee. When the Steelers won their first Super Bowl, in 1975, they were doing the bump and butting one another's heads like billy goats on the sideline in the closing seconds. This third set of Super Bowl victory closing seconds is more mature.

"I don't think it's really hit us yet," Blount says a few minutes later, in the dressing room. "It will take some hearing about it from others. It will take reading some articles about it. I don't really think we know just exactly what we've done."

□ 11 □

SUPER BOWL 1980:
STILL CAN'T COVER IT

Every year at this time, I go to the Super Bowl and fail to cover it. I might as well try to cover Christmas. Oh, I generally dig up some startling facts during Super Week. One year I learned that Ernie Holmes, the Steeler tackle, had bought his old high school. After hearing that it was closed down, he went back to Texas and bought it.

High school is where I realized that I was never, myself, going to play in anything like the Super Bowl. I came to that realization after quitting eighth grade football the first day of practice. The next thing I knew, I was a writer, and the Super Bowl was looming above me.

Time after time I have taken the Super Bowl's best shot and given it mine. I have sneaked down onto the sidelines, I have crouched in the end zone with the halftime show, I have hustled around the Superdome with a ticket scalper, I have drunk sangria on Super Saturday with the Pittsburgh defensive line, and in collaboration with Pete Axthelm, of *Newsweek*, I have bought out the stock of a flower girl (who wore a chenille bedspread and flip-flops) and covered the French Quarter streets on Super Bowl eve, dispensing free jonquils to Super fans and blowing on kazoos.

I have approached Super Week from just about every angle except the one that a guy came up with right after the '79 game. This unidentified fan somehow got past Super guard dogs and security men and entered the Steeler dressing room, where he undressed and took a shower with the Super victors. "We wondered who he was," Steeler tackle Larry Brown said later. "He didn't look anything like a football player. He was a little white guy." The infiltrator dried off and put his clothes on in front of Tight End Bennie Cunningham's locker, where, although Cunningham is a big black guy, he was interviewed as Cunningham by more than one reporter.

But I don't think that guy in the locker room really covered the Super Bowl either. You can't cover the Super Bowl; it is too manifold, too evocative, too

318

spurious, too self-regarding. Maybe this year the NFL will finally break down and admit that "Super Bowl" is too small a term; it ought to be "Stupendous Cauldron."

In '79 George Halas, the owner of the Bears, came into the press lounge and told how he invented pro football. Then, Bill Murray of "Saturday Night Live" came in and tore the Gucci buckles off the shoes of Axthelm's associate Max McGowan.

"Halas was good," one sportswriter said in the lounge. "Murray was good. But it's all hype."

But that *still* doesn't quite cover the Super Bowl. To be sure, the Bowl is Superhyped, but it also causes me, at least, to muse. "You know," I will often muse to someone at a Super wee hour, "Ernie Holmes bought his old high school."

This year Super Week is in Pasadena and environs, which is my third-favorite Super site. New Orleans is the best because you can sit in The Old Absinthe House and keep track of everything that goes on. Miami is next best because of Kelly's, a bar that Bill Murray discovered. The front of Kelly's is open to the street, so you can dance to the jukebox right out onto the roadway and watch such things as a Cuban-American car wreck. If you have never, while dancing, seen one Cuban-American family car running into another Cuban-American family car and the passengers spilling out arguing about who was at fault and telephoning for carloads of supporters who arrive avowing loudly that they were eyewitnesses, you have not partaken of the full spectrum of American experience. I don't know of any bar like Kelly's in or near Pasadena.

The last time the Super Bowl was in Pasadena, though, in '77, there were some interesting developments in the ongoing tradition of Super noncoverage. For one thing, the press lounge closed early every Super Week night. The reason, I was told, was that in Miami, the previous year, certain parties without official sanction (parties who, as it happened, included me) welcomed Jerry Jeff Walker, the modern cowboy singer and writer of "Mr. Bojangles," into that room late one night to play the guitar and sing various songs, including one he wrote called "Pissin' in the Wind." The disapproval of Jerry Jeff's appearance is one of the things that make it hard for me to comprehend the Super Bowl. That musical interlude seemed to me the most resounding part of Super Week '76 (except for the time Pittsburgh's Reggie Harrison blocked a punt with his face). But I understand that a writer from South Bend called it a desecration. And so, no more free drinks and onion dip from the NFL after midnight.

On the other hand, the '77 Super Bowl had the Polo Lounge. There I would cleave to the table of *Sports Illustrated*'s Dan Jenkins, who knew the head-waiter, and watch the heavy commingle. "See those two guys over there?" Jenkins said at one point. "They're network vice-presidents. They don't know they've been fired." At another point, someone indicated an unassuming but well-dressed and vaguely familiar-looking old gentleman and said, "You know who that is, don't you?"

I said no.

"That's God's brother."

"Oh . . . yeah, I heard something . . ."

"Never quite made it at anything," he said. "Still hanging around. Brother buys all his suits."

I'm sorry, but that kind of thing impresses me. Of course, I could see Gene Rayburn or Peter Lind Hayes and be impressed. During Super Week '77, I went to dinner with a group that included Mark Rydell, the director and actor. In *The Long Goodbye,* he played the hood who hits his girl friend in the face with a Coke bottle and says "And I *love . . . her*" to show Elliott Gould how tough he is. Well, in high school I knew a guy who really did hit somebody in the face with a Coke (actually, a Nugrape) bottle once (actually, twice), but I had never met anybody who'd done it on the screen. A local woman who had joined us for dinner had to leave early because, she said, she had to get up early so she could get depressed in time for an appointment with her shrink. I sincerely love Hollywood. At a CBS party on a Western movie lot, I ate raisin sorbet and watched a stunt man get set on fire.

Oh, '77 was a grand old Super Week in many ways. But coverable? By Super zero hour, many of us in the press corps were almost as weak as the Vikings turned out to be. (The Vikings were so superable, you will recall, that the game was as boring as most Super Bowls have been.) In the press box before the kickoff, I sat, bleary as an aged raven, next to George Kimball, of *The Boston Phoenix,* who had just watched people having pregame cocktails and brunch all around a man who was lying on the ground having a pregame heart attack. Kimball shook his head, looked out at the rather overbright greensward, dotted with gaily costumed Raiders and Vikes, and sighed, "I'm not even sure I'm *down.*"

Now, I am too thin-blooded when it comes to risking money (as opposed to spending it) to need a bookmaker myself, but if I'd had any semblance of my wits about me during that Super Week, I could have made a killing on the coin flip. I knew it was going to come up tails—former Steeler Warren Bankston, Oakland's special-teams captain and flip caller, had told me. "This year I've hit it seven out of seven," he had said. "Three tails, a head, two tails, a head. And Sunday it's going to be tails. I see it during the week. It's like I almost cheat. I see . . . like a coin flying. And it lands. And, just as big, it's tails. Sometimes I even argue with myself—it can't be three straight tails. But, naw, I have to go with my first instinct. I'll be taking a shower or something, and I'll just kind of *see it.*"

It was tails. And I didn't bet it. I was too busy trying to examine myself in a new light after talking to Bankston, not because of his coin prophecy but because of his self-image. In attempting to explain how the Raiders were going

320

to foil Minnesota's efforts to block their field goals, he drew a little circle with two dots in the middle of it.

"This is my body," he explained, "standing over my feet."

And there it was. Ever since then, I have been trying to firm up my own self-concept by drawing little pictures. This is my mind, standing off to one side of my mouth. This is my soul, standing in the need of something. This is my mission, standing under my misunderstanding.

It never works. It just looks like squiggles. That's what football has, that diagrammability. If you're a player, you have it until you get cut, and then you bleed out into the world at large and can't hold on to doodles anymore—unless you can get into a big company that has tables of organization or flow charts, which don't take into account your body, much less your feet.

As I write this, an eleven-day stretch of rain is ending in western Massachusetts, where I live, and a full moon has emerged. My lithe wife wants to take a walk and admire the moon, but I am dead set on trying to find the key to why nobody can find the key to the Super Bowl. I switch on the Monday-night game. Pro football still enjoys far and away the biggest TV sports market. People get *involved,* in spite of themselves, in all that diagrammable bumping and grinding. The Monday game, a thriller, begins to draw me in. I am ashamed of the extent to which I am drawn in and not drawn away by the moon. A pass receiver goes up, keeps a defender away from the oncoming ball and seizes it himself. "He knows," says Howard Cosell knowingly, "how to use . . . his body."

And this, on the chaise lounge, is my body, sitting level with my feet. Pete Gent, author and former receiver, in a visionary mood once told me, "I always wanted to win the Super Bowl so I could take it and hold it and see what lies beyond it. I think it may be the sun."

Ernie Holmes once came to practice on weigh-in day carrying a huge paper bag. He weighed himself, then tore open the sack and pulled out a big wooden bowl full of chef's salad, which he ate. There is nothing spectacular about chef's salad, of course, although in this case, there was a *lot* of it. The memorable thing was the bowl. The bowl itself. The bowl and the bag: the packaging.

My wife hardly ever watches TV football. Watching TV football is defined by many wives as what you do to avoid going person-to-person with your wife. Before becoming the coach of the Berkshire School field hockey team a couple of years ago, my wife had never seen a field hockey game, nor even a field hockey stick. Soon she was shouting, "Learn how to lunge!" at her charges and burning to play. One evening she headed for the door, saying, "I have to do that unicycle thing."

I asked, "What unicycle thing?"

"Behind the headmaster."

"What is the headmaster going to be doing?"

"Singing 'Molly Malone,' " she said.

High school must have changed. Oh, I wish I could purchase mine and go back to it and ride down its halls on a unicycle and start over. On this Monday night, the purpose of the Super Bowl begins to dawn on me. It is to make us feel unfulfilled by pro football. There are things, the Super Bowl hints, even harder to cover than this. I cry out, spring up, break away from the TV game as it is entering sudden-death overtime, and sprint out to walk foot-foot-foot with my wife in the drying, clearing night under the orbic moon. There are two dots in the middle of it.

P.S.:
Bradshaw threw big passes to Swann and Stallworth, Lambert made a big interception, and the Steelers beat the Rams 31–19. This was the Steeler's last Super Bowl, and the first one I didn't manage to watch at least in part from the sideline. I didn't even make it to the team party—it was a long drive away, for one thing, and I hadn't been invited, for another, and things weren't as loose as they used to be around the Steelers. Every time you saw a player, he was surrounded by Security surrounded by a crowd. Different scene from '75 in New Orleans when Reggie Jackson and I wandered into the defensive line's sangria-and-dancing klatch on Super Bowl eve.

The seventies—am I the only American who remembers them as a heady decade?—were over. The Steelers' dynasty was over. My marriage started breaking up.

□ **12** □

DWIGHT WHITE: MAD DOG RETIRED

Fall, 1980

It's Sunday afternoon and almost everybody in the Pittsburgh area is watching the Steeler game. But Dwight White, who used to be a *rabid* Steeler, has it behind him. He hasn't looked at the TV here on his patio since the first quarter, when he switched over to *The Wall Street Report*. White is peering in the opposite direction, downhill from his backyard in the prosperous suburb of Ross Township, through the telescopic sight of the Winchester 30–06 rifle he says he keeps ready. The Steelers intercept a pass. White pulls the trigger. Click. "Don't make me out to be the mad sniper now."

"Mad Dog" is what they called him when he was the all-pro right end of the Steel Curtain, Super Bowl history's most overwhelming Front Four. In Super IX White himself flattened Fran Tarkenton to score the first Super Bowl safety, and along with Joe Greene, L. C. Greenwood, Ernie "Arrowhead" Holmes (whom White calls the best defensive lineman he ever saw), the linebackers and defensive backs, he held the Vikings to *19 yards* rushing. And he had pleurisy at the time. Got out of a hospital bed, played, went straight back to the hospital for two weeks. ("God takes care of fools and little babies," he says.) That was one of four Super Bowls in which he played whole-hog and nasty.

"I was sick," he says with relish and bemusement (mostly relish), and it's not the pleurisy he's talking about. "I'd do *anything*. Late shot, that didn't mean anything to me. Push your damn face in, that didn't mean anything to me." But off the field he was the youngest-hearted, most ebullient on a team of high spirits. Round-faced, round-bodied (none of the front four looked like a Greek god), orotund and blithe. Now, at thirty-two, in his first season of retirement, he is a stockbroker. He handles security portfolios with the distinguished firm of Bache Halsey Stuart Shields. He was a delegate to President Reagan's Conference on Aging—although he looks about the same, just a little graver, as when he was whooping and dancing with recovered fumbles.

He can *sound* like a Republican stockbroker, too. But he hasn't grown staid.

"I got an arsenal here," he said. "A black family near here, somebody burned a cross in their yard, and the only one home was a teenage girl, and she got so upset, she had to go to the hospital.

"People said it was probably just local kids, a prank. But *I* didn't think it was funny. Went to the store and got this gun and the man said, 'Oh . . . Dwight White. Thirty-aught-six. Are you . . . going to shoot some deers?'

" 'Nope.'

" 'Going . . . hunting?'

" 'Nope.' "

He's *ready* for them. But it's prudent investors that White really wants to deal with; people who want to "get rich slow." What he tends to run into are people who want to talk about football. He will respond politely and turn the subject to securities and their FAB: Features, Advantages and Benefits.

"Being a football player is nice. But it ain't great in terms of twenty years down the road, can you feed your children? I happen to think that the ultimate test is not to play football, but to be something after football. It's a real challenge to wipe out that image, that stereotype. Everybody I talk to wants to ask me, am I going through withdrawal? 'Don't you miss it?' They *want* you to be crushed.

"But I'm completely desensitized to it. Whether you're getting out of a hospital bed, or breathing so hard you're breathing blood out of your lungs, busting capillaries just from the intensity of your breathing . . . whatever you do, when it's over, it's over. I was proud to be a player. It's a highly skilled employment. But it's men playing a kid's game. I'm more impressed with Wall Street than Three Rivers Stadium.

"I've got a lot of friends on the Steelers, but I never see 'em. We're on a different schedule. In football, you live in a society that's a bubble: work from 10 to 3, never experience traffic, never know what it's like to eat lunch at 12 o'clock. I'm competing with the *majority* now. There's not a football player in America up at 8:30. And that's not rolling into it yawning and stretching, fooling around putting on your warm-ups, getting ready to go into a meeting and listen to Chuck. That's 8:30 wide awake very alert talking business. I'll be doing this longer than I played football. You got to be an airhead not to tell the difference."

The Steelers are winning on TV and I keep sneaking looks, but White is restless. He's going into the house after wine, he's chasing down his little dog, Dusty, he's hollering over to the next-door neighbor, he's showing me his vegetable garden, he's talking to his pregnant wife, Karen, who is executive director of the local chapter of the Epilepsy Foundation. He's saying, "I want them to win, but I don't care about the details. I hear the announcers saying things about the guys, and they don't know what they're talking about, and I start yelling. . . . I'm not a fan. I was into *doing* it." There is the memory of White on the sidelines, chortling, sweating, pacing, fidgeting, groaning, going on and coming off; he didn't watch the game then either. For the Steeler exhibition games this year he was the local telecast's sideline reporter, but being around the bench in street clothes made him feel strange.

"It'll mess up your head. You have to sever . . . have to get away from it."

It's only later as we're riding in his Mercedes that he can quite bring himself to say it: "I'm not a football player anymore. It can make you toss and turn, thinking about that. But you accept it, get past it, a little period of—yeah, you can call it withdrawal. I'm not going to be a player anymore."

And isn't it a comedown? "I get off on what I'm doing. I can get off on anything I make some money behind."

Although he eventually made substantially more than $100,000 a year playing football, he says he didn't do that for the money. "I didn't play for the Steelers. I played for Dwight. People take that the wrong way. But if a player's not playing for himself . . . All the money in the world is not going to make me stick my head in there when I know it's going to get cut off. You got to *want* to do it."

And Dwight did. Later, extremely later, at night, we are in an after-hours spot in Pittsburgh's black Hill district, and Dwight is talking about how he felt when in college it suddenly came to him that he wanted to play pro ball. "I was sitting in this place with some guys and they were talking, and I wasn't even there with them. I was somewhere else. I was thinking about making it in the pros. And I squeezed the drink so hard, the glass broke."

Now he wants to make it as one of the few black stockbrokers in Pittsburgh, dealing mostly with the white upper-middle class. "You can't hardly be an investor if you got to rake and scrape to eat every day. The kind of business I do, not many black incomes are high enough to participate. Does that bother me? No. Because the fact I'm in it is one step closer to get more blacks into a sophisticated type of investing. I'm *infiltrating*. We got to quit hollering about the forty acres and a mule we ain't going to get. It's a capitalistic society we live in. I'd like to help you, but I can't help you if you're going to sleep on the ground."

Let it be said that White was not received as any kind of Oreo in those late-night ethnic places we went to, where whatever business might have been going on was not SEC-regulated. He is received with familiarity and extreme respect. "I like it," he says smiling, "that I can be on the top of the Steel Building during the day and down here swinging it with Leroy occasionally during the night."

Pittsburgh's Republican bigwigs no doubt had that in mind when they tried to talk White into running for sheriff recently. "That legitimatized the hell out of Dwight," says Dwight. "A lot of people of other persuasions—that made them say, well, he must be pretty legit. And I am legit. Allegheny County is heavily Democratic, but I'd get the black vote, which is a lot of Democrats. And I'd get the Jewish Republican vote. Plus I'd pick up a few stragglers. But I was just getting started at Bache, and I didn't know that much about Allegheny County politics, and . . . I didn't want to be sheriff."

325

The first time White took the SEC accreditation test, he failed it.

"Puts and calls, strips and straddles," he said at lunch high atop the U.S. Steel Building, where Bache's offices are. "Stuff will give you the blues. Thirty books. That's a hell of a lot of reading. In three months. And I been beaten in the head ten years, I got some rattles. Really."

But he passed the test on the second try. Now he's on salary, learning the ropes. After his first year he'll have to make it on commission, which won't be easy. "You don't generate business by losing money for people. Damn what the reason is."

But White spent ten years playing with a group that was "tough as a keg of nails" and didn't worry about reasons. "That defensive line we had. I felt a security about that. We reached a point where the game was really fun because we could whip everybody on the block. It wasn't even hard. Jack Tatum said in his book, you go out on the field and see those four dudes and think, boy oh boy, what's going to happen today?

"We *knew* what. We were very predictable. It's like the old thing about cotton and corn. It's going to be around. And us. You could go on the field and people would not bother you. Say to 'em, 'Fella, I am going to knock you out. And I don't need any help. But if I do, there's some fellas back there to clean up what's left.' Back there was Glen Edwards, John Rowser, J. T. Thomas, Jack Lambert, Jack Ham, Mel Blount, Mike Wagner, Andy Russell, they were all individually great. But us four—to be the best, most thorough group at that time made you feel good. We were so dominant, they changed the rules. Took away the headslap, wouldn't let Joe Greene crowd the ball. They couldn't beat us on the field, so they tried to beat us with the rules. And cut down on the bump and run because J. T. and Mel can bump and run *God*."

White wasn't happy as a Steeler last year. He was hurt and had slowed down, and people were saying he was being kept on the team because you couldn't cut a guy who got out of a hospital bed to help you win your first Super Bowl. He wasn't starting and he thought he wasn't getting a chance.

In the Steelers' last home game, Rocky Bleier, who had said he was retiring, scored a touchdown and got an ovation. After the game, White typically came up with the apt observation: "Like we used to say back home when somebody had a good funeral, 'They put him away real nice.' " It was White's last home game, too.

"When I came to the team, all the ingredients were right for Pittsburgh to win. Last year, all the ingredients were there for Dwight to get the hell out. There wasn't nearly as much hoopteraw about me as Rocky, but I hadn't announced my retirement ahead of time.

"I played on one of the best teams, in a great town. No point in me leaving on a negative note. I've still got the scars in my lungs. When the weather cools off, I can feel them grab. But for ten years I got beat on the head, and rained on, and snowed on, rolled on, and finally dumped on. And now . . . I feel *good* about Dwight."

326

□ **13** □

"FRANCO THINKS OUT EVERYTHING"

August, 1982

Franco Harris has, as they say, enormous presence. This is partly because he's enormous, partly because he has the face of a sheikh or a Moorish prince or a young Old Testament prophet, and partly because he doesn't seem to be entirely present. He looks *almost* as if he just woke up and isn't sure whether he slept well enough or not and is determined to make up his own mind about it.

"On a football field you don't have time to stop and think," says Harris's former teammate Joe Greene. "But Franco thinks out everything. You watch Franco run, he's not dancing. He's making decisions."

You watch Franco walk and it's as if he doesn't really believe in walking, he's beyond it; running is true discourse, walking is small talk. Yet he's notoriously in no hurry. In season and out he walks with the pained, stiffish amble of a powerful but sensitive and banged-up centurion, or a reflective cowboy just out of two weeks in the saddle.

His carriage suggests that his shoulders are connected to his feet by elastic cords that can only with effort be stretched. "Breaks down better than any big man I have seen," wrote a Steeler scout, on the plus side, when Harris was at Penn State. To break down is to maintain in action a good football position: balanced, gathered, cocked fluently at the knees and hips. Franco walks as if on the verge of that (and perhaps also the automotive) kind of breakdown. Or it may be more as though his body is a horse that feels like itself only in the strain of full stride, and his mind is a rider broodily aware that it's a long while between times to burst out.

Then on the field he does burst, and you'd forgotten that he, or anybody else, could flow as complicatedly but smoothly as that.

Fans may think they have Franco summed up: Immaculate Reception, all those Super Bowls, half-black–half-Italian. But his wife and Penn State Football Coach Joe Paterno have called him "an enigma," and this season vicariously hard guys in Pittsburgh bars will once again be watching Harris step out of bounds to avoid being needlessly crunched and will crunch their beer cans and exclaim, "What's his *story*?"

"There are no Franco stories!" says Lynn Swann, his Steeler roommate, with an air of illumination. "That's Franco. Franco likes to do things alone. Or with a few people he knows well. He's quiet.

"But then . . . you go somewhere and see him *surrounded*. Kids, all kinds of people, *flocking*."

Harris weighs anywhere from 220 pounds (his reckoning) to 240 (tacklers' estimates) and stands 6–2, and yet his running style has been described as "dainty." Which is why he has been able to play in 157 of a possible 166 games in 10 years, tie Jim Brown's record of seven 1,000-yard seasons, run for more yards and score more touchdowns in postseason games than anyone else ever, and gain more regular-season rushing yards (10,339) than anybody but Brown (12,312) and O. J. Simpson (11,236).

In 1972, when the Steelers first made the playoffs, Harris was AFC Rookie of the Year and came from nowhere in the first round of the AFC playoffs to grab a deflected pass just before it hit the ground and carry it 60 yards to beat Oakland in the last five seconds and go down in history as the Immaculate Receptor. In the Steelers' first Super Bowl, IX, in 1975, in which they beat Minnesota 16–6, he rushed for 158 yards and was named Most Valuable Player. In 1976 he was named NFL Man of the Year, and after the 1981 season he was presented the Byron R. (Whizzer) White Humanitarian Award.

Harris may, as they say, have lost a step. Or a fraction of one: He ran 40 yards in slightly under 4.8 seconds (from a bad start) in camp this year, compared to slightly more than 4.7 as a rookie. But, at thirty-two, he still moves in his own mysterious ways. He makes an estimated $350,000 a year from a Steeler contract he negotiated himself. So he no longer rides a municipal bus to Three Rivers Stadium and hitchhikes home the way he did when he was a rookie. Now he drives a Toyota that is always in the shop because he doesn't like to shift gears. Harris isn't a run-of-the-mill guy.

"I always say Franco is the one person I know of who's going to go straight up to heaven," says Dana Dokmanovich, the elegant Eastern Airlines flight attendant who has been an item with Harris since college, has been living with him for several years and is the mother of Franco Dokmanovich Harris, three, called Dok. Harris introduces Dana as his wife, but they have never felt compelled to make their union official, which is why Bess Dokmanovich—who lives with them in Pittsburgh and helps take care of Dok and serves as Harris's secretary—refers to herself amiably as "Franco's mother-in-law-so-to-speak."

"Franco and the Pope," says Dana, thinking of one other who will go straight to Glory. "Because of what Franco does for other people. To me he's a pain in the butt. He lets *anybody* in the house."

Franco, Dana, Dok and Bess don't live in a house you'd expect a football player to have. "When Franco first showed it to me, I thought it was a joke," says Dana. But that was when it was boarded up and in terrible shape inside.

Now it's the kind of townhouse a well-fixed San Francisco lawyer might have, with imposing marble mantels, rich-grained wainscoting, corkscrew balustrades, great hardwood floors and high ceilings. Franco walks around in it and says, "Feels *solid*." The house stands in an old part of Pittsburgh called the Mexican War Streets area (because its streets were laid out during that conflict), which is gentrifying, but not by leaps and bounds.

"It's an interesting neighborhood," says Harris in his deep murmur. "Not everyone would like it, but I like it. It has some interesting people." It reminds Bess of places she used to live. Dana, who doesn't remember that far back, would like to move somewhere "away from things." She says, "I'll tell you why he bought this house. Because it's so close to the stadium. Otherwise he'd never get there on time."

Near the house is a park. Steeler patriarch Art Rooney, who lives a few blocks away, once located Harris by going to this park, hailing the first little kid he saw playing basketball and saying, "Find Franco."

In this park, a young man comes up pushing a bent-limbed woman in a ramshackle wheelchair. Both of them look as if they've been down on their luck all their lives. "Here he comes again, with his mother," says Dana. "You should hear her holler at him when he hits a bump." The pair hails Franco, and Dana rolls her eyes.

"Did you find a place to live?" asks Harris in an elder-brotherish tone of concern. The last time he saw them, they were on his doorstep under the impression that his house, like most of the large dwellings in the vicinity, contained apartments for poor folks. Harris counsels with the pair for several minutes.

Meanwhile Dok, less reserved than his father, is dashing about like a Serbo-Italo-Afro-American butterfly.

"Dok goes up to people and says, 'Do you know who I am? Do you want to meet my daddy?' " says Dana (who's of Serbian descent). "When Franco signs autographs, Dok signs too—scribbles—on the same paper. We went into McDonald's and he saw Franco's picture on the glasses they're giving out. 'Give me my daddy's glass!' he yelled. Fortunately, Dok is hard to understand."

Harris is resigned to moving out of the inner city for Dok's sake, but he points out that no one has broken into the house.

"How would anyone break in?" says Dana. "There's always someone ringing the bell."

Dana adds: "He's never here, he's always away doing charity work. And I only know three-fourths of what he does for people. There are parts of himself he just won't share, and that's one. I don't think he wants to admit how much people get him to do for them."

One day, Pittsburgh sportscaster Myron Cope got a call about a local kid who'd been hit in the head by a line drive in a Little League game. The kid couldn't speak and could barely move. He had to do therapy on special walking boards to keep fluid from gathering in his lungs, but he couldn't get motivated. Would it be possible for Cope to arrange for the kid's No. 1 sports hero to visit him in the rehabilitation center? Cope said he'd try. He called and called but could never get the hero to call back.

Who was the kid's No. 2 hero? Cope inquired. Franco Harris. "Oh," said Cope, relieved. "No problem." After one call Franco was at the center with a huge bundle of coloring books and comics for the kids there.

"I sat down to wait while Franco and the doctor went into a room with the kid," says Cope. "I figured it'd be ten minutes or so. I sat there for an hour and fifteen minutes. Finally Franco came out. He'd been helping the kid on the walking boards. As we left he was telling the doctor, 'I'll be back with Swann and some other guys.' Franco is one guy who *really* does charity."

"Franco will go out of his way to help *anybody*," says Greene, the only Steeler other than Swann who knows Franco well, "but he isn't concerned with what anybody thinks. He's not concerned with what *I* think."

"We have plenty of arguments," Dana says, "but I'm the only one arguing. He will not argue. He has his own pace, and you can yell at him, but it doesn't make any difference."

That led to some problems during Harris's in-and-out career at Penn State. Steeler scouting reports said things like, "Can cut, slide, stop and go. Will lower the boom. Lots of movement and wiggle." But also things like this:

"Has all needs [scout talk for requirements] of a great pro but is not a hustler."

"Not a hard runner for his size."

"Question his top competitiveness."

And, finally, "Could be a great pro but might not even be a good one. However, I feel he is worth the gamble."

The Steelers took that gamble after considerable internal debate, but Harris didn't blow people away when he came to camp as the team's top draftee in '72. "I didn't think he could make the team," recalls retired Center Ray Mansfield. Rocky Bleier, who, with Franco, produced the Steelers' most effective running attack, says his first impression of Franco was "lazy."

Bleier's second impression: "I sat next to him in meetings and thought, 'Little thin arms . . . He's undeveloped. . . . What does he have that I don't have?' " Bleier was a committed weight lifter who had built up his chest, arms and legs enormously. "Franco's not all chiseled," observes a friend. "He's just sort of there." By the time Harris joined the Steelers, he thought of himself as being into serious lifting, but that was by his own standards. People who were in camp then recall that he didn't seem to know how to handle weights. Harris started lifting weights alone. About halfway through his rookie year the Steelers realized Franco was neither lazy nor weak but just unconventional.

As recently as 1979, however, Jack Tatum, then a feared Oakland defensive back, said in his book, *They Call Me Assassin*: "I have never seen a more imposing physical specimen of an athlete with less drive than Franco. . . . If

Franco doesn't run for the sidelines, slip and fall, or cake out before anyone gets near him, then . . . someone else is wearing his game jersey."

Of course, being criticized in those terms by Tatum is like being called effete by Stalin. But the kind of thing Tatum exaggerated is what makes Harris such a refreshing fullback. Most backs, says Bleier, would be embarrassed to run the way Franco sometimes does. "But you know Franco," Bleier says. "He could give a shit. And look what he's accomplished."

It all began in Pisa, Italy, where Sergeant Cad Harris of Jackson, Mississippi, who never talked much, met Gina Parenti, whose village had been destroyed and whose brother, an Italian soldier, had been chopped to pieces by Nazis, but who talked a great deal. She married Cad and went with him to Mount Holly, New Jersey.

Franco's father stayed in the army, at Fort Dix, New Jersey, after World War II, and Franco grew up in a firmly disciplined family of nine children. "He took after our father, because he was into his privacy," says Harris's younger brother Pete, who tried out unsuccessfully as a defensive back with the Steelers. "But I never saw Franco much when we were kids. He was always at Fort Dix shining shoes and bagging groceries. Too many kids to support."

Franco was also starring in baseball, basketball and football. But "nobody in our house talked about careers," he says. "In the seventh grade I got put into an A-track class, and the teacher went around the room asking whether we were going to take commercial or college prep, and everybody else said 'college prep, college prep,' so I said 'college prep.' But I never thought about going to college until my older brother Mario went to Glassboro State."

Franco did even better: made high school All-America and went to Penn State, where he wore a T-shirt, khakis and high-top black tennis shoes and hung out at the hoagie shop just like back home. But he also took his grades seriously. At the end of his first term, Harris had a 1.9, a tenth of a point under a C average. Many a jock would have been pleased, but Franco says, "I was *sick*. I couldn't get over it. I wasn't going to let *that* happen again"—possibly because he remembered the time one of his sisters came home with a bad grade "and my father tore her *up*. Whooo. A lot of time I didn't cross the fine line into getting in trouble because of fear of my father."

Which isn't to say that he toed every line. "The late sixties and early seventies was an era when I guess a lot of people didn't look at authority as very good no matter where it came from," Harris says. "Being in college then, you learned to read between the lines. Kent State, I think, was the most tragic thing in the history of our country. I couldn't believe our own countrymen shooting and killing. . . . If there were demonstrations or takeovers, I liked to go see what was happening. But I wasn't one to overthrow the university. At times I felt a lot of pressure, from people who thought it would be great to have a football player visible in a lot of things. But I still was kind of a punky kid from New Jersey and I didn't want anybody to tell me what to do, especially college kids.

"After I got to Penn State I heard that there had been a discussion among the coaches about whether I should shave my moustache. I'd never have gone there if I'd thought they'd tell me that. I never thought of my moustache as being a moustache. I thought it was just part of my face. I had hair on my lip at a very early age."

He also had a sense of how to play football at an early age, and in college he didn't test that sense enough. He was an All-America honorable mention his sophomore year, but tailed off after that. It's often said that Penn State relegated Franco to blocking for his friend and classmate Lydell Mitchell, who was a consensus All-America their senior year, but the situation wasn't that simple. John Morris, who was sports information director at Penn State then, says he promoted Harris and Mitchell equally as Mr. Inside and Mr. Outside, with the twist that Harris, the bigger of the two, was Mr. Outside. Their senior year, Harris got hurt and took a long time to get back in shape, and Mitchell became the primary ballcarrier. Years later, Morris says, "Franco told me, 'I wish I'd known as much about conditioning then as I do now. I'd have been unstoppable.' "

As it was, he made pro scouts doubt his mettle, and he ran afoul of coachly authority. Paterno was hollering at his troops trying to get them psyched at the beginning of practice one day when Harris, who had characteristically been the last player to get taped, came trotting up a few minutes late. In front of everyone, Paterno told him that if he did that again, he'd be demoted to second team.

The next day, Mitchell recalls, "I told Franco not to do it, but he did it anyway. Franco is the type of guy that I don't know how people cannot like him. But once he makes up his mind to do something, usually he does. Actually, Franco wasn't at practice late. But once we took the field, he sat inside. He came out late. He called Joe's bluff, and meanwhile Joe called his bluff."

Later Paterno blamed himself for challenging Harris in such a way, but the upshot was that Franco didn't start in the Cotton Bowl, and that raised questions about him in pro scouts' minds.

"I always thought I was an all right guy," says Harris. "But there was talk that I might be blackballed from the NFL. Joe was on vacation, out on a boat somewhere. I tracked him down and called him, asked him if he was saying anything negative about me. He assured me he wasn't.

"But it was going around that I might have been a problem. I remember wanting to send the Steelers a telegram not to draft me, because I didn't want to go where the fans threw snowballs at the players. But the guy who was my agent then told me not to send the telegram because I probably had a bad rap now, and it would just make it worse. I got a call that I'd been drafted by the Steelers, and I was in shock."

However, he was ready for the pros. For one thing, he was tired of trying to live on $15 a month laundry money. "I never did understand that," Harris

332

says. "How is somebody from a poor family supposed to get by? You're not supposed to scalp tickets. You're not supposed to get money from anybody else. You couldn't have a job. Somebody who doesn't have any rights is the college football player. Fortunately, I was able to scalp a few tickets."

And he'd had the maturing experience of working for Walter Conti, who has since become president of the Penn State board of trustees. Conti owns a restaurant in Doylestown, Pennsylvania, and he was prevailed upon to take Harris on as a summer worker because he was majoring in hotel and restaurant management.

"Around his junior year," says Conti, "Franco had become lax about some things. He was supposed to show up for an interview at 6. He showed up at 11. He said he'd be finished with school on the seventeenth of June. So I told him to call me on the first of June and I'd arrange for a place for him to live. On the sixteenth of June at 1 A.M., after I'd given up on him, he called. So I found him a nice place to live. He didn't like it. I found him another place. The first three days of work, he was supposed to be here at 8 in the morning. He'd show up at 5 P.M. I told him, 'Either you come or you're done.' And the guy responded.

"And he had a desire for perfection. I could see that with my liver. Every calf's liver has to be peeled, or when you cook it, it curls up. Peeling liver is not one of the better jobs that people like to do. Franco Harris cleaned my liver better than anybody else has."

Harris also played in the Senior Bowl and in the College All-Star game, "and I realized I was a better athlete than those other guys. Why had they accomplished more? I developed a total commitment to getting in shape. It made all the difference in the world. I told myself, when the other guys are tired, that's when you do it. I felt stronger, smarter, my feel for the game was sharper."

And the Steelers thought he was lazy. "I'm still trying to figure that out," Harris says. "After the first exhibition game the coaches came up saying, 'Good game,' like they didn't expect it from me. It was hard to believe they were disappointed in me the first week of practice. Maybe it was because I didn't allow people to beat on me."

Ah. The crux of Franco's peculiarity and strength. "I always feel that the easiest thing you can do," he says, "is run into somebody."

Call it common sense or call it elitist, such unabashed thinking is surprisingly rare in football. When asked how he responds when people accuse Harris of not running hard enough, Steeler Middle Linebacker Jack Lambert, headknocker nonpareil, doesn't say, "I wrench their torsos off." He says, "That's Franco's problem."

Of course, defenses and offenses have ever been uneasy allies. It's entirely possible that the Steeler defense would feel more comfortable if the team's mainstay running back were Chicago's Walter Payton, who says, "My running style is that I attack the defender."

Franco isn't the kind of humanitarian to take that approach, which, in the long run, is playing into the defenders' hands. It's like throwing fastballs to a fastball hitter so he'll respect you more.

"When I went to Buffalo in 1969," says O. J. Simpson, "I thought I had to show my macho, to go all out and play fierce. I did it for two or three games, and then I realized I wasn't going to be long for the NFL if I kept that up. Franco didn't have to prove himself, either. He's used his athletic gifts with discretion."

He has, in fact, been flagrant about it. Dana says that, although he has traditional notions about the roles of men and women, he's never shown any macho, and so do friends who've been in places where people told him he'd never be half the man Jim Brown was. Harris is so secure that he isn't afraid to say things like "If it's a matter of winding up in the same place, I'd rather not get hit than get hit, chicken as that may sound."

Defensive players would like runners to define themselves in terms of contact with the defense. But Harris knows what he's interested in, and it isn't being pounded by tacklers.

"I will always watch runners run," he says. "We're studying films, supposed to be watching defenses, and I find myself running along with the runner, putting myself in his shoes. I'm watching where other backs' feet are, how they move their hips. I see a certain move I like, and I run it over and over in my mind, and I'll try it.

"Every play is different. I can run 19-Straight ten times, and every time get a different read." He doesn't just read, he peruses: gliding laterally along the line, scanning it for a breakthrough. And if he winds up in the margin, he doesn't apologize.

He couldn't get away with that fancy stuff if it didn't work for the team, of course. For one thing, as Greene points out, "Franco is brushing a lot of people aside with a lot of authority. He just does it in such a smooth manner, it doesn't look like he's bowling them over."

And the Steelers learned that, as Harris says, "I take my shots. On first or second down, maybe I don't get an extra few feet that we didn't need, but if it's a third-down situation, I go as hard as anybody else."

"After a game," says one of the Steelers' physicians, Dr. Paul Steele, "Franco has big raw welts all across his back, as if somebody has beaten him with a truncheon, and he just gets up and goes again."

"When I first saw him," says Greene, "he reminded me of myself. He didn't like practice. Franco had a wonderful sense of timing; he could gauge the tempo of a play without going full speed in practice. He wasn't sloughing off. Every time he ran a play, he'd run the ball all the way to the goal line."

And if Harris didn't pump iron as lustily as some of his mates, he did do regular weight work, for tone rather than bulk, and he has habitually been the last Steeler out of the locker room after practice. He jumps rope, he lingers in the whirlpool, he kids around with the locker room boys, he does odd exercises no one else does, such as jumping up and down on a mat to develop his spring from a surface with no bounce.

When most of the other Steelers were in the showers after practice the first day the veterans reported to camp, Harris was catching short passes from a rookie quarterback, over and over and over—trying to snag the ball *perfectly,* with no element of bobble whatsoever. He would make little catching faces and catching noises, with a faraway look in his eyes, like a kid imagining himself a pro football player. When he dropped one he would go, "Awwww," and grimace and shudder with almost histrionically real feeling, as if in a pass-dropping-and-reaction drill. When he caught one he would hold the freshly received ball in his hands like cupped water, scrutinizing it, dwelling on it, as if it were a liver that had to be ideally peeled. ("The only thing about it," says Conti, "is he would take three and a half hours to peel one liver.")

"In the midst of our so-called dynasty," says Greene, "it was an era when if you couldn't run, you couldn't play, and we ran, and we ran with Franco. Ninety percent of the offense then was Franco."

"You can see the frustration sometimes," says Swann. That is, you can see Chuck Noll on the sidelines "wanting to say, 'Franco, run over the guy!' And Franco is getting up and . . ." Swann does an imitation of Franco moseying, preoccupied, with his back to the bench. "But Franco plays Chuck's offense. He does the job."

"If you want to get Franco jacked up," says Quarterback Terry Bradshaw, "just try to embarrass any one of us." In Super Bowl XIII, the Cowboys' Hollywood Henderson jostled and taunted Bradshaw between plays. Harris snatched Henderson away. On the next play Bradshaw picked up a safety blitz, called a trap, and Harris boomed through the hole for the deciding touchdown.

Harris still does things for his own reasons, though. Over the years there have been stretches when the team wondered when Harris was going to get going. There has been talk among the coaches of sitting him down to jolt him into intensity. In his career he has run for 100 yards or more in forty-four games, only thirteen of which have been in the first half of the season. "You don't really get into the thick of things until the last half," says Harris. Even during the juggernaut years, he could sometimes peel the thick awfully close.

That's because Harris isn't an automaton. He's a humanitarian. He has to have a certain kind of inspiration. Some players stoke their fires with amphetamines, but not Harris. Nor would he ever let anybody shoot him up so he could play hurt. In fact, well, he and Swann were working out at the University of Pittsburgh before camp this year and Swann found him in the locker room holding bloody ice on the back of his hand, where he had cut it on a light fixture. Swann talked him, with difficulty, into going over to the infirmary.

"He didn't want to. Didn't want them to take a stitch. And when they put antiseptic on it, he *screamed,*" says Swann. "There was a little kid sitting in there. He'd probably been sewed up a dozen times; he couldn't believe it."

"Then they had to put antiseptic on it again because Franco kept touching it, and then they put the stitches in and Franco is going like this. . . ." Swann makes a series of tight-lipped faces.

"Franco's saying, 'Is that all? Is that all?' And the doctor said he thought he ought to get a tetanus shot. Franco didn't want to. I told him *I'd* take one, I hadn't had one in a long time and we get those carpet burns on the turf. Franco still didn't want to. He said, 'How bad is it if you get tetanus?' The doctor said, 'You get like this. . . .' " Swann makes a series of tight-lipped faces just like the ones Franco was making when he got stitches.

"I'm saying, 'Franco, just go ahead and get the shot.'

" 'Well, what are the warning signs?' Franco wants to know. 'I could wait and get the shot if I start having them.'

"The doctor says, 'Put it this way, Franco, nine out of ten people who get the warning signs don't make it.'

" 'What if I get nauseous?' Franco says. 'Could I get the shot then?' He's still trying to talk the doctor out of the shot. Then finally he sits down, and he's like a high jumper crouched waiting for the wind to be just right. 'Got to get ready. Ah-right . . . mmm. Ah-right-ah-right-ah-right—wait a minute.' "

So. Maybe Harris *is* chicken. Maybe that's why he's so sympathetic to kids in hospitals, and why he has preserved himself so admirably, and even why he gets those sudden bursts. Walter Conti says Franco told him, after making his first long NFL run, "All of a sudden I saw a hole, cut through it, and saw these two big fellas coming after me. I was so scared I burst out fast, and the next thing I knew, I was 10 yards downfield. I don't like getting hit."

Maybe that's not the kind of humanitarianism Whizzer White seeks to foster, but one thing Harris has learned in his years of reading is this:

"The hole is never where it's supposed to be."

□ **14** □

BLOUNT IN GEORGIA

Summer, 1983

Hup! How often do we get to watch a black Georgia Steeler cowboy work? Mel Blount, the only such cowboy extant, is up on his cutting horse Straw King, and the two of them, in centaurial concert, are singling a calf out from the rest of a penned-up bunch.

Calf tries a move to his left. *Tharomble tharop, rrk,* dirt flying, Blount and Straw King are there. Calf cuts back to his right. *Tharomble tharop, rrk,* clods in the air, Blount and Straw King are there. Calf can't get open! Can't run his pattern! It's a bit like watching a distinguished NFL cornerback cow a receiver. "I've learned a lot from these horses," says Blount.

What, exactly?

He is silent for a moment, as if the answer is obvious. "Ways of moving."

Here in Toombs County, Georgia, a few miles south of the town of Vidalia, which is famous for its onions, is where Blount made his first moves in life, and where he now breeds quarter horses, and where he's starting Mel Blount Youth Home, Inc. The kids at the home, who would otherwise be in reform school, can save money for college by having their own horses to raise.

"I think I was blessed by growing up on a farm," Blount says. "My life has been like a storybook."

The story began two generations back with Mel's maternal grandfather— one-armed Charlie Sharpe, a great man who rated no obituary and seldom wore shoes. When Charlie was born, not far from this farm, he was a slave of the Sharpes, a family of cotton and corn farmers.

This is as far back as Blount's relatives can trace Charlie's line. "They say his mother was part Indian," says one of Blount's maternal relatives, Aunt Cooter, eighty-four, who has a lot of red in her coloring. "White people brought her from foreign lands. And she saw her sister there, at the place where she was being sold, so they brought the sister too."

When Charlie died in 1953, in his nineties (the family has no record of his birth date), he owned around 2,000 acres, the land that he acquired acre by acre while keeping out of white folks' way and working at a sawmill for as little as fifteen cents a day, and the land whence his youngest grandson sprang into football history.

When Mel introduces me to people, he often says, "We're brothers," to give them pause. Sometimes, while they're figuring out that it's a joke, I add, "-in-law."

But since Mel's and my people come from pretty much the same neck of the woods—Georgia just above Florida as far back as he can trace his, and Florida just below Georgia as far back as I can trace mine—the likelihood is that our Blount-hood derives, in one way or another, from the same folks.

My grandfather was a hard working man, too. He died at seventy while chopping down a tree from his seat in a wheelchair he'd made for himself. I'm proud of him and his forebears, who farmed respectably, if not lucratively, two hundred miles or so from Toombs County. But I despaired of discovering a heroic *Roots* saga for myself several years ago, when I went to the Calhoun County Public Library in Blountstown, Florida, not far from where my father and grandfather were born, and discovered that the town was named for a Seminole Indian, not related to me, who adopted an Anglo-Saxon name. The town bears his name, I was told, because it was founded on land granted to him in appreciation of his having helped Andrew Jackson fight other Indians— "and Negroes," according to the librarian. In 1834, after the United States government purchased his land and cattle and furnished him with a ship, Col. John Blount and some of his followers sailed from Florida to Texas. When I read a musty Blount family history in the same library and came to an enthusiastic account of a nineteenth-century lynching, I threw up my hands.

No doubt some ancestor of mine did own some of Mel's, but I have been unable to determine which one. Mel's father, James Blount, who died in 1967, married Charlie Sharpe's daughter, Alice, after coming to Toombs County from Lumber City, Georgia, where few of his relatives remain. Mel's paternal grandfather, Henry Blount, was a preacher. "They say he was the preachingest man, and the prayingest," says Mel's brother Isiah, who's called Jack. "One time he was praying at an outdoor service, and a mule hitched to a wagon went down in prayer with him. Kneeled right down. That's the truth. There's people around here who witnessed that." That's something I'll tell my grandchildren, whether I deserve to identify with Henry or not.

Mel and I both wanted to become great athletes, and he did. After visiting his farm, I know three reasons for that: work, food and—to put it mildly— sibling rivalry. Folks in Toombs County say Mel's brother Bobby may have been the best natural athlete among the seven Blount boys—people always say that about one of a sports star's brothers when the star has at least two—but Mel says matter-of-factly, "I always looked on myself as different." The last of eleven children who had been born at regular two-year intervals, he is also, by 2 or 3 inches, the tallest.

The most Olympian sports body I've ever seen belongs to Wilt Chamberlain, who, beginning at gracefully slim ankles, broadens in unhurried geometrical progression to shoulders the size of an ox yoke. Mel has the same body, only scaled down from 7–1 to 6–3. At the top of Blount's exquisite physique is his calmly erect, completely shaven head, which looks like a highly polished, bearded semiprecious stone.

He's a rich bay-auburn color. (I'm a sort of freckled off-peach.) At age thirty-five he weighs 205 pounds, about the same as he did at the end of his college career at Southern University in Baton Rouge, fourteen years ago. To use a scouting report phrase, he's "split high"; his pants are 36 inches in the inseam—5 inches longer than mine, although he is only 2½ inches taller—and 33 inches in the waist. "Really I take a 32 waist, but I have to have a size larger to be able to get them over my thighs," he says. My waist is 36. I asked him once whether he ever worried about his weight. "I don't worry about anything, man," he said. "It's not part of my makeup."

They say Charlie Sharpe was straight and streamlined like Mel, and nearly as tall. According to family lore, one time Charlie told a man, "Be careful of that axe," and just then the blade slipped and cut deep into the man's foot. Charlie tore off the sleeve that he didn't have any use for, bandaged the man's foot with it, put the man across his shoulders and trotted with him two miles to a doctor. Saved the man's life.

"Just think," says Mel with pleasure. "Someday people will be asking what kind of man I was. And people be lying. . . ." Self-effacement isn't part of his makeup either.

The fertile, highly tillable mixture of grayish-tan sand and red clay that he plowed with a mule when he was a boy is part of him, though. While he never moved a mule to pray, Mel was good with them, as was his mother, Alice Sharpe Blount, who is in her seventies. She's slightly bent now, but she moves smoothly, says, "I haven't forgot a thing," and is sure of herself. "I told Marlon," she says, referring to Mel's ball-of-muscle nineteen-year-old nephew, "I could get out there and ride a horse as well as he could, right now. I could see he didn't believe me. But I could.

"I don't think much of these tractors," she adds. "They cover the ground faster than a mule, but they don't turn it as well. Seems to me things have gone backwards. Time when we used mules, we could grow as much as we could eat and still put somethinother away. A mule, you could keep him fed. With this gasoline—and talk about $400 for a tractor tire!—you got to tie up your crop ahead of time."

Jack agrees that farming is hard to stay ahead of these days. "The government's lending farmers money and advising 'em to declare bankruptcy," he says.

"My father lost part of his right arm at the sawmill," Alice says. "I'd go out in the morning when I was a little girl to tie his hand rope. Tie his arm to the plow. And I'd get out early, be waiting in the field for him, and I'd try plowing myself. And I learned how.

"My father's mother had long, straight black hair she tied up in a big ball back of her head. She'd pick cotton and put it all in her apron—wore an old, long apron and tucked it up some way. And she'd pick 100 pounds a day, nearly every day. My daddy'd tell us what he gon' do to us if we let her outpick us. I'd be just apickin' cotton to keep up with that old lady.

"We'd get up ever' morning at four, and when they put you out in that field, you *worked.* My daddy could walk from here to everywhere. I'd be out in that field, thinking no one was watching whether I was working or not, and look up—way over on a hill, there'd be my daddy's eyes on me. Only thing kept you from working was if you was sick. And people in them days wasn't sick as much.

"We'd go to school couple of days, work the rest of the week and get behind in school so we couldn't ever catch up. It seemed rough at the time. But it's good to know how to do things. And you learned how on the farm.

"I raised eleven head of children, and the most of 'em went to college. Children and grandchildren together, I've had twenty-eight go to college."

If she'd had a chance, what would she like to have taken in college?

"Oh, I don't know," she says. "But what I *like* to do is plow. I just like to farm."

She lives on the family farm still, as do Mel's brothers, Jack, Bobby and Clint, and their families and Aunt Cooter and Uncle Son. Mel spends a good part of the off-season there in a three-bedroom trailer that forms a small compound with his twelve-stall horse barn (headquarters of his Cobb Creek Farms quarterhorse operation), the trailer that is the beginning of his youth home and his mother's house, which is decorated inside with photos of grand-children, framed passages of Scripture, the Last Supper painted on black felt, a souvenir scroll from the French Quarter and a sampler that says "BACHE-LORS ARE LIKE DETERGENT—THEY WORK FAST AND LEAVE NO RING."

Pine, oak, walnut, pecan, peach and fig trees shade the immaculate yard. The slightly rolling fields stretch across the horizon. Jack, forty-six, who lives over the hill, runs most of the farming operations, raising soybeans, oats, hay and cattle. Clint, thirty-seven, who lives just up the road and used to be a special-education teacher, helps Mel run the horse business and will be director of the youth home. Bobby, thirty-nine, who lives over on yet another part of the property, farms a little, drives a Toombs County school bus and runs his own pest-control business.

They all grew up working hard. "Didn't do anything *but* work," says Clint. When you had a lot of land to farm and didn't have a lot of equipment and couldn't afford to hire much help, you'd have eleven kids and put them out on the ground. "And we stayed on the place," says Clint. "When we'd get to go into Vidalia, it was like Christmas."

During the tobacco harvest, the kids might work twenty-two hours a day. But they all got their schooling—it was a forty-minute bus ride to the nearest black school, in the town of Lyons—and they played ball.

And they ate. Alice remembers James telling her, "Keep 'em fed. Keep 'em fed and they'll work." Every time I walked into her house, at 9 A.M., 11:30

340

A.M., 4:30 P.M. or 9:30 P.M., she was putting fried chicken, stewed chicken, butter beans, soupy white lima beans, grits, gravy, cornbread, rice, mashed potatoes, thick-sliced bacon, collard greens, biscuits, ham, black-eyed peas, sweet iced tea and hot sauce onto the table and saying, "Y'all about let it get cold." When I start eating food like that, it takes me back to when I was fourteen, could eat steadily for hours with impunity and figured I'd be a sports immortal.

Inside every thin Southern person is a fat person signaling to get out. Mine has partially emerged, as has Bobby's. One night Bobby leaned back from the table, slapped his stomach proprietarily with both hands and said, "Roy, this is all the savings I got."

There are food-related ways by which Mel stays in shape at the farm—like tossing 50- and 60-pound watermelons along a family bucket-brigade line— "And you can't stop," he says—to load them into a truck. But occasionally Mel skips one of his mother's meals, puts on a rubber bellyband that makes him sweat more around the middle and goes out and runs with the horses. Mel has received the NFL glory, but Bobby has received more food and looks like he is pleased with his end of the deal. Clint introduced me to Bobby as someone who "helps put out the magazines."

"Well," said Bobby, shifting his chew of tobacco and looking amused, "I guess there's got to be somebody for ever' thing."

Bobby is the easiest-going brother, but he can still play a mean game of what the Blounts call "country basketball." When they were growing up, the brothers played football using a tin can for the ball. It was tackle and no-holds-barred. And they played country basketball, after which the NFL never seemed particularly rough to Mel.

Country basketball is played on a pounded-dirt, one-basket court about the size of a boxing ring. I was *tempted* to join in. But I would have thrown everything off. It would have been like Pat Boone trying to sing with the Isley Brothers. I couldn't have jacked myself up to the level of the arguing, much less the shoving, slapping and in-your-facing.

To claim a foul, you pretty much have to have been thrown bodily out of bounds while in possession of the ball, and even then you have to be able to yell loud enough, long enough, to withstand all the accusations of pusillanimity.

I watched Mel and Bobby's stepson Frankie, fifteen, play Bobby's son Marlon, who will be a running back for Southern U this year, and Mel's son Norris, who's sixteen and ran back an interception 107 yards to help win a game 9–7 for his high school in Lubbock, Texas, last year. What appeared to be at stake was the championship of the world.

I have observed some vivid father-son struggles in my time—for instance, in performances of *Long Day's Journey Into Night*—but I've never seen one to match the sight of Mel and Norris thumping each other half to death under the family basket.

Norris's mother, Mary, was Mel's high school girl friend, whom Mel didn't marry. Norris spends his summers on the farm. Notre Dame has already written to him about playing football there. He's built like Mel, only—so far—two inches shorter.

It's clearly Mel's feeling that a son should never box a father out. Whump! Slap-slap-slap! Norris would go sprawling. And Norris would come right back. *"Show me!"* Norris would say. *"Show me!* I can be as rough as the next!" And they would be back into it again.

And Marlon, who looks like a Herschel Walker built lower to the ground, would be going up and changing directions twice in midair and popping in 12-foot jumpers or yelling at Mel, "You cheatin', Chuck!" (Marlon and Norris call Mel "Chuck," for Chuck Noll, or occasionally "Art Rooney," referring to the Steelers' owner.)

"I'm shooting the ball in the basket," Mel would say. "That cheating?"

"Way *you* do it," Marlon would say.

"Whining. Why you whining? You playing like the Dallas Cowboys," Mel would say. And I remembered watching Mel, in Super Bowl X, beat Cowboy Receiver Golden Richards up so bad that he staggered out of the game with broken ribs. In the Steelers' most dominant NFL years their bedrock strength was that they whipped people down into the dirt physically, and Blount was as big a part of that tradition as a defensive back can be.

In 1977 George Atkinson of Oakland sued Noll and the Steelers for slander, because Noll had accused Atkinson of being part of a "criminal element" in the NFL after Atkinson belted Steeler Receiver Lynn Swann in the head when Swann didn't even have the ball. During the trial, Noll conceded under cross-examination that some of his own players had struck blows as nasty as Atkinson's. Atkinson's lawyers showed a film of Blount hitting Branch when Branch didn't have the ball. Noll, no doubt with some sarcasm, said Blount's hit was a "dastardly" act. Blount was holding out at the time. He sued Noll for $5 million.

But when he signed, he dropped the suit. "I had just declared war on the Steelers in general," he says now. "Everything I know about football, Chuck taught me." During the '77 season, after the holdout, Blount hit Cincinnati's Bob Trumpy so hard that two of the bolts fastening Trumpy's face mask to his helmet were knocked off. For that, Blount was called into Commissioner Pete Rozelle's office, but he was cleared of using "unjust and improper force." "It's a game where you got to expect to be hit. It ain't a game for sissies," Blount says.

Nor is country basketball.

"Y'all wouldn't have been nothing back when I was in school," Mel told Norris and Marlon. "Wouldn't even have made the team."

"Naw," said Marlon. "'Cause we'd've been hurting everybody up too bad. Would've thought we was *gods*."

"Play him closer, Frankie!" Mel yelled. "You playing like a sissy." Frankie was in fact playing so hard that the bandage flew off the bad cut on his finger and the cut opened back up, and Frankie had about two-thirds of Marlon's body mass. But aunts and female cousins who were sitting around the court were saying, in dead earnest, "Frankie, you can't make the big play!" Frankie bore in on Marlon gamely, and Marlon said, "Yeah. He gon' go for that egg, and the chicken done gon' be gone!"

Marlon and Norris won the first two games. "OK," declared Mel. "*This* one's for the championship."

"OK," said Marlon. "You ain't *fair*. But we can live with it. We the best! We the best!"

"Gon' give us a break, huh?" said Mel.

"Ain't giving you a break," said Marlon. "Don't give nobody a break. If you got a two-month-old baby down, don't give him a break. Keep him down. Cause he's liable to get up and beat you."

"How come you letting this be the championship, then?"

"Cause y'all ain't going to beat us."

"What's wrong with you, Frankie! You lettin' him intimidate you! Keep your hand in his face!"

"Oh!" said Marlon sarcastically. "My face ain't ever going to forget that." There ensued half an hour of wrestling, flying through the air and full-tilt yelling, with Norris hollering, "All right, Big Boy!" at his father after Mel gave him a resounding whack, and Mel answering, "See what you made of, Norris? You playing a man's game now!" In large part because Mel called fouls on slaps that were hardly contact compared with some of his defensive assaults, Mel and Frankie won the championship by one basket.

And Mel and Marlon and Norris went straight up to the barn and took turns doing sets of repetitions of squats and jerks with 185 pounds, as the barn's stereo system played a disco song whose lyrics included, "I . . . love . . . to . . . see . . . you . . . sweat. Keep yo' body wet."

No hard feelings at all. "You ought to be loose," Mel said to Norris. "You been messing around with your daddy!"

A daddy has to do whatever it takes not to get beat by his son. "You don't know what kind of man I am," Mel told Norris. "I been before the public. You can look at my record."

"Uh-huh," said Norris, pumping iron and feeling strong.

"See why I like to come to the farm?" Mel asked me. "Every time I come down here I got to prove myself all over again. Get with these teenage kids; they want to fight me."

"I guess it's good for them," I said.

"I don't want them to get the idea," he said, "that things come easy."

I went through sixteen years of schooling in Georgia, Texas and Tennessee without ever having a black schoolmate. Mel never had a white one. "When I was growing up here," he says, "I wasn't really aware what life was all about. Went to an all-black school, always worked for my daddy, competed with black athletes. My whole world was black until I got into pro football. And then I realized that things I was told in college were true. There's differences between the way black people are treated and the way white people are treated. If you want to compete in white society, you've got to be twice as good. Can't ever take anything for granted. Because, let's face it, they're the ones making the decisions. You got to deal with reality. Being an athlete, I have that knack for meeting a challenge.

"There's no way in the world the North can touch the South. In the North people camouflage themselves so well when it comes to race. Black people are further ahead in the South. More aware what society is all about. Blacks in the North get a false security.

"And there's a difference between poor in the South and poor in the North. When you poor in the North, you poor, because you can't grow nothing in them concrete streets."

"The Blounts are very well thought of," whites in Vidalia told me, and everywhere I went with Blount, he was recognized and celebrated. (A hostess in a Savannah restaurant told me, however, "I thought he was that colored man on *The A-Team* without the jewelry.") But Blount says that although he has made speeches "all over the world, nobody has ever asked me to speak in my hometown." It's the Vidalia onion—which grows only in that area, is wonderfully sweet and is celebrated with an annual festival featuring a contest to see who can eat the most raw onions—that's referred to locally as "our favorite son." The 12,500 population of Vidalia is about one-third black, but in the two copies of the local paper, *The Advance,* that I saw, there were 134 white people in photographs (aside from an indistinct long shot of a graduating high school class) and five blacks. When I asked whether there had been an obituary or anything written about Charlie Sharpe in *The Advance* when he died, Jack looked surprised at the very notion.

I went with Clint to a local store, where he was served cordially. "Is there a big difference between the way blacks are treated in stores around here now and when you were a kid?" I asked him.

"When I was a little kid," he said, "if you didn't get out of whites' way fast enough, they'd kick you, slap you, knock you down. You just tried not to take their hate into you.

"The difference is, before they used a whip, now they're using a pencil. Used to beat you physically and get away with it, now they beat you legally and get away with it. You're still getting your butt beat. Now you get a little more respect—if they know you and want your business. I don't want to be treated different because of my name. I want to be treated the same way my neighbor is who maybe doesn't have any money. I want to be given respect because I'm a human being."

Charlie Sharpe, says Jack, "was the onliest Negro who got away with anything" in the old days. "Others lost their land all kinds of ways. He stayed back up here in the woods. Just came out to pay his taxes. Every white man he saw, he said 'Yassuh Captain, yassuh Captain,' just as nice as he could be. 'Captain would you please give me a drink of water?' Act like he didn't have anything.

"Had the prettiest stock in this part of the country. Built his own blacksmith shop and made his own tools. Don't know whether he ever went to school. He just had an X that he would sign. But he could figure up a bill in his head, fast as anybody."

Beginning more than a hundred years ago, Charlie would walk ten miles through the woods to the sawmill, save his pay, buy land with it for as little as twenty-five cents an acre and clear the new ground with his one arm by moonlight. Eventually he had several tenants working for him, besides the proliferating Blounts. When he died, there was over $150,000 in his bank account from decades of producing cotton, turpentine, hogs, cattle.

But he always wore just an old pair of overalls and a flannel or denim work shirt, and almost never wore shoes. To buy more land he'd borrow money from a white banker in town, Duncan McRae, who was straight and supportive in his dealings with him, but there was always the fear of getting the acreage tied up as collateral and losing it. "This land to my family is kind of like a sacred cow in India," says Blount. "We always had to overprotect what we had. I remember stories my mother told, when they were worrying about whether they could pay the mortgage. Sometimes shrewd businessmen wanted to come in and take the land. But my family knew the value of it.

"Now we got doctors and lawyers in this family, and entertainers. One of my brother Elijah's sons was the first black hired to teach law at the University of Georgia. Larry Blount. Another nephew's an engineer for Frito-Lay. His daddy's a doctor of philosophy. The right seed was planted in this family."

In 1936 Charlie paid off every penny he owed the bank. By way of celebration, McRae told him, "Charlie, go pick out any suit you want. I'm going to give it to you." Charlie picked out a pair of overalls and a denim jacket. He said he didn't think it would be right if he dressed different from the people who worked for him.

Charlie donated part of his land to the local black community, so that it would have a place to build Mt. Calvary Baptist Church. Blount was the special guest speaker in church one recent Sunday. He was announcing his youth home plans.

My religious roots are in traditional Southern white Protestantism, which is different from traditional Southern black Protestantism in more or less the way that Roy Acuff is different from Mahalia Jackson. Which is to say, different, but akin. To me religion that gets too far from washed-in-the-blood seems not to count at all, and yet salvation seems to me claustrophobic, a word I don't use lightly. But the hymns go deep. Inside every Southern person who is outside the church is someone who's signaling to get back in. For me, going to Mt. Calvary was a little bit like eating at Alice Blount's table.

Everyone was dressed the way people in my church dressed for Easter when

I was a kid, except more so. The hats on the women put tropical birds to shame, and Mel gleamed in a three-piece suit. Clint was videotaping everything.

Jack's wife, Minnie, got up after a couple of hymns and told the congregation it was "kinda tight. We're here for one reason, to praise His name, and some y'all sound like you think you're here on your own merits. If He didn't do nothing but wake us up this morning, we got reason to praise the Lord. Just loosen up. You know how these young ones do at the rock concerts, shoutin' and hollerin'. You know how to jump and shout for a home run. God done more for you than a home run when He died on that cross."

We put a lot more into "I Want to Go Where Jesus Is" and "Amazing Grace." Then we heard a pianist and three backup singers sing "You gotta get wrapped up . . . tied up . . . tangled up in Jeeesus. . . . Then the world can't do you no harm." The pianist got so loose that Clint's wife, Nell, went up, put an arm around the pianist's shoulders and cooled her off with a cardboard fan. I felt myself to be really in church for the first time in years and years.

Mel's former high school principal, T. R. Maxwell, the NAACP president in the area, introduced Mel. "Some people get the dust of the community on their shoes and dust it right off," said Maxwell. "He didn't do that. He has roots. His roots are here."

Maxwell said that Mel's "profession is very short-lived. After a few years they turn you out to pasture like an old animal."

"Mm-hm, mm-hm," people said. I was one of them.

Maxwell said he'd been an honorary board member of the Georgia Sheriffs' Association home for boys, but he had resigned when it became clear that there weren't going to be any black boys there. In 1969 I wrote a column for the *Atlanta Journal* about that home's nonintegration, but it did not have any appreciable effect on the home's policy.

"We have black boys in trouble, too," said Maxwell. "They don't need to be slammed in jail."

Blount then rose and began to speak. "God has lifted me out of the cotton fields of Toombs County. God took me from behind a plow and a mule and put me in the spotlight, to tell His word." He cited the Book of John, the story of Job, Noll, "who says if you stick with the basics, you'll come through all right," and the Apostle Paul, "who said to the Philippians, 'Don't worry about anything. Instead pray about everything. And if you do this, you get God's peace, which is more beautiful than the mind can understand.'"

Blount told of the home he was going to establish on his family land. One reason he was doing it, he said, was "to pull my family together. They struggling. I've made some progress. But the battle is not over with. We've had a history in my family of passing up opportunities. It's something wrong when each generation don't make progress. The Lord like to see us successful.

"Everywhere I go people know me. I just look at myself as a child of God. When I achieved things on the football field I realized it was not because I was such a specimen I could go out and outperform everybody else. I knew that God was watching over me.

"You could get out there on that road right now, and if you ain't got no direction, you could wind up anywhere. We need so much love among ourselves. Sure I cut the pathway, pushed some of the bushes out the way, but we all got to have love. Jesus didn't just exist, He went out and found Him some Disciples to spread the word. . . . In football, you can't let somebody else make the tackle; you make the tackle. You got to say, 'I'm not going to sit back and do the counting. I'm going to be one of the ones being counted.' "

The Rev. Woodrow Jones, pastor, responded to Blount's message, saying, "I felt like he was telling you something or reminding you of something that I been trying to tell you for years. . . . One reason a lot of folks haven't got anything is God knows they haven't got sense enough to use it. . . .

"We all can't be Mel Blount. We all can't be Jackie Robinson. Can't all be no Joe Louis. But we can all be a success. . . .

"I don't care how far you go, how far away, when it all boils down, it's Jesus. When you got Him, and other people be dying, you be flying."

"I think of myself as more of an entrepreneur than a ballplayer," Blount says, but when I asked him how many more years he was going to play ball, he said, "That's like asking me how many more years I'm going to live. Retiring's like dying: the time just comes."

The time is going to come for him, he's inclined to believe, at the end of this season. The Steelers timed him in camp last year at the same speed—4.5—in the 40 that he ran as a rookie. He can still, in the great Steeler defensive tradition, make a runner wish he were in some other line of work. But nobody—although you won't get Blount to admit it—has the same quickness against the pass at thirty-five that he had in his prime. When Blount turned one of his colts loose one afternoon on the farm and watched the animal cavort and frisk and leap around, he said, "Free at last."

"Do you feel like that horse on a football field?" I asked him.

"When I was a young boy," he said. "Still do sometimes. But not as often."

How will he continue to be a success after football, when he starts making $200,000 less a year? His business ventures have not always been profitable. His employment agency in New Orleans went bankrupt in 1978. "I don't think I lost much from this bankruptcy; I think I gained a lot," said Blount at the time, characteristically.

Now he has some real estate in Augusta, Georgia, and a diversified investment portfolio. But his horses are assets he can *ride*. "I'm going to make hundreds of thousands of dollars out of this horse," he says of his stud, Doc Blount. "Money on the hoof, man. Lot better than money in the bank." But the horse business is too unpredictable, he says, to be more than "a good side business."

So what's his main business going to be?

There's the youth home, he says, and maybe politics.

"How will you make money out of politics?" I asked.

He looked at me. "Why do you think people go *into* politics?" he said.

"But Clint says everything is districted around here so that whites are always in a majority," I said. "And there are still a lot of blacks working on farms around here who are afraid to register."

"To me, everything is politics," he says. "Politics is people. And I'm happiest working with people, all races and creeds. I'm going to make a lot of money with this farm. Going to build me a *city*. All you got to do is clear some land; pretty soon people be building and developing."

The land. Charlie's will has been probated, but the terms have never been administered. Relatives with possible claims are spread around the country. Title to the land has been up in the air for thirty years. Nobody knows exactly how many acres there are. That's why Mel talks about pulling the family together. Clearing, holding and using land is never easy.

With all those high-dollar horses around, I said to Clint, it must be a big change from the old days. "I think we got more in these horses than we've gotten out of them," Clint said. "It's hard times. It's always been hard times. It's no different now. Soon as we go out the door every morning, we're fighting. And soon as we close it behind us at night, we're licking our wounds.

"It's less physical work now. But between physical pressure and mental pressure, if I had a choice, I'd take physical. Because physical makes you feel closer to God, closer to nature. Physical keeps you young. My mother's seventy-six, and if it was a sprint from here to that fence post, I'd have a hard time beating her."

While I was visiting Blount, his friend Charlie Johnson, the Vikings' middle guard, came down. Johnson is getting into the horse business, too. The three of us were riding somewhere one night in Blount's truck. Willie Nelson was on the tape deck.

"Lot of black guys can't stand country music," I said.

"Lot of black guys can't stand their selves," said Blount. "My nickname in college was Country. I was country when country wasn't cool."

"I sort of wish I had been born in them cowboy days," said Johnson. "Carry a gun, ride a horse, shoot people when I had to."

"You want to be wild, huh?" said Blount. "Going after rustlers."

"Don't mess with me, I don't mess with you," said Johnson.

"I like it just the way it is," Blount said. "Got any better, I'd have to pay amusement tax."

"I can do without the world," said Johnson. "Give me two rottweiler dogs and a good horse. Rottweilers bite through bones."

"Would you rather be rich or have your health?" Blount asked.

"How rich?" said Johnson.

"You rather be a little bit rich and have your health, or . . ."

"Aw, no, not a little bit rich. I want to be rich—and have my health. Like a lot of people."

"I'd think the trouble with being a football player and planning your future financially is you never know how many more years you're going to play," I said.

"And you be thinking about it all the time, too," said Johnson. "We're just pieces of meat to them. They keep us long as they can use us."

"That game will make a man out of you," said Blount.

"When we had the head slap," said Johnson, "that's when they had some real football. Blood and stuff trickling down your legs. You don't hardly see no snaggle-tooth linemen anymore. Everything's changed. All of 'em got teeth."

But the mood was not wistful in Blount's truck, which cost $17,000 and was pulling a $15,000 horse in a $9,000 trailer. "I always wanted to be a football player," Blount said. "And I always wanted to have horses. And live in the country. And I got all three."

"I always wanted to play football, too," said Johnson. "And have a ranch. And I'm close. I haven't got the ranch yet, but I'm on my way."

"It's destiny," said Mel. "I believe a man is in control of his destiny. You can do what you want to in life."

"I saw a poll the other day," it occurred to me to say, "that said a big percentage of the population no longer believes in the American Dream."

There was a silence in the truck. Why did I have to say something like that? We drove along for a ways.

"Well," said Mel. "You got to be blessed, too."

Roy Blount Jr. is the author of seventeen books, including *Be Sweet, Roy Blount's Book of Southern Humor, If Only You Knew How Much I Smell You,* and, most recently, *Robert E. Lee,* a brief biography. He is a contributing editor of the *Atlantic* and a columnist for the *Oxford American,* and he appears regularly on NPR's *Wait, Wait . . . Don't Tell Me.* He was a staff writer at *Sports Illustrated* when he wrote his first book, *About Three Bricks Shy of a Load,* which he expanded into *About Three Bricks Shy . . . And the Load Filled Up* after covering the Steelers of the seventies for several publications, including *Esquire, Inside Sports,* and the *New York Times.*